THE MIND OF CHRIST

T. W. Hunt & Claude King

This book is a resource in the Personal Life subject area of the Christian Growth Study Plan.
Course CG-0174

ISBN: 978-1-4158-6615-3
Item 005173965

Dewey Decimal Classification: 248.4
Subject Heading: Christian Life

Unless otherwise indicated, Scripture quotations are from the King James Version.

Scripture quotations marked NASB are from the New American Standard Bible.
© The Lockman Foundation, 1960, 1962, 1963, 1968, 1971, 1972, 1973, 1975, 1977.
Used by permission.

Scripture quotations marked NIV are from the Holy Bible, New International Version,
copyright © 1973, 1978, 1984 by International Bible Society.

To order additional copies of this resource: WRITE LifeWay Church Resources Customer Service;
One LifeWay Plaza; Nashville, TN 37234-0113; FAX order to (615) 251-5933; PHONE
1-800-458-2772; E-MAIL *orderentry@lifeway.com*; order ONLINE at *www.lifeway.com*;
or visit the LifeWay Christian Store serving you.

Printed in the United States of America

COVER PAINTING: REMBRANDT VAN RIJN
Rembrandt was naturally attracted to the figure and personality of Jesus; he had a genuine love for
the Bible. Rembrandt painted a number of versions of Christ. The one used on the cover, entitled *Head
of Christ*, portrays Jesus as one whose face reveals intelligence as well as innocent concern. This is a
rendition of the private Jesus. He is about to speak, but not to multitudes of people. Instead, Jesus' quiet
words will be heard only by the listener close by. May that be so for you as you seek the mind of Christ.

Head of Christ, REMBRANDT VAN RIJN, Dutch, 1606-1669
Gemäldegalerie, Berlin-Dahlem, Oil on wood panel, 10 x 12"

Leadership and Adult Publishing
LifeWay Church Resources
One LifeWay Plaza
Nashville, TN 37234-0175

THE MIND OF CHRIST

CONTENTS

T. W. Hunt

For seven years prior to his retirement, T. W. Hunt served as prayer specialist in the Adult Discipleship and Family Development Department of the Baptist Sunday School Board. Before coming to this position, he was Professor of Church Music at Southwestern Baptist Theological Seminary in Fort Worth, Texas, for 24 years. He is the author of *Disciple's Prayer Life: Walking in Fellowship with God* (with Catherine Walker), *The Life-Changing Power of Prayer* (formerly *The Doctrine of Prayer*), *Music in Missions: Discipling Through Music, From Heaven's View* (written with his daughter), and has written numerous articles for a variety of periodicals. A native of Arkansas, Dr. Hunt graduated from Ouachita Baptist College; and received the Master of Music and Doctor of Philosophy degrees from North Texas State University. He lives in Spring, Texas with his wife Laverne. They have one daughter, Melana, and six grandchildren.

Claude King

Claude V. King is a discipleship specialist at LifeWay Christian Resources. In addition to this course, Claude worked with T. W. Hunt to develop *Growing Disciples: Pray in Faith* (formerly *In God's Presence*). He is coauthor of other books and courses including *Experiencing God, Fresh Encounter, Made to Count Life Planner,* and *Concentric Circles of Concern.* His most recent books include *Come to the Lord's Table* and *Growing Disciples: The Call to Follow Christ.* He is a graduate of Belmont College and New Orleans Baptist Theological Seminary. Claude lives in Murfreesboro, Tennessee, with his wife, Reta. They have two daughters, Julie and Jenny, and one grandson.

To be like Jesus! That is why God created us. "For whom he did foreknow, he also did predestinate to be conformed to the image of his Son, that he might be the firstborn among many brethren" (Rom. 8:29). God is in the process of "bringing many sons unto glory" (Heb. 2:10). The glory we are to have is the glory of being like God's perfect Son, Jesus Christ. This course is about learning to think the thoughts of Christ—to have the mind of Christ. It is based on the magnificent challenge in Philippians 2:5-11 which begins: "Let this mind be in you, which was also in Christ Jesus" (Phil. 2:5).

You may ask, "Isn't it presumptuous to speak on the mind of Christ?" That is exactly what I thought! I always have been overwhelmed with my unworthiness to deal with such an imposing topic. The only answer I have to that question is that, for some reason in His grace, God chose to arouse my interest and to answer my questions.

The Purpose of this Course

This course is not a biography of Christ. Large numbers of biographies already exist. The presentation is more topical than chronological. I generally follow the order of the concepts in Philippians 2:5-11. This course is intended to be practical and not theoretical. It should be studied with a view to immediate application.

You cannot study this course, however, apart from the help of the Holy Spirit. As Claude and I wrote it, we did not write a line without the Holy Spirit's help. We preceded every writing period with a prayer in which we pleaded that the Holy Spirit would direct the writing to reflect what God wants His Body to know about the mind of Christ. Prayer warriors and prayer ministries across the country undergirded this writing. I beg you to breathe a prayer every time you begin to study in this course.

My understanding of these concepts was forged out of the furnace of real life. Shortly after beginning to teach this message publicly, God impressed me that I never should teach an insight I had not applied to my own life and observed in practice. Because of these factors, I have written some portions of this course autobiographically. I

hardly could have done it any other way and remained faithful to the original calling and receiving of the message. I know from experience that application does work. I also want you to know it, and hope you will prove its validity by your own application.

No study can contain the whole of the mind of Christ. That is an impossibility, since His mind is infinite. This course is intended to be suggestive and helpful, but not exhaustive. It may initiate in your mind some topics you have not thought of. It may suggest others that I have not thought of. Those tangents may be the Holy Spirit taking you on a learning adventure all your own. I hope you will follow up on those other tangents as the Holy Spirit works to develop the mind of Christ in you.

Writing Preferences

For the most part, footnotes have been kept to a minimum. Occasionally I have used parentheses to avoid a footnote. I have followed this procedure in the hope that it would make for easier study. The footnotes I have included are intended to help you investigate further intriguing matters.

Scripture quotations usually are arranged in biblical order. In a few cases I placed them in chronological order as they occurred in Christ's life. I have attempted to give as much Scripture as possible so it will be readily available for your study. In cases where the text is not included, I have tried to give you references for your personal study.

I have preferred traditional terminology rather than a more sophisticated choice of words. For example, for the three cases in which Jesus restored a person to life, I have called them a *resurrection*. Some people prefer to reserve the term *resurrection* for Christ's conquering of death, and to use the term *resuscitation* for the restoration of life to the widow of Nain's son, Jairus's daughter, and Lazarus, since they died a normal death. However, the three were dead, and I have used *resurrection* to clarify the message.

Often I have used the masculine gender to refer to all of humanity, but I have tried to include both genders in the sections on the humanity of Christ. Simplicity sometimes indicated a masculine use to include all humanity. The Scriptures do this frequently. I have a profound respect for womanhood. I emphatically intend to include all women believers in the teaching.

Several of the virtues, such as purity, had to be treated from various viewpoints in different units. This gives a multi-faceted view of these virtues, like that of a diamond. Different contexts required another look at the virtues to serve the purpose of that context. Repetition should help you in the process of application.

Crucifixion and Resurrection

During the years that I have taught *The Mind of Christ* publicly, I always have included a narration of the crucifixion and the resurrection. The cross, more than anything else in Christ's life, presents the totality of His mind—His humility, His self-control, His servanthood, His faith. All that is Christ. We cannot comprehend God until we understand the dread cost of the cross. We also must look at the cross to know the bottomless depths of God's love. The glory of the cross also would be meaningless without the inseparable victory of the resurrection. We decided to include these two presentations as worship videos rather than in this interactive text format. I have made suggestions at the end of units 11 and 12 for the use of these two presentations.

My Personal Convictions About Christ

You might want to know my personal convictions about Christ. I simply say that He is fully God and fully Man. He is the only begotten Son of God, which means that He is of the same essence as God the Father. Christ also is the Second Person of the Holy Trinity. He was born of a virgin; lived a sinless, perfect life; died a sacrificial, substitutionary death for the sins of all who accept Him; and conquered death through the resurrection of His physical body. He is my personal Savior, and absolute Lord of my life: my every thought, my actions, my emotions, and my will. Christ is the Head of the church. Every Christian believer should submit to His lordship.

I have vivid memories of the criticisms of the Jesus Movement in the early 1970s. Certain persons who were antagonistic to the movement said that it centered too much on the Second Person of the Trinity—Jesus. The same criticism could be made about this course. My only answer is that we must be faithful to God's own method of Self-revelation. Any service to Him must be faithful to the patterns and procedures He establishes. God revealed and explained Himself by Jesus Christ. God chose that method. Knowing the Lord Jesus, we know God the Father and the Spirit, and we cannot know Jesus or the Father without the Spirit. The Spirit's job is to testify about Jesus and to glorify Him (John 15:26; 16:14). God has many means of Self-revelation, but His primary vehicle in history is the incarnation.

My Prayer for You

I sincerely hope that this course will suggest further studies to you. Ask God to help you study this course in His Spirit, and His Spirit will open up new worlds to you. My prayers are with you as you open-mindedly try to master the insights and concepts of this course.

Holy Father, exalt Your gracious Son to the one who studies this course. May Christ, and only Christ, be glorified as my friend reads and studies. I ask You to do this because You have given us the infinite worth of Jesus' name in which to offer our prayers. Through His Spirit, for His sake, and in His name I pray. Amen.

T. W. HUNT
Nashville, TN
January 1994

Overview of *The Mind of Christ*

Paul said, "Let this mind be in you, which was also in Christ Jesus" (Phil. 2:5). This course is to help you keep that command. In Luke 17:21 Jesus said, "the kingdom of God is within you." Jesus emphasized that the kingdom of God does not come with outward observance, but by an inner working that is not seen. That directs us to the mind, the area where God wants to work. The changes that He brings in your life are secret and inward, but they will bear fruit that will be visible in your life and lifestyle.

Moving toward that end, we will be looking at a poem in Philippians 2:5-11. This poem was actually a hymn and probably was sung during times of worship in the early church. I have divided the hymn into six parts for your study:

PHILIPPIANS 2:5-11

Part 1   Christ's Freedom

"Let this mind be in you, which was also in Christ Jesus" (v. 5).

Part 2   Christ's Lifestyle

"Who, being in the form of God, thought it not robbery to be equal with God" (v. 6).

Part 3   Christ's Servanthood

"But made himself of no reputation, and took upon him the form of a servant" (v. 7).

Part 4   Christ's Humanity

"And was made in the likeness of men: And being found in fashion as a man" (vv. 7-8).

Part 5   Christ's Holiness and Love

"He humbled himself, and became obedient unto death, even the death of the cross" (v. 8).

Part 6   Christ's Name

"Wherefore God also hath highly exalted him, and given him a name which is above every name: That at the name of Jesus every knee should bow, of things in heaven, and things in earth, and things under the earth: And that every tongue should confess that Jesus Christ is Lord, to the glory of God the Father" (vv. 9-11).

As we look at each part of this hymn, I will help you understand how God wants to work in you to transform you into the image of His Son Jesus.

• Unit 1 will help you understand a three-stage process through which God will guide you. You will see what the Christlike mind is like.

• God will begin His work by setting you free from the bondage of sin (units 2-3).

• In units 4-5 we will look at 17 virtues of the mind of Christ. God will be working to develop those virtues in your life.

• Unit 6 will help you understand the importance of servanthood, following the example of Christ. God will be working to develop in your life the characteristics of servanthood.

• Units 7-10 will help you focus on Christ's humanity. His earthly life is the perfect example of what God intended humanity to be. In these units we will study the Beatitudes, emotions, relationships with things and people, and living in the Spirit. God will be working to purify your mind and life to reflect the perfect humanity of Christ.

• Unit 11 will examine how love and holiness work together to enhance each other. God will be working in you to make you holy and to teach you to love with a Christlike love.

• The final unit (12) will reach the height of the hymn as we examine how God has exalted Christ through His names. You will be challenged to bow your knees by surrendering to the absolute lordship of Christ in your life.

This 12-unit study will serve as an introduction to a lifelong process for you as God continually renews your mind and life to reflect the image of His Son Jesus.

Studying *The Mind of Christ*

This book is different from most books. It is not designed for you to sit down and read from cover to cover. *The Mind of Christ* (Broadman & Holman) book takes that approach. In this approach, we want you to study, understand, and apply these biblical principles to your life. These challenging goals take time, and many people desire a personal guide or tutor to help them through the process. Claude and I have written this workbook to be your personal tutor.

To get the most out of this course, study only one daily lesson at a time. Do not try to study several lessons in a single day. You need time to let these thoughts sink in to your understanding and practice. You want to experience a Person—Jesus Christ. You want to develop His way of thinking and His way of living. Time and meditation are necessary to allow the Holy Spirit to make this renewal process real in your life.

Please do not skip any of the learning activities. They are designed to help you learn and apply these truths to your life. They will help you establish a personal daily walk with Christ. Many activities will lead you to interaction with God through prayer, meditation, and Bible study. If you leave out these activities, you may miss an encounter with God that could radically change your life. You will learn that your love relationship with God is the most important part of your spiritual life. Without an intimate relationship with God, you will miss what He wants to do in and through your life.

1. **The activities will begin (like this paragraph) with a flourish next to indented type. Follow the instructions given. After you have completed the activity you will return to the content.**

Answers might be given following the activity so you can check your work. Write your answer before reading ours. Sometimes your response to the activity will be your own response or opinion, and no right or wrong answer can be given. If you have difficulty with an activity or you question the answers given, write a note in the margin. Discuss this concern with your leader or small group.

Memorizing Scripture

One aspect of gaining the mind of Christ is implanting God's Word deeply in your mind. Memorizing Scripture is an important discipline you will be called on to use in your study. Use the cards in the back of this book to help you memorize the key passages in *The Mind of Christ*. Consider the following ideas to help you further develop Scripture memorization.

1. Read the verse and think about the meaning.
2. Write the verse on index cards, one phrase per line.
3. Glance at the first phrase and say it aloud. Glance at the next phrase and say both phrases aloud. Continue this process until you have said the whole verse.
4. Try to say the verse from memory later in the day. If you cannot remember the complete verse, glance at the cards to refresh your memory.
5. Repeat the verse several times each day for a week or until you feel that the verse is firmly implanted in your mind. Then review verses regularly.

Lifelong Helps

You will not finish this course in three months. This course is just an introduction to a lifelong process of allowing God to mold and shape your life into the image of Christ. Let God work with you day by day. That process never will be finished this side of heaven. You always will be in need of God's renewal process in your mind and in your life.

We have provided tools to help you in this lifelong process. The pages (pp. 224-259) and cards in the back of this book will help you regularly examine your mind and your life. In that process God will reveal things that should be removed from your life, and He will be transforming your thinking and your lifestyle to reflect Christ. The following three months will be your introduction to a lifelong process of becoming like Jesus.

Small-Group Sessions

Once each week you should attend a small-group session in which you will discuss the content you studied the previous week, share insights and testimonies, encourage one another, and pray together. You will miss much of the intended learning if you do not participate in a small-group study. Small groups should not have more than 10 members for maximum effectiveness. Larger groups will experience less closeness, less intimate sharing, more absenteeism, and more dropouts. If more than 10 people want to study the course, enlist additional leaders for each group of six to 10.

If you have started studying *The Mind of Christ* and you are not involved in a small group, enlist a few friends to study the course with you. You will discover that other members of the body of Christ can help you more fully know and understand God's working in your life. The small group becomes a place where you can practice Hebrews 10:23-25:

"Let us hold fast the confession of our hope without wavering, for He who promised is faithful; and let us consider how to stimulate one another to love and good deeds, not forsaking our own assembling together, as is the habit of some, but encouraging one another; and all the more, as you see the day drawing near" (NASB).

God intended for members of the body of Christ to help each other, stimulate each other to love and good deeds, and encourage one another. Don't try to develop the mind of Christ alone. Let the body of Christ help you in this process.

Seven Segments for Each Session

Each session is divided into seven segments. The following segment descriptions will give you an overview of the process suggested for each session. The purpose is to help you practice "being" the body of Christ.

1. Hearing What the Spirit Is Saying. "He that hath an ear, let him hear what the Spirit saith unto the churches" (Rev. 2:11). As you arrive before the session, review what God has been saying to you during the week. You will identify a Scripture and a name of Christ that have been most meaningful this week. You will identify and mark the issue or subject in which God seems to be working most actively to develop Christ's mind within you. You will use these bits of information at various points in the session. This is a standard part of each session; so you may want to watch for these items as you study each week.

2. Magnifying the Lord and Exalting His Name. "O magnify the Lord with me, and let us exalt his name together" (Ps. 34:3). As you open each session in prayer, you will worship God for Who He is and acknowledge

Him for what He has done. You may use the names of Christ to exalt His name together in prayer. Following the prayer time, you will have a chance to share any ways God may have revealed Himself this week through His names.

3. Transforming by the Word. "Christ also loved the church, and gave himself for it; that he might sanctify and cleanse it with the washing of water by the word, that he might present it to himself a glorious church, not having spot, or wrinkle, or any such thing; but that it should be holy and without blemish" (Eph. 5:25-27). Because the Scriptures reveal the nature, character, and standard for the mind and lifestyle of Christ, you will work with others to make two lists each week: (1) a list of things, actions, or attitudes identified in Scripture that need to be *cleansed from* one's mind and life, and (2) a list of things, actions, or attitudes that Scripture indicates need to be *incorporated into* one's mind and life. This is a standard activity each week; so you may want to watch for these items to remove and add to your life as you study each unit.

4. Stimulating One Another to Love and Good Deeds. "Let us consider how to stimulate one another to love and good deeds" (Heb. 10:24, NASB). Because God did not intend for Christians to live their lives independently from the rest of the body, He made us dependent on one another. You will help one another apply the truths of the Scriptures and the model of Christ to your own lives. This will be a time for discussion, testimony, encouragement, challenge, and accountability as you help one another respond to God's renewing process in your minds and lives.

Some people are far better at helping others than they are in receiving help themselves. For the body of Christ to function effectively, members need to learn to do both. Be willing to receive help when you need it. Also, keep in mind this is not to be a time for self-righteous people to "fix" everybody else. It is a time for humble servants to give and receive help.

5. Preparing the Bride for Her Bridegroom. "Let us be glad and rejoice, and give honour to him: for the marriage of the Lamb is come, and his wife hath made herself ready. And to her was granted that she should be arrayed in fine linen, clean and white: for the fine linen is the righteousness of saints. And he saith unto me, Write, Blessed are they which are called unto the marriage supper of the Lamb" (Rev. 19:7-9). As the marriage of Christ and His bride (the church) draws near, the bride must make herself ready. Christian churches must cleanse and purify themselves so they will be pleasing and acceptable to the Bridegroom. In each session, a Scripture will be examined that will help the bride prepare herself. You will discuss and apply the Scripture to your lives, families, and church.

6. Praying for One Another. "Confess your faults one to another, and pray one for another, that ye may be healed. The effectual fervent prayer of a righteous man availeth much" (Jas. 5:16). Because God intends for a church to be a house of prayer (see Luke 19:46), You will have an opportunity each session to share with one another in prayer. This will be an opportunity to share prayer requests for spiritual concerns; and confess faults, weaknesses, sins, struggles, and failures. But it will also be a time for praying fervently for one another for forgiveness, healing, encouragement, guidance, wisdom, knowledge, understanding, courage, strength, and faithfulness.

THE MIND OF CHRIST FAMILY

Resources have been developed for three primary approaches to developing the mind of Christ. You are holding one (the member book) in your hands. The family includes the following:

- *The Mind of Christ* member's book (item 005173965)
- *The Mind of Christ Leader Kit* (item 005156923) provides a copy of the member book for use in a 13-session group study, as well the viewer guide and four DVDs featuring author T. W. Hunt for use in an 8-session DVD conference.
- *The Mind of Christ Viewer Guide* (item 005174508) provides charts, diagrams, pages for participants to take notes on the DVDs, and a small-group discussion guide for 8 sessions.
- *The Mind of Christ* hardback book (Broadman/ Holman, item 001069699) Book version of T. W. Hunt's *The Mind of Christ*.

Learning Approaches
These resources provide three approaches for studying this message. You may want to consider participating in more than one approach as you allow God to continue

this lifelong process of conforming you to the image of Christ Jesus, His Son.

1. Individual Study. Individuals can study any of the resources at their own pace. They can either (1) read the Broadman & Holman book, (2) watch the DVD messages using the viewing guide or (3) study the member book. Making the resources available in the church media library and/or for sale to members will encourage individual study. Recommend that individuals consider participating in some group format to benefit from the encouragement and interaction with other believers.

2. DVD Conference. For years T. W. Hunt has led weekend conferences on *The Mind of Christ* in churches across the country. Now you can have Dr. Hunt in your church leading the conference through DVD messages. You are not limited, however, by his schedule and availability. You can conduct the conference on a weekend, weekdays, week nights, spread it out over 8 weeks, or do all of the above! Let Dr. Hunt do the teaching and preaching on the DVD messages during the evening worship services. Many people have found that one time through is not enough, so you can repeat the conference as often as you choose at your convenience. Members who miss a session can make it up by checking out the DVDs for home viewing. The DVD conference will require at least eight 75-minute sessions if you include time for discussion of the messages. Group members can help each other in making application to their lives.

3. Individual and Small-Group Study Combination. *The Mind of Christ* member book provides for an individual study with a small-group session once each week. This combination of more in-depth study and small-group interaction will enhance learning and contribute to greater application of the material. With this approach, you will need a small group for each eight to ten participants. If you have more than ten persons interested in the course, provide multiple groups in order to create the best possible learning environment. If you do not have sufficient leaders, start a waiting list for the next group. In the meantime, begin training new leaders within the group or groups you currently have.

If you are interested in ordering any of the additional resources, see page 260.

BECOMING LIKE CHRIST

Hymn Part 1

CHRIST'S FREEDOM

*"Let this mind be in you,
which was also in Christ Jesus"*
(Phil. 2:5).

DAY 1
Characteristics of a Christlike Mind, Part 1

DAY 2
Characteristics of a Christlike Mind, Part 2

DAY 3
Philippians 2:5-11

DAY 4
Developing the Mind of Christ

DAY 5
Fix Your Thoughts on Jesus

Why You Will Find This Unit Helpful
You will understand what God will be doing in you and expecting of you during this course (and for the rest of your life) to develop in you the mind of Christ. You will begin to cultivate a deeper intimacy with God in prayer and in His Word.

Lifelong Objective
In Christ you will set, renew, and gird up your mind in such a way that God will develop in you a spiritual mind characterized as alive, single-minded, lowly, pure, responsive, and peaceful.

Summary of God's Work in You

God's desire is that you be like Christ. The one aspect of your personality which He will measure constantly for Christlikeness is your mind. God helps in your growth by revealing through His Word the expectations He has for your mind. Through His Word, His work, His grace, and His Spirit, you can have the mind of Christ.

Unit Learning Goals

- You will understand the meaning of six characteristics of the Christlike mind.
- You will understand what God will be doing to develop Christlike qualities in your mind.
- You will understand three stages in the process of developing the mind of Christ.
- You will demonstrate your willingness to set your mind on Christ and submit to His renewing of your mind.
- You will understand the role you have in developing the mind of Christ.
- You will know the focus of your thoughts related to the Apostle and the High Priest roles of Christ.
- You will demonstrate your commitment to begin developing the mind of Christ.

What You Will Do to Begin Developing the Mind of Christ

- You will study the characteristics of a Christlike mind.
- You will set your mind and attention on Christ.
- You will begin to allow Christ to renew your mind.
- You will gird up your mind for action.

Scripture Memory Verse

"Be not conformed to this world: but be ye transformed by the renewing of your mind, that ye may prove what is that good, and acceptable, and perfect, will of God" (Rom. 12:2).

The Mind of Christ Cards Related to This Unit

1A. Scripture Memory—Philippians 2:5-8
1B. Scripture Memory—Philippians 2:9-11
2A. Six Characteristics of a Christlike Mind
2B. Three Stages in Developing the Mind of Christ
3A. Unit 1: Scripture Memory—Romans 12:2

Optional DVD Messages by T. W. Hunt

- Session 2, Part 1, Chapters 1-4: His Lifestyle

DAY 1
CHARACTERISTICS OF A CHRISTLIKE MIND, PART 1

Today's Bible Meditation
"Be not conformed to this world: but be ye transformed by the renewing of your mind, that ye may prove what is that good, and acceptable, and perfect, will of God" (Rom. 12:2).

Name of Christ for Today
The Bread of Life
(John 6:35)

Prayer to Begin the Lesson
Jesus, I am hungry and thirsty after Your righteousness. I do want to be like You. You are the Bread of life itself. Fill me with Yourself so that I may experience the abundant life You came to give. Amen.

1. Begin by reading in the left margin the Scripture for meditation and the name of Christ for today. Work on your memory verse. Then use the suggested prayer to begin your study. Reading those items each day will help prepare you for our time together.

Welcome to *The Mind of Christ*. You are beginning a lifelong process of developing the mind of Christ. Right now, that thought may be too big to understand. Through Paul, God has commanded His people to "Let this mind be in you, which was also in Christ Jesus" (Phil. 2:5). The mind of Christ! We are not told to have a good mind, not a mind purified by discipline, not a sharpened intellect, not even the highest of human attainment in godliness and virtue—but the very mind of Christ Himself! We are not merely to resemble Jesus. We are to think His very thoughts. This is not a wish but a command. We are to have the mind of the only perfect human who ever walked our earth—the mind of the God-man, Jesus Christ. Can you see why this will be a lifelong process? Let's get started.

2. If you have not read the introduction (pp. 8-11), you need to do that before continuing. Please check the box when you have read it. ❏

3. You will learn many names of Christ in this study. What name did you learn today? _____

These first three activities are simple. Future activities will become more meaningful. We began with these to get you off to a good start in our study together. Please complete each instruction or activity as best you can so God will have maximum opportunity to work in your life.

Six times the New Testament describes or implies what the Christian's mind is to be like. In each case, the word *mind* is mentioned. From these we can derive six adjectives that describe God's ideal for your mind. Let's begin our study by looking at these six characteristics.

SIX CHARACTERISTICS OF THE CHRISTLIKE MIND

1. **Alive**—"The mind set on the Spirit is life and peace" (Rom. 8:6, NASB).
2. **Single-minded**—"I am afraid, lest . . . your minds should be led astray from the simplicity and purity of devotion to Christ" (2 Cor. 11:3, NASB).
3. **Lowly**—"In lowliness of mind let each esteem other better than themselves" (Phil. 2:3).
4. **Pure**—"Unto the pure all things are pure: but unto them that are defiled and unbelieving is nothing pure; but even their mind and conscience is defiled" (Titus 1:15).
5. **Responsive**—"He opened their minds to understand the Scriptures" (Luke 24:45, NASB).
6. **Peaceful**—"The mind set on the Spirit is life and peace" (Rom. 8:6, NASB).

Throughout this course, you will look in detail at the life of Jesus. You will see that these six characteristics were true of His mind. Let's look at what each one means for your mind.

Alive

Paul tells us, "The mind set on the flesh is death, but the mind set on the Spirit is life and peace" (Rom. 8:6, NASB). Our first and last characteristics—alive and peaceful—come from this verse. Without Christ we are dead (Eph. 2:1). In Christ we have everlasting life (John 3:36). Jesus went further than saying we live. Jesus said that He came in order that we might have abundant life (John 10:10). You demonstrate this life (or death) constantly by the choices you make. When you set your mind on the Spirit, you experience life.

4. What is one characteristic of a Christlike mind? _____

You can choose what you will think about. That is why the will is so important. "The mind set on the flesh is death" (Rom. 8:6, NASB). The mind that is set on the Spirit is alive and active. Life is distinguished by activity. The mind of Christ is not lazy. It enjoys occupation. At times it reflects on the Person of God. At times it prays. At times it brings the intentions of God into our dialogue with another Christian or with a non-Christian. The mind that is alive chooses the spiritual in preference to the fleshly.

The mind that is alive chooses the spiritual in preference to the fleshly.

Single-minded

A second description of the mind occurs in 2 Corinthians 11:3: "I am afraid, lest as the serpent deceived Eve by his craftiness, your minds should be led astray from the simplicity and purity of devotion to Christ" (NASB). In other words, the mind of Christ is single-minded in devotion to Christ.

One of our spiritual problems is becoming distracted or being "led astray." Concentration is difficult because the mind is bombarded by so many distractions. Most of our minds dart off in hundreds of directions in the course of a day. Single-mindedness is an act of the mind. The single-minded Christian pays attention to Christ, His commands, His Person, and His ways.

Your mind must be preoccupied with sincere and pure devotion to Christ. Single-mindedness is the discipline of attention. We will see in more detail in future lessons the great importance of your will. You can direct or control your attention with a focus on Christ and His kingdom.

The single-minded Christian pays attention to Christ, His commands, His Person, and His ways.

5. What is a second characteristic of a Christlike mind? _____

Lowly

Paul gives another description of the godly mind in Philippians 2:3: "Let nothing be done through strife or vainglory; but in lowliness of mind let each esteem other better than themselves." The mind is to be lowly. Humility, a twin of lowliness, will be treated later in the study of servanthood (unit 6). One cannot be humble unless he is lowly. Humility follows lowliness of mind. Humility speaks of a relationship to others and to God. Lowliness is a state of mind.

The opposite of lowliness is haughtiness, pride, or arrogance. Lowliness is a trait which must be cultivated. Members of the body of Christ learn to submit to one another by lowliness. We can foster lowliness by concentrating on a genuine appreciation for the Person of God. We start there. Lowliness must come first, in order for the perspective to be right.

Those who encountered God in the Bible almost always first experienced genuine terror or fear before Him. This is a godly fear, not a carnal fear. Those who met God knew of the need for lowliness. They immediately recognized the vast difference between God and themselves. A clear view of God's greatness will lead you to a proper view of yourself. The lowly Christian has the security of understanding his position under the greatness of God.

The lowly Christian has the security of understanding his position under the greatness of God.

6. What is a third characteristic of a Christlike mind? _____

7. You have learned about three characteristics of a Christlike mind. Write the appropriate characteristic in front of its definition.

_____ A proper perspective of my position under the greatness of God.

_____ Disciplined attention on Christ and His kingdom.

_____ Activity of the mind that chooses the spiritual over _____ the fleshly.

8. Conclude today's lesson by focusing on Christ and His kingdom. Spend time in prayer.

- Talk to the Lord about what He is doing or preparing to do in your life and church.
- Thank God for the privilege of becoming like His Son Jesus Christ.
- Acknowledge your proper position of lowliness before His greatness.

DAY 2
CHARACTERISTICS OF A CHRISTLIKE MIND, PART 2

1. Begin today's lesson by reading the Bible verse and the name of Christ for today. Work on your memory verse. Then use the suggested prayer to begin your study.

2. Can you remember the three characteristics of a Christlike mind that you studied yesterday? Write the three below and check your work.

_____ _____ _____

Today's Bible Meditation
"To be carnally minded is death; but to be spiritually minded is life and peace" (Rom. 8:6).

Name of Christ for Today
Image of the Invisible God (Col. 1:15)

Prayer to Begin the Lesson
Jesus, Image of the Invisible God, show me the Father. Help me come to know the Father as You reveal to me what He is like. Since He is invisible, help me to focus my eyes on You and the example of Your life. Amen.

Pure

Paul speaks about the mind in Titus 1:15: "Unto the pure all things are pure: but unto them that are defiled and unbelieving is nothing pure; but even their mind and conscience is defiled." Purity is depicted as the natural state of the Christian. Impurity is reached by corruption of the mind and conscience.

3. What is one characteristic of a Christlike mind? _____

The natural spiritual state—one that is filled with God's Spirit and growing in Christ—is difficult to maintain. One reason is the constant assault of information on our senses. Tempters have opportunities to take us into realms of thought never known before. Television, for example, can channel impurities right into the privacy of our homes. Lust is grander. Jealousy is more treacherous. Greed is simply the road to an important position, and anxiety is more fashionable. Sin is everywhere.

In order to overcome the temptations toward impurity you must want to be pure. Until that desire becomes your passion, you will be overwhelmed by the impressions flooding into your senses. If your desire for purity is sincere, God will provide you with the way of overcoming impurities (1 Cor. 10:13). Your safest course is to escape temptation entirely. The psalmist used this approach when he said, "I will set no wicked thing before mine eyes" (Ps. 101:3). Strength comes prior to temptation, not during it. Overcoming is a prior act. It involves making a decision to remain pure before the temptation comes. If you haven't made up your mind before the temptation, you are going to be vulnerable.

4. *What is the safest way to maintain purity in the face of temptation?*

_____

Responsive

When Jesus appeared to His disciples on the evening of the resurrection, "He opened their minds to understand the Scriptures" (Luke 24:45, NASB). The Lord could not open some minds today! When Jesus chose the disciples, He recognized in them a quality that made them fit subjects for three and a half years of intensive training. The disciples did not always learn quickly, but they were teachable. They at least wanted to learn. We might call this quality open-mindedness, but modern connotations of that word give it a meaning foreign to the quality with which Jesus was working. They were responsive to His teaching.

We see the opposite of responsiveness in 2 Corinthians 3:12-16. Speaking of the Israelites in the desert, Paul says "their minds were blinded" (v. 14). Paul tells us that "Unto this day, when Moses is read, the veil is upon their heart" (v. 15). In Christ, however, the covering is taken away (v. 14). The spiritual dullness of the Pharisees and Sadducees was willful. They were smug in their self-righteousness and missed the coming of their Messiah. To be unresponsive to God is to be spiritually dull-witted.

Responsiveness must be to God. We must not be responsive to anything and everything. The disciples were sensitive when they asked, "Lord, teach us to pray" (Luke 11:1). In this petition, they were not merely envying the enormous ability of Jesus to perform miracles (earlier they had been given authority to heal the sick and cast out demons). Rather, they perceived in Jesus a relationship to His Father that they wanted to imitate. Jesus was intensely spiritual and they wanted that quality of spirituality in their own lives.

How can you cultivate that sensitivity? One way is to spend time in God's Word. Prayer also sensitizes your spirit.

Responsiveness to God is indispensable for progress in your spiritual life. You need to be sensitive to God's Holy Spirit. How can you cultivate that sensitivity? One way is to spend time in God's Word. Specifically, Jesus opened the minds of the disciples to Scripture. God wants you to understand His Word, but you cannot understand it if you do not spend time in it. Prayer also sensitizes your spirit. When the disciples wanted to imitate Jesus, it was His teaching on prayer that they asked for.

🖎 5. **What are two disciplines that can indicate a responsive mind?**

_____ _____

The Mind of Christ Cards in the back of this book are one of the tools provided to help you. You can carry these cards with you. Throughout the day you may have free time on a break, waiting in an office, or some other opportunity. Use the cards to memorize Scripture. Some of the cards will help you review the content you are studying. Saturate your mind with the things of God.

🖎 6. **Turn to the back of the book and tear out the following cards that relate to this unit:**

1A. Scripture Memory—Philippians 2:5-8
1B. Scripture Memory—Philippians 2:9-11
2A. Six Characteristics of a Christlike Mind
2B. Three Stages in Developing the Mind of Christ
3A. Unit 1: Scripture Memory—Romans 12:2

🖎 7. **While the idea is fresh on your mind, spend a few minutes to begin memorizing Romans 12:2 (Card 3A).**

Jesus was sensitive and responsive in the utmost degree to His Father. Jesus said, "I do nothing on My own initiative, but I speak these things as the Father taught Me" (John 8:28, NASB). He claimed to see what the Father was doing, to hear what the Father was saying, to do nothing independently of the Father, and to be taught by the Father. Jesus devoted Himself to reflecting the mind of the Father, and His reflection was exact. As the Father is to the Son, so Christ is to you.

• Jesus imitated the Father. You are to imitate Christ.
• Jesus saw the activity of the Father. You pay close attention to the known earthly activity of Jesus (also to His present activity).
• Jesus heard from the Father. You must hear from Jesus.
• Jesus was taught by the Father. You are taught by Jesus.
• Jesus could do nothing independently of the Father. and you cannot function independently of Jesus.
• Jesus was very close to the Father. You must remain close to Jesus.

Peaceful

Romans 8:6 already has given us the adjective *alive* to apply to the spiritual mind. It also gives another word: "The mind set on the Spirit is life and peace." The spiritual mind is peaceful. Peace is a fruit of the Spirit (see Gal. 5:22), not an attainment. Your work is setting your mind. God's work is providing the peace. Jesus had peace. His life was completely free from sin and the ravages of the world system. He promised rest to the weary and burdened (see Matt. 11:28). You find rest by taking His yoke.

Your work is setting your mind. God's work is providing the peace.

🖎 **8. Name the three remaining characteristics of a Christlike mind:**

1. Alive	3. Lowly	5. R _____
2. Single-minded	4. P _____	6. P _____

To summarize this week's unit, you are to do three things in developing the mind of Christ. You are to—

1. set your mind;
2. renew your mind;
3. gird up your mind.

In doing these things, you are imitating Christ. As you progress through this course, you will be engaging in one of these mental operations. The New Testament mentions six things your mind is to become—alive, single-minded, lowly, pure, responsive, and peaceful. As you engage in these mental operations, you are obeying the Scripture and becoming like Christ. Each of our units will relate to one of these key adjectives of a Christlike mind.

🖎 **9. Pray as you finish today's lesson. Review the six characteristics of a Christlike mind on Card 2A, and ask God to work in you to produce all six of those characteristics.**

DAY 3
PHILIPPIANS 2:5-11

Today's Bible Meditation
"Behold, the kingdom of God is within you" (Luke 17:21).

Name of Christ for Today
The Christ [Anointed One] (Matt. 16:16)

Prayer to Begin the Lesson
Christ Jesus, You are the Messiah—God's Anointed One. I'm anxious to see some progress in developing Your mind in me, but already I'm aware that this will be a long process. I am thankful that I don't have to do it alone. You dwell in me to help with the process. I love You. I look forward to deepening our relationship and to develop Your mind in me. Amen.

1. **Begin today's lesson by reading the Bible verse and the name of Christ for today. Work on your memory verse. Then use the suggested prayer to begin your study.**

You have studied six characteristics of a Christlike mind. They describe God's ideal for your mind. During your study of *The Mind of Christ*, God will be working to develop those characteristics in your mind.

As I have studied carefully our primary text for this course, Philippians 2:5-11, I have come to see six parts in the hymn. Each of the parts describes an aspect of Christ's life and mind. As we study each of those parts, God will be working to develop in you the six characteristics of a Christlike mind. During today's lesson, we will identify how each hymn part is related to what God will be doing in your life. God's kingdom (rule) is being realized as you become like Christ. The inner work God does in your mind will find expression outwardly in the way you live your life.

2. **Get out your Mind of Christ Cards for this unit and do the following:**

   • **Read the hymn in Philippians 2:5-11 on Cards 1A and 1B.**
   • **Begin memorizing the hymn at your own pace. It is an assignment over and above your weekly memory verse. Start today by working on verse 5. You may want to set a personal goal to memorize the hymn during the coming 12 weeks.**
   • **Review the Six Characteristics of a Christlike Mind on Card 2A.**

Now let's look in more detail at each part of the hymn in Philippians 2:5-11 and what God will be doing to develop a Christlike mind in you. The format we will use includes a hymn part and a title related to the mind of Christ. Beside each title is listed in parentheses the unit(s) related to that part of our hymn. Next you will read that part of the hymn text. Finally you will see the Christlike characteristic God will be developing in you.

PART 1—Christ's Freedom (Units 2-3)

Alive

Hymn: "Let this mind be in you, which was also in Christ Jesus" (Phil. 2:5).

Christlike Characteristic: Alive. Christians can experience mental battles occurring when the desires of the flesh clash with the desires of the Spirit. Christ intends to set you free from the dominion of sin in your life that causes such battles. Genuine freedom can occur only where spiritual life exists. Life is not fully spiritual until it is fully free. God will be working to give you life and freedom in Christ.

3. **Write this characteristic below and fill in the word to indicate what God will be doing in your life.**

   Characteristic—_____: God will be working to give me

   _____ and _____ in Christ.

PART 2—Christ's Lifestyle (Units 4-5)

Hymn: "Who, being in the form of God, thought it not robbery to be equal with God" (Phil. 2:6).

Christlike Characteristic: Single-minded. The human mind tends to waver like a ship on a stormy sea. Distractions are plentiful. The world works to shape you into its mold. Single-mindedness means that you set your mind and heart on seeking first God's kingdom. As you determine to put His kingdom first, God will begin to give you the virtues of godly wisdom and the fruit of the Spirit.

Single-minded

🖎 4. **Write this characteristic below and fill in the word to indicate what God will be doing in your life.**

Characteristic—_____: God will be working to give me the virtues of godly _____ and the _____ of the Spirit.

PART 3—Christ's Servanthood (Unit 6)

Hymn: Jesus "made himself of no reputation, and took upon him the form of a servant" (Phil. 2:7).

Christlike Characteristic: Lowly. Pride has been a foe of right living since Adam and Eve sinned in the garden. God despises the proud, but He dwells with the lowly. Lowliness does not mean belittling yourself. Rather, it means esteeming others. God will be working to help you see His greatness. With a lowly spirit you will take on the characteristics of servanthood.

Lowly

🖎 5. **Write this characteristic below and fill in the word to indicate what God will be doing in your life.**

Characteristic—_____: God will be working to help me see His _____, and with a _____ spirit I will take on the characteristics of _____.

PART 4—Christ's Humanity (Units 7-10)

Hymn: Jesus "was made in the likeness of men;" He was "found in fashion as a man" (Phil. 2:7-8).

Christlike Characteristic: Pure. When God became man, He demonstrated His intention that human beings have great authority and nobility. To have these two attributes, you must be pure. This purity will show in the way you express your humanity: in your emotions, in your relationships to things and people, and in your daily walk in the Spirit. God will be working in you to cleanse the impurities of your life and establish right patterns for living.

Pure

🖎 6. **Write this characteristic below and fill in the word to indicate what God will be doing in your life.**

Characteristic—_____: God will be working in me to cleanse the _____ of my life and establish _____ patterns for living.

PART 5—Christ's Holiness and Love (Unit 11)

Hymn: Jesus "became obedient unto death, even the death of the cross" (Phil. 2:8).

Responsive

Christlike Characteristic: Responsive. Jesus "became obedient unto death." His obedience purchased for us our holiness. Which death did Jesus die? "Even the death of the cross." This was the ultimate expression of God's love. Because of what Jesus did, we gladly obey Him. Responsiveness is not "doing your duty." In being responsive, you choose to share Christ's nature of holiness and love. God will be working to make you holy and to teach you to love with a Christlike love.

7. Write this characteristic below and fill in the word to indicate what God will be doing in your life.

Characteristic—_____: God will be working to make

me _____ and to teach me to _____ with a Christlike love.

PART 6—Christ's Name (Unit 12)

Hymn: "Wherefore God also hath highly exalted him, and given him a name which is above every name: That at the name of Jesus every knee should bow, of things in heaven, and things in earth, and things under the earth; And that every tongue should confess that Jesus Christ is Lord, to the glory of God the Father" (Phil. 2:9-11).

Peaceful

Christlike Characteristic: Peaceful. Jesus' love bought peace for us. Peace is not the absence of conflict, but the harvest of love. Christ's love took Him to Calvary. But in His death Jesus bought peace for us—peace with God. The resurrection was Christ's victory over sin and death. His victory made peace a reality. Through Christ's death, resurrection, and exaltation we can experience genuine peace. Peace doesn't come while your flesh battles God for control. The peace comes when you finally bow your knees to Christ and allow Him to be absolute Lord of your life. God will be working to exalt Christ before you so you will surrender completely to His lordship.

8. Write this characteristic below and fill in the word to indicate what God will be doing in your life.

Characteristic—_____: God will be working to exalt Christ

before me so I will _____ completely to His _____.

9. Close your study today in prayer. Of all the characteristics, which one do you sense God most wants to work on in your life? Ask God. Open your life to Him and give Him permission to mold you into the image of His Son. Thank God for the model He has given you in Jesus.

DAY 4
DEVELOPING THE MIND OF CHRIST

1. **Begin today's lesson by reading Bible verse and the name of Christ for today. Work on your memory verse. Then use the suggested prayer to begin your study.**

The New Testament uses three verbs concerning the mind. Becoming like Christ is accomplished in a process. If we were to think of the operations of the mind as a process, the three verbs can neatly classify themselves as beginning, middle, and ending parts of the process. I define these three stages in the following way:

THREE STAGES IN DEVELOPING THE MIND OF CHRIST

Beginning Stage	The Will Principle	*Set* your mind on things above.
Growing Stage	The River Principle	Allow God to *renew* your mind.
Qualified Stage	The Readiness Principle	*Gird up* your mind for action.

The Will Principle

The first verb, or the beginning of the process, is found in Colossians 3:2: "Set your mind on the things above, not on the things that are on earth" (NASB). A similar idea occurs in Philippians 4:8: "Finally, brethren, whatever is true, whatever is honorable, whatever is right, whatever is pure, whatever is lovely, whatever is of good repute, if there is any excellence and if anything worthy of praise, let your mind dwell on these things" (NASB).

We call this stage the Will Principle. You must set your mind. You must decide, choose, or determine the focus of your mind. That is where you start in developing the mind of Christ. The opposite of *will* is *instinct* or *unwilled reactions*. Decision making is not a problem with animals. But with human beings, the will is that part of your mind over which you have control. The will enables you to obey in spite of your feelings or intuitions. Often you cannot control your emotions, but you always have control over your will. What you want to do is take "every thought captive to the obedience of Christ" (2 Cor. 10:5, NASB). Giving God your will is the first step in having the mind of Christ.

2. **What do you do during the first stage—the Beginning Stage?**

   I (a verb) _____ my mind.

3. **What does it mean to set your mind? Define it in your own words.**

   _____

   _____

In the Beginning Stage you set your mind on Christ. You give your will to God and seek His will as your own. Christ repeatedly identified His will with that of His

Father. In the last week of His earthly life, as He faced the cross, Jesus said, "Now is my soul troubled; and what shall I say? Father, save me from this hour: but for this cause came I unto this hour. Father, glorify thy name" (John 12:27-28). Jesus openly confessed that His emotions were one place, but His will was in another. This decision to let His will rule over His emotions or feelings also is seen in Christ's plea in Gethsemane, "Father . . . take away this cup from me: nevertheless not what I will, but what thou wilt" (Mark 14:36). Jesus' performance was flawless, because He set His will from the beginning. Jesus' mind was given to God. Therefore, His actions worked out the implications of a blameless mind. Jesus' mind was set on things above.

I was asked once to take a position that would involve tremendous personal sacrifice as well as a huge salary cut. It also offered opportunity to expand God's kingdom in a way that nothing else offered. My feelings said *no* but my will chose the will of God. Only the will can choose beyond feelings.

The River Principle

Our second verb is *renew*. In Romans 12:2 Paul says, "Be transformed by the renewing of your mind." The Christian lives in a constant state of renewal! After you give your will to God, you must continue to allow your mind to be changed (transformed) by a renewing process. This part of the process is a time of growth.

Growing Stage
Allow God to renew your mind.

We call this middle or growing stage of the process the River Principle. Jesus said, "He who believes in Me, as the Scripture said, 'From his innermost being shall flow rivers of living water' " (John 7:38, NASB). Fresh living water flows in and washes out the old and the dead. Most of us do not work on the River Principle. We work on the Pond Principle! Ponds become stagnant, but rivers flow. Ponds become puddles, but rivers become oceans. You are to grow spiritually, and your growth in Christ ultimately is to be enormous.

Your body grows by producing new cells. As long as life continues, your body constantly is producing new cells. That newness is a sign of life. Failure to produce newness is a sign of death. The spiritual life, too, is to be characterized by a constant renewing. Lack of renewal or growth is a sign of death. I have learned to expect spiritual newness and not to be surprised at what form the newness takes. Sometimes the newness comes in the shape of new insights, previously unknown. Sometimes it comes in the form of spiritual energy. At times it is a new and deeper meaning applied to an old familiar verse. Newness may occur as you move into a new and deeper relationship to the body of Christ, or to another Christian. Newness may involve a new commitment of some kind. At times newness takes the form of a new strength or a new way to resist temptation. Newness is the way of progress as you are moving from one glory to another (see 2 Cor. 3:18).

2 Corinthians 3:18
"We all, with open face beholding as in a glass the glory of the Lord, are changed into the same image from glory to glory, even as by the Spirit of the Lord."

4. **What do you do during the second stage—the Growing Stage?**

I (a verb) _____ my mind.

5. **Which of the following indicate renewal? Check all that apply.**

❑ a. Newness of spiritual growth.
❑ b. Failure to show any signs of spiritual growth.
❑ c. New insights into the meaning or application of the Scripture.

❑ d. Failure to understand or apply Scriptures to my life.
❑ e. Sensing fresh spiritual energy to work for the Master.
❑ f. Weakness, tiredness, and lack of spiritual energy to work
   for the Master.

Allow God to renew your mind in the Growing Stage. Do you see the contrast between the River and the Pond Principles? Renewal brings newness, new insights, and fresh spiritual energy (a., c., e.). Christ's life demonstrated progress and growth. "Jesus increased in wisdom and stature, and in favour with God and man" (Luke 2:52). "Although He was a Son, He learned obedience from the things which He suffered" (Heb. 5:8, NASB). If you are to have the mind of Christ, you must expect newness. That is the way of growth. That is renewal.

The Readiness Principle

Our third verb associated with the mind takes us to the climax of the process. We are to *gird up* our minds for action (see 1 Pet. 1:13). The reference is to the long, flowing robes people wore in the first century. People could not run or move quickly in such dress. To do anything athletic, a person had to lift the edge of the robe and tuck it under the belt to free the lower legs for action. This was called girding up the robe. In this command is the Readiness Principle. Your mind is to be prepared for action.

> **Qualified Stage**
> *Gird up your mind for action.*

> **1 PETER 1:13**
> "GIRD UP THE LOINS OF YOUR MIND, BE SOBER, AND HOPE TO THE END FOR THE GRACE THAT IS TO BE BROUGHT UNTO YOU AT THE REVELATION OF JESUS CHRIST."

📖 6. What do you do during the third stage—the Qualified Stage?

   I (a verb) _____ my mind.

📖 7. What does that mean? Define it in your own words.

   _____

In the Qualified Stage you prepare your mind for action by girding it up. Jesus was alert, or ready, as various groups attempted to trap Him with trick questions in Luke 20:20-40. The scribes and the chief priests asked whether Jews should pay taxes to the foreign Roman government. Their trap failed as Jesus answered that they should give both God and Caesar their just due. When the Sadducees questioned Him about resurrection, Jesus skillfully corrected their wrong ideas about the nature of the future life. Jesus demonstrated a mental readiness at all times. Readiness means being qualified for service. If your will is set and your mind has grown through constant renewal, you will be qualified for any test God allows to come your way. Be alert and ready.

📖 8. Write each verb (gird up, renew, set) beside its description below.

   _____ focused attention

   _____ growth and newness

   _____ prepared for action

9. Match the verbs on the right to the proper stage and principle listed on the left. Write the letter of the verb on the line beside the stage.

_____ 1. Beginning: The Will Principle   a. Gird up

_____ 2. Growing: The River Principle   b. Set

_____ 3. Qualified: The Readiness Principle   c. Renew

10. Close this session by setting your mind on the Lord in prayer.

• Ask God to give you a focused attention to things above.
• Offer your will to God. Seek His will as you begin this three-stage process of developing the mind of Christ.

DAY 5
FIX YOUR THOUGHTS ON JESUS

Today's Bible Meditations
"Thou wilt keep him in perfect peace, whose mind is stayed on thee: because he trusteth in thee" (Isa. 26:3).

"Holy brothers, who share in the heavenly calling, fix your thoughts on Jesus, the apostle and high priest whom we confess" (Heb. 3:1, NIV).

Name of Christ for Today
Apostle and High Priest of Our Profession (Heb. 3:1)

Prayer to Begin the Lesson
Lord Jesus, I confess that You are the Apostle and High Priest of my profession. I have decided to study this course because of my desire to know You better. I want

1. Begin today's lesson by reading the Bible verses and the name of Christ for today. Work on your memory verse. Then use the suggested prayer in the left margin to begin your study.

Developing the mind of Christ involves a three-stage process. In nature we see the development of the mind in a little child as a process. So in the spiritual world, developing the mind of Christ is also a process. Even at spiritual birth, we have the mind of Christ (see 1 Cor. 2:16). But in subsequent growth that mind must contend with established habits, the culture in which we live, and the work of Satan to keep it from growing (and other factors to be mentioned later). In us, the mind of Christ matures in a process of growth.

2. Based on yesterday's study, what are the three verbs that describe the three stages of that process? Write the verbs in the blanks.

Beginning: S_____

Growing: R_____

Qualified: G_____

The apostle John says, "We know that, when He appears, we shall be like Him, because we shall see Him just as He is" (1 John 3:2, NASB). Whatever degree of Christlikeness we attain on earth will not match that final perfection of being just like Him. Jesus will return some day to claim His own. In His presence we will become like Him without spot or blemish. Our destiny is to be like Christ. God intends it. He has commanded it, and the Scriptures call on us to participate in the process of becoming like Him.

*3. As a child of God, what is your ultimate destiny?

_____

Yes, you are to be like Christ in eternity. Jesus said, "A disciple is not above his teacher, nor a slave above his master. It is enough for the disciple that he become as his teacher, and the slave as his master" (Matt. 10:24-25, NASB). Plainly, Jesus expected you to become like Him. Peter tells us "You have been called for this purpose, since Christ also suffered for you, leaving you an example for you to follow in His steps" (1 Pet. 2:21). Not only are you to think like Christ, but you are to follow His lifestyle. Peter also gives this command: "As Christ hath suffered for us in the flesh, arm yourselves likewise with the same mind" (1 Pet. 4:1). In the process of becoming like Christ, you are to accept suffering as a tool to put the flesh to death. Developing the mind of Christ will be costly. Yet its value is far beyond any cost that may be required.

Jesus expected you to become like Him.

*4. If you had to be honest with yourself, what are you feeling about developing the mind of Christ? Check all that apply or write your own.

❏ I'm overwhelmed. This is too much. I can't do it.
❏ I'm fearful. The idea of suffering sounds scary.
❏ I'm excited. I understand some of the cost, but I know the results will be well worth it all.
❏ I'm confused. I still don't quite understand what I'm getting into.
❏ Other: _____

God Is at Work

You may be feeling all of the above emotions right now. I have felt them all at one time or another. Paul tells us that those "He did foreknow, He also did predestinate to be conformed to the image of his Son" (Rom. 8:29). That is God's goal for us—the image of His Son. Later Paul wrote, "We all, with unveiled face beholding as in a mirror the glory of the Lord, are being transformed into the same image from glory to glory, just as from the Lord, the Spirit" (2 Cor. 3:18, NASB). What an awesome thing—to become like Christ!

We do have good news for you, though. Passages in the New Testament suggest that the process of being molded into Christ's image is primarily the work of God. We are the subjects; God is the active agent. You are not in this process alone. It does not solely depend on you. Paul indicates that God does two things for you: "It is God which worketh in you both to will and to do of his good pleasure" (Phil. 2:13). God causes you to want the mind of Christ and He enables you to develop it. Then Paul tells us: "Being confident of this very thing, that he which hath begun a good work in you will perform it until the day of Jesus Christ" (Phil. 1:6). We are commanded to "[fix] our eyes on Jesus, the author and perfecter of faith" (Heb. 12:2, NASB). God is the initiator of our faith and He will complete its perfect work. Each of us will meet many discouraging circumstances in the process of becoming like Him, but we need not despair. We do not complete the work. Jesus does. Our eyes are fixed on Him specifically as the Perfecter of our faith.

God wants us to develop the mind of Christ. He causes you to want it. He enables you to do it. Then one day Christ perfects the work that God began. What a guarantee! That should be encouraging news for you.

5. **Which of the following statements describes the role you have in developing the mind of Christ? Check one.**

❏ I'm in this work all alone. If anything happens, I'll have to do it. If I don't do it, nothing will get done.

❏ I'm not alone; God is my helper. But I carry the main assignment. God will help out if I get in a jam. The whole burden is on me.

❏ God is at work in me molding me into the image of His Son. As I submit to His work and cooperate with Him, God will bring it to pass.

Apostle and High Priest

The writer of Hebrews commands us to "consider Jesus, the Apostle and High Priest of our confession" (Heb. 3:1, NASB). The name *Apostle* indicates one who has been sent. Jesus was sent from Heaven to earth. We are to consider Jesus. To consider means to fix your mind, thoughts, and attention on Him—to set your mind on Christ. We are to fasten our attention on His earthly life as revealed in the gospels. Then we are to follow in Christ's steps (see 1 Pet. 2:21).

HEBREWS 7:25

"HE IS ABLE ALSO TO SAVE THEM TO THE UTTERMOST THAT COME UNTO GOD BY HIM, SEEING HE EVER LIVETH TO MAKE INTERCESSION FOR THEM."

We also are to consider Him as High Priest. Jesus served as our High Priest when He offered His life as the perfect sacrifice for us. But presently Jesus is High Priest as He makes intercession for us (Heb. 7:25). Much of that high priestly role is revealed in the New Testament epistles.

If we are to consider both the Apostle and the High Priest, we must know the gospels (for the apostle life) and the New Testament letters (for the high priestly life). The gospels show us Jesus in action on earth. When we fix our thoughts on His lifestyle we can pattern our lives after His example. The letters describe for us both the meaning of the Apostle and also the present intercessory role of the High Priest in heaven. We are to fix our thoughts on His divine work in our behalf.

6. **Match the roles of Christ in the left column with the intended focus of our thoughts in the middle column. Then indicate where we learn about that focus by matching the names to an item in the other columns. (Write two letters in front of each name.)**

_____ _____ Apostle   a. His divine work   x. Gospels
                            in heaven

_____ _____ High Priest   b. His earthly life   y. New Testament
                                                     Letters

Summary

Our goal is to become like Christ. We have a role in that process: we are commanded to think like Christ. The main work in the process, however, belongs to God. Our Christlikeness is His intention. God has predetermined it and currently is transforming us "from glory to glory" (2 Cor. 3:18) into the likeness of Christ. In working with God in the process, we study carefully all the revealed aspects of the human life of Christ and seek to follow in His steps. (Answers: Apostle—b., x.; High Priest—a., y.)

7. As you finish this first unit, review your memory verse. Work at hiding God's Word in your heart so that you will be better prepared to face temptation when it comes. Ask God to be at work in you during this course to open your mind and heart to the Scriptures. Commit to God your intention of responding to all that He may reveal to you during your study. Consider praying this prayer:

I am both frightened and thrilled by the command to become like Jesus. I agree with You that He is a "Lamb without blemish and without spot." Am I really to be without blemish and without spot like Him? At this point, that seems almost unfathomable. But I truly want to be obedient. I want to be like Jesus.

Thank You for a starting place. For Jesus' sake and in His name, I give my mind to You. I have set my mind on things above, so far as I know how to do that. I seek continuing renewal, and thank You for it. I will gird up my mind and live in a state of readiness to witness to the glories of Jesus. It seems that my mind must be alive, or I would not want to be like Him. Thank You that Jesus was single-minded, lowly, pure, responsive, and peaceful. Help me to be like Him in those specific ways. Amen.

BECOMING LIKE CHRIST

SESSION GOALS

This session will help you understand how God will be working in your life during this course to develop the mind of Christ. You will demonstrate a willingness to help one another become like Christ.

PSALM 34:3

"O MAGNIFY THE LORD WITH ME, AND LET US EXALT HIS NAME TOGETHER."

EPHESIANS 5:25-27

"CHRIST ALSO LOVED THE CHURCH, AND GAVE HIMSELF FOR IT; THAT HE MIGHT SANCTIFY AND CLEANSE IT WITH THE WASHING OF WATER BY THE WORD, THAT HE MIGHT PRESENT IT TO HIMSELF A GLORIOUS CHURCH, NOT HAVING SPOT, OR WRINKLE, OR ANY SUCH THING; BUT THAT IT SHOULD BE HOLY AND WITHOUT BLEMISH."

HEBREWS 10:24, NASB

"LET US CONSIDER HOW TO STIMULATE ONE ANOTHER TO LOVE AND GOOD DEEDS."

Hearing What the Spirit Is Saying (as you arrive)

1. (Individuals) Review what God has been saying to you during the study of unit 1.
   • Identify a Scripture and a name of Christ that have been meaningful this week.
   • Identify and mark the issue or subject in which God seems to be working most actively to develop the mind of Christ. (These will be shared later in the session.)
2. (Individuals) Write out any questions related to this unit you would like answered.

Magnifying the Lord and Exalting His Name (5 minutes)

1. (Leader) Open the session in prayer. Ask God to work in the minds and lives of group members that you may reflect the mind of Christ. Acknowledge the presence of the Holy Spirit and ask Him to be your Teacher during the session.
2. Read Psalm 34:3.
3. Pray as you feel led to worship God for Who He is and acknowledge Him for what He has done. Use the names of Christ to exalt His name together in prayer.
4. After prayer, share ways God revealed Himself to you this week through His names. Which name of Christ has been most meaningful to you and why?

Transforming by the Word (15 minutes)

1. (Pairs) Pair up and quote this week's memory verse, Romans 12:2.
2. Share what God said to you through this week's memory verse or other Scripture that has been especially meaningful.
3. Read Ephesians 5:25-27.
4. (Quads—or two groups) Distribute poster board or newsprint and markers to each of two groups. Make two lists related to characteristics of a Christlike mind. Focus on this unit's Scriptures only.
   • Group 1: Make a list of things, actions, or attitudes identified or implied in Scriptures during this unit that need to be cleansed from one's mind and life.
   • Group 2: Make a list of things, actions, or attitudes identified or implied in Scriptures during this unit that need to be incorporated into one's mind and life.
   • For example: We need to transform ourselves from being *carnally minded* (group 1) to being *spiritually minded* (group 2) (see Rom. 8:6).
5. Call on quads to read and comment on their lists. Place one on the Transformed From Wall and the other on the Transformed To Wall.
6. (Volunteer) Pray that God will cleanse members of your group and church.

Stimulating One Another to Love and Good Deeds (20 minutes)

1. Read Hebrews 10:24 from your session segment poster. How can we help each other as we seek the mind of Christ together?
2. Share testimonies of what God has done this week in your life that has been meaningful, challenging, or instructive.
3. State questions or concerns you have written for consideration. As time permits, seek to answer the questions as a group.

4. As time permits, discuss one or more of the following questions:
   - Why do you want to develop the mind of Christ? or Why have you decided to participate in this course?
   - Which of the six characteristics of the Christlike mind seems to be the most rare in the church today? Why do you think that is true? What do you think could be done better to develop that characteristic in believers' lives?
   - Which of the three principles (Will, River, or Readiness, pp. 23-25) is most needed in your life right now and why? What are some ways we can: (1) set our minds on things above? (2) experience the renewing of our minds? (3) gird up our minds for action?
   - What role do you have in developing the mind of Christ? What is God's role? (See "God Is at Work," pp. 27-28)
5. Turn to page 27 and share your response to the activity 4.

Preparing the Bride for Her Bridegroom (5 minutes)

1. Read Revelation 19:1-9. Listen for ways the bride (church) needs to prepare for the return of Christ.
2. As time permits, discuss these questions:
   - What needs to be done between now and the marriage supper of the Lamb in order for the bride to be ready?
   - What cleansing, purifying, or preparation is needed in our church?
   - How can we apply this Scripture to our lives, families, and church?
3. Pray for your church to continue to prepare for the Lord's return.

Praying for One Another (10 minutes)

1. (Quads) Read James 5:16 and confess your need to become more like Christ in specific ways. Share personal, family, church, or work-related prayer requests that primarily focus on developing the mind of Christ or purifying the bride.
2. (Quads) Pray specifically for one another for forgiveness, healing, encouragement, guidance, wisdom, knowledge, understanding, courage, strength, faithfulness, and/or for specific requests you shared above.

Closing the Session (5 minutes)

1. Share questions or concerns discussed during the session that we should remember in prayer.
2. Preview unit 2 on the following pages. Notice that the Lifelong Helps (Bondage to Freedom Lists on pages 224-226) will be used for the first time during unit 2.
3. Close by praying that God will work throughout this study to set, renew, and gird up the minds of group members to grow more like Christ.

REVELATION 19:7-9
"LET US BE GLAD AND REJOICE, AND GIVE HONOUR TO HIM: FOR THE MARRIAGE OF THE LAMB IS COME, AND HIS WIFE HATH MADE HERSELF READY. AND TO HER WAS GRANTED THAT SHE SHOULD BE ARRAYED IN FINE LINEN, CLEAN AND WHITE: FOR THE FINE LINEN IS THE RIGHTEOUSNESS OF SAINTS. AND HE SAITH UNTO ME, WRITE, BLESSED ARE THEY WHICH ARE CALLED UNTO THE MARRIAGE SUPPER OF THE LAMB."

JAMES 5:16
"CONFESS YOUR FAULTS ONE TO ANOTHER, AND PRAY ONE FOR ANOTHER, THAT YE MAY BE HEALED. THE EFFECTUAL FERVENT PRAYER OF A RIGHTEOUS MAN AVAILETH MUCH."

EXPERIENCING FREEDOM IN CHRIST

Hymn Part 1
Christ's Freedom
"Let this mind be in you,
which was also in Christ Jesus"
(Phil. 2:5).

❧

DAY 1
Disordered Mind

DAY 2
Making a List of Your Desires

DAY 3
Christ Sets You Free

DAY 4
The Ordered Mind of Christ

DAY 5
One Great Passion

Why You Will Find This Unit Helpful
You will learn that the control of sin in your life causes mental conflicts as your flesh wars against the Spirit. As you begin to let Christ's desires become your desires, you will experience genuine freedom and peace. Christ will set you free to live abundantly.

Lifelong Objective
In Christ you will live in peace with freedom from the control of sin. As you seek first His kingdom, you will develop Christ's desires as your desires.

Summary of God's Work in You

Christ's desires within you facilitate the work of the Father in your life. God's goal is Christ's fullness in your life. Your growth in holy desires is attainable only by seeking the Kingdom above all other things. Christ helps you develop that desire by His example. Christ wants you to share His wants.

Unit Learning Goals

- You will understand that your desires can cause conflict with Christ's desires.
- You will understand that a disordered mind leads to ungodly living.
- You will understand how Christ sets you free from mental conflict and the control of sin.
- You will know 17 Christlike virtues that are true of Christ's mind.
- You will demonstrate a willingness to seek the kingdom of God above all other things.

What You Will Do to Begin Experiencing Freedom in Christ

- You will begin making a private list of your wants or desires.
- You will evaluate your list of wants to see if they conflict with Christ's desires.
- You will begin to study 17 virtues of Christ's mind to understand what His mind is like.
- You will ask God to renew your mind and give you the desires of Christ in place of your desires.

Scripture Memory Verse

"Seek ye first the kingdom of God, and his righteousness; and all these things shall be added unto you" (Matt. 6:33).

Lifelong Helps Related to This Unit

Bondage to Freedom Lists (pp. 224-26)

The Mind of Christ Cards Related to This Unit

3A. Unit 2: Scripture Memory—Matthew 6:33
7A. Eight Virtues of Godly Wisdom
7B. Fruit of the Spirit

Optional DVD Messages by T. W. Hunt

- Session 1, Part 1: His Freedom

DAY 1
A Disordered Mind

1. Begin today's lesson by reading the Bible verse and the name of Christ for today. Work on your memory verse. Then use the suggested prayer to begin your study.

I want to tell you one of the ways God worked in my life to begin developing the mind of Christ in me. Read my story and then make your own list like the one I describe below.

A Time for Meditation

I was alone on a Saturday in August of 1972. My wife had gone to the beauty shop and my daughter was at an orchestra practice. I took advantage of this time alone to focus on my walk with the Lord. I had memorized the Book of James, so I spent that Saturday morning meditating on James 3:13–4:3. James says:

> The fruit of righteousness is sown in peace of them that make peace. From whence come wars and fightings among you? come they not hence, even of your lusts that war in your members? Ye lust, and have not: ye kill, and desire to have, and cannot obtain: ye fight and war, yet ye have not, because ye ask not. Ye ask, and receive not, because ye ask amiss, that ye may consume it upon your lusts.

2. Have you ever asked God for something that primarily was for selfish reasons? Check one: ❏ Yes ❏ Not that I recall

3. If you answered yes, name one thing you asked for.

_____

As I was meditating on the words of James, I realized that my lusts (my wants, desires, pleasures, or passions) would create war within me. The phrase "war in your members" is a military phrase that indicates my passions act like opposing soldiers in battle.

4. Have you ever had a mental battle within yourself when two different wants argued with each other? Check one: ❏ Yes ❏ Not that I recall

5. If you answered yes, briefly describe one such battle. For instance you might have wanted to buy an expensive outfit that you couldn't afford, but you also wanted to be faithful to pay your rent on time.

_____

_____

_____

Testing the Scripture in My Life

I decided to test this idea by listing all my lusts (wants, desires, pleasures, or passions), good and bad. Then I would see if they really did war against each other. I got a legal pad and began to list my desires just as they occurred to me. I decided to be totally honest before the Lord in making this list. Then I planned to burn the list before anyone came home! My list began like this:

> I want:
> 1. a new suit
> 2. a washer and dryer
> 3. Jesus Christ to be honored on the seminary campus where I teach
> 4. _____ (an itch)
> 5. a consistent faith
> 6. _____ (another thing)

The first two desires had been on my mind because we had been without either for four years. The Laundromat was very inconvenient. I am ashamed to say that Jesus' honor was third on my list and not first. I will not tell you what the fourth item was, but I will tell you that it was like an itch. Once I thought about this desire, resisting it was like trying to resist an itch; it had an irresistible appeal. I did not want to honor the itch, but often it surfaced in my mind. Have you ever had an itch like that? Satan knows that if he can get our attention for five seconds, he may have our mind for five minutes! Neither the itch nor its persistent clamor was good.

Once I thought about this desire, resisting it was like trying to resist an itch; it had an irresistible appeal.

The fifth desire I wrote down was a desire for a consistent faith like I saw in a friend's life. I had a friend who had been through a series of trials through which he demonstrated a consistent faith. He did not fluctuate up or down as the trials could have carried him. He remained faithful to the Lord regardless of circumstances. At that time I was experiencing a series of ups and downs in my life. I wanted the quality of consistent faith, like that of my friend.

My sixth desire, like my first and second, was for a material thing. I would have argued that I had settled the issue of materialism in my mind. But, under the leadership of the Holy Spirit, I found that I still wanted many things. I was a materialist in areas I did not consciously suspect.

And so it went. I filled the page with desires. I mixed the good with the bad. I listed them randomly just as they came to mind. I realized the good and the bad were all mixed up in my mind just as they were on my list. I had a picture of how my mind normally worked. My mind was inconsistent and disordered.

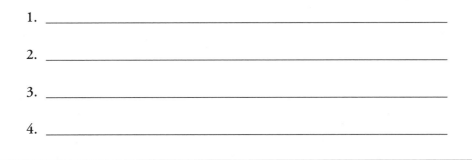

6. If you made a list like mine, what are four desires or wants that would be on your list? I want:

1. _____

2. _____

3. _____

4. _____

The Inner Conflict

Next I asked the question: Do my desires "war" with one another? I took a look at how my desires interacted with one another. My fourth desire had been an unholy itch, unwelcome but often present. My third desire, on the other hand, was a desire that Christ be honored. Between the unholy itch and the desire to honor Christ was a conflict! I truly wanted to honor the Lord but sometimes violated that desire by allowing an opposite, conflicting desire to surface. One desire fought the other!

Next I realized that the reason my faith was inconsistent (my fifth desire) was that I had not resolved the issue of materialism. My concern for things increased my tendency to go up and down with the circumstances around me. Again, one desire created friction with another desire. I was a divided person. Some of my wants actively opposed other wants. I realized that if I made a choice concerning what to think about, the lower often won over the higher. My choices concerning what to think about were themselves thoughtless. I had spent most of my life unconscious of the process of thinking. Little of my thinking was controlled by my will. The Bible was right! My passions produced conflict in my mind, that is, within me, or in my heart.

7. **According to James, what is the reason a Christian has mental conflict or battles?**

_____

_____

8. **Check each of the following items that describes a disordered mind.**

❑ a. only good desires

❑ b. good and bad desires mix together

❑ c. clear choices are made regarding what to think about

❑ d. little thought is given to what to think about

❑ e. the will is in control of thinking

❑ f. the will is not in control of thinking

Our thoughts often lead to actions—godly thoughts to godly actions, wrong thoughts to wrong actions.

According to James, the war that rages in our minds as Christians is due to our desires that battle against each other. The disordered mind has both good and bad (higher and lower) desires jumbled together with little order. The will is not in control of thinking. Therefore, little thought is given to what we think about. (Answers: b., d., f.) Then our thoughts often lead to actions—godly thoughts to godly actions, wrong thoughts to wrong actions.

The mind of Christ was not disordered but ordered. He controlled His thinking in such a way that only godly actions came through His life. This is one reason you and I need the mind of Christ.

9. Close this lesson in prayer, asking Jesus to begin doing the work He needs to do in you to set you free from the effects of a disordered mind.

DAY 2
MAKING A LIST OF YOUR DESIRES

1. Begin today's lesson by reading the Bible verses and the name of Christ for today. Work on your memory verse. Then use the suggested prayer to begin your study.

Yesterday, you learned that your desires can war against each other causing great mental conflict. This results in a disordered mind. A mind with conflicting desires can lead to ungodly or evil actions. Look at the conflict Paul described in Romans 7:18-25.

18I know that in me (that is, in my flesh,) dwelleth no good thing: for to will is present with me; but how to perform that which is good I find not. 19For the good that I would I do not: but the evil which I would not, that I do. 20Now if I do that I would not, it is no more I that do it, but sin that dwelleth in me. 21I find then a law, that, when I would do good, evil is present with me. 22For I delight in the law of God after the inward man: 23But I see another law in my members, warring against the law of my mind, and bringing me into captivity to the law of sin which is in my members. 24O wretched man that I am! Who shall deliver me from the body of this death? 25I thank God through Jesus Christ our Lord. So then with the mind I myself serve the law of God; but with the flesh the law of sin.

2. Which kind of mind do you think Paul was describing? Check one:
   ❏ A disordered mind dominated by the flesh.
   ❏ An ordered mind dominated by the Spirit.

3. Draw a line matching the mind on the left with the kind of living it produces on the right.

   A disordered mind   • godly living
   An ordered mind   • ungodly living

4. Who or what can deliver you from such mental conflict so you can serve God more effectively (verse 25)?

_____

Today's Bible Meditation
"Who shall deliver me from the body of this death? I thank God through Jesus Christ our Lord. So then with the mind I myself serve the law of God" (Rom. 7:24-25).

Name of Christ for Today
Jesus Christ Our Lord (Rom. 7:25)

Prayer to Begin the Lesson
Jesus Christ, My Lord, I thank my heavenly Father for You. You are the God-man who made it possible for me to be free from bondage to sin and death. Guide me to get rid of my desires that are in conflict with Your desires. You are my Lord. I will do whatever You ask. Amen.

As you read about Paul's struggle in Romans 7, you likely realized that a disordered mind can lead to an ungodly life. But you also learned the good news that Jesus can set you free from this conflict so that you can serve God more effectively. Jesus Christ is the One who can set you free!

An ordered mind, like the mind of Christ, must be controlled by the will. You must make mental decisions concerning what you think about. You must get to the place that you choose to deny your desires that conflict with God's desires. You must choose to want what God wants so that Christ's desires become your desires. As this begins to happen in your life, you will begin to experience a freedom in Christ that will allow you to live life to its fullest dimensions. Let me show you where we are headed.

A PROCESS TOWARD FREEDOM

1. Make your own **list of desires**. This will be the beginning of an ongoing process for your life.
2. **Identify desires that** may **conflict** with other desires.
3. Pray that Christ will help you **get rid of desires** that are in conflict with His.
4. Pray that **Christ will give you His desires**.
5. Begin to **make decisions to follow after Christ's desires** rather than your own desires.

To get you started, I want you to identify your desires—the good ones as well as the bad. Then you will evaluate which of those desires may be causing conflict with godly desires.

⁂ 5. **Follow these instructions to begin making a list of your lusts, wants, desires, and passions.**

INSTRUCTIONS FOR MAKING A LIST OF DESIRES

1. Obtain several sheets of paper or a notebook. I recommend a notebook that you can keep at home for reference as we work on this project together. Write the title "My List of Desires" and today's date at the top of a sheet.
2. Decide to be thoroughly honest with God as you make your list. Pray and ask God to help you identify the desires, wants, lusts, and passions in your life.
3. Begin making your list. Include everything that comes to mind. I suggest that you number the items. Start with the four desires you listed in yesterday's lesson.

4. If you want to maintain greater privacy, you may want to list items as *itch A* or *thing 2* and so forth. Give yourself enough information so that you can remember what you are listing. Ask yourself: *What do I really want in life? What are my desires or passions?*

5. Write down everything that comes to mind. Don't try to evaluate them right now; that comes later.

6. If you have difficulty, turn to page 224 and use the guide to help you make your list more complete.

7. Take what time you can today. You probably will not finish your list, just begin. You may want to carry a note pad with you throughout the day to jot down other desires that come to mind. Once you start your list, sign and date on the line below.

I have started making a list of my desires, being as honest with God as I can.

Signature:_____ Date:_____

You will continue to process this list over a period of time. Add to it any time during the course that you become aware of additional desires.

6. Close your study today by asking Jesus to give you unbiased spiritual eyes to begin seeing the desires you have that conflict with His desires.

DAY 3
CHRIST SETS YOU FREE

1. **Begin today's lesson by reading the Bible verses and the name of Christ for today (on the right). Work on your memory verse. Then use the suggested prayer on the following page to begin your study.**

2. **Review the list of desires you made yesterday. What desires conflict with each other? On your list, write down the number of conflicting desires. Identify several pairs. You may not have time to cover your entire list today. That is OK. Remember, you are beginning a lifelong process. You will continue to process these conflicts over the coming months.**

Let me share an example with you. My fourth desire was an unholy itch, unwelcome but often present. My third desire was that Christ be honored where I taught. A conflict existed between the unholy itch and the desire to honor Christ. Therefore, I would write down 4 versus 3.

Today's Bible Meditations
"The law of the Spirit of life in Christ Jesus hath made me free from the law of sin and death" (Rom. 8:2).

"It was for freedom that Christ set us free" (Gal. 5:1, NASB)

Name of Christ for Today
The Deliverer (Rom. 11:26)

3. Describe below one of the conflicts you identified.

_____

_____

_____

_____

_____

_____

Let me remind you about the source of many mental conflicts. James 4:1 says, "From whence come wars and fightings among you? come they not hence, even of your lusts that war in your members?" When your desires conflict with godly desires you will experience mental battles. When you have ungodly desires mixed with godly desires you have a disordered mind that can lead to ungodly living.

The mind of Christ can help you resolve those conflicts. This is not, however, some method or program that will straighten out your thinking. Christ Himself is the One who will set you free. Remember from yesterday's lesson that Paul said Jesus Christ is the One who sets you free.

**A Process Toward
Freedom**
1. List your desires.
2. Identify conflicting
desires.
3. Get rid of wrong desires.
4. Receive Christ's desires.
5. Decide to follow
His desires.

4. Review in the left margin "A Process Toward Freedom."

This process relates to what you do. But Christ is the One at work in you throughout this process. Here is what He is doing.

• Christ creates in you the desire to be like Him.
• Christ begins to give you desires for the things He wants.
• Christ's desires within you enable the Father to work in your life.
• God's goal is for you to experience Christ's fullness so that He becomes your life.
• You grow in having holy desires by seeking the Kingdom (the rule of Christ) above all other things.
• Christ helps you develop that desire by His example.
• Christ wants you to share His wants.

5. Which of the following best describes what needs to happen for you to be set free from conflicting desires? Check one.

❏ a. I review an approved list of desires, get rid of desires that are not on the list, and replace them with desires that are on the list.

❑ b. I sit back and wait and do nothing until God changes me to be all He wants me to be.

❑ c. Christ encourages me to become like Him. I release my desires and allow Him to give me His desires.

God does not automatically change you *(b)*. God will not violate your will. You must be involved in the process by your own choice. However, you cannot do this alone *(a)*. You cannot become what God wants apart from His work in your life. The correct answer is *(c)*. Christ takes the initiative to cause you to want to be like Him. When you respond and submit your desires to Him, Christ gives you a new set of desires. As you will see in tomorrow's study, His desires do not conflict with themselves.

Alive in Christ

In unit 1 we saw that the word *mind* is described six places in the New Testament. From those passages we identified six characteristics of the godly mind. The first characteristic is *alive*. True life is in the Spirit. Those persons without the Spirit are dead spiritually. You need a mind that is alive in the Spirit.

6. Read Romans 8:1-17 below and circle words related to life and death: *life, live, quicken* (make alive), *death, dead, die, mortify* (put to death).

There is therefore now no condemnation to them which are in Christ Jesus, who walk not after the flesh, but after the Spirit. For the law of the Spirit of life in Christ Jesus hath made me free from the law of sin and death. For what the law could not do, in that it was weak through the flesh, God sending his own Son in the likeness of sinful flesh, and for sin, condemned sin in the flesh: That the righteousness of the law might be fulfilled in us, who walk not after the flesh, but after the Spirit. For they that are after the flesh do mind the things of the flesh; but they that are after the Spirit the things of the Spirit. To be carnally minded is death; but to be spiritually minded is life and peace. Because the carnal mind is enmity against God: for it is not subject to the law of God, neither indeed can be. So then they that are in the flesh cannot please God. But ye are not in the flesh, but in the Spirit, if so be that the Spirit of God dwell in you. Now if any man have not the Spirit of Christ, he is none of his. And if Christ be in you, the body is dead because of sin; but the Spirit is life because of righteousness. But if the Spirit of him that raised up Jesus from the dead dwell in you, he that raised up Christ from the dead shall also quicken your mortal bodies by his Spirit that dwelleth in you. Therefore, brethren, we are debtors, not to the flesh, to live after the flesh. For if ye live after the flesh, ye shall die: but if ye through the Spirit do mortify the deeds of the body, ye shall live. For as many as are led by the Spirit of God, they are the sons of God. For ye have not received the spirit of bondage again to fear; but ye have received the Spirit of adoption, whereby we cry, Abba, Father. The Spirit itself beareth witness with our spirit, that we are the children of God: And if children, then heirs; heirs of God, and joint-heirs with Christ; if so be that we suffer with him, that we may be also glorified together.

7. This passage describes spiritual life and death. Each of the following words or phrases relates to either life or death. On the line in front of each word or phrase write *L* for *Life* and *D* for *Death*.

_____ a. bondage to fear   _____ g. mortify the deeds of the body

_____ b. carnally minded   _____ h. righteousness

_____ c. enmity against God   _____ i. sin

_____ d. in the Spirit   _____ j. Spirit of adoption

_____ e. led by the Spirit of God   _____ k. spiritually minded

_____ f. live after the flesh   _____ l. walk after the Spirit

Christ's Freedom

Genuine freedom can occur only where spiritual life exists.

This first characteristic of the Christian mind—*alive*—corresponds to the first part of the hymn in Philippians 2. Being spiritually alive is related to Christ's freedom. Genuine freedom can occur only where spiritual life exists. Life is not fully spiritual until it is fully free. This is why we have begun our study with an emphasis on freedom in Christ. This is the first step in the process of having the mind of Christ.

A person in Christ is free to live in the fullest sense of the word! Spiritual life is not the absence of death, but the presence of Christ—Christ in you. When you allow Christ to make you like Himself, He sets you free to fully live. (Answers: *L*—d., e., g., h., j., k., l.; *D*—a., b., c., f., i.)

8. Pause now and ask Jesus to begin renewing your mind in such a way that you walk after the Spirit.

DAY 4
THE ORDERED MIND OF CHRIST

Today's Bible Meditations
"The wisdom that is from above is first pure, then peaceable, gentle, and easy to be entreated, full of mercy and good fruits, without partiality, and without hypocrisy"
(Jas. 3:17).

1. Begin today's lesson by reading the Bible verses and the name of Christ for today. Work on your memory verse. Then use the suggested prayer on the following page to begin your study.

In developing the mind of Christ in you, God guides you to get rid of wrong desires and replace them with His desires. Knowing how Jesus thought and what He showed concern for can help you understand what He wants to develop in you. Today we want to introduce you to 17 virtues that are true of Christ's mind. We will take a more in-depth look at each one in later units. These virtues describe some of the ideal qualities of the mind of Christ that God wants you to exhibit also.

As I meditated on James 3:13–4:3, I noticed that godly wisdom was described by eight virtues. These are words that describe godly thinking and, therefore, describe a part of the mind of Christ.

ᔥ 2. **Read James 3:13-17 and circle the eight virtues of godly wisdom in verse 17.**

¹³Who is a wise man and endued with knowledge among you? let him shew out of a good conversation his works with meekness of wisdom. ¹⁴But if ye have bitter envying and strife in your hearts, glory not, and lie not against the truth. ¹⁵This wisdom descendeth not from above, but is earthly, sensual, devilish. ¹⁶For where envying and strife is, there is confusion and every evil work. ¹⁷But the wisdom that is from above is first pure, then peaceable, gentle, and easy to be entreated, full of mercy and good fruits, without partiality, and without hypocrisy.

ᔥ 3. **Verse 14 also describes the conflict or battles that can rage inside your mind and heart. When you have such envy and strife what should you do?**

_____

_____

ᔥ 4. **Where does that kind of wisdom come from? (see v. 15)**

_____

ᔥ 5. **What is present where this envy and strife exist? (see v. 16)**

_____

The kind of mental conflict we have been describing should not cause you to glory. To do so is to lie against the truth. The kind of wisdom that results in envy and strife is earthly, sensual, and devilish. When this kind of wisdom is present, confusion and evil work (ungodly actions) are present. Do you see why we need to be set free from a disordered mind by Christ Himself? We need to be set free from this earthly, sensual, and devilish way of thinking and have it replaced by God's wisdom.

Eight Virtues in James 3:17

Verse 17 lists eight virtues of godly wisdom. As I was meditating on this passage, I realized that these eight virtues are a partial picture of the mind of Christ. Since Christ is God, He had this godly wisdom. Jesus Christ was pure, peaceable, gentle, entreatable, merciful, fruitful, steadfast, and honest. He was perfect in each one.

"The fruit of the Spirit is love, joy, peace, long-suffering, gentleness, goodness, faith, meekness, temperance: against such there is no law" (Gal. 5:22-23).

Name of Christ for Today
Our Hope
(1 Tim. 1:1)

Prayer to Begin the Lesson
Jesus, You are my hope. If I am ever to be set free to live fully, You are the One to do it. Please continue Your work of producing freedom in me. Amen.

Eight Virtues
(Jas. 3:17)
pure
peaceable
gentle
entreatable
merciful
fruitful
steadfast
honest

6. Read the list of virtues in the left margin. These are so important I want you to begin memorizing them. Read through the list several more times and then try to write the eight virtues from memory.

1. P _____   5. M_____

2. P _____   6. F _____

3. G _____   7. S _____

4. E _____   8. H _____

Remember that the conflict I experienced was because of my own desires. When I realized this, my mind turned back to the Christ I saw in the eight virtues of James 3:17. These eight virtues describe His mind. They do not describe all of the mind of Christ, but they describe important parts of it. Then I asked myself: What if I had the characteristics of James 3:17—perfectly pure as Christ is, perfectly peaceable, gentle, and all the rest?

7. Do any of those qualities conflict with any of the others? Does purity ever conflict with peace? Or peace with gentleness, or entreatability with mercy, or fruitfulness with honesty? Check one:
❏ Yes, they can conflict.   ❏ No, they do not conflict.

No they do not conflict. They do not clash with one another. They blend and harmonize with each other. All these qualities work with, not against one another. As a matter of fact, each works on behalf of the others. They enhance one another!

Fruit of the Spirit in Galatians 5:22-23
In 1959 the Lord graciously granted me a profound renewal of spiritual life. At that time I wanted more than anything for God to work out in my life the nine qualities or virtues in Galatians 5:22-23, the fruit of the Spirit.

8. Read Galatians 5:22-23 and circle the nine qualities or fruit of the Spirit.

The fruit of the Spirit is love, joy, peace, longsuffering, gentleness, goodness, faith, meekness, temperance: against such there is no law.

Jesus is God, but the Holy Spirit is God also. Whatever the Spirit produces as His fruit shows what God is like. I knew that these nine virtues were, therefore, true of Christ also. I wrote the nine virtues in a vertical column like the one in the right margin on the next page. Then I inspected these virtues to see if they worked together as harmoniously as those of James 3:17. Look for yourself!

9. Does love: ❏ make war against joy or does it ❏ produce joy?

10. Do peace and gentleness: ❏ give a harsh discord, or do they
    ❏ work together?

Love produces joy. Peace and gentleness work together. The same comparison could be made for each of the virtues. Each virtue complements and even increases the power of the others. They form a symphony, perfect in unity. No one of them distracts from the glory of another. A life is glorious in its harmony and unity when all these virtues are present.

11. This list of nine virtues is also important. I want you to begin
    memorizing the virtues. Read through several times the list of virtues
    (fruit) in the right margin on this page. Then try to write from memory
    the nine virtues.

Nine Virtues
(Gal. 5:22-23)
love
joy
peace
longsuffering
gentleness
goodness
faith
meekness
temperance

1. L _____

2. J _____

3. P _____

4. L _____

5. G _____

6. G _____

7. F _____

8. M _____

9. T _____

An Integrated Mind

Now I had two lists of virtues, those in James 3:17 and those in Galatians 5:22-23. Each was complete in itself. Each demonstrated perfect unity within itself. Then I asked: Can the two lists harmonize with one another? I realized that the virtues in James are all adjectives, and those in Galatians are all nouns. I decided to apply each of the adjectives (James) to each of the nouns (Galatians) to determine if the combinations made sense.

12. Does it make sense to talk about a pure love, peaceful love, gentle love,
    or entreatable love? ❏ Yes ❏ No

It certainly does! You may also talk about a lovely peace, loving joy, peaceful gentleness, longsuffering mercy, faithful honesty, and many other combinations. The two lists combined show many possible and reasonable combinations—merciful gentleness, fruitful faith, or any combination you like. Regardless of the direction, the two lists work together perfectly.

I saw that the mind of Christ is an integrated mind—it has order, harmony, and unity. Each virtue works perfectly with all other virtues. In fact, the virtues enhance one another. The mind of Christ has no inner conflicts.

I looked again at the conflicts on my list of desires, and felt helpless against the itches and the materialism that God had revealed. God knew it all along, and now I knew it. But how was I to change it? We speak lightly of changing our minds, but what if you really had to change the qualities of your mind? Tomorrow I will share how I responded to God.

🙠 13. Conclude your study today by asking God to produce these 17 virtues in your life more clearly day by day.

DAY 5
ONE GREAT PASSION

🙠 1. Begin today's lesson by reading the Bible verse and the name of Christ for today. Work on your memory verse. Then use the suggested prayer to begin your study.

Did Jesus ever express a desire of any kind? Below are three statements illustrating His desires beginning with His earliest recorded words spoken at the age of 12.

Age 12: "I must be about my Father's business" (Luke 2:49).
Age 30: "My meat [food] is to do the will of him that sent me, and to finish [accomplish] his work" (John 4:34).
Age 32: "I came down from heaven, not to do mine own will, but the will of him that sent me" (John 6:38).

🙠 2. What was Jesus' one great passion or desire? Check one.

❏ Jesus wanted to be popular and please men.

❏ Jesus wanted to do His Father's will and please Him.

❏ Jesus wanted to do things to please Himself.

Jesus' One Passion

Jesus' one passion was to do His Father's will. Scripture indicates this one desire dominated His life from at least His 12th year, through the beginning of His ministry at age 30, and then to about age 32. The night before Jesus died, He prayed, "I glorified Thee on the earth, having accomplished the work which Thou hast given Me to do" (John 17:4, NASB). To the very end, Jesus was concerned primarily with the things of His Father. Jesus had no unholy want. He allowed no other desire to interfere. Jesus had an ordered mind focused on His one great passion of doing the will of His Father.

Because Jesus was dominated by this one great passion, all His attributes work hand-in-glove with one another. His purity can only result in peace. His peace makes His gentleness more winsome. He is unmixed; nothing in Him contradicts anything anywhere else in His mind or His personality. Everything in Christ is integrated and all is unity.

Fix My "Wanter"

The more I thought about my conflicting desires, I felt entrapped by my own weaknesses. Then I remembered Romans 6:14: "Sin shall not be master over you" (NASB). Could I ever master my mind so that sin could not master me? The rest of the verse tells why sin is not to have dominion: "You are not under law, but under grace." Mastery over my mind cannot be done by will power, but by the power of the Holy Spirit—by His grace.

Mastery over my mind cannot be done by will power, but by the power of the Holy Spirit— by His grace.

3. **What are you feeling about the conflicting desires that you may have uncovered this week? Check your response.**

❏ I feel almost helpless to win the victory. I feel trapped by my weakness.

❏ I feel hopeful that God is already working in me to set me free by His grace.

❏ I don't really care that I have these conflicting desires. So what?

❏ Other: _____

Feeling both helpless and hopeful that God was at work in me, I took the sheet with the list of my desires. I knelt, held the list up toward heaven, and cried to the Lord, "Lord, what I need is to get my 'wanter' fixed. In my own strength, I am captive to my own lusts. But I am under grace. I want grace to be operative in my life. In Jesus' name, I ask you to 'fix my wanter.' "

I knew from past experience the requirements of the Lord in accomplishing real change. I then gave the Lord a significant addendum: "And in Jesus' name, I free You to do anything You have to do to 'fix my wanter.' I will not quarrel with any procedure You deem necessary, but will accept the fact that You really do want me to be like Jesus, regardless of the cost."

I Needed Help

I had intended to destroy the list. But facing one of the greatest challenges of my Christian growth, I felt I could not do it alone. When my wife Laverne returned that morning, I shared with her the list, the insights, and the prayer I had prayed. I asked her to pray with me that God would completely free me from the mastery of any sin in my mind. This was one step toward achieving an integrated (harmonious, united, ordered) mind like the mind of Christ.

4. Is there someone you need to ask to pray for you in this process? It could be a spouse, a friend, a teacher, a pastor, a relative, a person in your *Mind of Christ* small group, or a fellow believer. If you sense a need for a prayer partner in this, who is this person?

_____

God Began His Work

The Lord immediately began a process of answering my prayer. To accomplish His purpose, He began using a single verse, Matthew 6:33—"Seek first His [God's] kingdom and His righteousness" (NASB). The Holy Spirit so haunted me with that verse that it followed me night and day. It echoed constantly, like a refrain in the back of my mind. If I got into an argument, the Spirit would remind me of my greater seeking. If an unholy lust popped into my mind, I found myself turning quickly to another thought, seeking God's righteousness.

Romans 12:2 commands us to be "transformed by the renewing of [our] mind." This was precisely what was happening to me now. In myself I could not change my mind, but God the Spirit knew how to give me a greater passion. My self-seeking was now being transformed into seeking God's kingdom and righteousness. By the end of the fall, I was conscious of a complete renewal of my mind in the area of my wants.

One of God's desires for you is that you seek His kingdom and His righteousness.

One of God's desires for you is that you seek His kingdom and His righteousness. Our prayer for you is that by now you have that desire also. Having the desire and seeking the Kingdom, however, are not the same thing. How can you live in a way that indicates you are seeking the Kingdom? Listed below are some ways you could demonstrate your willingness to seek God's kingdom first. You could do such things as:

- choose to deny self and follow Christ;
- memorize Matthew 6:33 and ask God to do what is necessary to help you live that way;
- pray to seek God's guidance and follow it rather than doing only what you think you ought to do without any guidance from Him;
- ask God how to use excess money rather than buying things you want (but don't really need) and having little left for Kingdom work;
- choose to follow God's desires rather than your desires;
- rush away from temptations, impure thoughts, and lusts and focus on godly living, righteousness, and pure thoughts.

5. Ask God now how He would have you to begin seeking first His kingdom in your life. Agree to do whatever He impresses you to do.

The Rest of the Story

That is not the end of the story that began in August of 1972! Laverne and I discovered before the end of the fall that we had saved enough to buy a new suit—the first item on my original want list. Then I judged some music auditions and happened to be paid the exact amount we needed for a sale-priced washer! So we got the washer—part of want number two.

Late that fall, I went to teach at a missionary orientation center. While there, I was having lunch with Norman Coad, whose calling was to Africa. As we talked, He told me that he and his family were going to Upper Volta (now Burkina Faso). In my ignorance I asked, "Where is Upper Volta?"

Norman told me that it was inland and sub-Sahara. "As a matter of fact," he added, "we have been told that it is so hot and dry that we should not bring our dryer, so now we need to get rid of it. You couldn't use a dryer, could you?" Almost in disbelief, I assured him that we most certainly could! But then he asked, "What kind of dryer connections do you have?" I answered that they were electric. Norman then gave me the bad news that his dryer connections were gas.

The next morning we were preparing to have a worship service when a missionary going to Brazil came in and pleaded, "Wait, my wife and I have an emergency. We've been packing our crates for shipping, and we just got a letter out of our post office box telling us that our dryer connections are gas—but we have an electric dryer! Is there anyone here who would be willing to exchange a gas dryer for an electric dryer?"

So God provided us with a dryer!

We had both installed, and I commented to Laverne, "This certainly has a surprising twist. We used to pray for things, and often didn't get them. Now I find myself attending to kingdom matters and not concerned about things. Yet God provided all the items on my original want list of last August—the new suit, the washer, and the dryer. Still, we haven't prayed for them. Why did we fail to get them when we prayed, but got them when we didn't pray?"

She asked me, "What is that verse that has meant so much to you this fall?"

I reminded her of Matthew 6:33: "Seek ye first the kingdom of God, and his righteousness."

Then she asked, "But what does the rest of the verse say?" Of course the verse assures us, "And all these things shall be added unto you."

Suddenly, with a burst of insight, I told my wife, "All my life I have been about the wrong business. I thought my things were my business, and I've tried to attend to them. Now I find out that God's kingdom and righteousness are my business, and God's business is my things. When I released my things to God, and started attending to my business (God's kingdom and righteousness), I freed God to attend to His business (my things). As long as I insisted on attending to my things, I tied God's hands so that He could not do His business. Now I have released the hand of God to work in what He loves to work in—our things. Our things are His business."

God's kingdom and righteousness are my business, and God's business is my things.

6. **As you conclude this lesson and this unit, consider praying this prayer.**

Lord, what I need is to get my 'wanter' fixed. In my own strength, I am captive to my own lusts, but I am under grace. I want Your grace to be at work in my life. In Jesus' name, I ask You to fix my wanter. And in Jesus' name, I free You to do anything You have to do to fix my wanter. I will not quarrel with any procedure You know is necessary. I will accept the fact that You really do want me to be like Jesus, regardless of the cost. Because that is what You want, that is what I want. Make me like Jesus—whatever it takes. Amen.

GROUP SESSION 2

FREEDOM IN CHRIST

SESSION GOALS

This session will help you understand how your conflicting desires can produce a disordered mind and how Christ can set you free from bondage to sin. You will demonstrate a willingness to seek first the kingdom.

Hearing What the Spirit Is Saying (as you arrive)

1. (Individuals) Review what God has been saying to you during the study of unit 2.
   - Identify a Scripture and a name of Christ that have been meaningful this week.
   - Identify and mark the issue or subject in which God seems to be working most actively to develop the mind of Christ. (These will be shared later in the session.)
2. (Individuals) Write out any questions related to this unit that you would like to have answered.

Magnifying the Lord and Exalting His Name (5 minutes)

1. (Volunteer) Open the session in prayer by asking God to use this study to set members free from bondage to sin, especially the lusts and desires that are contrary to the mind of Christ.
2. Pray as you feel led to worship God for Who He is and acknowledge Him for what He has done. Use the names of Christ to exalt His name together in prayer.
3. After prayer, share ways God revealed Himself to you this week through His names. Which name of Christ has been most meaningful to you and why?

Transforming by the Word (15 minutes)

1. (Pairs) Pair up and quote this week's memory verse, Matthew 6:33.
2. Review last week's memory verse by quoting Romans 12:2 in unison.
3. Share what God said to you through this week's memory verse or other Scripture that has been meaningful.
4. Read Ephesians 5:26.
5. (Quads—or two groups) Distribute poster board or newsprint and markers to each of two groups. Make two lists related to characteristics of a Christlike mind. Focus on this unit's Scriptures only.
   - Group 1: Make a list of things, actions, or attitudes identified or implied in Scriptures during this unit that need to be cleansed from one's mind and life.
   - Group 2: Make a list of things, actions, or attitudes identified or implied in Scriptures during this unit that need to be incorporated into one's mind and life.
   - For example: We need to abandon *living after the flesh* (group 1) and embrace *living after the spirit* (group 2) (see Rom. 8:1).
6. Call on quads to read and comment on their lists. Place one on the Transformed From Wall and the other on the Transformed To Wall.
7. (Volunteer) Pray that God will cleanse members of your group and church.

EPHESIANS 5:26
"THAT HE [CHRIST] MIGHT SANCTIFY AND CLEANSE IT WITH THE WASHING OF WATER BY THE WORD."

HEBREWS 10:24, NASB
"LET US CONSIDER HOW TO STIMULATE ONE ANOTHER TO LOVE AND GOOD DEEDS."

Stimulating One Another to Love and Good Deeds (20 minutes)

1. Read again Hebrews 10:24.
2. Share what God has done this week in your life that has been meaningful, challenging, or instructive.
3. State questions or concerns you have written for consideration. As time permits, seek to answer the questions as a group.
4. As time permits, discuss one or more of the following questions:

- What are some examples of conflicting desires that you found as you developed your desires lists? Do these conflicting desires cause mental conflict?
- What are some overall observations you made about your desires after you completed your list? Were your desires primarily God-honoring or self-serving?
- How can the "Process Toward Freedom" (p. 38) help you let Christ set you free? How did you respond to activity 3 on page 40?
- What is the value of asking Christ to "fix your wanter"?
- What, if anything, has God impressed you to begin to do to begin seeking His kingdom first?

Preparing the Bride for Her Bridegroom (5 minutes)

1. Read Matthew 25:1-13. Listen for ways the bride (church) needs to prepare for the return of Christ. List them in the margin.
2. As time permits, discuss these questions:
   - Though the bridegroom may tarry, how important is it for us to be ready?
   - What cleansing, purifying, or preparation is needed in our church?
   - How can we apply this Scripture to our lives, families, and church?
3. Call on one member to pray for your church to continue to prepare for the Lord's return.

Praying for One Another (10 minutes)

1. (Quads, preferably same gender) Share personal, family, church, or work-related prayer requests that primarily focus on developing the mind of Christ or purifying the bride. Read James 5:16 and suggest that members may want to confess struggles they are having between the flesh and the spirit.
2. (Quads) Pray specifically for one another for forgiveness, healing, encouragement, guidance, wisdom, knowledge, understanding, courage, strength, faithfulness, or for specific requests.

Closing the Session (5 minutes)

1. Share questions or concerns that came up during the session that we should remember in prayer.
2. Preview unit 3 on the following pages. [Note for this next week: You may want to keep the lists you will be making in a journal or loose leaf binder so you can review and update them periodically.]
3. Close by praying Matthew 6:33. Ask God to enable every member to seek His kingdom first.

JAMES 5:16
"CONFESS YOUR FAULTS ONE TO ANOTHER, AND PRAY ONE FOR ANOTHER, THAT YE MAY BE HEALED. THE EFFECTUAL FERVENT PRAYER OF A RIGHTEOUS MAN AVAILETH MUCH."

MATTHEW 6:33
"SEEK YE FIRST THE KINGDOM OF GOD, AND HIS RIGHTEOUSNESS; AND ALL THESE THINGS SHALL BE ADDED UNTO YOU."

Hymn Part 1
CHRIST'S FREEDOM

"Let this mind be in you, which was also in Christ Jesus" (Phil. 2:5).

DAY 1
God's Goal: Your Freedom

DAY 2
Habits, Loyalties, Relationships, and Prejudices

DAY 3
Ambitions, Duties, Debts, and Possessions

DAY 4
Fears and Weaknesses

DAY 5
Hurts or Grudges

Why You Will Find This Unit Helpful
You will learn about 11 more areas in which you can experience bondage. In each area you will begin to experience the freedom of Christ as He renews your thinking, mind-set, and outlook on life.

Lifelong Objective
In Christ you will live in peace with freedom from the control of sin.

Summary of God's Work in You

Christ's freedom within you facilitates the mental quality of attention. God's goal is your complete freedom from any bondage to this world system. Your growth in freedom from sin can be measured only by Christ's sinlessness. He gives freedom in His office as Deliverer. Christ sets you free.

Unit Learning Goals

- You will demonstrate a willingness to be set free from areas of bondage.
- You will understand why God wants you to be free from bondage to sin.
- You will understand ways God wants to set you free in the areas of habits, loyalties, relationships, prejudices, ambitions, duties, debts, and possessions.
- You will demonstrate a continued willingness to seek the kingdom of God above all other things.
- You will understand the damaging nature of fears, weaknesses, and hurts.
- You will demonstrate submission to God's work in your life to set you free from the damage caused by fears, weaknesses, and resentment.
- You will begin to demonstrate forgiveness toward those who have hurt you.

What You Will Do to Continue Growing in Christ's Freedom

- You will ask Christ to continue His work of producing freedom in you until you are free indeed.
- You will begin making lists of your habits, loyalties, relationships, prejudices, ambitions, duties, debts, possessions, fears, weaknesses, and hurts.
- You will begin to evaluate your lists to identify items that lead to bondage.
- You will seek Christ's help to be set free in those areas of bondage.

Scripture Memory Verses

"Ye shall know the truth, and the truth shall make you free . ... If the Son therefore shall make you free, ye shall be free indeed" (John 8:32,36).

Lifelong Helps Related to This Unit

Bondage to Freedom Lists (pp. 224-26)

The Mind of Christ Cards Related to This Unit

3B. Unit 3: Scripture Memory—John 8:32,36

Optional DVD Messages by T. W. Hunt

- Session 1, Part 2: His Freedom

DAY 1
GOD'S GOAL: YOUR FREEDOM

Today's Bible Meditation
"It was for freedom that Christ set us free; therefore keep standing firm and do not be subject again to a yoke of slavery" (Gal. 5:1).

Name of Christ for Today
The Truth (John 14:6)

Prayer to Begin the Lesson
Jesus, You are the Truth. You are the One who sets me free—free indeed. Please continue to work in me, producing the freedom You desire. Amen.

1. Begin today's lesson by reading the Bible verse and the name of Christ for today. Work on your memory verse. Then use the suggested prayer to begin your study.

God's Purpose in Freedom

Freedom has a purpose. We are free to serve Christ. We either must be servants of the world or servants of Christ. Freedom in one area means servanthood in the other. If you want to serve Christ, you must choose freedom from the world.

God inspired Peter to say, "Live as free men, but do not use your freedom as a cover-up for evil; live as servants of God" (1 Pet. 2:16, NASB). This means you could misinterpret the purpose for your freedom. You could see your experience of God's grace and freedom from the law as an invitation to live like the world—to do evil. That is not what God intended by setting you free in Christ. God has given His commandments as guidelines for right living. You are free to live within those guidelines and experience the fullness of life God intends for you. But when you cross over those boundaries, you become a slave to sin. As a slave to sin, you cannot be an effective servant of Christ. You will miss God's best for you.

2. Make the two statements below correct by crossing out the incorrect word inside each pair of parentheses ( ).
   • When I live like the world and do (right/evil), I am a slave to sin.
   • When I live like a servant of God and do (right/evil), I am truly free.

3. Read John 8:31-36 below and underline statements that describe what a servant (a disciple) of God does and what a servant of sin does.

   [31]Then said Jesus to those Jews which believed on him, If ye continue in my word, then are ye my disciples indeed; [32]And ye shall know the truth, and the truth shall make you free. [33]They answered him, We are Abraham's seed, and were never in bondage to any man: how sayest thou, Ye shall be made free? [34]Jesus answered them, "Verily, verily, I say unto you, Whosoever committeth sin is the servant of sin. [35]And the servant abideth not in the house for ever: but the Son abideth ever. [36]If the Son therefore shall make you free, ye shall be free indeed."

4. Verses 32 and 36 are your memory verses for this week. As a way to begin memorizing them, write the verses below.

   _____

   _____

   _____

A servant of sin is one who commits sin (v. 34). Such a person is in bondage, not to men, but to sin. He or she becomes a slave of sin. The disciple of Jesus, on the other hand, is one who continues in Christ's Word (v. 31). He or she knows the truth (v. 32). This is a person who lives according to Christ's commands. When you are Christ's disciple, He sets you free!

God's Process Toward Freedom

Last week I explained a process God has taken me through to move me toward freedom in Christ. For a long time, I thought these things were happening to me just for my sake. I never planned to share them publicly. However, the unusual series of events that led to my public sharing of these insights convinced me that God wants His children free from all bondage to sin. God wants you to be free.

To begin that process, I asked you to make a list of your desires or lusts. You already have begun to evaluate your desires and remove those that conflict with Christ's desires. During this unit, I want you to look at some other areas where bondage occurs. Some are neutral areas of bondage. Items in these areas can be good or bad depending on how they measure up against God's desires for you.

During this week, I suggest that prayerfully you begin making lists in the last eight areas. You already have started the first. We begin with the neutral areas first, because they are easier to deal with. Then I will guide you to tackle your fears, weaknesses, and hurts. These last three are the damaging areas of bondage. They are more difficult to deal with. I will explain each of these neutral and damaging areas in more detail during your study this week.

Neutral Areas
- lusts
- habits
- loyalties
- relationships
- prejudices
- ambitions
- duties
- debts
- possessions

Damaging Areas
- fears
- weaknesses
- hurts

5. **Read through the list of 12 areas of bondage in the right margin. Circle the one or two that you think may be most difficult for you to deal with.**

Two Cautions

Don't rush God! It took me more than 14 months to make and process the lists the first time. That is why I see this course as an introduction for you to a lifetime of developing the mind of Christ. For each list, I had to pray for freedom and allow God time to guide me in working out the requirements for real freedom. Pray as you make each list. After you make the list, give God the liberty to do anything He needs to do to give you complete freedom. Don't be surprised if the Holy Spirit requires you to remake the lists from time to time. He may direct you to areas I have not named. He may work your transformation in a completely different direction from the one He took me through. Let God direct you through this process in His way and on His time schedule.

Don't give up your responsibilities. God does assign us responsibilities that limit us. For example: no spouse is completely free. Each is responsible to his or her vows. No Christian father or mother can declare freedom from the obligations for children. The limitations which God assigns are a training ground for Christlikeness.

6. **Are you willing to give God all the time He needs to work out your freedom?** ❏ Yes ❏ No.

If you checked yes, tell God so right now.
If you checked no, ask Him to make you willing.

Christ's Mind-set

Anyone can be free in the 12 areas of bondage I have listed. God's intention is that you be free from this world's mind-set. In doing that, you become bound to His mind-set—the mind of Christ. In being bound to God's way of thinking, you are free from the bonds of Satan and sin.

Jesus Christ was the freest human being who ever walked on earth. As His ministry moved into various phases, Jesus had to make decisions—ministry decisions— about what to say and when to say it, where to go and when to go, always watching the timing of His Father. Jesus spoke often of His hour. His decisions were always perfect. Only in freedom can we make correct spiritual decisions.

Only in freedom can we make correct spiritual decisions.

Christ greatly desires your freedom. He promised, "If therefore the Son shall make you free, you shall be free indeed" (John 8:36, NASB). Nothing outside of you can disturb the freedom Christ gives. His freedom can endure. Paul cautioned, however, "It was for freedom that Christ set us free; therefore keep standing firm and do not be subject again to a yoke of slavery" (Gal. 5:1, NASB). Paul was talking about freedom from Jewish legalism, but sin also enslaves you.

Why is your freedom from the bondage of sin so important to having the mind of Christ? The person with the mind of Christ has focused attention. When you are in bondage, your attention is on your lusts, loyalties, ambitions, grudges, and all those things that bind you to the world. Christ's freedom within you allows and assists the mental quality of attention—attention to God, to His Word, to prayer, and to His voice. God's desire is our freedom.

Focused Attention
- to God
- to His Word
- to prayer
- to His voice

🖎 7. **Why is freedom from the bondage of sin important?**

_____

🖎 8. **What is God's desire for you?**

My f _____

This freedom God desires for you has no earthly measures. Its only measure is the Lord Jesus Christ Himself. Your growth in freedom from sin can be measured only by Christ's sinlessness—not by yourself, by other people, or by any other standard.

🖎 9. **What is the standard for measuring your growth in freedom?**

_____

We are not talking about righteousness that God gives through faith in Christ. We are talking about the outworking of your faith. Fruitful faith is practical, and God indeed wants you free. Christ wants you to be free, just as He is.

🖎 10. **Close this session in a time of prayer asking Christ to set you free indeed. Ask the Father to make you fruitful and faithful like Jesus His Son.**

DAY 2
HABITS, LOYALTIES, RELATIONSHIPS, AND PREJUDICES

1. Begin today's lesson by reading the Bible verse and the name of Christ for today. Work on your memory verse. Then use the suggested prayer to begin your study.

Habits

One afternoon I was to pick up my wife, Laverne. I forgot the appointment. I often did that kind of thing. I usually made the excuse that I was a professor, and my mind was on deeper things. When I remembered the appointment, Laverne had been waiting on me for an hour. I arrived to pick her up with profuse apologies. I begged her to forgive me. Of course she granted forgiveness immediately. Then she said, "If you were serious about sin not being master over you, don't you think you ought to pray about your absent-mindedness? After all, does a bad habit honor the indwelling Spirit?"

That got my attention. A few days later I came across this statement in Mark 10:1: "According to His custom, He once more began to teach them" (NASB). Jesus had habits! He was in the habit of going to the synagogue on the Sabbath (see Luke 4:16). Gethsemane must have been a favorite place, because He had the custom of going to the Mount of Olives when He was in Jerusalem (see Luke 22:39). Prayer was one of Jesus' habits (see Mark 1:35; Luke 6:12). But all of His habits were good. I knew that mine were not. The Lord clearly was showing me another area of bondage—my habits.

We need to take action the moment the Lord reveals to us a necessary action if we are to be doers and not merely hearers of the word. In my next quiet time, I prayed for the Lord to reveal to me all my habits, good and bad. I wrote down these habits, and it was obvious which ones needed to go. Again, in my helplessness, I prayed for the Lord to show me those paths which would eliminate all that was displeasing to Him. A bad habit (like absent-mindedness) reveals an area of life which is not under the control of the Holy Spirit. Most of my bad habits resulted from carelessness. I had to take certain measures for some of my bad habits, but essentially the changes were effected not by personal discipline but by greater consciousness of the constant rule of the Holy Spirit. My habits were changed from being careless to being Spirit-ruled.

> God's desire is to move your habits
> from being careless to Spirit-controlled.

2. In your notebook, journal, or separate sheets of paper, begin to prepare a list of your habits. Write the title "My Habits List" and today's date at the top of a sheet. If you have difficulty, turn to page 224 and use the guide to help you make your list more complete. You will be making four lists today, so budget your time. List at least five or six habits as a start.

3. As you begin to evaluate your habits, ask God to help you identify which ones are careless and which ones are Spirit-controlled. Write a *C* beside the ones that are careless and need to come under the Spirit's control.

Today's Bible Meditation
"Commit thy works unto the Lord, and thy thoughts shall be established" (Prov. 16:3).

Name of Christ for Today
The Way (John 14:6)

Prayer to Begin the Lesson
Jesus, You are not only the Truth. You are the Way to the truth about life. I don't really know the way apart from You. Please guide me in the way I should go. Amen.

Loyalties

One day I found myself arguing a certain matter with a friend. I became defensive. At that point the Holy Spirit whispered in my spirit that defensiveness was a tell-tale sign of the world's mind-set. Here was another signal from God, so I responded. The conviction was strong enough that I prayed through the matter. We usually think of loyalty as a good quality. The Lord seemed to say that I had been defending a false loyalty.

Jesus had loyalties. He was certainly loyal to His Father. Jesus loyally protected the disciples at the time of His arrest. Since I am to be like Jesus, the Lord was bringing to light the fact that not all my loyalties were Christlike. I had not realized that a loyalty could be false or unnecessary.

I made a list of all my loyalties, and then prayed through each one on the list. My list was too long! Loyalties, like wants, should be pure before the Lord. I discovered that my loyalties, even the legitimate ones, were not weighed according to spiritual value. Some of them I eliminated as valueless. I assigned others a new value according to their spiritual weight. Basically, I found that I could be loyal to anything I could pray for. The final result was an almost complete restructuring of my value system. My loyalties were changed from being scattered to being prayerful.

> God's desire is to move your loyalties
> from being scattered to being prayerful.

✍ 4. **In your notebook, begin to prepare a list of your loyalties. Title and date the list. If you have difficulty, turn to pages 224-25 and use the guide to help you make your list more complete. List a few loyalties to get started.**

✍ 5. **As you begin to evaluate your loyalties, ask God to help you identify which ones are scattered and which ones are prayerful. Write an _S_ beside the ones that seem to be scattered or unnecessary.**

Relationships

MARK 12:30-31

"THOU SHALT LOVE THE LORD THY GOD WITH ALL THY HEART, AND WITH ALL THY SOUL, AND WITH ALL THY MIND, AND WITH ALL THY STRENGTH: THIS IS THE FIRST COMMANDMENT. AND THE SECOND IS LIKE, NAMELY THIS, THOU SHALT LOVE THY NEIGHBOUR AS THYSELF."

Relationships was the next area in which the Holy Spirit began working to free me from the bondage of sin. Since I am not a possessive person, I genuinely felt that I was free from any bondage in relationships. Still, the Spirit may see areas of ownership of which we are not conscious. Deliberately I gave my wife to the Lord by saying, "Lord, I ask You to make her love You more than she loves me." I asked God to make her priorities those of Mark 12:30-31. Our love for God must be first, far above all earthly loves. When I prayed that same prayer about my daughter, I had to add, "And this means that if You want to take her to Africa or some other distant field, her love and service to You must outrank her love and service to us." I have prayed this same prayer about each of my grandchildren.

I found the Spirit leading me to make a list of all my relationships—to my boss, my friends, my colleagues, and others. Then I gave each one to the Lord to serve whatever purposes He had in bringing them into my life. Slowly I came to realize that every relationship in my life was to be one of service to God. I really was being transformed. My relationships had changed from serving self to serving God.

God's desire is to move your relationships
from serving self to serving God.

6. In your notebook, begin to prepare a list of your relationships. Title and date the list. If you have difficulty, turn to page 225 and use the guide to help you make your list more complete. List three or four relationships as a start.

7. As you begin to evaluate your relationships, ask God to help you identify which ones are serving self and which ones are serving God. Write an *S* beside the ones that seem to be serving self.

Prejudices

Next the Holy Spirit began working on my prejudices. I didn't think I had any! Under the leadership of the Spirit, I found deep, hidden prejudices.

In the Bible Naaman was angry when Elijah told him to bathe in the Jordan. Naaman asked, "Are not Abana and Pharpar, rivers of Damascus, better than all the waters of Israel?" (2 Kings 5:12). The Pharisees showed their prejudices when they asked Jesus' disciples, "Why is your Teacher eating with the tax-gatherers and sinners?" (Matt. 9:11, NASB).

Many believers have taken care of the better known prejudices (concerning race or ethnic groups) through the work of the Holy Spirit in their thinking. However, under the holy supervision of God's Spirit, you may find unsuspected prejudices. For example, some believers unconsciously think that if God works a certain way in their life, He is bound to work that same way in other believers. Most of us are prejudiced about natural or spiritual gifts. We sometimes think that the use of our particular gift or gifts is the only way God can work legitimately in any other person's life. Some Christian leaders think that all people are called to their same calling.

If God is sovereign, no prejudice of any kind on our part can exist which would limit His working n our lives.

If we are prejudiced about the way God works in anyone's life, we are limiting the sovereignty of God. If God is sovereign, no prejudice of any kind on our part can exist which would limit His working in our lives. Once again, I had to make a list. I had not suspected their lurking presence, but prejudices limit God's control.

God's desire is to move your prejudices
from being accidental to being scriptural.

8. In your notebook, begin to prepare a list of your prejudices. Title and date the list. If you have difficulty, turn to page 225 and use the guide to help you make your list more complete. To get you started, list three or four prejudices.

9. As you evaluate your prejudices, ask God to help you identify which ones are accidental and which ones are scriptural. Write an A beside the ones that seem to be accidental or contrary to Scripture.

In each of the areas named so far—false lusts, habits, loyalties, relationships, and prejudices—I had to make a list and pray fervently about the bondage inherent in each. I prayed fervently over each list as a prelude to the Spirit's deep work in freeing me from these areas of bondage.

ᔐ 10. Close today's session by praying about the areas God seems to emphasize that need changing first or most. Give Him permission to do whatever is necessary to help renew your mind in these areas.

DAY 3
AMBITIONS, DUTIES, DEBTS, AND POSSESSIONS

Today's Bible Meditation
"It is required in stewards, that a man be found faithful" (1 Cor. 4:2).

Name of Christ for Today
The Life (John 14:6)

Prayer to Begin the Lesson
Lord Jesus, You are my Life. Without You, I would be dead in my sin. Please set me free from the things that keep me from living life to the fullest extent You have planned for me. Amen.

ᔐ 1. Begin today's lesson by reading the Bible verse and the name of Christ for today. Work on your memory verse. Then use the suggested prayer to begin your study.

Ambitions

The Lord next led me to the bondage that comes from my ambitions. Ambitions include goals, purposes, objectives, hopes, and dreams. These are what drive us to achievement. A deep sin can lurk hidden from the conscious mind in ambitions. Our ambitions reveal sin in the area of pride. Being honest with the Lord is difficult in this matter, so I had to pray that the Lord would help me be open to Him as I made the list of my ambitions. I had not described carefully certain ambitions. They were really unconscious hopes or dreams. As I prayed, I became aware of ambitions I never had admitted openly, even to myself.

After I made the list, I tried sincerely to give these ambitions to the Lord. Again I freed God to do anything He needed to do to accomplish His aim. Many of my ambitions would have brought honor to me. Now the transformation began. The Spirit wanted me to put to death my personal ambitions and to develop ambitions that would honor the Lord or advance His kingdom.

> God's desire is to move your ambitions
> from honoring self to honoring God.

ᔐ 2. In your notebook, begin to prepare a list of your ambitions. Title and date the list. If you have difficulty, turn to page 225 and use the guide to help you make your list more complete. You will be making four lists today, so budget your time. List at least two or three in each category during this lesson to get started.

ᔐ 3. As you evaluate your ambitions, ask God to help you identify which ones are honoring self and which ones are honoring God. Write an *S* beside the ones that honor self or have pride as a root cause.

Duties

Next, the Spirit began to convict me that some of my duties were an obstacle to complete freedom. One of the works of the Spirit is to produce in us a sense of "ought to" about our basic Christian works. He convicted me that I was carrying on a number of busy activities for which I was not gifted or called. I am a dutiful person, so this area shocked me. Under the close supervision of the Holy Spirit, I discovered I was being driven by duties I was performing that I had no business doing.

This does not mean all duties are wrong. We should feel certain divine obligations. We are not saved by works, but works are a fruit of our faith. I studied the times when Jesus said "I must." "I must be about My Father's business. . . . I must preach to other cities also: for therefore am I sent. . . . I must journey on [to Jerusalem] … a prophet [cannot] perish outside of Jerusalem." I sensed an eternal ring about all His duties. Jesus knew from the beginning the course and ultimate outcome of His life. Certainly at Caesarea Philippi Jesus knew of His coming death and resurrection (see Matt. 16:21), and He never veered from that course, even if it meant rebuking Peter (see Matt. 16:23). Jesus showed resolution in His final walk to Jerusalem and the cross (see Mark 10:32). He had duties and was relentless in performing them.

Indeed, God expects us to do certain things. We are, for example, to be certain that we love God supremely. We are to honor our parents and pay our tithes. Many of God's commands outline the "ought tos" or duties that God has intended for us. To be valid, each duty must be part of eternal work for the Kingdom. "For we are his workmanship, created in Christ Jesus unto good works, which God hath before ordained that we should walk in them" (Eph. 2:10). Only God knows what He wants us to do. God's will is discernable through the patterns He establishes in our lives, the teaching of Scripture, the authorities He places over us, and the counsel of wise Christians.

> **EPHESIANS 2:10**
> "WE ARE HIS WORKMANSHIP, CREATED IN CHRIST JESUS UNTO GOOD WORKS, WHICH GOD HATH BEFORE ORDAINED THAT WE SHOULD WALK IN THEM."

To have the mind of Christ, we must know what God wants us to do, just as Jesus knew what the Father wanted Him to do—"I must work the works of Him who sent Me" (John 9:4). But we must also know what we are not required to do. I made my list of duties, and arduously discovered through much prayer how many of them were not of God. Ridding myself of superfluous duties was difficult and even, at times, painful. This exercise required an unexpected determination, but in the process, I found myself thinking in terms of eternity and my place in it.

> God's desire is to move your duties
> from compulsion to eternity.

4. **In your notebook, begin to prepare a list of your duties. Title and date the list. If you have difficulty, turn to page 225 and use the guide to help you make your list more complete. Remember to budget your time.**

5. **As you evaluate your duties, ask God to help you identify which ones are based on compulsion and which ones are based on eternity. Write a *C* beside the ones that seem to be based on compulsion.**

Debts

Now the Lord began to speak to me about the bondage of debt. Previously I had worked myself out of monetary debt, so I felt no bondage in this area . . . until the Spirit introduced a new way of looking at debt. I found that I "owed" many people for favors. We certainly should feel gratitude when someone is gracious to us, and we should express that gratitude. We also should demonstrate grace (giving what has not been earned by the recipient) without expecting to be repaid. We are gracious because of our nature, not because of what it will bring us.

I made a list of these debts and discovered that God was a part of each one. I am profoundly, eternally indebted to God for all He has done for me. Because of that, I am indebted to carry out His work. "I am a debtor to the Jew first, and also to the Greek." Paul used *debt* to indicate the ministry to which he was called. In other words, my debts were transformed from secular ones (temporal ones) to the ministry God had given me (eternal ones).

> God's desire is to move your debts
> from the temporal to the eternal.

6. In your notebook, begin to prepare a list of your debts—both those that are financial and those that are interpersonal. Title and date the list. If you have difficulty, turn to page 225-26 and use the guide to help you make your list more complete.

7. As you evaluate your debts, ask God to help you identify which ones are temporal and which ones are eternal. Write a *T* beside the ones that seem to be temporal or secular.

Possessions

More than we know, most of us are bound by the things we own.

Now it was time for the Lord to free me from my possessions. More than we know, most of us are bound by the things we own. We protect them and take measures to safeguard their security. Few Western Christians know the kind of life that Christ lived. He owned nothing except the clothes He wore.

Our house was the first thing the Lord required that I give Him. Laverne agreed that the Lord should dictate our use of our house. We were not owners but stewards of what He had provided. So we dedicated our house to God. He quickly sent a series of students, friends, street people (usually homeless), and others for us to host—obviously as a test of the commitment we had made. Moreover, I had to disciple or teach these guests as well as I could under the circumstances. Later, we were required to sell the house as a part of God's call to a new job assignment.

At the time we owned two cars. We had a young friend who was about to be married and had no car. The Lord led me to go to the filing cabinet, get the title to one of the cars, and give it (as a gift from God, not us) to the young man. The Lord seemed either to find unusual uses for our possessions or to rid us of them. Little by little, our thinking was transformed from a mind set of ownership to a mind set of stewardship.

> God's desire is to move your possessions
> from ownership to stewardship.

8. Using your notebook, begin to prepare a list of your possessions. You may want to place some in large categories like "furniture." Title and date the list. If you have difficulty, turn to pages 226 and use the guide to help you make your list more complete.

9. As you evaluate your possessions, ask God to help you identify which ones you relate to as an owner and which ones you relate to as a steward.

In all these transformations, my family and I were being freed from:
• the world as we had known it;
• inhibitions;
• the necessity to look a certain way at our friends and the world;
• time-worn, but false conceptions of happiness and well-being;
• the restraints of secret bonds we had not realized were there.

We were being freed to:
• let God have first place;
• minister to His body; and,
• move into new and deeper lessons on Christlikeness.

Sin shall not be your master in any area (see Rom. 6:14). Its dominion in your life is to be zero.

10. Close today's session by praying about the areas God seems to emphasize that need changing first or most. Give Him permission to do whatever is necessary to help renew your mind in these areas.

DAY 4
FEARS AND WEAKNESSES

1. Begin today's lesson by reading the Bible verses and the name of Christ for today. Work on your memory verse. Then use the suggested prayer on the following page to begin your study.

Damaging Areas of Bondage
All of the areas of bondage we have examined so far are neutral. They can be good or they can be bad. Even Jesus, in all His magnificent freedom, had wants, habits, loyalties, and relationships—but His were all good. Mine were not—at least, not all of them. The Lord patiently and gently took me from area to area and transformed my mind and my thinking. This process required more than a year of consistent work of the Spirit to transform my psyche and outlook about the items in these first nine lists. That year was a time of continual examination, probing, and reshaping of my outlook, even of my philosophy of life.

2. How much time do you think you should give the Spirit to do His renewing work in your mind? Check your response.
❏ Probably less than a year. I'm a fast learner.
❏ Hopefully about a year.
❏ Several years. I'm awfully messed up.
❏ As long as God needs, maybe a lifetime.

Today's Bible Meditations
"God hath not given us the spirit of fear; but of power, and of love, and of a sound mind" (2 Tim. 1:7).

"He said unto me, 'My grace is sufficient for thee: for my strength is made perfect in weakness.' Most gladly therefore will I rather glory in my infirmities, that the power of Christ may rest upon me" (2 Cor. 12:9).

Name of Christ for Today
Spiritual Rock
(1 Cor. 10:4)

Renewing of my mind during that year was only a beginning which continues even now. Periodically, I remake the lists. Each time I discover that the Lord is taking me deeper into His freedom. I would even say He is taking me into His holiness. The Lord's freedom is, after all, freedom from sin. I hope you will not put God under a time limit for renewing your mind. Give Him all the time He needs. Renewing of your mind will be a lifelong process.

By now the Lord had prepared me for a step I could not have taken the year before. He had taken me through the neutral areas of bondage to prepare me for three areas that were not neutral, but damaging. The probing was going deeper and requiring more.

Fears

The first of these damaging areas was my fears. I wrote down all the fears I could think of. Immediately I saw that most of them grew out of my desire to protect myself. Even though I had given my debts and possessions to the Lord, some of my fears had to do with money or the lack of it. I had fears about my family and job security. In all of them I discovered the element of self-protectiveness. This revealed a lack of trust in God, so I prayed about the depth of my faith. To have the mind of Christ is to trust in the Father's provision. Only He can protect us. Only He can protect our families.

Fears indicate a lack of trust in God's provision and protection.

3. When you have fears and are self-protective, what does that reveal about your belief in God? _____

Yes, fears indicate a lack of trust in God's provision and protection. They also may indicate a misunderstanding of God's purposes which are far beyond our understanding. For instance, Jesus allowed Lazarus to die from his sickness rather than heal him. But Jesus had a greater purpose in mind that would bring glory to God when He raised Lazarus from the dead. (See John 11:1-45.)

Paul seemed to demonstrate the mind of Christ in his letter to the Philippians. He was in prison and some were seeking his death.

According to my earnest expectation and hope, that I shall not be put to shame in anything, but that with all boldness, Christ shall even now, as always, be exalted in my body, whether by life or by death. For to me, to live is Christ, and to die is gain (Phil. 1:20-21, NASB).

Paul was ready for life or death. Whatever God permitted was OK. Paul faced both life and death without fear because he had trust and confidence in God. That is why Paul could write Timothy and say, "God hath not given us the spirit of fear; but of power, and of love, and of a sound mind" (2 Tim. 1:7).

After I had written down all the fears I could think of, I gave them to the Lord and asked Him to transform my mind in whatever direction He wished. Christ began to develop in me a unique sense of security. The only security I now am allowed to have is in Christ. In God's process, I realized that I was manipulative in ways I had not suspected. Some of my behavior was a false bravery that covered a fear of being perceived as simple or naive. Sometimes my innocent remarks were really self-protective or self-securing. Slowly the Lord became the only security on which I could count. In spite of my fears, I was being changed from one who is self-protective to one who is secure in Christ.

> God's desire is to change you from being one who is self-protective
> to one who finds his only security in Christ.

4. In your notebook, begin to prepare a list of your fears. Title and date the list. If you have difficulty, turn to page 226 and use the guide to help you make your list more complete. Today list two or three fears to get started.

5. As you begin to evaluate your fears, ask God to reveal ways you seek security through being self-protective. Ask Him to begin moving you toward finding your only security in Christ.

Weaknesses

Weaknesses were the next area of damaging bondage. We often excuse our weaknesses by saying we were born that way. For example, one of my weaknesses was that I could not speak effectively in public. The guidance God was giving me at that time demanded that I do just that. I felt like Moses who used that excuse. I also am basically a shy person, so I had developed ways to cover my shyness. I had found ways to make up for other weaknesses, too. I did not want them to be known publicly.

Three times Paul asked the Lord to remove his "thorn in the flesh" or a weakness. God's response was: "My grace is sufficient for thee: for my strength is made perfect in weakness" (2 Cor. 12:9). Paul showed his responsiveness to the Lord when he said: "Most gladly therefore will I rather glory in my infirmities, that the power of Christ may rest upon me. Therefore I take pleasure in infirmities, in reproaches, in necessities, in persecutions, in distresses for Christ's sake: for when I am weak, then am I strong" (2 Cor. 12:9-10).

I had never talked to the Lord about my weaknesses. I made my list. Then I prayed carefully about it and asked the Lord to strengthen me where necessary. I asked Him to use my weak points for His glory. In this way, my weaknesses were transformed from being a tool of Satan to being a tool of God.

My weaknesses were transformed from being a tool of Satan to being a tool of God.

> God's desire is to move your weaknesses from
> being tools of Satan to being tools of God.

6. Using your notebook, begin to prepare a list of your weaknesses. Title and date the list. If you have difficulty, turn to page 226 and use the guide to help you make your list more complete. Today list several of your weaknesses to get started.

7. As you begin to evaluate your weaknesses, ask God to help you identify the ones which are being used against you as tools of Satan. Write an S beside the ones that seem to be tools of Satan. Ask God to transform these weaknesses into tools that bring Him glory.

DAY 5
HURTS OR GRUDGES

Today's Bible Meditation
"If thy brother trespass against thee, rebuke him; and if he repent, forgive him. And if he trespass against thee seven times in a day, and seven times in a day turn again to thee, saying, I repent; thou shalt forgive him" (Luke 17:3-4).

Name of Christ for Today
Physician (Luke 4:23)

Prayer to Begin the Lesson
Jesus, I have many hurts. Some of them go way back in time. I want to be healed of those hurts. I want to be set free from the damaging bondage to the past that they bring. As the great Physician, please perform Your healing work in my life. Amen.

1. **Begin today's lesson by reading the Bible verses and the name of Christ for today. Work on your memory verse. Then use the suggested prayer in the margin on the left to begin your study.**

The Holy Spirit had one area of bondage yet to deal with—my hurts, or grudges. I am grateful that the Spirit saved this area for last. Hurts are perhaps the most difficult of all to deal with. As with all the other areas of bondage, I made my list of hurts or grudges. My list was long.

In 1959, while I was working on my Ph.D., I had a life-changing renewal experience in the Lord. Prior to the renewal, I had been very successful in the area of musicology. I had achieved a reputation for knowledge and sophistication in that field. Then I found myself with a new set of values. The reputation I had sought so eagerly was now hollow. From being a witness for the world and its values, I was becoming a witness for Christ. That was not fashionable on the campus of North Texas State University in 1959. Fellow students who once looked up to me now looked down on me.

One of the men who recognized this new direction in my life was also a Christian. After we finished our doctoral work, I occasionally saw him at professional meetings. He seemed to work it into the conversation that I was a religious fanatic. I bottled it up and resented him. Another man lied in order to worm his way into a position I was occupying. Others took advantage of me. I was dismayed at the depth of the resentments that were bottled up within me.

By 1973 the Lord had been preparing me for over a year to deal with these grudges. I finished the list and prayed over each one. I asked the Lord to forgive me for the resentment I felt and to forgive them for the wrongs they had done in selfishness.

2. **In your notebook, begin to prepare a list of your hurts, resentments, or grudges. Title and date the list. If you have difficulty, turn to page 226 and use the guide to help you make your list more complete.**

> God's desire is to move your hurts from
> producing resentment to producing love.

Later that morning I was praying as I walked to the school where I taught. I asked the Lord, "How well do I really understand forgiveness?" Immediately I remembered Matthew 5:43-44: "You have heard that it was said, 'You shall love your neighbor, and hate your enemy.' But I say to you, love your enemies, and pray for those who persecute you" (NASB).

What could I legitimately pray for the fellow who made fun of my relationship to Christ? I told the Lord, "I must ask for something he would understand, and the only thing he seems to understand is money!" I groped for an understanding of the Christlike thing to ask for him. Repeatedly money was brought back to my mind.

Then it occurred to me: I have various degrees, certificates, and awards which I could hang on the wall if I wanted to (I don't). But I had no certificates, no outer or visible proof of the changes in my mind and outlook that had taken place the previous year. I had no tangible evidence that the changes were genuine and that they were of God. I wholeheartedly wanted to pray spiritually and intelligently (see 1 Cor. 14:15), but I needed a sign from God that I was on the right track.

So I prayed, "Lord, speak to Bill about Yourself through money. I ask that You cause an unexpected windfall so miraculously that he will know that You are working in his life, that You care for him. Then, Lord, make him call me about what happened. If he calls me, I won't need a certificate! I will know that You are signaling me and that You really want me free from these resentments and from all the other areas of bondage!"

Almost immediately, I received a call from him! Bill said, "T. W., you will not believe what has happened." And then he told me about an unexpected windfall so miraculous that he knew God had done it. The moment was high joy for him and for me, too. I told him, "Bill, you can't imagine how much this means to me." At first he didn't believe me. My sincerity finally came through, however. We became good friends. As we talked, I realized that God had worked through my resentment and the renewing of my mind to perform a miracle in Bill's life. What had been my resentment was changed into love!

What had been my resentment was changed into love!

3. As you evaluate your hurts, ask God to help you identify which ones you respond to with resentment and which ones you respond to with love. Write an *R* beside the ones over which you still carry a grudge, resentment, or bitterness.

4. As you conclude this lesson:
   • Ask God to forgive you for any resentment or bitterness in your life.
   • Ask God to enable you to forgive those who have hurt you.
   • Ask God to forgive those who have hurt you.
   • Ask God to begin changing your resentment to love.

GROUP SESSION 3

FREE INDEED

SESSION GOALS

This session will help you understand areas of bondage to sin and how Christ wants to work to set you free. You will demonstrate submission to God's working in your life.

Hearing What the Spirit Is Saying (as you arrive)

1. (Individuals) Review what God has been saying to you during the study of unit 3.
   • Identify a Scripture and a name of Christ that have been meaningful this week.
   • Identify and mark the issue or subject in which God seems to be working most actively to develop the mind of Christ. (These will be shared later in the session.)
2. (Individuals) Write out any questions related to this unit you would like answered.

Magnifying the Lord and Exalting His Name (5 minutes)

1. (Volunteer) Open the session in prayer by asking God to continue the process of setting members free from bondage to sin in every area of life.
2. Pray as you feel led to worship God for Who He is and acknowledge Him for what He has done. Use the names of Christ to exalt His name together in prayer.
3. After prayer, share ways God revealed Himself to you this week through His names. Which name of Christ has been most meaningful to you and why?

Transforming by the Word (15 minutes)

1. (Pairs) Pair up and quote this week's memory verse, John 8:32,36. As time permits, alternate quoting verses from previous units. Use your Scripture memory cards as a reference.
2. Share what God said to you through this week's memory verse or other Scripture that has been meaningful.
3. (Quads—or two groups) Distribute poster board or newsprint and markers to each of two groups. Make two lists related to characteristics of a Christlike mind. Focus on this unit's Scriptures only.
   • Group 1: Make a list of things, actions, or attitudes identified or implied in Scriptures during this unit that need to be cleansed from one's mind and life.
   • Group 2: Make a list of things, actions, or attitudes identified or implied in Scriptures during this unit that need to be incorporated into one's mind and life.
   • For example: We need to cleanse ourselves from our *love for the world and the things of the world* (group 1) and incorporate love for God (group 2) (see 1 John).
4. Call on quads to read and comment on their lists. Place one on the Transformed From Wall and the other on the Transformed To Wall.
5. (Volunteer) Pray that God will cleanse members of your group and church.

Stimulating One Another to Love and Good Deeds (20 minutes)

1. Share testimonies of what God has done this week in your life that has been meaningful, challenging, or instructive.
2. State questions or concerns you have written for consideration. As time permits, seek to answer the questions as a group.
3. As time permits discuss one or more of the following questions:
   • Why should we not rush God in the process of receiving freedom from bondage to sin? (p. 55)

- How could giving up your responsibilities hinder or thwart what God wants to do in developing in you the mind of Christ? (p. 55)
- What experiences have been meaningful this week as you have prepared your lists? What has God been doing in your life to set you free?

4. Turn to page 65 and share your responses to the activity 7.
5. Remember you are only receiving an introduction to a lifelong process. You should not expect a quick fix or instant success in all areas. Let God work on His schedule as you are responsive to Him.

Preparing the Bride for Her Bridegroom (5 minutes)

1. Read 2 Peter 3:1-14. Listen for ways the bride (church) needs to prepare for the return of Christ. List them in the margin.
2. As time permits, discuss these questions:
   - Seeing that the world will come to an end, what kind of persons ought we be?
   - What cleansing, purifying, or preparation is needed in our church?
   - How can we apply this Scripture to our lives, families, and church?
3. Call on one member to pray for your church to continue to prepare for the Lord's return.

Praying for One Another (10 minutes)

1. (Quads, preferably same gender) Share the one general area where you face your greatest challenge for being freed from bondage to sin. You do not have to be specific. Share personal, family, church, or work-related prayer requests that primarily focus on developing the mind of Christ or purifying the bride.
2. (Quads) Pray specifically for one another for forgiveness, healing, encouragement, guidance, wisdom, knowledge, understanding, courage, strength, faithfulness, or for specific requests.

Closing the Session (5 minutes)

1. Share questions or concerns that came up during the session that we should remember in prayer.
2. Preview unit 4 on the following pages.
3. Close by praying that God will work this week to develop in each member the virtues of godly wisdom.

VIRTUES OF GODLY WISDOM

Hymn Part 2
CHRIST'S LIFESTYLE
*"Who, being in the form of God, thought
it not robbery to be equal with God"*
(Phil. 2:6).

❧ ❧

DAY 1
Cleansing Your Mind with God's Word

DAY 2
Pure

DAY 3
Peaceable

DAY 4
Gentle, Entreatable, and Merciful

DAY 5
Fruitful, Steadfast, and Honest

Why You Will Find This Unit Helpful

God's goal is for you to become like His Son Jesus. That is a high standard, and it is unreachable without God's help. God wants you to have the virtues of Christ. The good news is that He stands ready to help! In this unit you will study eight virtues of Christ. He is your Model. God will be working in you and with you to give you the mental quality of discernment. As you begin to measure your thoughts and actions against the perfection of Christ, God will be at work renewing your mind to reflect the virtues of Christ.

Lifelong Objective

In Christ you will develop the mental quality of discernment and use it to become pure, peaceable, gentle, entreatable, merciful, fruitful, steadfast, and honest.

Summary of God's Work in You

Christ's lifestyle in you springs from the mental quality of discernment. God's goal is your virtue. Your growth in Christ's character can be measured only by Christ's perfection. Christ enables your virtue in His office as Model. He makes your virtue possible.

Unit Learning Goals

- You will understand the importance of God's Word as a tool for cleansing your mind and keeping you from sin.
- You will demonstrate your submission to God's cleansing work through His Word.
- You will understand the difference between the eight virtues of godly wisdom in James 3:17 and their opposites and perversions.
- You will know eight virtues of godly wisdom.
- You will demonstrate a spiritual hunger for Christ to establish these virtues in your mind.

What You Will Do to Begin Developing the Virtues of Godly Wisdom

- You will study eight virtues, along with their opposites and perversions.
- You will become familiar with the Lifelong Helps on pages 224-259.
- You will focus your attention on one of the virtues and begin using the helps to move toward maturity in that virtue.

Scripture Memory Verse

"The wisdom that is from above is first pure, then peaceable, gentle, and easy to be intreated, full of mercy and good fruits, without partiality, and without hypocrisy" (Jas. 3:17).

Lifelong Helps Related to This Unit

Christlike Virtues (pp. 227-39)

The Mind of Christ Cards Related to This Unit

3B. Unit 4: Scripture Memory—James 3:17
7A. Eight Virtues of Godly Wisdom

8A. Pure	10A. Merciful
8B. Peaceable	10B. Fruitful
9A. Gentle	11A. Steadfast
9B. Entreatable	11B. Honest

Optional DVD Messages by T. W. Hunt

- Session 2, Part 1, Chapter 5: His Lifestyle

DAY 1
CLEANSING YOUR MIND WITH GOD'S WORD

Today's Bible Meditations
"Who, being in the form of God, thought it not robbery to be equal with God" (Phil. 2:6).

"Christ also loved the church, and gave himself for it; That he might sanctify and cleanse it with the washing of water by the word, That he might present it to himself a glorious church, not having spot, or wrinkle, or any such thing; but that it should be holy and without blemish" (Eph. 5:25-27)

Name of Christ for Today
The Word (John 1:1)

Prayer to Begin the Lesson
Jesus, You are the Word of God. You are God. I want my life to be saturated with You. Please cleanse me and fill me with Yourself. Amen.

1. Begin today's lesson by reading the Bible verses and the name of Christ for today. Work on your memory verse. Then use the suggested prayer in the margin to the left to begin your study.

Hymn Part 2—Christ's Lifestyle

If God came to earth and walked among us, how would He behave? What would His actions be like? We have the answer to that question in the poem found in Philippians 2:5-11. God came to earth in the Person of Jesus Christ. He came to act out in visible form God's purpose for humanity. "Being in the form of God, [He] thought it not robbery to be equal with God" (Phil. 2:6). Since we can see the actions of God in Christ's lifestyle, we can learn about His mind. "For as he thinketh in his heart, so is he" (Prov. 23:7). Outward actions are a reflection of inner thoughts. During the next two units we will look at the virtues of Christ that were reflected in His lifestyle.

2. Read the account of Jesus' temptation in the wilderness. As He was tempted by Satan, Jesus responded in a way that tells us something about His mind. As you read the following verses, underline the words of Jesus.

Then was Jesus led up of the Spirit into the wilderness to be tempted of the devil. And when he had fasted forty days and forty nights, he was afterward an hungered. And when the tempter came to him, he said, If thou be the Son of God, command that these stones be made bread. But he answered and said, "It is written, Man shall not live by bread alone, but by every word that proceedeth out of the mouth of God" [see Deut. 8:3]. Then the devil taketh him up into the holy city, and setteth him on a pinnacle of the temple, And saith unto him, If thou be the Son of God, cast thyself down: for it is written, He shall give his angels charge concerning thee: and in their hands they shall bear thee up, lest at any time thou dash thy foot against a stone. Jesus said unto him, "It is written again, Thou shalt not tempt the Lord thy God" [see Deut. 6:16]. Again, the devil taketh him up into an exceeding high mountain, and sheweth him all the kingdoms of the world, and the glory of them; And saith unto him, All these things will I give thee, if thou wilt fall down and worship me. Then saith Jesus unto him, "Get thee hence, Satan: for it is written, Thou shalt worship the Lord thy God, and him only shalt thou serve" [see Deut. 6:13]. Then the devil leaveth him, and, behold, angels came and ministered unto him (Matt. 4:1-11).

3. In all three responses Jesus used a phrase to begin His response. What was it?

Jesus quoted Scripture when He was tempted to sin. He said, "It is written. …" Jesus had memorized Scripture. By knowing God's commands, Jesus knew how to respond in each temptation so He did not sin. The psalmist said, "Thy word have I hid in mine heart, that I might not sin against thee" (Ps. 119:11).

🖎 **4. Why should we become familiar with what God has said in the Bible?**

_____

One thing we learn about the mind of Christ is that Christ filled His mind with the Scriptures. Jesus knew the will of His Father and was prepared to resist temptation when it came. Scripture helped Jesus keep His mind clean and unpolluted.

God's Word Cleanses

The Word of God has a cleansing effect on the mind. Jesus told the disciples, "You are already clean because of the word which I have spoken to you" (John 15:3, NASB). Later Jesus prayed, "Sanctify [the disciples] in the truth; Thy word is truth" (John 17:17, NASB). The Lord cleanses the church by "the washing of water with the word" (Eph. 5:26, NASB).

Our minds often are so mixed with the world's way of thinking that we need to be reoriented to God's way of thinking. We begin by a thorough cleansing with God's Word. God's Word cleanses as it washes away things that are wrong or impure. God's Word cleanses as it replaces wrong with right ways of thinking. One step in developing the mind of Christ is to let God cleanse your mind through His Word.

God's Word cleanses as it washes away things that are wrong or impure.

Humanism Hindered Me

After I had been working on my areas of bondage lists, I set out to study what the Bible says about each of the 17 virtues of James 3:17 and Galatians 5:22-23. These virtues partially represent that ideal mind of Christ toward which I was striving. I knew that once I was free from the bondage of sin, God would move me toward these virtues in my life. Using my concordance, I compiled passage after passage about the virtues mentioned in the two Scriptures.

In the process, I began to discover factors which hampered my gaining the virtues. At various points in my education, I had been exposed to aspects of humanism in subtle ways. Humanism teaches that we have a capacity for self-realization through reason. It glorifies what man can do apart from God. At that time, I had difficulty believing that the biblical virtues are simply a gift, native equipment born in us at spiritual birth (as implied in 1 Cor. 2:16 below). My humanistically trained mind wanted to work hard to achieve the virtues.

> The natural man receiveth not the things of the Spirit of God: for they are foolishness unto him: neither can he know them, because they are spiritually discerned. But he that is spiritual judgeth all things. . . . For who hath known the mind of the Lord, that he may instruct him? But we have the mind of Christ (1 Cor. 2:14-16).

5. Correctly identify the two statements below by marking them *God's* perspective or *humanism's* perspective.

_____ I can develop these godly virtues in my life by study and hard work.

_____ Godly virtues are a gift to me at spiritual birth and show when I allow Christ to live His life in me.

I needed God to do a work in me that would allow Christ's presence and mind to show through my life.

Knowledge does help, and my Bible studies defined the virtues enough to enable me to recognize them. My spiritual knowledge was growing, but I had been taught to be proud of knowledge. When we achieve certain things in the world system, that act of achieving becomes a part of our unconscious mind. The virtues could not be developed by hard work. Humanism teaches this. I needed God to do a work in me that would allow Christ's presence and mind to show through my life.

A Special Vow

For some reason, I could not simply "let go and let God have His way." But I earnestly wanted to. In order to overcome the deep, unconscious presence of humanism, I made a vow to the Lord: from that time on, I would not read anything but the Bible until God signalled me that I had begun to think in biblical terms. I determined to saturate my mind with God's way of thinking. Other Christians may not need to go to such an extreme. Certain aspects of humanism were radically rooted in me. Even today, I believe that the vow was inspired by the Lord and was a necessary part of my development at that time.

That period lasted four years. During that time I read nothing but the Bible. I did not even read commentaries. I memorized several books and many passages and chapters of the Bible. I studied exhaustively, prayed constantly, and found a real change taking place in the deepest parts of my mind. I felt that I actually was understanding the deeper meaning and implications of the virtues in James 3:17 and Galatians 5:22-23. The Word of God reaches into the deepest recesses of the mind. God's Word impacts every part of our mind, including the subconscious, especially when the Word is stored there.

I want you to allow God to begin a cleansing work in your mind through His Word. I am providing several opportunities in this course for you to begin this process. The following are some ways you can allow God the opportunity to cleanse your mind with His Word.

6. As you read through this list, check the ballot box beside the items you do already. Circle any item to which you sense God wants you to devote more time and attention.

❑ Daily read a part of God's Word.
❑ Study passages closely to see what God may want you to believe or do in response to His Word.
❑ Study related topics in Scripture to understand more clearly what God is saying on a particular subject.

❏ Memorize verses, passages, chapters, and even books of the Bible.

❏ Meditate on God's Word. Think about what He is saying to you through it.

❏ Pray through passages of Scripture discussing with God the implications for your life.

❏ Discuss God's Word with other believers. God may give you insight through a fellow believer.

7. Pray as you conclude today's study. Ask God to use the reading, studying, and memorizing of Scripture in this course to cleanse your mind. If you sense God calling you to devote more time to His Word (instead of sports, TV, movies, or other reading), tell Him about your intentions.

DAY 2
PURE

1. Begin today's lesson by reading the Bible verse and the name of Christ for today (in the right margin). Work on your memory verse. Then use the suggested prayer in the margin on the right to begin your study.

During the remainder of this week we will study the virtues of godly wisdom listed in James 3:17. We will look at three aspects of each virtue:

1. What it is (Christlike Virtue).
2. What it is not (Satanic Opposite).
3. How it can be distorted (Perversion).

Each virtue is a Christlike quality. For each virtue, Satan has one or several opposites. For example, lust is the opposite of purity. The carnal mind tends to adopt this opposite quality. In the same way, Satan also has a perversion of each virtue. We who attempt to develop the virtues into maturity are in danger of perverting them. For example, in trying to develop purity we can get sidetracked into being puritanical.

The mental quality God will be developing in you is discernment. This is a spiritual process of discerning right actions and thoughts from wrong actions and thoughts. God wants to help you know the difference between pure, lustful, and puritanical. The Holy Spirit will help you begin to discern between Christlike virtues, Satanic opposites, and perversions.

2. Read the chart on the following page. Ask God to guide you to the virtue He would like to work on first in your life. Circle the one you sense God wants you to focus on first.

Today's Bible Meditation
"Finally, brethren, whatsoever things are true, whatsoever things are honest, whatsoever things are just, whatsoever things are pure, whatsoever things are lovely, whatsoever things are of good report; if there be any virtue, and if there be any praise, think on these things" (Phil. 4:8).

Name of Christ for Today
A Refiner and Purifier (Mal. 3:3)

Prayer to Begin the Lesson
Purest Lord Jesus, I worship and adore the purity I see in Your life. I want to be pure like You are pure. You are a refiner and purifier. Refine and purify me so I can be like You. Burn away anything in my life that is impure. Amen.

Satanic Opposite	Christlike Virtue	Perversion
Lustful	*Pure*	Puritanical
Fussy	*Peaceable*	Compromising
Harsh	*Gentle*	Unkind restraint
Unapproachable	*Entreatable*	Yes-person
Merciless	*Merciful*	Indulgent
Fruitless	*Fruitful*	Fruit-obsessed
Wavering	*Steadfast*	Inflexible
Lying	*Honest*	Brutal

I have prepared a special tool for each of these virtues to help you in your study. Titled "Lifelong Helps for Developing the Mind of Christ," they are located in the back of this book. Though certainly not complete, they serve as a starting point as you allow God to bring these virtues to maturity in your life.

3. **Turn to pages 227-39 and find the page for the virtue you circled above. Place a bookmark at this place or fold down the corner of the page so you can refer to it this week. Write the page number here:** _____

4. **Now turn to the perforated cards in the back of the book. Tear out the card that relates to the virtue you have selected. Carry it with you this week to focus your attention on this virtue and its opposites and perversions.**

Pure

One Friday morning in October 1973, I was reviewing the insights I had gained on purity. My heart was filled with gratitude as I observed that God had enabled me to make progress in purity of heart.

5. **Read the list of words in the left margin to help you understand what** *purity* **is and what it is not (opposites). Below write your definition of** *purity*.

Purity **is** _____

_____

Pure
blameless, clean, chaste, pristine, spotless, unblemished, innocent, unadulterated, stainless, not contaminated, beyond reproach

Opposites of *Pure*
lustful, carnal, fleshly, lewd, contaminated, tainted, corrupt, depraved, immoral, impure

As I reflected on the progress I had made, I became keenly aware that my environment contained an abundance of impurities. Immediately I thought of a friend whose speech reflected an impure mind. I had been offended by his occasional lewd comments. I prayed for the Lord to purify his mind. Then I thought of another friend who had a different kind of impurity. I sensed that she cultivated friendships for what they could do for her. She had impure motives. I asked the Lord to purify her. Next I thought of a fellow who seemed to be backsliding and was showing a distaste for spiritual matters. I began praying for him.

The longer I thought about it, the more impurity I seemed to find in the people I knew. I was thinking about believers! The list of impure people grew long, and the kinds of impurity grew complex. The longer I prayed, I realized that I was experiencing grief. I knew that this particular grief usually indicated some sort of sin in my mind. So I asked the Lord to show me if I had sin in my heart. He spoke quite clearly!

One Satanic opposite of purity is lust. Spiritual Christians try to avoid that. God has given a perfect example of purity in the Lord Jesus, so we are to flee lust and pursue the goal of Christlikeness. But Satan has a perversion of purity. We overshoot our goal. Instead of being pure, we become puritanical—my source of grief. God was showing me that I was becoming puritanical.

We encounter many degrees of this perversion. It often involves pride and may involve scorn for others. In its early stages, however, it may surface as a simple opinion. I think I was in the opinion stage at that time. I honestly did not feel any scorn in my heart for the persons involved. I felt genuine affection. But God convicted me that I was judging them.

I was heartbroken. I asked the Lord, "How could I go so wrong when I have read nothing but the Bible for more than a year?" Then I remembered that the Pharisees knew far more of their Torah than I did my Bible. Yet they were puritanical. I had defined the virtues in biblical terms, but I was using my progress as the measuring stick for their definitions. Puritanicalism is using self as a measure of purity rather than Christ.

6. **Read the list of words in the margin to help you understand the perversion of *purity*. Can you think of an experience when you have observed this kind of behavior? If so, who was involved and when?**

Perversions of *Pure*
puritanical, pharisaical, rigid, severe, overly strict, prudish, austere, self-righteous

_____

_____

Jesus Is the Standard

All the virtues must be defined in terms of the life and personality of Jesus. Jesus is the definition of the virtues. The Bible has a purpose in telling us to "consider" Him (Heb. 3:1) and to "fix our eyes" on Him (Heb. 12:2, NASB). All of the biblical passages on purity are important, but understanding them apart from their manifestation in the life of Christ can lead to perversion.

Jesus was absolutely pure. I am sometimes asked if Jesus ever was tempted to lust. Without doubt He had that opportunity. Luke 8:3 tells of a group of women who followed Jesus and supported Him out of their own means. Few men have had more adoring women around them than Jesus. Yet Peter, who was in Jesus' inmost circle and watched Him closely for three and a half years, described Him as a "lamb without blemish and without spot" (1 Pet. 1:19). John, another of Jesus' inner circle, said that "in him is no sin" (1 John 3:5). Those who knew Him best recognized Jesus had perfect mental self-command.

Jesus knew no lust, but neither was He puritanical. Puritanical people are narrow in their selection of friends. Jesus befriended so many tax collectors, prostitutes, and down-and-outs that He was called a Friend of sinners. He accepted invitations to eat with self-righteous Pharisees as well as with sinful tax-collectors. Jesus never yielded to lust or to any other impurity; yet, He also never perverted purity. Jesus was simply and absolutely pure.

7. **What is one virtue of the mind of Christ?**

P_____	Peaceable	Gentle	Entreatable
Merciful	Fruitful	Steadfast	Honest

How did Jesus live such a clean life? He constantly practiced the presence of God! Jesus was never out of the conscious presence of the Father. His Father was His constant conscious point of reference (see Luke 2:49; John 4:34; 5:19-23; 6:38; 17:4). In the same way, you can practice the continual presence of Christ. Christ is with you always (see Matt. 28:20). He is your reference point.

8. **Turn to pages 227-28 and scan the *Pure* list in the Lifelong Helps. Notice some practical suggestions for practicing the presence of God. Conclude your study today by asking God to enable you to be more aware of His presence in your life moment by moment.**

DAY 3
PEACEABLE

Today's Bible Meditation
"Whosoever will be great among you, let him be your minister; And whosoever will be chief among you, let him be your servant" (Matt. 20:26-27).

Name of Christ for Today
The Prince of Peace
(Isa. 9:6)

1. **Begin today's lesson by reading the Bible verses and the name of Christ for today. Work on your memory verse. Then use the suggested prayer on the left to begin your study.**

Peaceable
The second virtue is *peaceable*. *Peaceable* describes a way of acting. The opposite of *peaceable* is *fussy*. Seeking peace can be perverted into compromise. Jesus cautioned:

"Do not think that I came to bring peace on the earth; I did not come to bring peace, but a sword. For I came to SET A MAN AGAINST HIS FATHER, AND A DAUGHTER AGAINST HER MOTHER, AND A DAUGHTER-IN-LAW AGAINST HER MOTHER-IN-LAW; AND A MAN'S ENEMIES WILL BE THE MEMBERS OF HIS HOUSEHOLD" (Matt. 10:34-36, NASB).

In all of His peacefulness, Jesus drew hard lines. He did not compromise on His expectations to maintain peace. We must not misuse or distort His qualities or His ideas. We must not go beyond being peaceable to compromising.

2. Read the list of words in the margin to help you understand what *peaceable* is and what it is not (opposites). Below write your definition of *peaceable*.

Peaceable is _____

_____

3. Read the list of words in the left margin that help you understand the perversion of *peaceable*. Can you think of an experience when you have observed this kind of behavior? If so, who was involved and when?

_____

_____

Jesus Was Peaceable

A quarrel broke out among the disciples when James and John, requested favored positions in the Kingdom. Competition is found throughout history wherever fallen man expresses himself. Pride feeds the need to compete for position, power, or fame. Pride characterizes human life as we know it and does not make for peace. But in this situation Jesus was peaceable.

> Then came to him the mother of Zebedee's children with her sons, worshipping him, and desiring a certain thing of him. And he said unto her, "What wilt thou?" She saith unto him, Grant that these my two sons may sit, the one on thy right hand, and the other on the left, in thy kingdom. But Jesus answered and said, "Ye know not what ye ask … to sit on my right hand, and on my left, is not mine to give, but it shall be given to them for whom it is prepared of my Father." And when the ten heard it, they were moved with indignation against the two brethren. But Jesus called them unto him, and said, "Ye know that the princes of the Gentiles exercise dominion over them, and they that are great exercise authority upon them. But it shall not be so among you: but whosoever will be great among you, let him be your minister; And whosoever will be chief among you, let him be your servant: Even as the Son of man came not to be ministered unto, but to minister, and to give his life a ransom for many" (Matt. 20:20-28).

Jesus pointed out that "whosoever will be chief among you, let him be your servant." Jesus announced that He "did not come to be served, but to serve, and to give His life a ransom for many" (Matt. 20:28, NASB). Our world is full of quarrels and war because we are seeking positions. Peace comes when we serve one another mutually just as Jesus served others.

4. What are two virtues of the mind of Christ?

P_____   P_____   Gentle   Entreatable

Merciful   Fruitful   Steadfast   Honest

Prayer to Begin the Lesson

Prince of Peace, I live in a world that knows very little of peace. I ask You to shape my life to be peaceable like You. Then as You see fit, place me among people who need a peacemaker—and work through me to show peace to my world. Amen.

Peaceable

peaceful, friendly, harmonious, orderly, quiet, content, reconciling, calm, agreeable, compatible

Opposites of *Peaceable*

fussy, nit-picking, ornery, contentious, combative, competitive, argumentative, cantankerous, controversial, litigious, contrary, mean, cranky, disagreeable, picky, obstinate

Perversions of *Peaceable*

compromising, wishy washy, goes with the flow, people-pleaser

Competition in the body of Christ does not reflect this quality of being peaceable. If we were like Jesus, all our attributes would harmonize with those of others in the body of Christ, and peace would prevail. Our attributes, callings, gifts, and functions will complement each other and work together when we are like Jesus. Differences in personality will blend together so that they will cause praise rather than blame.

> 5. In the statement below, circle the word or words in parentheses that make the following sentence true.
>
> If everyone in the body of Christ were to live like Jesus, our attributes would (compete with, complement) each other.

Our attributes would complement each other. My love, joy, and peace will work with your love, joy, and peace to accomplish great things for the Kingdom even though we function differently. On one hand, we are to be Christlike, and in that measure we will bear certain similar attributes. On the other hand, we also are to make an individual contribution. No one can make that unique contribution except the one God designed to do it (Eph. 2:10). Competition in the body of Christ is unnecessary. It is not a part of the divine design to bring in the Kingdom.

> 6. Yesterday we asked you to identify one virtue in your life that God would want to work on. We suggested you mark the Lifelong Helps in the back of your book for that virtue. As you conclude today's study, turn to that page and prayerfully read through the section "Becoming _____." Ask God to show you any attitudes or actions that are not like this virtue. Seek God's forgiveness. Then ask God to renew your mind and actions so that you will more nearly reflect that virtue in your life.

DAY 4
GENTLE, ENTREATABLE, AND MERCIFUL

Today's Bible Meditation
(to be selected at the end of today's lesson)

_____

_____

_____

_____

Name of Christ for Today
A Merciful and Faithful High Priest (Heb. 2:17)

> 1. Begin today's lesson by reading the name of Christ for today in the left-hand margin. Work on your memory verse. Then use the suggested prayer on the following page to begin your study.

Gentle

The third virtue in James 3:17 is *gentle*. Several Greek words are often translated as *gentle*. Matthew 16:15-23 describes gentleness in action. Jesus was gentle and showed accomplished skill in dealing with Peter. Jesus gently could beckon Peter to walk on water, and moments later reprimand Peter's little faith (see Matt. 14:28-32). He could lavishly call Peter blessed for his insight, only to rebuke him for refusing to embrace God's plan for Jesus:

> He saith unto them, "But whom say ye that I am?" And Simon Peter answered and said, Thou art the Christ, the Son of the living God. And

Jesus answered and said unto him, "Blessed art thou, Simon Barjona: for flesh and blood hath not revealed it unto thee, but my Father which is in heaven. ..." From that time forth began Jesus to shew unto his disciples, how that he must go unto Jerusalem, and suffer many things of the elders and chief priests and scribes, and be killed, and be raised again the third day. Then Peter took him, and began to rebuke him, saying, Be it far from thee, Lord: this shall not be unto thee. But he turned, and said unto Peter, "Get thee behind me, Satan: thou art an offense unto me: for thou savourest not the things that be of God, but those that be of men" (Matt. 16:15-23).

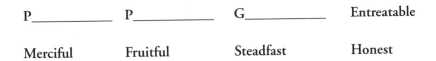 2. **What are three virtues of the mind of Christ?**

P_____	P_____	G_____	Entreatable
Merciful	**Fruitful**	**Steadfast**	**Honest**

Satan's opposite of gentle is harsh; the perversion is negligence. Think of a good parent dealing gently with a child. But suppose, in the attempt to be gentle, the parent was too lax for the child's good. The perversion could be negligence, or it even could be an unkind restraint.

3. **Read the list of words in the margin to help you understand what *gentle* is and what it is not (opposites). Below write your definition of *gentle*.**

Gentle is _____

_____

_____

4. **Read the list of words in the left margin that help you understand the perversion of *gentle*. Can you think of an experience when you have observed this kind of behavior? If so, who was involved and when?**

_____

_____

_____

Entreatable

The next virtue in James 3:17 is *entreatable*. An entreatable person is glad to serve. He or she does not object to being asked to do a favor for someone. The opposite of this virtue is *being unapproachable*. We encounter people who retreat from every opportunity to serve. The perversion is to be a yes-man or a yes-woman.

Prayer to Begin the Lesson

Lord Jesus, You are my High Priest. You are perfectly merciful and faithful. Because You have been merciful and faithful to me, help me to be merciful and faithful to others. Amen.

Gentle
fitting, equitable, fair, moderate, forbearing, considerate, humane, reasonable, pleasant, nurturing, tender, delicate, tactful, affable, amiable, genial, gracious, considerate, kindhearted

Opposites of *Gentle*
harsh, caustic, rough, abusive, hard, stiff, bitter, cruel, fierce, violent, blunt, brash, rude, short, snippy, grating

Perversions of *Gentle*
unkind restraint, negligent, laxity, derelict, heedless, careless, delinquent, neglectful, inattentive, reckless, unchecked, unbridled, reticent

Entreatable
approachable, cordial, affable, helpful, accessible, available, open, reachable, cooperative, willing, inclined, amenable, accommodating, responsive

5. Read the list of words in the left margin to help you understand what *entreatable* is and what it is not (opposites). Below write your definition of *entreatable*.

Entreatable is _____

_____

Opposites of *Entreatable*
unapproachable, distant, cold, cool, reticent, uncooperative, inaccessible, closed, unresponsive, frigid, restrained, introverted

6. Read the list of words in the left margin that help you understand the perversion of *entreatable*. Can you think of an experience when you have observed this kind of behavior? If so, who was involved and when?

_____

_____

Perversions of *Entreatable*
yes-person, pushover, easy mark, dupe, chump, stooge, sucker

Jesus was approachable and entreatable. On the way to heal the daughter of Jairus, He interrupted His trip to deal with the woman with the issue of blood (see Mark 5:34). Jesus knew a delay would result in the little girl's death, which gave Him something different to deal with.

> A certain woman, which had an issue of blood twelve years, And had suffered many things of many physicians, and had spent all that she had, and was nothing bettered, but rather grew worse, When she had heard of Jesus, came in the press behind, and touched his garment. For she said, If I may touch but his clothes, I shall be whole. And straightway the fountain of her blood was dried up; and she felt in her body that she was healed of that plague. And Jesus, immediately knowing in himself that virtue had gone out of him, turned him about in the press, and said, "Who touched my clothes?" And his disciples said unto him, Thou seest the multitude thronging thee, and sayest thou, Who touched me? And he looked round about to see her that had done this thing. But the woman fearing and trembling, knowing what was done in her, came and fell down before him, and told him all the truth. And he said unto her, "Daughter, thy faith hath made thee whole; go in peace, and be whole of thy plague" (Mark 5:25-34).

Jesus never turned down a request for healing, although He tested the faith of the Syrophoenician woman (Matt. 15:21-28) and delayed going to Lazarus in order to perform a greater miracle (John 11:4). When others were rebuking Bartimaeus, Jesus heard him (Mark 10:48-49). Jesus came when the centurion called for Him (Matt. 8:5-7). The whole story of Jesus is one of constant availability.

Merciful

The fifth virtue is *merciful*. This, of course, is an attribute of God, and therefore of Jesus. The opposite of *merciful* is *merciless*. The perversion is *indulgent*. Christians rarely are merciless, but we meet the perversion often.

7. Read the list of words in the margin to help you understand what *merciful* is and what it is not (opposites). Below write your definition of *merciful*.

Merciful is _____

_____

Merciful
caring, forgiving, gracious, decent, chivalrous, noble, forbearing, sympathetic, tolerant, compassionate, charitable, benevolent

8. Read the list of words in the left margin that help you understand the perversion of *merciful*. Can you think of an experience when you have observed this kind of behavior? If so, who was involved and when?

_____

_____

Opposites of *Merciful*
merciless, unmerciful, unsympathetic, compassionless, hardened, uncaring, pitiless, spiteful

Perversions of *Merciful*
indulgent, lenient, permissive

We want mercy as Christ demonstrated. Mercy often is equated with compassion. The repeated healings Jesus performed clearly demonstrate a profound sympathy for the hurt, the impaired, and the suffering. At times, Jesus was determined to heal in spite of official opposition (Mark 3:1-5). Matthew often mentions the compassion that a large crowd aroused in Jesus (see Matt. 9:36; 14:14; 15:32). The tears at Lazarus's tomb were partially a result of the empathy He felt for Mary and Martha. Through Jesus we know the great, compassionate heart of God.

Mercy is supremely demonstrated in forgiveness. Forgiveness requires a personal greatness and stature beyond compassion. In forgiveness, a person who has been offended pardons the offender. Sin is a dreadful offense to the absolute holiness of God. Because of this, God often exercises mercy in unsuspected ways. We exercise mercy in a supernatural way when we are able to convince an errant human of the reality of God's mercy. Jesus performed a miracle in the heart of the sinful woman who washed His feet when He told her, "Your sins have been forgiven" (Luke 7:48). The ultimate reach of mercy is in Jesus' great prayer from the cross: "When they were come to the place, which is called Calvary, there they crucified him. . . . Then said Jesus, Father, forgive them; for they know not what they do. And they parted his raiment, and cast lots" (Luke 23:33-34).

9. What are five virtues of the mind of Christ?

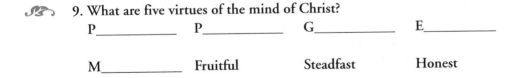

P_____   P_____   G_____   E_____

M_____   Fruitful   Steadfast   Honest

10. Turn in the Lifelong Helps to the virtue you are focusing on this week. Read the Scriptures for Meditation and select one that is particularly meaningful. Write it in the left margin under "Today's Bible Meditation" at the beginning of this lesson. Spend time with God seeking understanding of the verse and the virtue. Ask God to assist you in making that virtue evident in your living.

DAY 5
FRUITFUL, STEADFAST, AND HONEST

1. Begin today's lesson by reading the Bible verse and the name of Christ for today. Work on your memory verse. Then use the suggested prayer to begin your study.

Fruitful

The sixth virtue in James 3:17 is *fruitful*. The opposite is *fruitless* and the perversion is to be *fruit-obsessed*. The term can apply both to the fruit of the Spirit (Gal. 5:22-23) or to bearing fruit by bringing persons to God. In the latter sense, Jesus' own fruitfulness is the most easily demonstrated of the virtues named in James 3:17. Two thousand years of Christian history have produced millions of "fruits" of the Lord Jesus. He changed the course of world history. Jesus was the most fruitful Man who ever walked the earth. Here is one example.

They bring unto him one that was deaf, and had an impediment in his speech; and they beseech him to put his hand upon him. And he took him aside from the multitude, and put his fingers into his ears, and he spit, and touched his tongue; And looking up to heaven, he sighed, and saith unto him, "Ephphatha," that is, Be opened. And straightway his ears were opened, and the string of his tongue was loosed, and he spake plain. And he charged them that they should tell no man: but the more he charged them, so much the more a great deal they published it; And were beyond measure astonished, saying, He hath done all things well: he maketh both the deaf to hear, and the dumb to speak (Mark 7:32-37).

Fruitful
productive, fertile, prolific, constructive, high yield

Opposites of *Fruitful*
fruitless, unproductive, nonproductive, ineffective, ineffectual, unyielding, worthless, empty, hollow, profitless

Perversions of *Fruitful*
fruit-obsessed, success-driven, obsessed with numbers, vain, showy

2. Read the list of words in the left margin to help you understand what *fruitful* is and is not (opposites). Below write your definition of *fruitful*.

Fruitful is _____

_____

3. Read the list of words in the left margin that help you understand the perversion of *fruitful*. Can you think of an experience when you have observed this kind of behavior? If so, who was involved and when?

_____

_____

4. What are six virtues of the mind of Christ?

P_____   P_____   G_____   E_____

M_____   F_____   Steadfast   Honest

Steadfast

The seventh virtue in James 3:17 is *without wavering*, or *steadfast*. The opposite would be *wavering*, and the perversion would be *inflexible*. Jesus was neither of these. Once Jesus set His face toward the cross, nothing—not the pleas of a beloved disciple nor the dread of the process—deterred Him from carrying out the divine intention. He did not waver. Notice the agony of facing the cross and His reverent submission to the Father's will:

> He went a little farther, and fell on his face, and prayed, saying, "O my Father, if it be possible, let this cup pass from me: nevertheless not as I will, but as thou wilt. He went away again the second time, and prayed, saying, "O my Father, if this cup may not pass away from me, except I drink it, thy will be done" (Matt. 26:39,42).

Jesus was steadfast, but He was not inflexible. Entreatable persons cannot be inflexible. They can be interrupted. For example, Jesus' prayer time was interrupted by Simon and his companions (see Mark 1:35-37).

5. **Read the list of words in the left margin to help you understand what *steadfast* is and what it is not (opposites). Below write your definition of *steadfast*.**

   Steadfast is _____

   _____

6. **Read the list of words in the margin that help you understand the perversion of *steadfast*. Can you think of an experience when you have observed this kind of behavior? If so, who was involved and when?**

   _____

   _____

Honest

The last virtue in James 3:17 is *without hypocrisy*, *honest*, or *sincere*. The opposite is lying, or hypocritical. No one can attribute any lie or play-acting to Christ. Christ is Truth (John 14:6). The perversion of honesty is being brutal. Brutality is a real possibility to those of us required to deal with apathetic Christianity or unreal Christianity. We must watch our exasperation with those who lack sincerity. This is not to say that honesty must never confront. Real honesty can be courageous and bold with genuine integrity. Jesus insisted on inner perfection and confronted inner hypocrisy with crisp honesty (Luke 11:37-54). Only wisdom knows how to integrate honesty, integrity, and confrontation. Notice how Jesus identified the hypocrisy of the scribes and Pharisees:

Steadfast
firm, unshakable, sure, never-failing, enduring, abiding, resolute, constant, adamant, devoted, staunch, steady, immovable, resolved, uncompromising

Opposites of *Steadfast*
wavering, unsure, unstable, vacillating, weak, wobbly, waffling, fickle, volatile, flimsy, shaky, faltering, halting, hesitant, indecisive, reluctant, wayward, capricious

Perversions of *Steadfast*
inflexible, rigid, narrow-minded, obstinate, stubborn, unbendable, bullheaded, hardheaded, hard-line, inelastic, despotic, authoritarian, tyrannical, severe, iron-handed, intransigent

As he spake, a certain Pharisee besought him to dine with him: and he went in, and sat down to meat. And when the Pharisee saw it, he marvelled that he had not first washed before dinner. And the Lord said unto him, "Now do ye Pharisees make clean the outside of the cup and the platter; but your inward part is full of ravening and wickedness. Ye fools, did not he that made that which is without make that which is within also? But rather give alms of such things as ye have; and, behold, all things are clean unto you. But woe unto you, Pharisees! for ye tithe mint and rue and all manner of herbs, and pass over judgment and the love of God: these ought ye to have done, and not to leave the other undone. Woe unto you, Pharisees! for ye love the uppermost seats in the synagogues, and greetings in the markets. Woe unto you, scribes and Pharisees, hypocrites! for ye are as graves which appear not, and the men that walk over them are not aware of them." Then answered one of the lawyers, and said unto him, Master, thus saying thou reproachest us also. And he said, "Woe unto you also, ye lawyers! for ye lade men with burdens grievous to be borne, and ye yourselves touch not the burdens with one of your fingers. Woe unto you! for ye build the sepulchres of the prophets, and your fathers killed them. Truly ye bear witness that ye allow the deeds of your fathers: for they indeed killed them, and ye build their sepulchres. Therefore also said the wisdom of God, I will send them prophets and apostles, and some of them they shall slay and persecute: That the blood of all the prophets, which was shed from the foundation of the world, may be required of this generation; From the blood of Abel unto the blood of Zacharias, which perished between the altar and the temple: verily I say unto you, It shall be required of this generation. Woe unto you, lawyers! for ye have taken away the key of knowledge: ye entered not in yourselves, and them that were entering in ye hindered." And as he said these things unto them, the scribes and the Pharisees began to urge him vehemently, and to provoke him to speak of many things: Laying wait for him, and seeking to catch something out of his mouth, that they might accuse him (Luke 11:37-54).

Honest
sincere, true, genuine, ethical, sound, trustworthy, upright, straightforward, factual, candid, forthright, real, plain-dealing

Opposites of *Honest*
lying, dishonest, hypocritical, counterfeit, fake, fraudulent, crooked, deceitful, scheming, shady, unscrupulous, corrupt

Perversions of *Honest*
brutal, cruel, callous, pitiless, unkind, ferocious, hard-hearted, indifferent, ruthless, spiteful, unrelenting, vicious

7. **Read the list of words in the margin to help you understand what *honest* is and what it is not (opposites). Below write your definition of *honest*.**

   Honest is _____

   _____

8. **Read the list of words in the margin that help you understand the perversion of *honest*. Can you think of an experience when you have observed this kind of behavior? If so, who was involved and when?**

   _____

   _____

9. What are eight virtues of the mind of Christ?

P_____   P_____
G_____   E_____

M_____   F_____
S_____   H_____

10. Conclude this unit of study by asking God to continue molding and shaping your life to discard every behavior or attitude that does not measure up to the standard set by Christ. Ask God to perfect these virtues in your life.

GROUP SESSION 4

VIRTUES OF GODLY WISDOM

SESSION GOALS

This session will help you understand the difference between the virtues of godly wisdom in James 3:17 and their opposites and perversions. You will demonstrate a spiritual hunger for Christ to establish these virtues in your mind and your life.

Hearing What the Spirit Is Saying (as you arrive)

1. (Individuals) Review what God has been saying to you during the study of unit 4.
   • Identify a Scripture and a name of Christ that have been meaningful this week.
   • Identify and mark the issue or subject in which God seems to be working most actively to develop the mind of Christ. (These will be shared later in the session.)
2. (Individuals) Write out any questions related to this unit you would like answered.

Magnifying the Lord and Exalting His Name (5 minutes)

1. (Volunteer) Open the session in prayer by asking God to work through each member to develop the virtues of godly wisdom.
2. Pray as you feel led to worship God for Who He is and acknowledge Him for what He has done. Use the names of Christ to exalt His name together in prayer.
3. After prayer, share ways God revealed Himself to you this week through His names. Which name of Christ has been most meaningful to you and why?

Transforming by the Word (15 minutes)

1. (Pairs) Pair up and quote this week's memory verse, James 3:17. Then, as time permits, alternate quoting verses from previous units. Use your Scripture memory cards as a reference.
2. Share what God said to you through this week's memory verse or other Scripture that has been meaningful.
3. (Quads—or two groups) Distribute poster board or newsprint and markers to each of two groups. Make two lists related to characteristics of a Christlike mind. Focus on this unit's Scriptures only.
   • Group 1: Make a list of things, actions, or attitudes identified or implied in Scriptures during this unit that need to be cleansed from one's mind and life.
   • Group 2: Make a list of things, actions, or attitudes identified or implied in Scriptures during this unit that need to be incorporated into one's mind and life.
   • For example: We need to abandon *youthful lusts* (group 1) and embrace *righteousness, faith, charity, and peace* (group 2) (see 2 Tim. 2:22).
4. Call on quads to read and comment on their lists. Place one list on the Transformed From Wall and the other on the Transformed To Wall.
5. (Volunteer) Pray that God will cleanse members of your group and church.

Stimulating One Another to Love and Good Deeds (20 minutes)

1. Share testimonies of what God has done this week in your life that has been meaningful, challenging, or instructive.
2. State questions or concerns you have written for consideration. As time permits, seek to answer the questions as a group.
3. As time permits discuss one or more of the following questions:

- What is a good reason for becoming familiar with what God has said in the Bible? (p. 73)
- How has humanism affected your thinking and living? What can we do to let God renew our thinking?
- Which of the virtues does God seem to be working on in your life right now?
- With all the impurity surrounding us, what can we do as Christians to develop and maintain purity?
- Which of the perversions do you see most frequently in the Christian community? Why do you think that is true?
- If God were to measure our church by the standards of these virtues, what do you think He would have to say to us as a church? What can we do to help each other? to help our families?

4. Turn to pages 74-75 and share how you responded to activity 6.

Preparing the Bride for Her Bridegroom (5 minutes)

1. Read 1 Thessalonians 4:1–5:11. Listen for ways the bride (church) needs to prepare for the return of Christ. List them in the margin.
2. As time permits, discuss these questions:
   - With what words should we comfort each other regarding the second coming?
   - What cleansing, purifying, or preparation is needed in our church?
   - How can we apply this Scripture to our lives, families, and church?
3. Call on one member to pray aloud for your church to continue to prepare for the Lord's return.

Praying for One Another (10 minutes)

1. (Quads, preferably same gender) Share personal, family, church, or work related prayer requests that primarily focus on developing the mind of Christ or purifying the bride.
2. (Quads) Pray specifically for one another for forgiveness, healing, encouragement, guidance, wisdom, knowledge, understanding, courage, strength, faithfulness, or for specific requests.

Closing the Session (5 minutes)

1. Share questions or concerns that came up during the session that we should remember in prayer.
2. Preview unit 5 on the following pages. [Note for this next week: God's agenda is far more important than just following a course outline. Study unit 5, but spend time working on any area in which God seems to be focusing your attention. For instance, God may want you to continue working on purity. Spend time on God's agenda, even if you are distracted from the current unit of study.]
3. Close by praying that God will manifest His Spirit and reveal His fruit in the lives of all your group members this next week.

Hymn Part 2
CHRIST'S LIFESTYLE
*"Who, being in the form of God,
thought it not robbery to be equal with God"*
(Phil. 2:6).

DAY 1
Love

DAY 2
Joy and Peace

DAY 3
Longsuffering and Gentleness

DAY 4
Goodness and Faith

DAY 5
Meekness and Temperance

Why You Will Find This Unit Helpful
The nine virtues in Galatians 5:22-23 are the fruit of the Spirit that dwells in you.
As you develop the mind of Christ, you will display less of your old nature; and you
will allow the Spirit to display more of His nature. In this unit you will study nine
more qualities of Christ. God will be working in you and with you to give you the
mental quality of discernment. As you begin to measure your thoughts and actions
against the perfection of Christ, God will continue to renew your mind to reflect the
virtues of Christ.

Lifelong Objective
In Christ you will develop the mental quality of discernment and use it to display
love, joy, peace, long-suffering, gentleness, goodness, faith, meekness, and temperance.

Summary of God's Work in You

Christ's lifestyle in you springs from the mental quality of discernment. God's goal is your virtue. Your growth in Christ's character can only be measured by Christ's perfection. Christ enables your virtue in His position as Model. He makes your virtue possible.

Unit Learning Goals

- You will understand the difference between the nine virtues in Galatians 5:22-23 and their opposites and perversions.
- You will know the nine virtues that are the fruit of the Spirit.
- You will demonstrate a spiritual hunger for Christ to establish these virtues in your mind.

What You Will Do to Begin Developing the Fruit of the Spirit

- You will study nine virtues, their opposites and perversions.
- You will become familiar with the Lifelong Helps on pages 224-259.
- You will focus your attention on one of the virtues and begin using the Lifelong Helps to move toward maturity in that virtue.

Scripture Memory Verses

"The fruit of the Spirit is love, joy, peace, longsuffering, gentleness, goodness, faith, meekness, temperance: against such there is no law" (Gal. 5:22-23).

Lifelong Helps Related to This Unit

Christlike Virtues (pp. 227-39)

The Mind of Christ Cards Related to This Unit

4A. Unit 5: Scripture Memory—Galatians 5:22-23
7B. Fruit of the Spirit

12A-B. Love	15B. Gentleness
13A-B. Love Is—1 Cor. 13	16A. Goodness
14A. Joy	16B. Faith
14B. Peace	17A. Meekness
15A. Longsuffering	17B. Temperance

Optional DVD Messages by T. W. Hunt

- Session 2, Part 1, Chapter 6: His Lifestyle
- Session 2, Part 2: His Lifestyle

DAY 1
LOVE

Today's Bible Meditation
"God commendeth his love toward us, in that, while we were yet sinners, Christ died for us" (Rom. 5:8).

Name of Christ for Today
The Bridegroom
(John 3:29)

Prayer to Begin the Lesson
Jesus, You are the Bridegroom of the church. You gave us a new command that we should love each other as You have loved us. Teach me to love others that way. Amen.

1. Begin today's lesson by reading the Bible verse and the name of Christ for today. Work on your memory verse. Then use the suggested prayer to begin your study.

Last week you studied the eight virtues of godly wisdom in James 3:17. We trust that God has been developing in you the mental quality of discernment. This is a spiritual process of discerning right actions and thoughts from wrong actions and thoughts. For each of these virtues you studied three aspects:

1. What it is (Christlike virtue).
2. What it is not (Satanic opposite).
3. How it can be distorted (perversion).

2. Let us give you a little test. We've jumbled a list of virtues, their opposites, and their perversions. See if you can place them in the right category (virtue, opposite, or perversion). First read through the list and circle the virtues. Next cross through the opposites. Finally underline the perversions.

brutal	entreatable	gentle	harsh
honest	indulgent	lustful	lying
merciful	merciless	pure	puritanical
unapproachable	unkind restraint	yes-person	

After you finish, check your answers with the chart on page 76.

The Holy Spirit will help you discern between the virtues, Satanic opposites, and perversions. This week we will take a similar look at the nine virtues in Galatians 5:22-23, the fruit of the Spirit. Jesus was "full of the Holy Spirit" (Luke 4:1, NASB). Jesus described His life's mission in terms of the leadership of the Holy Spirit (Luke 4:18). The close relationship of Jesus and the Holy Spirit will be described in unit 10, but keep in mind that Jesus is God. The Holy Spirit is also God. They are not two Gods but different persons of the Trinity. One True God who has expressed Himself in three persons: Father, Son, and Holy Spirit. Thus, the fruit of the Spirit is also a reflection of Christ.

3. Pray as you read this chart of the virtues in Galatians 5:22-23. Ask God to guide you to one virtue He would like you to work on this week. Circle that virtue.

SATANIC OPPOSITE	CHRISTLIKE VIRTUE	PERVERSION
Hate, fear	Love	Possessive, permissive
Pain	Joy	Frenzy
War	Peace	Neutral
Impatient	Long-suffering	Lenient
Hard	Gentleness	Soft
Badness	Goodness	Finicky nice
Unbelief	Faith	Presumption
Arrogance	Meekness	Weakness
Undisciplined	Temperance	Fleshly effort

4. **Now turn to pages 227-39 and fold down the corner or place a bookmark at the page corresponding to the virtue you selected. Then turn to the cards in the back and tear out the one that relates to this virtue. Carry it with you this week and refer to it often to focus your attention on this virtue.**

Love

The first fruit of the Spirit is *love.* Jesus loved. That was His life. "Having loved His own which were in the world, he loved them unto the end" (John 13:1). The clearest expression of love in the Bible is unlimited giving of self to others. Jesus described the action of perfect love: "Greater love hath no man than this, that a man lay down his life for his friends" (John 15:13). Then Jesus proceeded to the most monumental expression of love of all ages—the cross on which He died. Paul tells us that nothing in all creation "shall be able to separate us from the love of God, which is in Christ Jesus our Lord" (Rom. 8:39). No superlative can capture the essence of Christ's love. Paul says that this love "surpasses knowledge" (Eph. 3:19, NASB). Small wonder that Christ's love controls us (2 Cor. 5:14, NASB). Christ's love is the motivating factor in the Christian life.

Christ's love is the motivating factor in the Christian life.

5. **What is one virtue of the mind of Christ?**

L_____	Joy	Peace
Long-suffering	**Gentleness**	**Goodness**
Faith	**Meekness**	**Temperance**

One opposite of love is *hate.* The perversions such as permissiveness, protectiveness, and possessiveness are numerous. The opposites also are numerous. For example, fear is also an opposite of love: "There is no fear in love; but perfect love casteth out fear" (1 John 4:18). Satan's road is wide. He has many opposites and perversions. The Christlike road is narrow (see Matt. 7:14).

Love
affection, charity, compassion, benevolence, adoration, fondness, commitment, caring deeply

Opposites of *Love*
hate, animosity, antipathy, aversion, dislike, enmity, hostility, ill-will, malice, vindictiveness, fear, dread, fright

Perversions of *Love*
possessive, overly protective, permissive, smothering love, manipulative

6. Read the list of words in the left margin to help you understand what *love* is and what it is not (opposites). Below write your definition of *love*.

Love is _____

_____

7. Read the list of words in the margin that help you understand the perversion of *love*. Can you think of an experience when you observed this kind of behavior? If so, who was involved and when?

_____

_____

Love probably is the greatest virtue of all. Loving God and loving others are the essence of the two greatest commands (Mark 12:30-31). We will focus more attention on love in unit 11.

> Thou shalt love the Lord thy God with all thy heart, and with all thy soul, and with all thy mind, and with all thy strength: this is the first commandment. And the second is like, namely this, Thou shalt love thy neighbour as thyself. There is none other commandment greater than these (Mark 12:30-31).

8. If time permits, read the Scriptures for Meditation under *Love* in the Lifelong Helps (pp. 233-34). Close your study today by asking God to show His love through you to a watching world. Ask God to give you specific assignments or opportunities to demonstrate love toward another person.

DAY 2
JOY AND PEACE

Today's Bible Meditation
"If ye keep my commandments, ye shall abide in my love. … These things have I spoken unto you, that my joy might remain in you, and that your joy might be full" (John 15:10-11).

Name of Christ for Today
Our Peace
(Eph. 2:14)

1. Begin today's lesson by reading the Bible verses and the name of Christ for today. Work on your memory verse. Then use the suggested prayer on the following page to begin your study.

Joy

The second virtue in Galatians 5:22 is *joy*. You may be surprised to think of joy as a virtue. However, it is a virtue of Jesus; and we are noble when we aim for Christ's joy. At times Jesus knew joy derived from the occasion (Luke 10:21). He obviously enjoyed the fellowship of Lazarus, Mary, and Martha in their home in Bethany (Luke 10:38-39; John 11:3,5). Nevertheless, Jesus' highest joy was a constant experience. It did not depend on circumstances but on a deep reality of His being. Jesus spoke of His obedience to His Father, and then He told the disciples, "These things I have spoken to you, that My joy may be in you, and that your joy may be made full" (John 15:11, NASB).

Jesus wants His disciples to have a full joy. Later He promised that their joy after His resurrection would be indestructible—a permanent feature in their lives (John 16:22). From this time with the disciples He went to the cross.

Jesus realized joy when He sought to glorify His Father in every circumstance. "For the joy set before Him, [Jesus] endured the cross" (Heb. 12:2). In His high priestly prayer Jesus prayed,

> Father, the hour is come; glorify thy Son, that thy Son also may glorify thee: As thou hast given him power over all flesh, that he should give eternal life to as many as thou hast given him. And this is life eternal, that they might know thee the only true God, and Jesus Christ, whom thou hast sent. I have glorified thee on the earth: I have finished the work which thou gavest me to do (John 17:1-4).

Facing that hideous punishment, Jesus' experience of joy was undisturbed. His joy was, in fact, full. In the parable of the talents, the master commanded the industrious servants to "enter into the joy of your master" (Matt. 25:21,23, NASB). This is the joy we will enter into—the joy of Jesus.

2. **What are two virtues of the mind of Christ?**

L_____	J_____	Peace
Long-suffering	Gentleness	Goodness
Faith	Meekness	Temperance

The opposite of joy would be *sadness* or even *hurt*. The perversion is *frenzy*. Like all emotions, joy is under the control of a temperate person. Christian joy is a superlative. It cannot depend on outward circumstances, although circumstance may produce a particular expression of joy. Many people settle for pleasure, but joy is more than pleasure. Pleasure in itself is not wrong because Jesus enjoyed His friends. Joy, however, is higher and grander than pleasure. It is a constant experience that comes from your inner being. It is the joy of Christ in you.

3. **Read the list of words in the margin to help you understand what** *joy* **is and what it is not (opposites). Below write your definition of** *joy*.

Joy is _____

_____

4. **Read the list of words in the margin that help you understand the perversion of joy. Can you think of an experience when you have observed this kind of behavior? If so, who was involved and when?**

_____

_____

Prayer to Begin the Lesson

Jesus, the angels proclaimed Your joy when You came into the world. You are the Prince of Peace. You are my Peace. Guide me to live in such a way that I will know Your joy and Your peace. Amen.

JOHN 16:22

"YE NOW THEREFORE HAVE SORROW: BUT I WILL SEE YOU AGAIN, AND YOUR HEART SHALL REJOICE, AND YOUR JOY NO MAN TAKETH FROM YOU."

Joy
delight, gladness, calm, cheerfulness, bliss, enjoyment, contentment, radiance

Opposites of *Joy*
pain, hurt, wound, agony, anguish, distress, misery, torment, woe

Perversions of *Joy*
frenzy, crazed excitement, hysteria

Peace

The third fruit of the Spirit is peace. Jesus is the Prince of Peace (see Isa. 9:6). We usually think of Him as a King, but He also is a Prince. Jesus knows more about peace than anyone else. He rules over it. Peace is His to give, and He gives it to His disciples (John 14:27).

Jesus cautioned against worry (Matt. 6:25,34). His own demeanor was never troubled by insecurity or instability. Insecurity cannot be decisive, and Jesus always acted decisively. His words and His actions were conclusive. Each healing was final; the leprosy, blindness, deafness, or lameness did not reoccur. Only peace can move forward, and Jesus always progressed. He never went backward in the phases of His life. Jesus had peace.

5. **What are three virtues of the mind of Christ?**

L_____	J_____	P_____
Long-suffering	Gentleness	Goodness
Faith	Meekness	Temperance

Jesus was able to give His kind of peace to His disciples. This gift was given at the end of His life after the disciples had observed Him for about three and a half years. Jesus talked with them at length on important information they would need after His death:

- the Holy Spirit
- the treatment they would receive at the hands of the world

- abiding in Him
- His departure and its significance for them

Then He concluded:

> Behold, the hour cometh, yea, is now come, that ye shall be scattered, every man to his own, and shall leave me alone: and yet I am not alone, because the Father is with me. These things I have spoken unto you, that in me ye might have peace. In the world ye shall have tribulation: but be of good cheer; I have overcome the world (John 16:32-33).

This is one of the great declarations of all time. The world will always trouble us, but we are in Christ. And Christ has overcome the world!

Peace is resting in the character and achievements of Christ.

Peace
rest, quietness, tranquility, harmony, concord, repose, serenity

Opposites of *Peace*
war, rage, havoc, discord, conflict, strife, rivalry, clash, feud, brawl, fracas, hassle, melee, rift

The James 3:17 *peaceable* describes an outer way of acting; the quality in Galatians 5:22 is an inner peace. Its opposite is *war*. In unit 2 we saw that our own lusts produce war within us. The mind of Christ, however, is integrated, at one with itself. Peace is to be whole, not fragmented by warring inner factions.

6. **Read the list of words in the left margin to help you understand what *peace* is and what it is not (opposites). Below write your definition of *peace*.**

Peace is _____

_____

The perversion is *being neutral.* Jesus cautioned against lukewarmness (see Rev. 3:15-16). What is wrong with being lukewarm? In this tepid, halfhearted condition, we are both trying to be cold (perhaps to impress certain people) and also trying to be hot (perhaps for other people). Lukewarm persons are trying to be opposite things at the same time! Bland neutrality is not what Jesus meant by *peace.*

7. **Read the list of words in the margin that help you understand the perversion of *peace.* Can you think of an experience when you have observed this kind of behavior? If so, who was involved and when?**

_____

_____

Perversions of *Peace*
neutrality, lukewarmness, indifference, detached, uncommitted, uninvolved

8. **Yesterday we asked you to identify one virtue in your life that God would want to work on. We suggested you mark the Lifelong Helps in the back of your book for that virtue. As you conclude today's study, turn to that page and prayerfully read through the section "Showing _____." Ask God to show you any attitudes or actions that are not like this virtue. Seek God's forgiveness. Ask God to renew your mind and actions so that you will more nearly reflect that virtue in your life.**

DAY 3
LONG-SUFFERING AND GENTLENESS

1. **Begin today's lesson by reading the name of Christ for today. Work on your memory verse. Then pray using the prayer on the following page to begin your study.**

Today's Bible Meditation
(to be selected at the end of today's lesson)

_____

_____

_____

_____

_____

_____

_____

_____

Long-Suffering
The next virtue in the Galatians verse is *long-suffering. Long-suffering* is an old English word that means *patient.* A long-suffering person suffers for a long time! Let's look at one example of Jesus demonstrating long-suffering or patience. Even under the great stress of facing His impending death, Jesus was patient and long-suffering with His disciples:

> Then cometh Jesus with them unto a place called Gethsemane, and saith unto the disciples, "Sit ye here, while I go and pray yonder." And he took with him Peter and the two sons of Zebedee, and began to be sorrowful and very heavy. Then saith he unto them, "My soul is exceeding sorrowful, even unto death: tarry ye here, and watch with me." And he went a little further, and fell on his face, and prayed, saying, "O my Father, if it be possible, let this cup pass from me: nevertheless not as I will, but as thou wilt." And he cometh unto the disciples, and findeth them asleep, and saith unto Peter, "What, could ye not watch with me one hour? Watch and pray, that ye enter not into temptation: the spirit indeed is willing, but

Name of Christ for Today
A Quickening Spirit
(1 Cor. 15:45)

Long-suffering

patience, endurance, constancy, steadfastness, perseverance, forbearance, slow in avenging wrongs

Opposites of Long-Suffering

impatient, edgy, chafing, crabby, nagging, touchy, impetuous, restless, quick to avenge wrongs

Perversions of Long-Suffering

lenient, indulgent, permissive

the flesh is weak." He went away again the second time, and prayed, saying, "O my Father, if this cup may not pass away from me, except I drink it, thy will be done." And he came and found them asleep again: for their eyes were heavy. And he left them, and went away again, and prayed the third time, saying the same words. Then cometh he to his disciples, and saith unto them, "Sleep on now, and take your rest: behold, the hour is at hand, and the Son of man is betrayed into the hands of sinners. Rise, let us be going: behold, he is at hand that doth betray me" (Matt. 26:36-46).

The opposite of *long-suffering* is *impatient*. Impatience reveals anxiety, intolerance, irritability, and a host of other un-Christlike qualities. The perversion is lenience.

2. **Read the list of words in the left margin to help you understand what *long-suffering* is and what it is not (opposites). Below write your definition of *long-suffering*.**

Long-suffering is _____

_____

3. **Read the list of words in the left margin that help you understand the perversion of *long-suffering*. Can you think of an experience when you have observed this kind of behavior? If so, who was involved and when?**

_____

_____

Jesus was long-suffering, but never lenient. The disciples were slow to learn. Three times they got into arguments over the matter of personal greatness in the Kingdom (see Mark 9:34; 10:35-45; Luke 22:24-27) in spite of the Lord's repeated teachings on humility. Ironically, the first of these arguments occurred just after Jesus taught on His approaching humiliation and death. The last one occurred on the last night of His life when He was preparing to die. The disciples did not learn humility in spite of Jesus' efforts to teach them. They were not chosen for their brilliance!

Jesus bore with them and often retaught material He had covered already. For example, the Lord scolded them for their lack of faith (see Matt. 8:26; 14:31; 16:8; Mark 4:40). As early as the Sermon on the Mount, Jesus announced that God would provide for the needs of His own (see Matt. 6:25-34). The disciples heard Him say repeatedly that the faith of those healed was the effective force in some of His miracles (see Matt. 9:29; Luke 7:50). They heard Jesus commend highly the rare faith of the centurion (see Matt. 8:10) and of the Syrophoenician woman (see Matt. 15:28). Yet, in spite of their slowness, Jesus did not give up. On the way to Jerusalem, He still taught on faith (see Luke 17:6). Even in the final week of His life, Jesus struggled to convey the importance and the nature of faith (see Matt. 21:18-22). Perhaps we should be grateful that the disciples were slow to learn and that Jesus was long-suffering! His repeated teaching of faith is a help to us.

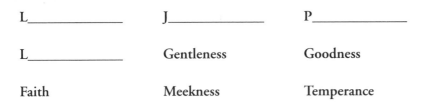

4. What are four virtues of the mind of Christ?

L_____   J_____   P_____

L_____   Gentleness   Goodness

Faith   Meekness   Temperance

Gentleness

The fifth fruit of the Spirit is *gentleness*. The Greek word for *gentleness* in Galatians is different from the word for *gentle* in James. The word in Galatians describes an attitude or disposition that is more than action. Biblical gentleness is demonstrated in a sensitive balance that does not go too far yet demonstrates the tender touch of God when it is really needed. Jesus displayed gentleness. Jesus dealt tenderly with children, with the helpless, with the lame and impaired. The prophecy of the Servant of the Lord in Isaiah 42:3 had said of Him that "a battered reed He will not break off, and a smoldering wick He will not put out" (Matt. 12:20, NASB). With those who needed firmness, Jesus was uncompromising and firm. With the vulnerable, He dealt sympathetically. We see one of the gentlest actions from His hand when He healed the leper after the Sermon on the Mount.

> [1]When he was come down from the mountain, great multitudes followed him. [2]And, behold, there came a leper and worshipped him, saying, Lord, if thou wilt, thou canst make me clean. [3]And Jesus put forth his hand, and touched him, saying, "I will; be thou clean." And immediately his leprosy was cleansed. [4]And Jesus saith unto him, "See thou tell no man; but go thy way, shew thyself to the priest, and offer the gift that Moses commanded, for a testimony unto them" (Matt. 8:1-4).

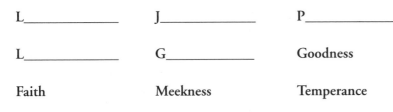

5. What are five virtues of the mind of Christ?

L_____   J_____   P_____

L_____   G_____   Goodness

Faith   Meekness   Temperance

The opposite of *gentleness* is *hardness* or *hard*. Jesus warned the Pharisees that Moses only permitted them divorce "because of the hardness of your hearts" (Matt. 19:8). The perversion is to be *soft*. Jesus was not soft when He pronounced repeated woes on the Pharisees and teachers of the law in the temple (see Matt. 23:13-36).

6. Read the list of words in the margin to help you understand what *gentleness* is and what it is not (opposites). Below write your definition of *gentleness*.

Gentleness is _____

_____

Gentleness
kindness, goodness of heart, integrity, goodness in deeds or actions, kindly disposition toward others

Opposites of *Gentleness*
hard, severity, harsh, caustic, rough, abusive, hard, stiff, bitter, cruel, fierce, violent, blunt, brash, rude, short, snippy, grating

Perversions of *Gentleness*
soft, mushy, negligence, laxity, dereliction, heedless, careless, inattentive, unchecked, unbridled, reticent

7. Read the list of words in the left margin that help you understand the perversion of *gentleness*. Can you think of an experience when you have observed this kind of behavior? If so, who was involved and when?

_____

_____

_____

_____

8. Turn to the Lifelong Helps to the virtue you are focusing on this week. Read the Scriptures for Meditation and select one that is particularly meaningful. Write it in the left margin under "Today's Bible Meditation" at the beginning of today's lesson. Spend some time with God to seek understanding of the verse and the virtue. Ask God to assist you in making that virtue evident in your life.

DAY 4
GOODNESS AND FAITH

Today's Bible Meditation
"Moreover it is required in stewards, that a man be found faithful"
(1 Cor. 4:2)

Name of Christ for Today
The Good Shepherd
(John 10:11)

Prayer to Begin the Lesson
Jesus, Good Shepherd, guide me to the paths of righteousness. Feed me on the riches of Your truth. Quench my thirst for fellowship with You! Amen.

1. Begin today's lesson by reading the Bible verse and the name of Christ for today. Work on your memory verse. Then use the suggested prayer to begin your study.

Goodness

The next virtue is *goodness.* As Jesus used the word, *good* indicated that something or someone was functioning. If we said, "This watch is no good anymore; it won't keep time," we would mean that the watch did not work, it did not function. This is how Jesus used the word. Of the two servants who invested well, Jesus said, "Well done, *good* and faithful slave" (Matt. 25:21, 23, NASB; italics mine). These servants functioned; they produced. Jesus said that a good tree produces good fruit (see Matt. 7:17); that is, the tree functions. Something is good when it works.

Jesus obviously produced. He never failed. His teaching made a profound and lasting impression. After the healing of the deaf man in the Decapolis, "They were utterly astonished, saying, 'He has done all things well; He makes even the deaf to hear, and the dumb to speak'" (Mark 7:37, NASB). Jesus' success rate was 100 percent! The supreme evidence, however, is from the Father Himself. Jesus said,

I have greater witness than that of John: for the works which the Father hath given me to finish, the same works that I do, bear witness of me, that the Father hath sent me. And the Father himself, which hath sent me, hath borne witness of me (John 5:36-37).

The success rate of Jesus testifies that God the Father was endorsing all His works. He functioned. Jesus was good.

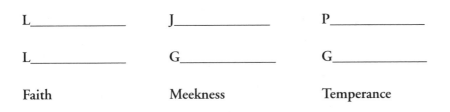 2. **What are six virtues of the mind of Christ?**

L_____   J_____   P_____

L_____   G_____   G_____

Faith   Meekness   Temperance

The opposite of *goodness* is *badness*. One perversion is to be *finicky nice*. Jesus was far more than merely *nice*. He certainly was not choosy or persnickety. Jesus was the most wholesome man who ever lived. He loved His friends and cultivated friendship. He even loved to eat! Behind every charge of the Pharisees was some element of truth. They called Jesus a glutton (see Matt. 11:19), so obviously they had observed that He enjoyed eating. Some of them even invited Him for meals. Jesus was no more a glutton than He was a drunkard, but He evidently ate with delight. But Jesus also knew when the next bite would be sin! To Him, human life was good, and worthy of His blessing. Jesus blessed the wedding at Cana. He was a real Man, and He was wholesome. Jesus showed goodness at its best.

3. **Read the list of words in the right margin to help you understand what** *goodness* **is and what it is not (opposites). Below write your definition of** *goodness.*

Goodness is _____

_____

4. **Read the list of words in the right margin that helps you understand the perversion of** *goodness.* **Can you think of an experience when you have observed this kind of behavior? If so, who was involved and when?**

_____

_____

Goodness
uprightness of heart and life, moral, wholesome, productive, functioning, working order

Opposites of *Goodness*
badness, unwholesome, evil, corruption, depravity, immorality, wickedness, nonproductive

Perversions of *Goodness*
finicky nice, self-righteous

Faith or Faithfulness

The seventh fruit of the Spirit is faith or faithfulness. Jesus was faithful in His love for His disciples (see John 13:1). Jesus is faithful in His promises:

• "If ye shall ask any thing in my name, I will do it" (John 14:14).
• "I will not leave you comfortless: I will come to you" (John 14:18).
• "Because I live, ye shall live also" (John 14:19).

Jesus showed His faithfulness to the Scripture and in the work of His Father until His death:

> After this, Jesus knowing that all things were now accomplished, that the scripture might be fulfilled, saith, "I thirst." Now there was set a vessel full of vinegar: and they filled a sponge with vinegar, and put it upon hyssop, and put it to his mouth. When Jesus therefore had received the vinegar, he said, "It is finished" (John 19:28-30).

He is faithful as High Priest (see Heb. 3:1). John calls Him the "faithful witness" (see Rev. 1:5). He is the "same yesterday and today, yes and forever" (Heb. 13:8, NASB). He is the standard for faithfulness by which we measure ourselves.

5. What are seven virtues of the mind of Christ?

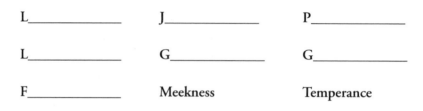

L_____	J_____	P_____
L_____	G_____	G_____
F_____	Meekness	Temperance

The opposite of *faith* or *faithfulness* is *faithlessness* or *fickleness*. Many Christians would be horrified if they were accused of fickleness, and yet they do not live up to the high standard of Jesus for faithfulness. The perversion of faith is legalism—doing the right things for the wrong reasons.

Faith
faithfulness, trustworthiness, integrity, reliability, fidelity, ardor, loyalty, dependability, consistency

6. Read the list of words in the left margin to help you understand what *faith* is and what it is not (opposites). Below write your own definition of *faith*.

Faith is _____

_____

Opposites of *Faith*
faithlessness, fickleness, untrustworthiness, inconsistency, uncertainty, waywardness, capriciousness

7. Read the list of words in the left margin that helps you understand the perversion of *faith*. Can you think of an experience when you have observed this kind of behavior? If so, who was involved and when?

_____

_____

Perversions of *Faith*
legalism, workaholism, overcommitted, fanatical, overly zealous, extremism

8. Close your study today in prayer. Ask God to wash away those things in your mind and life that are not good and those things that are faithless. Invite God to complete His good work in you and show goodness and faith through your life.

DAY 5
MEEKNESS AND TEMPERANCE

1. **Begin today's lesson by reading the Bible verse and the name of Christ for today. Work on your memory verse. Then use the suggested prayer to begin your study.**

Meekness

Jesus claimed *meekness* for Himself, and, significantly, coupled it with being "lowly in heart" (Matt. 11:29, KJV). His meekness is worthy of our imitation.

Come unto me, all ye that labour and are heavy laden, and I will give you rest. Take my yoke upon you, and learn of me; for I am meek and lowly in heart: and ye shall find rest unto your souls. For my yoke is easy, and my burden is light (Matt. 11:28-30).

2. **What are eight virtues of the mind of Christ?**

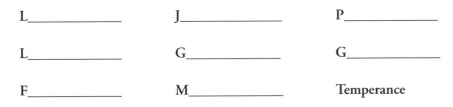

L_____   J_____   P_____

L_____   G_____   G_____

F_____   M_____   Temperance

One opposite of meekness is *arrogance*. The perversion is *weakness*, and many think of meekness in terms of its perversion. True meekness is a humility coupled with inner strength. We will look more thoroughly into meekness in unit 6 on servanthood and unit 7 on the Beatitudes.

3. **Read the list of words in the margin to help you understand what** *meekness* **is and what it is not (opposites). Below write your definition of** *meekness*.

Meekness is _____

_____

4. **Read the list of words in the margin that help you understand the perversion of** *meekness*. **Can you think of an experience when you have observed this kind of behavior? If so, who was involved and when?**

_____

_____

Today's Bible Meditation
"Take my yoke upon you, and learn of me; for I am meek and lowly in heart: and ye shall find rest unto your souls" (Matt. 11:29).

Name of Christ for Today
The True Vine
(John 15:1)

Prayer to Begin the Lesson
Heavenly Father, You are the Gardener and Jesus is the True Vine. Help me to abide in Christ more. Prune away things and activities in my life so I can be most fruitful. Holy Spirit, please bear Your fruit through me. Amen.

Meekness
accepting God's dealings with us as good without resistance, a fruit of power, lowly before God and humble before man

Opposites of *Meekness*
arrogance, haughtiness, pride, cockiness, egotism, vanity, conceit

Perversions of *Meekness*
weakness, wimpy, cowardly, spinelessness, timidity

Temperance

The final virtue—*temperance*—is rendered in Greek by a compound which refers to inner strengthening. The translation *self-control* captures some of the idea. Temperance also is a discipline, but it cannot be imposed from an outside source. Temperance cannot be achieved by energy or by training. Rather, temperance is a *fruit* of the Spirit. The spiritual Christian has this quality, not as a result of will power or effort, but as a result of the work of the Holy Spirit in our lives. Temperance grows like fruit grows.

Temperance is observable in such disciplines as prayer, Bible study, and witness. In Jesus, we see it in His night of prayer prior to choosing the disciples (see Luke 6:12) and in His rising early to pray (see Mark 1:35). Jesus' discipline also is obvious in His enormous knowledge of the Old Testament and in His constant proclamation of the Kingdom of God. Certainly in Jesus' temperance was a fruit, because of His intimate acquaintance with and dependence on the Holy Spirit. Notice the self-control Jesus exhibited during His trial before Pilate:

> Jesus stood before the governor: and the governor asked him, saying, Art thou the King of the Jews? And Jesus said unto him, "Thou sayest." And when he was accused of the chief priests and elders, he answered nothing. Then said Pilate unto him, Hearest thou not how many things they witness against thee? And he answered him to never a word; insomuch that the governor marvelled greatly (Matt. 27:11-14).

MARK 1:35

"IN THE MORNING, RISING UP A GREAT WHILE BEFORE DAY, HE WENT OUT, AND DEPARTED INTO A SOLITARY PLACE, AND THERE PRAYED."

🕮 5. **What are nine virtues of the mind of Christ?**

L_____   J_____   P_____

L_____   G_____   G_____

F_____   M_____   T_____

The opposite of temperance is to be *undisciplined*, referring to a lack of self-control. Another opposite would be *self-indulgent*. Paul cautioned against self-seeking people in the church who mislead the body of Christ (see Rom. 16:18). The perversion is *fleshly effort* or *self-effort*. The spiritual Christian always remembers that "It is God [not self] who is at work in you, both to will and to work for His good pleasure" (Phil. 2:13, NASB). Temperance, or self-control, rests in God's work in our lives. We cooperate with or work with God in the accomplishing of His aims.[1]

🕮 6. **Read the list of words in the left margin to help you understand what** *temperance* **is and what it is not (opposites). Below write your definition of** *temperance*.

Temperance is _____

_____

Temperance
strength, controlling power of the will under the operation of the Spirit of God, self-control, mastery over desires or sensual appetites, endisciplined by God

Opposites of *Temperance*
undisciplined, self-indulgent, slothful, lazy, lackadaisical, sluggish, laid back

7. Read the list of words in the right margin that help you understand the perversion of *temperance*. Can you think of an experience when you have observed this kind of behavior? If so, who was involved and when?

Perversions of *Temperance*
fleshly effort, self-effort

_____

_____

Perhaps first-century Christians found it natural to expect such work of the Spirit in their lives because the idea of self-control was taught carefully in their poetry and wisdom literature (see Ps. 141:3; Prov. 16:32; 25:28). While they did not express in New Testament language the idea of the Holy Spirit working in them, they knew well that outcomes were in God's hands (see Prov. 3:5-6; 20:24, Jer. 10:23).

8. Conclude this unit of study by reviewing the nine virtues that are fruit of the Holy Spirit. Pray and ask God to do whatever is necessary in you so that your life will bear the fruit of the Spirit on every occasion.

---

1. This does not mean we are passive in the exercise of the spiritual disciplines. But the Holy Spirit is their Author. The Holy Spirit should be credited properly as the One who initiates and directs the disciplines. The disciplines are not a result of self-control but of Spirit control. We play an active part. The Spirit is the Director and Energizer of all true prayer, Bible study, witnessing, and all spiritual disciplines. For further study on the disciplines see Richard Foster, *Celebration of Discipline*, revised edition (New York: Harper and Row, 1988); Dallas Willard, *The Spirit of the Disciplines* (New York: Harper and Row, 1988); Donald S. Whitney, *Spiritual Disciplines for the Christian Life* (Colorado Springs: Navpress, 1991); and Claude King, *Growing Disciples: The Call to Follow Christ* (Nashville: LifeWay Press, 2006).

GROUP SESSION 5

FRUIT OF THE SPIRIT

SESSION GOALS

This session will help you understand the difference between the virtues in Galatians 5:22-23 and their opposites and perversions. You will demonstrate a spiritual hunger for Christ to establish and manifest these virtues in your mind and your life.

Hearing What the Spirit Is Saying (as you arrive)

1. (Individuals) Review what God has been saying to you during the study of unit 5.
   • Identify a Scripture and a name of Christ that have been meaningful this week.
   • Identify and mark the issue or subject in which God seems to be working most actively to develop the mind of Christ. (These will be shared later in the session.)
2. (Individuals) Write out any questions related to this unit you would like answered.

Magnifying the Lord and Exalting His Name (5 minutes)

1. (Volunteer) Open the session in prayer asking God to so cleanse lives that His Spirit will be seen clearly in every life as He manifests His fruit.
2. Pray as you feel led to worship God for Who He is and acknowledge Him for what He has done. Use the names of Christ to exalt His name together in prayer.
3. After prayer, share ways God revealed Himself to you this week through His names. Which name of Christ has been most meaningful to you and why?

Transforming by the Word (15 minutes)

1. (Pairs) Pair up and quote this week's memory verse, Galatians 5:22-23.
2. Ask volunteers to quote each of the verses from previous units: Romans 12:2; Matthew 6:33; John 8:32,36; and James 3:17.
3. Share what God said to you through this week's memory verse or other Scripture that has been meaningful.
4. (Quads—or two groups) Distribute poster board or newsprint and markers to each of two groups. Make two lists related to characteristics of a Christlike mind. Focus on this unit's Scriptures only. *Make sure members have a chance to work on different lists occasionally rather than always working on Transformed From or Transformed To.*
   • Group 1: Make a list of things, actions, or attitudes identified or implied in Scriptures during this unit that need to be cleansed from one's mind and life.
   • Group 2: Make a list of things, actions, or attitudes identified or implied in Scriptures during this unit that need to be incorporated into one's mind and life.
   • For example: We need to eliminate *hate for our enemies* (group 1) and cultivate *love for our enemies* (group 2) (see Matt. 5:43-44).
4. Call on quads to read and comment on their lists. Place one on the Transformed From Wall and the other on the Transformed To Wall.
5. (Volunteer) Pray that God will cleanse members of your group and church.

Stimulating One Another to Love and Good Deeds (20 minutes)

1. Someone quote Hebrews 10:24.
2. Share testimonies of what God has done this week in your life that has been meaningful, challenging, or instructive.
3. Encourage members to ask questions or state concerns that they have written for consideration. As time permits, guide the group in answering the questions.
4. As time permits, discuss one or more of the following questions:

- What are some of the things God has been doing in your life this week to develop any of the 17 Christlike virtues?
- Which of the virtues does God seem to be working on in your life right now?
- Which of the virtues is most lacking in our church today? Which is most visible?
- Which of the perversions do you see most frequently in the Christian community? Why do you think that is true?
- If God were to measure our church by the standards of these virtues, what do you think He would He have to say to us as a church? What can we do to help each other? to help our families?
- How clearly do we allow the Spirit to manifest this fruit through us? If we don't measure up very well, what do you sense God would have us do as a church? as individuals? as families?

Preparing the Bride for Her Bridegroom (5 minutes)

1. Read 2 Timothy 3:1-17. Listen for ways the bride (church) needs to prepare for the return of Christ. List them in the margin.
2. As time permits, discuss these questions:
   - What are the marks of the last days and what can the church do to prepare for that time?
   - Do you see any evidences that could indicate we may be living in the last days? What?
   - What cleansing, purifying, or preparation is needed in our church?
   - How can we apply this Scripture to our lives, families, and church?
3. Someone pray for our church to continue to prepare for the Lord's return.

Praying for One Another (10 minutes)

1. (Quads, preferably same gender) Share personal, family, church, or work-related prayer requests that primarily focus on developing the mind of Christ or purifying the bride.
2. (Quads) Pray specifically for one another for forgiveness, healing, encouragement, guidance, wisdom, knowledge, understanding, courage, strength, faithfulness, or for specific requests.

Closing the Session (5 minutes)

1. Share questions or concerns that came up during the session that we should remember in prayer.
2. Preview unit 6 on the following pages. Watch for ways this week to demonstrate a spirit of servanthood.
3. Close by praying that God will help you follow the model of Jesus in being His servants.

Hymn Part 3
Christ's Servanthood
Jesus "made himself of no reputation,
and took upon him the form of a servant"
(Phil. 2:7).

DAY 1
Two Reasons for Servanthood

DAY 2
Serving God and Others

DAY 3
Characteristics of a Servant Mind, Part 1

DAY 4
Characteristics of a Servant Mind, Part 2

DAY 5
Characteristics of a Servant Mind, Part 3

Why You Will Find This Unit Helpful
You will learn that having the servant mind of Christ frees God to do mighty works in and through your life. As you study the characteristics and example of Christ's servanthood, God will be working to conform you to that same image of servanthood.

Lifelong Objective
In Christ you will take on the form of a servant and serve God and others with the heart and mind of a servant.

Summary of God's Work in You

Christ's servant-mind in you facilitates the mental quality of willingness. God's goal is Kingdom business. Your growth in servanthood can be measured only by Christ's example. Christ enables your servanthood in His role as Master. Christ leads you.

Unit Learning Goals

- You will know two reasons for being a servant.
- You will demonstrate your lowliness before God.
- You will understand the importance of serving God and others.
- You will know 14 characteristics of servanthood.
- You will indicate your willingness for God to develop these characteristics in your life.
- You will demonstrate your submission to God as your Master.

What You Will Do to Begin Developing a Servant Mind

- You will ask God to mold you into the image of His Righteous Servant—Jesus Christ.
- You will look at how Jesus demonstrated 14 characteristics of servanthood.
- You will see how the characteristics of servanthood free God to do His work in and through you.
- You will give God permission to give you any assignment as His servant.

Scripture Memory Verse

"It is enough for the disciple that he be as his master, and the servant as his lord" (Matt. 10:25).

Lifelong Helps Related to This Unit

Servanthood Instrument (p. 240)

The Mind of Christ Cards Related to This Unit

4A. Unit 6: Scripture Memory—Matthew 10:25
18A. The Servant Mind 1
18B. The Servant Mind 2
19A. The Servant Mind 3
19B. The Servant Mind 4

Optional DVD Messages by T. W. Hunt

- Session 3, Part 1: His Servanthood
- Session 3, Part 2: His Servanthood

DAY 1
TWO REASONS FOR SERVANTHOOD

Today's Bible Meditations
Jesus "made himself of no
reputation, and took upon
him the form of a servant"
(Phil. 2:7).

"From everyone who has
been given much shall
much be required; and to
whom they entrusted
much, of him they will ask
all the more"
(Luke 12:48, NASB).

Name of Christ for Today
Righteous Servant
(Isa. 53:11)

**Prayer to Begin
the Lesson**
*Jesus, Your life here on earth
reflected Your
identity as the Righteous
Servant. You were
righteous and You were a
servant. I want to be like
You. Please work in me to
help me develop a servant
mind-set. Amen.*

1. Begin today's lesson by reading the Bible verses and the name of Christ for today. Work on your memory verse. Then use the suggested prayer to begin your study.

At the center of the mind of Christ is the servant mind. The third part of the hymn focuses on Christ's servanthood: He "made himself of no reputation, and took upon him the form of a servant" (Phil. 2:7). Christ's entire life was one of a Servant. The great messianic passages predicted Jesus as a servant: "Behold my servant, whom I uphold; mine elect, in whom my soul delighteth" (Isa. 42:1). Isaiah identified Christ as a Righteous Servant: "As a result of the anguish of His soul, He will see it and be satisfied; by His knowledge the Righteous One, My Servant, will justify the many, as He will bear their iniquities" (Isa. 53:11, NASB).

Many people in the Bible were called servants or assumed a deliberate servant role. The list includes Abraham, Isaac, Israel, Moses, Samuel, David, Job, Simeon, Paul, Peter, Timothy, James, Jude and others. They were servants because they chose to worship the one true God.

2. If God were preparing a list of His servants today, would you want to be included on that list? Check your response: ❏ Yes ❏ No

Servanthood—a Lost Concept

We have difficulty understanding the real meaning of servanthood. When domestic servants were common, the aspects of servanthood—humility, subjection to authority, obedience—were evident. Our need for human servants has lessened with technology such as computers, microwave ovens, washing machines, and no-wax floors. Even though any employee of another is a servant, the understanding of servanthood often is missing in democracies. Democracies emphasize equality. Employees are more concerned with rights than responsibilities or submission.

Rulers do not have the authority they once had. A dictatorship is a horror in public opinion. Few kings have absolute authority. From the standpoint of democracy, these developments have provided increased comfort and happiness. But they have caused us to lose an understanding of biblical servanthood. Social environment denounces a willing subjection to another person. Refusal to submit ourselves to others often carries over in our refusal to submit to other believers, the church, or perhaps even to God.

3. Which of the following is true in your opinion? Check one.

   ❏ Most Christians have a good view of servanthood and they regularly practice mutual submission to one another.
   ❏ Most Christians have a poor understanding of servanthood, and they resist submission to one another.

Many Christians are more concerned with the provision of privileges and personal rights than the joy of service.

Two Reasons for Servanthood

The Bible gives two reasons why we should be a servant. First, it is a command. Philippians 2:7 tells us to think like Jesus, who "took upon him the form of a servant." We are to think like a servant. Many of Jesus' parables describe the relationships in God's kingdom as that of servants with a king or master. One truth of the parables is that servants will be called to give an account of their servanthood. In like manner Jesus will call His servants to give account of their servanthood. He expects us to be His servant.

1. It is a command.

✍ 4. State one reason you should be a servant.

_____

✍ 5. How would Jesus evaluate your servanthood today? Check one:

❏ Well done. You have been a faithful servant and a good manager.
❏ Poorly done. You have been wicked and lazy in your service and
   a poor manager.
❏ Other: _____

A second reason we should be a servant is because Jesus is our model. This is the main point of the hymn we are studying. We are to become like Christ. Jesus washed the disciples' feet before the Lord's Supper. Then He told them: "If I then, the Lord and the Teacher, washed your feet, you also ought to wash one another's feet. For I gave you an example that you also should do as I did to you" (John 13:14-15, NASB). Jesus was not as interested in clean feet as He was in the disciples assuming servant roles.

2. Jesus is our model.

✍ 6. What is a second reason you should be a servant?

_____

God does not need our service. He does not need anything—not our talent, our intelligence, our money, or our service. If God wants something, He is quite able to supply it. God demands service not out of His need, but out of our need.

✍ 7. Conclude today's study by starting to learn your memory verse, Matthew 10:25. Agree with God that it is enough for you to be like your Master. Then pray and ask the Lord to work in a special way this week to develop in you an attitude of servanthood.

DAY 2
SERVING GOD AND OTHERS

1. Begin today's lesson by reading the Bible verse and the name of Christ for today. Work on your memory verse. Then use the suggested prayer to begin your study.

Unlike the world's system, in Christ's kingdom servanthood is the key to greatness, not position or influence. Salome requested that her sons James and John sit at Jesus' right and left hand in His kingdom. The disciples were furious, probably because they were not the first to make the request. Jesus explained Kingdom greatness.

2. Read below what Jesus said in Matthew 20:25-28. Circle the world's ways to greatness. Underline the Kingdom way to greatness.

You know that the rulers of the Gentiles lord it over them, and their great men exercise authority over them. It is not so among you, but whoever wishes to become great among you shall be your servant, and whoever wishes to be first among you shall be your slave; just as the Son of Man did not come to be served, but to serve, and to give His life a ransom for many (NASB).

Greatness coming through lowly servanthood is beyond our comprehension. This part of Jesus' teaching has not become a part of the attitude of most Christians. If men such as Abraham, Moses, Elijah, David, Paul, and especially Jesus, were servants, then God really means what He says. The last will be first, the least will be the greatest, and the servant will be regarded highly.

On earth the elite often are determined by heredity. In the business world *nobility* comes from ambition, drive, energy, or ability. Jesus, however, says that the truly great in heaven—the servants—will be those that are humble.

3. In God's kingdom which is the most important role for greatness? Check one.

❏ High position of authority
❏ Influence of a charismatic personality
❏ Power backed by masses of supporters or weapons of destruction
❏ Servanthood

Surprisingly, this truth reverses many of the values we have learned. Yet it hardly could be any other way if heaven is to be heaven. Genuine oneness of spirit is feasible only if every member of the society is submissive to all others. We cannot imagine a world with no rivalry. In a world with no competition, joy will come from the privilege of serving others.

God Is Supreme

A society based on servanthood could have only one supreme authority. Jesus tells us that "no servant can serve two masters; for either he will hate the one, and love the other, or else he will hold to one, and despise the other" (Luke 16:13, NASB). We can please only one Master. That Master must be God. Paul knew this lesson. He wrote, "Am I now seeking the favor of men, or of God? Or am I striving to please men? If I were still trying to please men, I would not be a bond-servant of Christ" (Gal. 1:10, NASB). We must be servants of Christ. Our one passion must be to please Christ and do His will.

Serving Each Other

We are to serve Christ supremely, but we are also to serve one another. "You were called to freedom, brethren; only do not turn your freedom into an opportunity for the flesh, but through love serve one another" (Gal. 5:13, NASB). This seems contradictory: we are to serve only one Master, and yet we also are to serve one another. The solution is that we are not to serve each other as master. Our mutual service is an act of love and submission. Our obedience is to Christ as Master.

4. Draw a line matching the service on the left with the motive on the right.

Serve God •   • In order to become great

Serve each other •   • Because He is Supreme

        • Because of love

We serve God because He is supreme. He has the right and authority to demand our service. God is the sovereign Ruler of the universe. We serve, not out of a selfish desire to become great, but because God loves us and commands us to love one another. Love serves others by meeting needs.

5. You are almost halfway through this 12-week introduction to the mind of Christ. Today's lesson is a little shorter than most. Take time today to review.

- Review all your memory verses.
- Glance back over your Bondage to Freedom Lists to see the progress you are making.
- Review the Lifelong Helps regarding Christlike virtues. Which one is God working on in your life? _____

6. Conclude your study time in prayer. Let God guide your praying according to His desires for you. The Holy Spirit can help you pray when you do not know what to ask for (see Rom. 8:26-27). Ask Him to guide you now.

ROMANS 8:26-27
"THE SPIRIT ALSO HELPETH OUR INFIRMITIES: FOR WE KNOW NOT WHAT WE SHOULD PRAY FOR AS WE OUGHT: BUT THE SPIRIT ITSELF MAKETH INTERCESSION FOR US WITH GROANINGS WHICH CANNOT BE UTTERED. AND HE THAT SEARCHETH THE HEARTS KNOWETH WHAT IS THE MIND OF THE SPIRIT, BECAUSE HE MAKETH INTERCESSION FOR THE SAINTS ACCORDING TO THE WILL OF GOD."

DAY 3
CHARACTERISTICS OF A SERVANT MIND, PART 1

Today's Bible Meditation
"When ye shall have done all those things which are commanded you, say, We are unprofitable servants: we have done that which was our duty to do" (Luke 17:10).

Name of Christ for Today
An Offering and Sacrifice to God (Eph. 5:2)

Prayer to Begin the Lesson
Jesus, You paid it all. Your perfect offering and sacrifice of Your life make my spiritual life possible. Thank You. I love you. I exalt Your name as an Offering and Sacrifice to God. Amen.

1. Begin today's lesson by reading the Bible verse and the name of Christ for today. Work on your memory verse. Then use the suggested prayer to begin your study.

The New Testament describes what a servant is like. From these passages, we can derive 14 characteristics that describe the servant mind. These characteristics also secure the work of God in our lives. They free God to do His work. We become a servant first not by what we do, but by what we are. Each of these 14 characteristics applies to every servant of God.

CHARACTERISTICS OF THE SERVANT MIND

1. Humble	5. Faithful	8. Not Quarrelsome	11. Patient
2. Obedient	6. Watchful	9. Gentle	12. Meek
3. Willing	7. Courageous	10. Able to Teach	13. Good
4. Loyal			14. Wise

2. **Which of the following is first in importance for a servant of God? Check one.**

❏ His work: What the servant does.
❏ His character: What the servant is.

3. **Turn to the back of your book and tear out The Mind of Christ Cards 18 and 19. Review these characteristics during the next few days.**

God's first desire for your servanthood is your character. Jesus said, "The disciple is not above his master, nor the servant above his lord. It is enough for the disciple that he be as his master, and the servant as his lord" (Matt. 10:24-25). Your character is far more important than what you do. Doing grows out of your being. Let's take a closer look at each of the 14 characteristics that should be true of your mind.

The Bible says that Jesus was the Righteous Servant. Our final authority in all matters is the Lord Jesus Christ—not only what He said, but His example. These 14 characteristics can be applied to His life. What you are seeking is the mind of Christ as He exhibited it in His role as the Righteous Servant.

4. **Who is your standard and model for these qualities of servanthood?**

1. Humble

The fundamental servant characteristic is *humble* (Acts 20:19). The servant must be humble before God in order to obey God, and must be humble before others to fit in with their works of service. Humble persons do not seek recognition for their work. They would rather advance the Kingdom than look good to others, and see their work as part of a bigger picture. The bigger picture is more important to them than their own piece of it. Knowing that service often depends on the complementary work of others, humble persons learn from others and seek to facilitate others' work.

Humble
Proper attitude toward the Master's work in others.
- Fleshly attitude: "Who do you think you are?"
- When you are a humble member (Acts 20:19), you free God to manifest Himself to you and through you (Isa. 57:15).

5. Write one characteristic of the servant mind.

1. _____   3. Willing   5. Faithful

2. Obedient   4. Loyal

The quality of humility establishes the fact that we really are *members* of the Body of Christ. The Body seldom has functioned as a unit in the past because it has been divided by many would-be leaders. One day the church will become what it was intended to be—an association of the lowly. Unity of spirit is possible in a true association of the lowly; it is impossible among the proud.

Humility frees God to manifest Himself. God says, "I dwell on a high and holy place, and also with the contrite and lowly of spirit in order to revive the spirit of the lowly and to revive the heart of the contrite" (Isa. 57:15, NASB). Jesus demonstrated disdain for the proud but a special affection for the lowly and despised. God manifests His presence to the humble.

6. When you are humble, what does that free God to do?

Humility frees God to _____

Jesus was humble. Jesus' friends were lowly, common people. He did not normally cultivate close relationships with influential people, although Jesus did not turn them away. A first-century custom was to have a servant wash the feet of arriving guests. Jesus assumed that humble servant role before the Lord's Supper and washed the feet of His disciples. Jesus commended this kind of humble service to them (see John 13:14-17). Jesus showed a humble spirit of servanthood.

2. Obedient

The second servant characteristic is *obedient* (see Eph. 6:5). Obedience is an attitude which draws no limits on what the Master can order. True obedience is instant, not delayed. At times we need to question the voices that seem to speak to us or to give us commands. Once God's will is known, however, the obedient servant does not question the Master's will. We obey God because He is God, regardless of consequences. Obedience is the one quality which understands the meaning of God's authority. Obedience signifies that truly you are a servant. "To obey is better than sacrifice, and to heed than the fat of rams" (1 Sam. 15:22, NASB). Obedience is always the best thing you can do.

Obedient
Understanding the authority of the Master over my time and life.
- Fleshly attitude: "OK, in a minute." "I'll get around to it."
- When you are an obedient servant (Eph. 6:5), you free God to do mighty acts (Judg. 7).

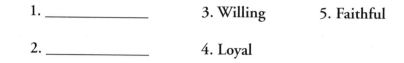 7. **Write two characteristics of the servant mind.**

1. _____   3. Willing   5. Faithful

2. _____   4. Loyal

Obedience frees God to act in mighty ways. Gideon obeyed promptly when God told him to reduce his army of 32,000 to 300 (Judg. 7:2-7). The defeat of the Midianites was a great victory for the forces of God, but God was credited with the victory. The victory would not be memorable had Gideon fought with his original army. God may require strange things as He did of Joshua at the Battle of Jericho (Josh. 6:1-20). God's grand intentions can be realized only when we are obedient.

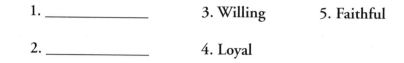 8. **When you are obedient, what does that free God to do?**

Obedience frees God to _____

Jesus was obedient. Jesus' obedience was manifest throughout His life. After Jesus' appearance in the temple at age twelve, Luke tells us that "He went down with them [Joseph and Mary], and came to Nazareth; and He continued in subjection to them" (Luke 2:51, NASB). Jesus said whatever the Father told Him to say (see John 12:50). He obeyed precisely. At the end of His life, Jesus declared, "That the world may know that I love the Father, and as the Father gave Me commandment, even so I do" (John 14:31, NASB). He did not choose words carelessly. Jesus obeyed perfectly.

Willing

Identity with the Master's attitudes.
• Fleshly attitude: "You have to look out for yourself."
• When you are a willing child (Eph. 6:7), you free God to reward divinely (Col. 3:22-24).

3. Willing

The third servant characteristic we consider is *willing* (see Eph. 6:7). Our service must be wholehearted. Our behavior often depends on our feelings rather than our will. Feelings often are confusing. Only the will can be single-minded. Only the will can override feelings. Continuing obedience cannot be a result of feelings, but of the will. Even when feelings are out of control, you can give your will to God. You are to do the will of God with "singleness of your heart" (Eph. 6:5).

The will can exist in one of three ways: weak-willed, strong-willed (self-willed), or God-willed. To be God-willed a person identifies his will with God's. Weak-willed persons too easily submit the will to others. Strong-willed persons seldom submit to anyone. Both weak-willed and strong-willed persons are independent of God. If your will insists on independence, your entire personality is independent. Only the will can truly identify with Jesus. That identification is what having the mind of Christ is all about. You are to do the will of God from your heart. Christ's will becomes your will.

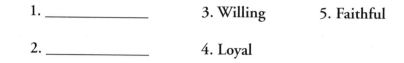 9. **Which type of will is most characteristic of you at this point in your spiritual life? Check one. Most frequently I am:**

❏ Weak-willed
❏ Strong-willed (self-willed)
❏ God-willed

✍ 10. Write three characteristics of the servant mind.

1. _____   3. _____   5. Faithful

2. _____   4. Loyal

Your willingness frees God to reward divinely. You are to obey with all your heart, "knowing that from the Lord you will receive the reward of the inheritance" (Col. 3:24, NASB). Identifying your will with that of God establishes a spiritual likeness.

✍ 11. When you are willing, what does that free God to do?

Willingness frees God to _____

Jesus was willing. Christ's identification of His will with that of the Father is one of the striking aspects of His life. We already have seen that the dominating desire of Jesus' life was to do the will of His Father. His passion was the Father's will. The Father's will was Jesus' will. In the greatest trial of His life, Jesus remained consistent in seeking the Father's will: "My Father, if this cannot pass away unless I drink it, Thy will be done" (Matt. 26:42, NASB). The will of the Master must be the will of the servant, or the work will not get done.

✍ 12. Pray and indicate to the Lord your willingness to obey and follow Him. Ask God to remove any pride that gets in the way of your faithful service to Him and to others.

DAY 4
CHARACTERISTICS OF A SERVANT MIND, PART 2

✍ 1. Begin today's lesson by reading the Bible verse and the name of Christ for today. Work on your memory verse. Then use the suggested prayer on the following page to begin your study.

✍ 2. As a review, write three characteristics of the servant mind.

1. H_____   3. W_____   5. Faithful

2. O_____   4. Loyal

4. Loyal

The next servant characteristic is *loyal* (see Luke 16:13). Loyalty means that you have an undivided heart. Only the loyal servant is truly dependable. Loyalty is indispensable for a servant. Obedience may require sacrifice and even death. Only loyalty remains steadfast regardless of cost. Loyalty is exclusive. It says, "As for me and my house, we will serve the Lord" (Josh. 24:15). God demands loyalty. God is jealous

Today's Bible Meditation
"Hath the Lord as great delight in burnt offerings and sacrifices, as in obeying the voice of the Lord? Behold, to obey is better than sacrifice, and to hearken than the fat of rams" (1 Sam. 15:22).

Name of Christ for Today
A Teacher Come from God (John 3:2)

Loyal
Unswerving devotion to the Master.
• Fleshly attitude: "You scratch my back, I'll scratch yours."
• When you are a loyal citizen (Luke 16:13), you free God to promote you (Gen. 39–41).

(see Ex. 20:5), for He is absolute. Lordship, by definition, cannot be partial. You cannot say no and call Him Lord.

Loyalty is an indispensable requirement for citizenship in the Kingdom of heaven. We are "fellow citizens with the saints, and are of God's household" (Eph. 2:19, NASB). Loyalty says, "I have been very zealous for the Lord, the God of hosts" (1 Kings 19:10,14, NASB). Only loyalty praises the Father for whatever might be "well-pleasing in [His] sight" (Matt. 11:26, NASB).

3. What is a fourth characteristic of the servant mind?

1. Humble	3. Willing	5. Faithful
2. Obedient	4. _____	

Loyalty frees God to promote you within Kingdom work. In Genesis 37-41, Joseph was betrayed by his brothers, Potiphar's wife, and the cupbearer; yet, he remained faithful to his brothers, to Potiphar, and to God. Because he was loyal to God, God was free to promote Joseph. Joseph became the prime minister of Egypt.

4. When you are loyal, what does that free God to do?

Loyalty frees God to _____

Jesus was loyal. His loyalty to the Father is seen in the dedication of His life to the Father's will. Jesus was loyal to His disciples. In His great High Priestly prayer, Jesus said to the Father, "While I was with them in the world, I kept them in thy name" (John 17:12). Jesus was loyal to death on the cross.

Faithful
Confidence that anticipates the Master continuing His plan.
• Fleshly attitude: "I'm tired of this."
• When you are faithful (1 Cor. 4:2), you free God to expand your ministry (Matt. 25:21).

5. Faithful

The fifth servant characteristic is *faithful* (1 Cor. 4:1-2). Through Moses God commanded His people to be faithful: "Thou shalt fear the Lord thy God; him shalt thou serve, and to him shalt thou cleave" (Deut. 10:20). Faithfulness reflects the fidelity of a God who says, "I will never break my covenant with you" (Judg. 2:1). Faithfulness is reflected in statements like: "We must obey God rather than men" (Acts 5:29, NASB). Jesus praised the faithful servants in His parables.

Jesus described us as branches abiding in Him, the True Vine (see John 15:1-7). In faithfulness you establish your "branchhood." Only an abiding branch produces fruit. Obedience cannot be a one-time act. Obedience must be a continuing process. Faithfulness also is inclusive—it applies both to small and great matters (Luke 16:10).

5. Write five characteristics of the servant mind.

1. _____	3. _____	5. _____
2. _____	4. _____	

Faithfulness frees God to expand your ministry. The five-talent man and the two-talent man were "faithful with a few things" and so the master put them "in charge of many things" (Matt. 25:21,23, NASB). God rewards trustworthiness with greater trust.

✍ 6. When you are faithful, what does that free God to do?

Faithfulness frees God to _____

Jesus was faithful. He was faithful to the Father, even to death. Jesus also was faithful to His disciples: "Having loved His own who were in the world, He loved them to the end" (John 13:1, NASB). Jesus continues to be faithful as our High Priest. He is "with you always, even to the end of the age" (Matt. 28:20, NASB). Even Jesus' name is "Faithful and True" (Rev. 19:11).

6. Watchful

The sixth servant characteristic is *watchful* (see Luke 12:35-48). The emphasis is both on alertness and being prepared for the master's return. Watchfulness indicates an attitude toward the master. Watchful means you want to know what God says or what He wants you to do. In Jesus' parables, good servants spent much time waiting. They were expected to be alert at all times. Such watchfulness was what made them good servants rather than wicked servants.

The psalmist wrote, "As the eyes of servants look to the hand of their master, as the eyes of a maid to the hand of her mistress; so our eyes look to the Lord our God, until He shall be gracious to us" (Ps. 123:2). Paul wrote Titus, "Remind them to be . . . ready for every good deed" (Titus 3:1, NASB). The quality of watchfulness proves whether you are God's watchman. Paul wrote the Thessalonians, "You are all sons of light and sons of day. We are not of night nor of darkness; so then let us not sleep as others do, but let us be alert and sober" (1 Thess. 5:5-6, NASB).

Watchful

Attentiveness to the Master's voice.
- Fleshly attitude: "I wish I had not said that."
- When you are a watchful watchman (Luke 12:35-48), you free God to speak (Hab. 2:1).

✍ 7. Write one characteristic of the servant mind.

6. _____   **8. Not Quarrelsome**

7. **Courageous**   9. **Gentle**

Watchfulness frees the Lord to speak. Habakkuk demonstrated the watchman spirit: "I will stand on my guard post . . . I will keep watch to see what He will speak to me" (Hab. 2:1, NASB). God is not likely to speak to servants who are not watchful. Only those alert for action will hear the voice of the Lord.

✍ 8. When you are watchful, what does that free God to do?

Watchfulness frees God to _____

Jesus was watchful. His eye was always on the Father to know the Father's direction: "Truly, truly, I say to you, the Son can do nothing of Himself, unless it is something He sees the Father doing; for whatever the Father does, these things the Son also does in like manner" (John 5:19, NASB). "I can do nothing on My own initiative.

As I hear, I judge; and My judgment is just, because I do not seek My own will, but the will of Him who sent Me" (John 5:30, NASB). Christ always depended on direction from the Father. Jesus spent the night in prayer before He chose His disciples (see Luke 6:12). A watchful servant remains alert to the Master.

7. Courageous

Our next servant characteristic is *courageous*. Zechariah's song proclaimed that the "horn of salvation" (the Messiah) would "grant us that we … might serve Him without fear, in holiness and righteousness before Him all our days" (Luke 1:74-75, NASB). David was called a servant, and "David said to Saul, 'Let no man's heart fail on account of him; your servant will go and fight with this Philistine' " (1 Sam. 17:32, NASB). Daniel was a servant of God and he defied the king's edict in order to pray before God (see Dan. 6:10). Just before his shipwreck, Paul told the crew, "This very night an angel of the God to whom I belong and whom I serve stood before me, saying, 'Do not be afraid. …' Therefore, keep up your courage, men, for I believe God" (Acts 27:23-25, NASB). Courage is a servant quality that demonstrates conviction.

9. Write two characteristics of the servant mind.

6. _____   8. Not Quarrelsome

7. _____   9. Gentle

Courage proves that you are one of God's soldiers. Courage frees God to protect you. As David faced Goliath, he claimed, "The battle is the Lord's" (1 Sam. 17:47). No wound was found on Daniel "because he had trusted in his God" (Dan. 6:23, NASB). Paul's faith in God was justified as the entire crew made it safely to shore (Acts 28:1).

10. When you are courageous, what does that free God to do?

Courage frees God to _____

Jesus was courageous. He endured persecution, suffering, and death. Having predicted His own death, Jesus knew what that fateful last trip to Jerusalem would produce. Jesus headed toward His death with the disciples like frightened chicks behind Him: "They were on the road, going up to Jerusalem, and Jesus was walking on ahead of them; and they were amazed, and those who followed were fearful" (Mark 10:32, NASB). Jesus was courageous.

8. Not Quarrelsome

Five servant characteristics are found in 2 Timothy 2:24: "And the servant of the Lord must not strive; but be gentle unto all men, apt to teach, patient, in meekness instructing those that oppose themselves." The first of these is a negative: the servant of the Lord must not strive. He must not be quarrelsome. Servants often are assigned to work together, especially in the Kingdom of God. Every true calling from God will complement and enhance the genuine callings of others. Can you imagine what a church would be like if no one quarreled?

11. Write three characteristics of the servant mind.

6. _____   8. _____

7. _____   9. Gentle

If you possess this quality not to be quarrelsome, you are a peacemaker. This frees the Lord to focus on the main thing. Martha was quarrelsome, but when Mary sat at Jesus' feet and listened to His word, Jesus said, "One thing is needful: and Mary hath chosen that good part, which shall not be taken away from her" (Luke 10:42).

12. When you are not quarrelsome, what does that free God to do?

Not being quarrelsome frees God to _____

Jesus was not quarrelsome. He did not start arguments although He was swift to reply when challenged by either secret hypocrisy or open confrontation. When asked by a man in the crowd, "Teacher, tell my brother to divide the family inheritance with me," Jesus replied, "Man, who appointed Me a judge or arbiter over you?" Then He warned, "Beware, and be on your guard against every form of greed; for not even when one has an abundance does his life consist of his possessions" (Luke 12:13-15, NASB).

13. Just as Mary sat at Jesus' feet to learn the more needful things, spend time now and throughout the day with Jesus in prayer. Watch. Wait. Listen. Prepare to obey.

DAY 5
CHARACTERISTICS OF A SERVANT MIND, PART 3

1. Begin today's lesson by reading the Bible verse and the name of Christ for today. Work on your memory verse. Then use the suggested prayer on the following page to begin your study.

2. As a review write three characteristics of the servant mind.

6. W_____   8. N_____

7. C_____   9. Gentle

9. Gentle

The next characteristic *gentle* suggests congenial and mild. It has a soothing quality. To be a peacemaker, we must be soothing. Some of our servant tasks will require gentleness.

Today's Bible Meditation
"Truly, truly, I say to you, the Son can do nothing of Himself, unless it is something He sees the Father doing; for whatever the Father does, these things the Son also does in like manner" (John 5:19, NASB).

Name of Christ for Today
The Only Wise God
(1 Tim. 1:17)

Gentle
Respect that enhances the work of others for the Master.
• Fleshly attitude: "I've had it up to here!"
• When you are a lover of gentleness (2 Tim. 2:24), you free God to strengthen you (Luke 22:32).

Able to Teach
Understanding of the Master's work.
• Fleshly attitude: "I don't have time for Bible study."
• When you are able to teach (2 Tim. 2:24), you free God to establish divine authority (Matt. 7:28-29).

3. Write the ninth characteristic of the servant mind.

6. Watchful   8. Not Quarrelsome

7. Courageous   9. _____

Just as courage frees God to protect you, gentleness frees God to strengthen you. Jesus was gentle with Peter when He predicted Peter's fall. Jesus told him, "Simon, Simon, behold, Satan has demanded permission to sift you like wheat; but I have prayed for you, that your faith may not fail; and you, when once you have turned again, strengthen your brothers" (Luke 22:31-32, NASB). Perhaps that prayer was responsible for Peter's courageous stand before the Sanhedrin in Acts 4:8-12. Gentleness is a perversion if it does not come from strength. But strength is also a perversion if it is not coupled with gentleness.

4. When you are gentle, what does that free God to do?

Gentleness frees God to _____

Jesus was gentle. He was gentle and forbearing. One of the most tender pictures we have of Jesus is His declaration, "I am the door of the sheep. … If anyone enters through Me, he shall be saved, and shall go in and out, and find pasture" (John 10:7-9, NASB). Here is a case of gentleness growing out of great strength.

10. Able to Teach

Paul's next servant characteristic in 2 Timothy 2:24 is *able to teach*. This seems an extraordinary requirement, since teaching is listed as a spiritual gift in Romans 12:6-7. The ability to teach also is required of a pastor or bishop (see 1 Timothy 3:2). However, ability to communicate God's message is expected of all servants of the Lord. A person may not be a great speaker but can nevertheless teach. The key to this mystery is found in the verse following our servant verse: "With gentleness correcting those who are in opposition" (2 Tim. 2:25, NASB).

5. Write one characteristic of the servant mind.

10. _____   12. Meek   14. Wise

11. Patient   13. Good

Christians are light for this world because the Light of the World dwells in us. (Matt. 5:14). Being able to teach frees God to establish divine authority. Peter told us, "Always being ready to make a defense to everyone who asks you to give an account for the hope that is in you" (1 Pet. 3:15, NASB).

6. When you are able to teach, what does that free God to do?

Being able to teach frees God to _____

Jesus was able to teach under divine authority. Early in His ministry, "He came down to Capernaum, a city of Galilee. And He was teaching them on the Sabbath; and they were amazed at His teaching, for His message was with authority" (Luke 4:31-32, NASB). Later, as He ended the Sermon on the Mount, "the multitudes were amazed at His teaching; for He was teaching them as one having authority, and not as their scribes" (Matt. 7:28-29, NASB). On occasion Jesus' skillful and wise teaching silenced those who opposed Him.

11. Patient

The next servant characteristic is *patient*. In the Kingdom, waiting is not a waste of time. We must wait on the Lord (see Ps. 130:5-6) and we also must learn to be patient with others. Being patient goes hand in hand with being watchful. You will not continue to be watchful if you are not also patient.

Patient
Forbearance that values the Master's purposes for others.
- Fleshly attitude: "Enough is enough!"
- When you are a patient ruler (2 Tim. 2:24), you free God to answer prayer. (John 14:8-14).

> 7. **Write two characteristics of the servant mind.**

    10. _____   12. Meek   14. Wise

    11. _____   13. Good

In patience you demonstrate your nobility. "He who is slow to anger is better than the mighty, and he who rules his spirit, than he who captures a city" (Prov. 16:32). Patience frees the Lord to answer prayer in His way and in His time. God never is in a rush even though we usually are. Waiting on God allows Him to provide the best answer. We are to become like God, who is patient with us.

> 8. **When you are patient, what does that free God to do?**

    Patience frees God to _____

Jesus was patient. Jesus' patience with His disciples is notable. They repeatedly were slow to understand. Again and again He scolded the disciples for their lack of faith (Matt. 8:26; 14:31). Although Jesus taught repeatedly on humility, the night before He died, "there was also a strife among them, which of them should be accounted the greatest" (Luke 22:24). Jesus explained patiently one last time the importance of humility and servanthood (see Luke 22:24-27).

12. Meek

The last servant characteristic in 2 Timothy 2:23-25 is *meek*. Only two persons in the Bible are called meek. Numbers 12:3 tells us, "Now the man Moses was very meek, above all the men which were upon the face of the earth." In Matthew 11:29, Jesus used the word to describe Himself. The context in each case does indicate lowliness. The only two men described as meek, however, are the two strongest personalities in the Bible. Think of Moses confronting Pharaoh repeatedly, or of Jesus reproving the Pharisees in Matthew 23:13-36. No weakness is found in either of these two great examples! We can be lowly, yet strong. Only strength submits voluntarily. Involuntary submission has nothing to do with meekness.

Meek
Disciplined sensitivity to the Master.
- Fleshly attitude: "I'll show them!"
- When you are meek like sheep (2 Tim. 2:24), you free God to guide you (Ps. 25:9).

✍ 9. Write three characteristics of the servant mind.

10. _____   12. _____   14. Wise

11. _____   13. Good

Meekness frees the Lord to guide you. "The meek will he guide in judgment: and the meek will he teach his way" (Ps. 25:9).

✍ 10. When you are meek, what does that free God to do?

Meekness frees God to _____

Jesus was meek. We already have described His meekness. Jesus could have come as a king, a high priest, or in some other exalted position. Jesus came as a lowly carpenter, but with great spiritual strength.

Good

Applied trust in the Master's excellence.
• Fleshly attitude: "It was just a little mistake."
• When you are a good servant (Matt. 25:21), you free God to produce fruit (Matt. 7:17).

13. Good

The parable of the talents gives us another characteristic: "Well done, thou good and faithful servant" (Matt. 25:21). Note how Jesus uses the word in the parable. Once again, it implies that the servant had accomplished Kingdom work. A good servant has practical worth.

✍ 11. Write four characteristics of the servant mind.

10. _____   12. _____   14. Wise

11. _____   13. _____

Goodness frees the Lord to produce fruit in you. It proves that you really are the servant you were redeemed to be. "You will know them by their fruits" (Matt. 7:20, NASB). A good servant produces fruit.

✍ 12. When you are good, what does that free God to do?

It frees God to _____

Jesus was good. Jesus' goodness is reflected in the two thousand years of Christian history. He claimed, "I am the good shepherd" (John 10:11). We could apply this characteristic to all His roles: He is the Good Teacher, the Good Savior, the Good Brother, the Good Bridegroom, the Good Priest, and all the others. In all that Jesus is, He functions. Jesus is good.

14. Wise

The last servant characteristic comes from the parable of the unjust steward in Luke 16:1-13. In the King James Version, the servant was *wise*, but perhaps the New American Standard Version comes closer to Jesus' idea—the servant must be shrewd!

This seems a strange quality to require of us, especially since the manager in the story was devious.

Jesus is not commending deceitful behavior. He sent the 70 out as "lambs in the midst of wolves" (Luke 10:3, NASB). Yet Jesus cautioned, "The sons of this age are more shrewd in relation to their own kind than the sons of light" (Luke 16:8, NASB). In Jesus' mind, no conflict exists. We can be childlike and yet resourceful. The servant must use good judgment, keen discernment, and, at times, intelligent discrimination. Certainly Jesus was innocent and keenly perceptive. He could not be caught off guard. This same word, *wise,* is used in Matthew 7:24 of the wise man who built his house on a rock.

Wise
Dependence on the Master's method.
• Fleshly attitude: "I don't know what to do."
• When you are a wise disciple (Luke 16:1-13), you free God to invest you with authority (Matt. 24:45).

13. **Write five characteristics of the servant mind.**

10. _____ 12. _____ 14. _____

11. _____ 13. _____

Wisdom frees God to invest you with authority. Wisdom establishes that you are a disciple, learning from the Master and becoming like Him. Jesus asked, "Who then is the faithful and sensible slave whom his master put in charge of his household to give them their food at the proper time?" (Matt. 24:45, NASB). The authority of the wise will be increased greatly.

Wisdom establishes that you are a disciple, learning from the Master and becoming like Him.

14. **When you are wise, what does that free God to do?**

Wisdom frees God to _____

Jesus was wise. When we see shrewdness in Jesus' life, we expect it to accomplish desirable and eternal goals. Most of Jesus' great works were accomplished in Galilee. Little is recorded of miracles in Judea in comparison with the Galilean and Perean ministries. This is an indication of wisdom. Jesus had opposition from the beginning. Jesus wisely chose to work where the religious officials did not live. Wisdom placed His work among the receptive, the poor, and the lowly. Even His name is "wisdom of God" (1 Cor. 1:24).

15. **Conclude this week's study by praying:**

Heavenly Father, thank You that these qualities are attainable. They are within my grasp. Being a servant goes against the grain of everything I have been taught in my culture. I have been taught to "hitch my wagon to a star" and to look out for number one in all that I do. You teach me that I am at my greatest when I stoop to serve. With my background, I find it hard to believe that.

Yet I do believe You. You always are right, no matter how strange Your Word may seem by worldly standards. Lord, I am conscious of the great distance between what I am and what the Lord Jesus lived out on the earth. Make me like Him, no matter what I have to do. In Jesus' name. Amen.

GROUP SESSION 6

THE SERVANT MIND

SESSION GOALS

This session will help you understand the characteristics of the servant mind. You will demonstrate submission to God as your Master and Lord.

Hearing What the Spirit Is Saying (as you arrive)

1. (Individuals) Turn to the Servanthood Instrument in the Lifelong Helps section (p. 240). Read the instructions and complete the test as a personal evaluation of your attitudes about servanthood. Use notebook paper provided by your leader.
2. (Individuals) If you finish the test before the beginning of the session, review what God has been saying to you during the study of unit 6. Identify a Scripture and a name of Christ that have been meaningful this week. Identify and mark the servant attitude, issue, or subject in which God seems to be working most actively to develop the mind of Christ. These will be shared later in the session.
3. (Individuals) Write out any questions for which you would like to find answers.

Magnifying the Lord and Exalting His Name (5 minutes)

1. (Volunteer) Open the session in prayer by asking God to develop the attitude of servanthood in every member.
2. Pray as you feel led to worship God for Who He is and acknowledge Him for what He has done. Use the names of Christ to exalt His name together in prayer.
3. After prayer, share ways God revealed Himself to you this week through His names. Which name of Christ has been most meaningful to you and why?

Transforming by the Word (15 minutes)

1. (Pairs) Pair up and quote this week's memory verse, Matthew 10:25. Then, as time permits, alternate quoting verses from previous units. Use your Scripture memory cards as a reference.
2. Share what God said to you through this week's memory verse or other Scripture that has been meaningful.
3. (Quads—or two groups) Distribute poster board or newsprint and markers to each of two groups. Make two lists related to characteristics of a Christlike mind. Focus on this unit's Scriptures only.
   - Group 1: Make a list of things, actions, or attitudes identified or implied in Scriptures during this unit that need to be cleansed from one's mind and life.
   - Group 2: Make a list of things, actions, or attitudes identified or implied in Scriptures during this unit that need to be incorporated into one's mind and life.
   - For example: We need to stop *ruling by exercising authority* (group 1) and start *serving humbly* (group 2) (see Matt. 20:25-28).
4. Call on quads to read and comment on their lists. Place one on the Transformed From Wall and the other on the Transformed To Wall.
5. (Volunteer) Pray that God will cleanse members of your group and church.

Stimulating One Another to Love and Good Deeds (20 minutes)

1. Share testimonies of what God has done this week in your life that has been meaningful, challenging, or instructive.
2. State questions or concerns you have written for consideration. As time permits, seek to answer the questions as a group.

3. As time permits discuss one or more of the following questions:
   • What are some of the clearest ways Jesus demonstrated the servant mind by His actions?
   • Why should Christians want to become servants?
   • Why has the art of being a servant disappeared from our society?
   • How do most people outside the church seek greatness? How do most people inside the church seek greatness? Do Christians live more by God's ways or the world's ways?
   • Would people in our community see our church as one that serves people? Why or why not? Is there anything we need to do to change that perception?
   • Which of the characteristics of the servant mind is God working on in your life?
4. Think about each of the characteristics, one at a time. How can we help each other develop these characteristics? What is God's role, and what is our role?

Preparing the Bride for Her Bridegroom (5 minutes)

1. Read Matthew 25:31-46. Listen for ways the bride (church) needs to minister to others as they await the return of Christ. List them in the margin.
2. As time permits, discuss these questions:
   • What kinds of service characterize true believers who willingly serve the Lord?
   • What areas of service are we neglecting that as a church Christ is expecting?
   • What cleansing, purifying, or preparation is needed in our church?
   • How can we apply this Scripture to our lives, families, and church?
3. Someone pray for our church to minister in the name and character of Christ to those who have needs.

Praying for One Another (10 minutes)

1. (Quads, preferably same gender) Share personal, family, church, or work-related prayer requests that primarily focus on developing the mind of Christ or purifying the bride.
2. (Quads) Pray specifically for one another regarding the specific requests made and for the development of a servant spirit in every member.

Closing the Session (5 minutes)

1. Share questions or concerns that came up during the session that we should remember in prayer.
2. Preview unit 7 by using the looking at the Beatitudes in the Lifelong Helps section (pp. 241-50).
3. Discuss the option of a mid-course get-together. Enlist help in planning and preparing for the event if you choose to do it.
4. Close by praying that God will use circumstances to develop the character of Christ and the attitudes described in the Beatitudes in our group members.

Hymn Part 4
CHRIST'S HUMANITY
"[Jesus] was made in the likeness of men:
and . . . found in fashion as a man"
(Phil. 2:7-8).

DAY 1
Two Halves of a Whole, Part 1

DAY 2
Two Halves of a Whole, Part 2

DAY 3
Poor in Spirit, Mourn, Meek

DAY 4
Hungry, Merciful, Pure in Heart

DAY 5
Peacemakers, Persecuted for Righteousness

Why You Will Find This Unit Helpful
You will come to understand that God uses circumstances, even difficult or hurtful ones, to develop in you qualities that He in turn blesses. God will be working in you to develop the qualities described in the Beatitudes. God also will work through you to manifest Himself to others as you give of yourself.

Lifelong Goal
In Christ you will become a reflection of Christ's perfect humanity as you develop and manifest the qualities described in the Beatitudes.

Summary of God's Work in You

Christ's humanity in you facilitates the mental quality of authority. God's goal for you is royal princeliness. Your growth in humanity can be measured only by Christ's nobility of spirit. Christ enables your perfect humanity in His role as Brother. Christ transforms you.

Unit Learning Goals

- You will know some of the differences between the first four and the second four Beatitudes.
- You will understand ways God uses circumstances to develop the Beatitudes in your life.
- You will understand what the Beatitudes are and are not.
- You will understand eight ways you can worship God because of what He does in and through you.
- You will demonstrate an openness to God's work of developing the Beatitudes in your life.

What You Will Do to Begin Developing the Beatitudes

- You will contrast the first four Beatitudes with the second four to understand what they mean and how God uses them.
- You will begin to use the Lifelong Helps and The Mind of Christ Cards to guide the process of developing the Beatitudes in your life.
- You will examine your life to identify past and present circumstances that God uses to mold you into the image of His Son.
- You will surrender self to allow God to work in and through you to reflect the qualities of Christ's humanity.

Scripture Memory Verse

"Blessed are the poor in spirit: for theirs is the kingdom of heaven" (Matt. 5:3).

Lifelong Helps Related to This Unit

Beatitudes (pp. 241-50)

The Mind of Christ Cards Related to This Unit

4B. Unit 7: Scripture Memory—Matthew 5:3
6A-B. Scripture Memory—Matthew 5:3-10

20. A-1: Poor in Spirit	24. B-1: Merciful
21. A-2: Mourn	25. B-2: Pure in Heart
22. A-3: Meek	26. B-3: Peacemakers
23. A-4: Hungry	27. B-4: Persecuted

Optional DVD Messages by T. W. Hunt

- Session 4, Part 1: His Manhood
- Session 4, Part 2: His Manhood

DAY 1
TWO HALVES OF A WHOLE, PART 1

Today's Bible Meditations

"Be ye kind one to another, tenderhearted, forgiving one another, even as God for Christ's sake hath forgiven you" (Eph. 4:32).

"[Jesus] was made in the likeness of men: and ... found in fashion as a man" (Phil. 2:7-8).

Name of Christ for Today

An Advocate with the Father (1 John 2:1)

Prayer to Begin the Lesson

Jesus, the Father has forgiven me because You are my Advocate. I do not deserve what You do for me, but I thank You for Your mercy. Because I have been given much, I, too, want to give. Amen.

1. Begin today's lesson by reading the Bible verses and the name of Christ for today. Work on your memory verse. Then use the suggested prayer to begin your study.

Hymn Part 4: Christ's Humanity

The fourth part of our hymn in Philippians 2:5-11 describes Christ's humanity: "[Jesus] was made in the likeness of men: and . . . found in fashion as a man" (Phil. 2:7-8). Yes, Jesus was God; but Jesus also was fully human. One of the reasons Jesus came to earth was to show us how to live. Jesus gave us a view of God's original intention for man. He displayed what perfect humanity was intended to be. Jesus described Himself as the good Shepherd (see John 10:14) who leads us. He said, "I am come that they might have life, and that they might have it more abundantly" (John 10:10). In units 7-10, we will look at the humanity of Jesus and how He lived His life. We must learn the rules for humanity.

Blessings for Right Living

God's program for human conduct is contained in the Sermon on the Mount (see Matt. 5–7). That is Jesus' New Law, the law for perfected humanity, the laws of the Kingdom of heaven. The sermon begins with a description of a Kingdom person. Since Jesus began His great sermon on Kingdom living with these eight blessings for right living, they assume real importance.

2. Several Lifelong Helps will assist you in following God's pattern for blessed living. Let us introduce you to them. Place a check beside each assignment as you complete it.

❑ First, tear out Scripture Memory Cards 4A and 6A/6B. Notice that your memory verse for this unit is the first of the eight Beatitudes. The others are found on card 6. You are not expected to memorize them all this week. Begin hiding in your mind and heart these rules and promised blessings so God can call attention to them any time He wants.

❑ Next, tear out the Mind of Christ Cards related to the Beatitudes (cards 20-27). Notice that you have one card for each Beatitude. This will allow you to focus on them one at a time as God works to develop these qualities in your life.

❑ Finally, turn to pages 241-250. Notice that we have given you detailed information on each Beatitude. Place a bookmark at page 241 or fold down the corner of the page so you can turn to it easily.

The eight Beatitudes describe a whole person blessed by God, living as God intended. The first four and the second four display symmetry between two halves. All parts are necessary, and the whole represents a complete human being in God's design for humanity.

3. Turn to page 241 and spend a few minutes studying the Lifelong Help that compares and contrasts the first four Beatitudes with the second four. Identify which one of the items in each pair goes with the first four (A) and which one goes with the second four (B). Write A beside one item in each pair and B beside the other.

Basis for Happiness   _____ Your Giving
      _____ Your Need

Keys to   _____ God's Heart
      _____ Christ's Character

Focus   _____ Turn your mind toward others.
      _____ Turn your mind toward God.

Command   _____ Love God
      _____ Love Others

Object   _____ God gives according to your need to mold and shape you into the image of Christ.
      _____ God works through you to reveal Himself to a watching world.

Greatness   _____ The practice
      _____ The door

Worship   _____ Higher levels of worship as you bring God glory by revealing Christ's character to others.
      _____ Lower levels of worship as your praise to God comes out of His meeting of your needs.

Basis for Happiness

The first four Beatitudes demonstrate need. The poor in spirit need God. The mourners need the Holy Spirit of God. That is one reason why God breaks them—to create the need, or to make them aware of the need. The meek need others. The hungry for righteousness need spiritual food.

The second four Beatitudes focus on giving. The merciful give God's grace to the world. The pure in heart give holiness to the world. The peacemakers give wholeness. The persecuted give themselves.

The two halves of the Beatitudes are in balance. God gives of Himself because of our desperate need. The greater the need, the more abundant His giving. After receiving Christ, we move into the area of self-giving (the second four). We often cycle through these two sides so God can continue to grow and develop our character for greater service.

God gives of Himself because of our desperate need. The greater the need, the more abundant His giving.

4. As you look at your spiritual life, are you more on the needy side or the giving side?

The Keys

The first four Beatitudes—poor in spirit, mourning (brokenness), meekness, and hungry for righteousness—are the keys to God's heart. God loves the needy. Persons who meet these conditions are more receptive than persons who do not. Our need and consequent receiving in the first four Beatitudes prepare our character for something greater.

The second four Beatitudes—mercy, pure, peacemakers, and persecuted—are the keys to Christ's character. Because we needed God, He gave us Himself, and we are becoming like Christ. These second four qualities are Christlike. In them, we practice perfect giving because we have so much of God.

5. Conclude today's study by thanking God for His work in you. Ask God to show you which qualities He would like to work on in your life. Read the eight Beatitudes on page 241. If God directs your attention toward one in particular, circle it.

DAY 2
TWO HALVES OF A WHOLE, PART 2

Today's Bible Meditation
"My brethren, count it all joy when ye fall into divers temptations; Knowing this, that the trying of your faith worketh patience. But let patience have her perfect work, that ye may be perfect and entire, wanting nothing" (Jas. 1:2-4).

Name of Christ for Today
Man of Sorrows (Isa. 53:3)

1. Begin today's lesson by reading the Bible verses and the name of Christ for today. Work on your memory verse. Then use the suggested prayer on the following page to begin your study.

2. As you read the following contrasts between the first *(A)* and second *(B)* groups of four Beatitudes, circle key words for each topic. Then write A or B beside the word to indicate the group of Beatitudes to which it belongs.

Focus

The first four Beatitudes turn the mind to God. In poverty of spirit, brokenness, meekness, and hunger we instinctively turn to God. The second four Beatitudes turn the mind to others. We do not direct our mercy toward God, but toward our neighbor. We demonstrate peace, purity, and grace under persecution to those around us.

This order (the first four Beatitudes turning our mind to God and the second four turning our mind to others) follows the order of the two greatest commandments. The most important commandment is to love God above all, and the second is to love our neighbor (see Mark 12:29-31).

Greatness

The first four Beatitudes are the door to greatness. They produce those qualities that Jesus said make us greatest in the Kingdom (see Mark 9:35; 10:43; Luke 22:26-27). Spiritual greatness allows no room for pride. We become the little children Christ told us to be (see Matt. 18:1-4). We can see examples of these qualities in great yearners of the Bible such as Abel, Enoch, Noah, and Jeremiah.

The second four Beatitudes are the practice of greatness. The practice of these are filling the world's need for grace and holiness. The Bible furnishes examples of the great practitioners—Abraham, Joseph, Moses, David, Daniel, and Paul.

Object

God changes our inner life with the first four Beatitudes. Our need for God and for others grows profoundly. As we desperately reach to God in our needs, He trains us in our inner being. In the second four Beatitudes, God uses our outer life to affect the world around us.

In the first four Beatitudes, God uses circumstances to manifest our need of Him and His supply. When we find ourselves poor in spirit or broken, God offers us a deeper spiritual blessing than could be known in the smoother roads of life. Life may not always be comfortable. Many of us tend to blame God for our troubles, but God's intention is to use our hurt for our own maturation. God expresses Himself to others through the outworking of the second four Beatitudes in our lives. God allows us to use circumstances for His glory.

God uses circumstances to manifest our need of Him and His supply. When we find ourselves poor in spirit or broken, God offers us a deeper spiritual blessing than could be known in the smoother roads of life.

3. **Can you think of a time when God used a difficult or hurtful time to help you mature spiritually? If so write a brief note about that time.**

_____

_____

4. **Beginning with the next lesson, you will be using the Lifelong Helps on the Beatitudes. Read the instructions in preparation for tomorrow. Underline any ideas that you may want to refer to later. Based on this page of instructions, answer the following question:**

   God uses circumstances to develop the Beatitudes in your life. For what is He training you?

_____

5. **Conclude your study in prayer. Ask God to open your mind to understand His activity in your life. Ask God to reveal when and how He has worked in the past and is working in the present to develop in you these qualities. If God reveals specific instances in the past, record them in your journal for later use.**

DAY 3
POOR IN SPIRIT, MOURN, MEEK

Today's Bible Meditation
"God be merciful to me a sinner" (Luke 18:13).

Name of Christ for Today
All (Col. 3:11)

Prayer to Begin the Lesson

Jesus, I am a needy person. Without You I am lost and undone. I am nothing apart from You. You are described by Paul as "All." Just as the Father was the "I Am that I Am" to Moses, You are everything I need. You are my Source. I praise You for being all sufficient for my every need. Work in me today to meet my needs, even those I may not be aware of. Amen.

1. Begin today's lesson by reading the Bible verse and the name of Christ for today. Work on your memory verse. Then use the suggested prayer to begin your study.

We want to change our learning pattern. We want you to begin using the Lifelong Helps for the Beatitudes. We will give you assignments that will call for you to study and begin using the helps on pages 241-250. You may want to keep a bookmark here and in the back so you can flip back and forth as needed. You will also need The Mind of Christ Cards 20-27.

The Poor in Spirit

2. Read *Poor in Spirit* (p. 243) and answer the following questions.

What is the principle for this Beatitude? _____

To what is this quality of life a key? _____

How would you define poor in spirit? _____

_____

Has God used a circumstance to develop this quality in you? Write a brief note to describe the situation.

_____

_____

What response in worship does this Beatitude prompt? _____

_____

Mourn

3. Read *Mourn* (p. 244) and answer the following questions.

What is the principle for this Beatitude? _____

To what is this quality of life a key? _____

How would you define mourn? _____

_____

Has God used a circumstance to develop this quality in you? Write a brief note to describe the situation.

_____

_____

What response in worship does this Beatitude prompt? _____

_____

_____

Meek

4. Read Meek (p. 245) and answer the following questions.

What is the principle for this Beatitude? _____

To what is this quality of life a key? _____

How would you define meek? _____

_____

_____

Has God used a circumstance to develop this quality in you? Write a brief note to describe the situation.

_____

_____

What response in worship does this Beatitude prompt? _____

_____

_____

5. Close today's lesson in prayer. Talk to the Lord about what He has done, is doing, or wants to do in your life regarding these three Beatitudes.

DAY 4
HUNGRY, MERCIFUL, PURE IN HEART

Today's Bible Meditation
"God, thou art my God;
early will I seek thee: my
soul thirsteth for thee, my
flesh longeth for thee in a
dry and thirsty land, where
no water is" (Ps. 63:1)

Name of Christ for Today
Head of the Church
(Eph. 5:23)

**Prayer to Begin
the Lesson**
*Lord Jesus, I do hunger and
thirst after You. You are
satisfying my needs and I
thank You. I sense my
church needs a deeper hunger and thirst after you. You
are working in me in that
area. As Head of the Church,
would You create that same
hunger and thirst in others?
If You want to use my life in
any way in the process, You
have my permission.
Continue filling me
today! Amen.*

1. Begin today's lesson by reading the Bible verse and the name of Christ for today. Work on your memory verse. Then use the suggested prayer to begin your study.

Continue using the Lifelong Helps for the Beatitudes and complete the following assignments.

Hungry for Righteousness

2. Read Hungry (p. 246) and answer the following questions.

What is the principle for this Beatitude? _____

To what is this quality of life a key? _____

How would you define hunger and thirst for righteousness? _____

_____

_____

Has God used a circumstance to develop this quality in you? Write a brief note to describe the situation.

_____

_____

What response in worship does this Beatitude prompt? _____

_____

Merciful

3. Read *Merciful* (p. 247) and answer the following questions.

What is the principle for this Beatitude? _____

To what is this quality of life a key? _____

How would you define *merciful?* _____

_____

_____

Has God used a circumstance to develop this quality in you? Write a brief note to describe the situation.

_____

_____

What response in worship does this Beatitude prompt? _____

_____

_____

Pure in Heart

🖋 4. Read *Pure in Heart* (p. 248) and answer the following questions.

What is the principle for this Beatitude? _____

To what is this quality of life a key? _____

How would you define *pure in heart?* _____

_____

_____

Has God used a circumstance to develop this quality in you? Write a brief note to describe the situation.

_____

_____

What response in worship does this Beatitude prompt? _____

_____

_____

🖋 5. Close today's lesson in prayer. Talk to the Lord about what He has done, is doing, or wants to do in your life regarding these three Beatitudes. Thank God for what He is doing to develop these qualities in your life.

DAY 5
PEACEMAKERS, PERSECUTED FOR RIGHTEOUSNESS

Today's Bible Meditation
"All things are of God, who hath reconciled us to himself by Jesus Christ, and hath given to us the ministry of reconciliation" (2 Cor. 5:18).

Name of Christ for Today
Righteous Judge
(2 Tim. 4:8)

Prayer to Begin the Lesson
Righteous Judge, my world often condemns those who serve You. I have heard of some that have been persecuted for claiming Your name. I ask You to Judge such actions with Your righteous justice. Strife is all about me. Help me to be the peacemaker You want me to be. Help me to carry out faithfully the ministry of reconciliation You have given me. Amen.

1. Begin today's lesson by reading Bible verse and the name of Christ for today. Work on your memory verse. Then use the suggested prayer to begin your study.

Continue using the Lifelong Helps for the Beatitudes and complete the following assignments.

Peacemakers

2. Read *Peacemaker* (p. 249) and answer the following questions.

What is the principle for this Beatitude? _____

To what is this quality of life a key? _____

How would you define *peacemaker?* _____

_____

_____

Has God used a circumstance to develop this quality in you? Write a brief note to describe the situation.

_____

_____

What response in worship does this Beatitude prompt? _____

_____

_____

Persecuted for Righteousness

3. Read *Persecuted* (p. 250) and answer the following questions.

What is the principle for this Beatitude? _____

To what is this quality of life a key? _____

How would you define *persecuted for righteousness?* _____

_____

_____

Has God used a circumstance to develop this quality in you? Write a brief note to describe the situation.

_____

_____

What response in worship does this Beatitude prompt? _____

_____

_____

4. Review the eight Beatitudes using The Mind of Christ Cards 20-27. Select one in which God is working in your life. Spend some extra time today meditating on the Scriptures in the Lifelong Helps section for that Beatitude.

5. Conclude your study of this unit praying for God to use any circumstance He chooses to develop the first four qualities in your life. Give God permission to call on you to manifest the second four qualities whenever or wherever He needs to show the world what He is like. Pray for your group members as they seek to develop the mind of Christ in these areas.

GROUP SESSION 7

THE BEATITUDES

SESSION GOALS

This session will help you understand ways God uses circumstances to develop the Beatitudes in your life. You will demonstrate an openness to God's work of developing the Beatitudes in your life.

Hearing What the Spirit Is Saying (as you arrive)

1. (Individuals) Review what God has been saying to you during the study of unit 7.
   * Identify a Scripture and a name of Christ that have been meaningful this week.
   * Identify and mark the issue or subject in which God seems to be working most actively to develop the mind of Christ. (These will be shared later in the session.)
2. (Individuals) Write out any questions related to this unit you would like answered.

Magnifying the Lord and Exalting His Name (5 minutes)

1. (Volunteer) Open the session in prayer by asking God to reveal to members how He works through circumstances to develop the Beatitudes in believers.
2. Pray as you feel led to worship God for Who He is and acknowledge Him for what He has done. Use the names of Christ to exalt His name together in prayer.
3. After prayer, share ways God revealed Himself to you this week through His names. Which name of Christ has been most meaningful to you and why?

Transforming by the Word (15 minutes)

1. (Pairs) Pair up and quote this week's memory verse, Matthew 5:3. Then, as time permits, alternate quoting verses from previous units. Use your Scripture memory cards as a reference.
2. Share what God said to you through this week's memory verse or other Scripture that has been meaningful.
3. (Quads—or two groups) Distribute poster board or newsprint and markers to each of two groups. Make two lists related to characteristics of a Christlike mind. Focus on this unit's Scriptures only.
   * Group 1: Make a list of things, actions, or attitudes identified or implied in Scriptures during this unit that need to be cleansed from one's mind and life.
   * Group 2: Make a list of things, actions, or attitudes identified or implied in Scriptures during this unit that need to be incorporated into one's mind and life.
   * For example: We need to stop *exalting self* (group 1) and start *humbling self* (group 2) (see Luke 18:10-14).
4. Call on quads to read and comment on their lists. Place one on the Transformed To Wall and the other on the Transformed From Wall.
5. (Volunteer) Pray that God will cleanse members of your group and church.

HEBREWS 10:24, NASB

"LET US CONSIDER HOW TO STIMULATE ONE ANOTHER TO LOVE AND GOOD DEEDS."

Stimulating One Another to Love and Good Deeds (20 minutes)

1. Review Hebrews 10:24 in the margin.
2. Share testimonies of what God has done this week in your life that has been meaningful, challenging, or instructive.
3. State questions or concerns you have written for consideration. As time permits, seek to answer the questions as a group.
4. Using page 241 that contrasts the first four and the second four Beatitudes, discuss the helpfulness of these divisions. Use the material in activity 3 on page 131 as a guide for your questions and discussion.

5. Turn to page 133. Ask volunteers to share their responses to activity 3.

6. As time permits, discuss one or more of the following questions:
   • How does God use circumstances to develop the Beatitudes in a person's life? Give an example.
   • In the second four Beatitudes, why is it important for a person to identify with Christ by expressing the Beatitude? Give an example.
   • Why do you think God repeatedly guides us through the cycle of developing the Beatitudes?
   • What can we do to help one another respond to God's activity in developing the Beatitudes?
   • Which of the Beatitudes is God working on in your life right now? Would some of you share how He seems to be working in or through you?

Preparing the Bride for Her Bridegroom (5 minutes)

1. Read Matthew 24:1-35. Listen for ways the bride (church) needs to prepare for the return of Christ. List them in the margin.

2. As time permits, discuss these questions:
   • What evidences do you observe that may indicate Christ's return may be drawing near?
   • What cleansing, purifying, or preparation is needed in our church?
   • How can we apply this Scripture to our lives, families, and church?

3. Someone pray for our church to continue to prepare for the Lord's return.

Praying for One Another (10 minutes)

1. (Quads, preferably same gender) Review James 5:16 in the margin and share personal, family, church, or work-related prayer requests that primarily focus on developing the mind of Christ or purifying the bride.

2. (Quads) Pray specifically for one another for forgiveness, healing, encouragement, guidance, wisdom, knowledge, understanding, courage, strength, faithfulness, or for specific requests.

Closing the Session (5 minutes)

1. Share questions or concerns that came up during the session that we should remember in prayer.

2. Preview unit 8 on the following pages. This next, week watch for ways you exhibit both positive and negative emotions.

3. Close by praying that this week God will help all your group members learn to control emotional impulses that do not reflect the mind or character of Christ.

JAMES 5:16
"CONFESS YOUR FAULTS ONE TO ANOTHER, AND PRAY ONE FOR ANOTHER, THAT YE MAY BE HEALED. THE EFFECTUAL FERVENT PRAYER OF A RIGHTEOUS MAN AVAILETH MUCH."

Hymn Part 4
CHRIST'S HUMANITY
"[Jesus] was made in the likeness of men: and ...
found in fashion as a man"
(Phil. 2:7-8).

DAY 1
Jesus' Identification with Humanity

DAY 2
Jesus' "Negative" Emotions

DAY 3
Jesus' Positive Emotions

DAY 4
Controlling Emotional Impulses

DAY 5
Jesus and Wisdom

Why You Will Find This Unit Helpful
You will understand how and why Jesus was able to express His emotions without sinning. You will discover ways to prepare yourself to control emotional impulses and show godly wisdom in your everyday world. God will be at work helping you to will and to do His pleasure.

Lifelong Goal
In Christ you will express your emotions in ways that honor God.

Summary of God's Work in You

Christ's life in you springs from the mental quality of sincerity, which deals only with reality. God's goal for you is found in His original intention for a perfect humanity. Your spiritual growth can be measured only by Christ's relations with His Father and with other people. Christ enables your growth as God intended it in His role as Son of Man.

Unit Learning Goals

- You will understand why you should imitate Jesus' humanity.
- You will identify some "negative" and positive emotions Jesus expressed.
- You will demonstrate your desire for control in expressing negative emotions in ways that honor Christ.
- You will understand one way you can miss the mind of Christ regarding the experience of joy.
- You will understand reasons you might demonstrate the mind of Christ by showing compassion.
- You will understand how to control emotional impulses with godly wisdom and your will.
- You will understand the importance of biblical wisdom for right living.
- You will demonstrate a renewed commitment to be a faithful student of God's Word.

What You Will Do to Begin Godly Expression of Emotions

- You will study the way Jesus expressed both "negative" and positive emotions.
- You will seek God's help in developing godly wisdom for right living.
- You will review your Bondage to Freedom Lists to see areas God is still working to set you free.
- You will review the Lifelong Helps for Christlike Virtues and The Beatitudes for the purpose of letting God continue to mold you into the image of His Son.

Scripture Memory Verse

"The Word was made flesh, and dwelt among us, (and we beheld his glory, the glory as of the only begotten of the Father,) full of grace and truth" (John 1:14).

Lifelong Helps for Review in This Unit

Bondage to Freedom Lists (pp. 224-26)
Christlike Virtues (pp. 227-39)
The Beatitudes (pp. 241-50)

The Mind of Christ Cards Related to This Unit

4B. Unit 8: Scripture Memory—John 1:14

DAY 1
JESUS' IDENTIFICATION WITH HUMANITY

Today's Bible Meditation
"Christ also suffered for us, leaving us an example, that ye should follow his steps: Who did no sin, neither was guile found in his mouth" (1 Pet. 2:21-22).

Names of Christ for Today
Son of Man (Matt. 12:40)
The Last Adam
(1 Cor. 15:45)
The Second Man
(1 Cor. 15:47)

Prayer to Begin the Lesson
Son of Man, thank You for choosing to become human. As I observe Your life in Scripture, I see what You intended for human life to be like. You lived with all the same temptations that I experience, yet You did not sin. You lived victoriously over temptation and sin. You showed what perfect human-ity looks like. You were holy, spotless, and blameless. Teach me and help me to fol-low in Your steps. I want to be like You. Amen.

1. **Begin today's lesson by reading the Bible verses and the names of Christ for today. Work on your memory verse. Then use the suggested prayer on the left to begin your study.**

In this unit we will continue to look at the fourth part of the hymn: Christ's humanity. This unit will focus on the emotions of Christ. Jesus displayed a broad range of human emotions. Yet, Jesus never sinned in the way He expressed His emotions. This is an area where avoiding sin is difficult. We have emotional outbursts. We express emotions inappropriately. We allow our emotions to govern our behavior and lead us into sinful acts. We want you to learn how to handle your emotions by following the example of Jesus.

God's Emphasis on the Inner Person

The mind always has been more important to God than outward actions. In the Old Testament, the emphasis was on the heart. At times, the Bible uses the word *heart* where we would use the word *mind*. For instance: "Apply your heart to discipline" (Prov. 23:12, NASB) and "As he thinketh in his heart, so is he" (Prov. 23:7).

Jesus used the word *heart* in the same sense: "Jesus knowing their thoughts said, 'Why are you thinking evil in your hearts?'" (Matt. 9:4, NASB).

2. **Which is more important to God? Check one.**

   ❏ My inner being   ❏ My outward actions

Often we are satisfied if our outer, visible actions fulfill the expectations of society and the requirements of God. God looks on the inner person. He told Samuel: "Man looketh on the outward appearance, but the Lord looketh on the heart" (1 Sam. 16:7). In the somewhat stricter emphasis of the New Testament, we can say the Lord looks at the mind. God is more concerned with the inner person than with outer actions.

Outward actions reflect what is on the inside. We may not commit the overt act of adultery, but Jesus says: "that everyone who looks on a woman to lust for her has committed adultery with her already in his heart" (Matt. 5:28, NASB). Christians who have a horror of committing murder are still in sin if they hate in their heart (see Matt. 5:21-22). The greed of Ahab—a mental sin—preceded the overt act of murder and stealing Naboth's vineyard (see 1 Kings 21:1-15). Cain was first guilty of the invisible sin of jealousy before he committed the visible sin of killing Abel (Gen. 4:5). God knows your heart and your thoughts. His primary concern is your mind.

3. **Which comes first? Check one.**

   ❏ Thoughts/emotions   ❏ Outward actions

The primary purpose in Jesus' coming to earth was to die for our sins. Jesus, however, did not come merely to die. He also came to live and to show us how to live. The way Jesus lived His life has enormous consequences for us.

Jesus deliberately identified with the common life of ordinary human beings, so that we will be able to identify with Him. He said, "The Son of Man came eating and drinking, and they say, 'Behold, a gluttonous man and a drunkard, a friend of tax-gatherers and sinners!' " (Matt. 11:19, NASB). Jesus chose the lowest human beings to identify with. One problem we face is that we find Jesus too grand or too lofty to imitate. Yet, Jesus went out of His way to identify with the most humble and insignificant persons in order to invite us to identify with Him.

To make this identification strong Jesus submitted to baptism—a baptism normally for sinners. Clearly, Jesus was placing Himself in the mainstream of common humanity. He met John's objection by saying, "Suffer it to be so now: for thus it becometh us to fulfil all righteousness" (Matt. 3:15). Jesus was not baptized for personal sin, but to identify with sinners. In His sinless life, Jesus showed the perfect nature of humanity as He created us to be. A perfect God became perfect Man for our sake. We can and must be like Him.

4. Why should you want to be like Jesus in His humanity?

_____

_____

5. You do not have additional Lifelong Helps for use this week. Review the helps related to Christ's virtues (pp. 227-39) and the Beatitudes (pp. 241-50). Ask God to identify the area in your life He would like to work on. Spend time this week studying and praying through the Lifelong Help related to the area God identifies.

_____

6. As you conclude today's lesson, pray to Jesus—the Son of Man. Express your gratitude and appreciation for His example. Tell Jesus of your desire to be like Him. Ask Him to prepare your mind and heart for the study of emotions.

_____

_____

_____

_____

DAY 2
JESUS' "NEGATIVE" EMOTIONS

Today's Bible Meditation
"Jesus wept" (John 11:35).

Name of Christ for Today
The Express Image of His [God's] Person (Heb. 1:3)

Prayer to Begin the Lesson
Jesus, I have negative emotions that sometimes are destructive to my relationships with others. I want to learn from Your example to express emotions in good ways. You are the perfect image of God. Teach me to reflect Your image in my life so that You will be honored. Amen.

1. **Begin today's lesson by reading the Bible verse and the name of Christ for today. Work on your memory verse. Then use the suggested prayer to begin your study.**

Jesus experienced many human emotions, both negative and positive. In so doing, Jesus affirmed a normal and healthy emotional life. God has emotions, as the Old Testament clearly demonstrates. God can be angry, (see Num. 25:3) jealous (see Ex. 20:5), loving (see Jer. 31:3), and compassionate (see Lam. 3:22). Jesus did not deny any legitimate emotion. His life shows us the wholesome range of human emotions.

Three times the New Testament records Jesus as being angry. The earliest one occurs in the first casting out of the money changers. Jesus repeated this action in the last week of His earthly life (see Matt. 21:12-13; Mark 11:15-17; Luke 19:45-46). Notice as you read the following account that Jesus did not just throw a temper tantrum. He expressed zeal for His Father's house. Jesus carefully planned His actions and took time to make a whip before displaying the anger He and His Father had for desecration of the temple.

> [Jesus] found in the temple those that sold oxen and sheep and doves, and the changers of money sitting: And when he had made a scourge of small cords, he drove them all out of the temple, and the sheep, and the oxen; and poured out the changers' money, and overthrew the tables; And said unto them that sold doves, 'Take these things hence; make not my Father's house an house of merchandise.' And his disciples remembered that it was written, The zeal of thine house hath eaten me up (John 2:14-17).

Anger

Jesus' anger is recorded again in Mark 3:1-5. The Pharisees were watching Jesus to see if He would heal on the Sabbath a man with a shriveled hand. "Looking around at them with anger, [He was] grieved at their hardness of heart" (v. 5, NASB). Anger can be expressed illegitimately. These violations of holiness and justice, however, were occasions for the appropriate expression of holy anger. Holy anger comes from such a pure fountain that we probably would do well not to try to imitate it.

2. **What is a "negative" emotion that Jesus expressed in an appropriate way?**

_____

Indignant

On one occasion, Jesus was indignant with His own disciples. They had attempted to keep people from bringing children to Him for blessing. Often when they failed to understand His ways, Jesus was temperate and longsuffering. But on this occasion "He was indignant" (Mark 10:14, NASB). He rarely expressed this emotion. Evidently this particular offense was serious. Jesus desired that children come to Him.

One time the Pharisees came to Jesus and asked for a sign from heaven. Jesus already had given abundant signs through His healings and miracles. Ironically, this demand followed immediately after Jesus' feeding of the four thousand. What greater sign could they want? Mark tells us that Jesus "sighed deeply in his spirit" (Mark 8:12)—a rare example of displeasure. Even God's patience is limited by His own perfect holiness.

Displeasure

Four times the New Testament pictures Jesus as being troubled. The first of these occurred at the death of Lazarus. On this occasion, Jesus "groaned in the spirit, and was troubled" at the sight of Mary's weeping (John 11:33). Jesus was "troubled in spirit" when He announced the betrayal of Judas (John 13:21). The prospect of monumental human failure and the betrayal by a close friend were understandably troubling. In Gethsemane the night before His death, Jesus "began to be very distressed and troubled" (Mark 14:33, NASB). Jesus even verbalized His over-whelming sorrow: "My soul is exceeding sorrowful unto death" (Mark 14:34). Later in Gethsemane, He was "in an agony" and probably sweated blood (Luke 22:44). Jesus was unquestionably capable of profound and deep human emotion. He expressed it openly and straightforwardly.

Troubled

Distressed
Sorrow
Agony

🔊 **3. Below list some of the other "negative" emotions Jesus expressed.**

_____

_____

_____

_____

We get a hint of God's grief over the reign of sin and death when Jesus wept at the grave of Lazarus (see John 11:35). Jesus gave a "deep sigh" when He was healing the deaf man (see Mark 7:34).

Wept
Deep Sigh

Jesus was capable of profound grief. The two cries of sorrow over Jerusalem indicate an intense love that has been wounded deeply: "O Jerusalem, Jerusalem, the city that kills the prophets and stones those sent to her! How often I wanted to gather your children together, just as a hen gathers her brood under her wings, and you would not have it!" (Luke 13:34, NASB). Jesus also wept over the city of Jerusalem during the triumphal entry. We almost hear the sigh in His breath as Jesus said, "If you had known in this day, even you, the things which make for peace! But now they have been hidden from your eyes" (Luke 19:41-42, NASB). No more eloquent cries of rejection are found in all literature.

Grief

🔊 **4. What are some negative emotions you have expressed?**

_____

_____

_____

_____

5. How would you evaluate the way you normally express negative emotions? Check one or write your own response.

❏ I always act in appropriate (good) ways.
❏ Sometimes I do OK, but other times I explode.
❏ I am afraid that I usually express negative emotions in bad ways.
❏ Other: _____

6. Pray about the way you express negative emotions. Ask Jesus to assist you in responding to your negative emotions in ways that would honor Him and never displease Him.

DAY 3
JESUS' POSITIVE EMOTIONS

Today's Bible Meditation
"When he saw the multitudes, he was moved with compassion on them, because they fainted, and were scattered abroad, as sheep having no shepherd" (Matt. 9:36).

Name of Christ for Today
A Righteous Man
(Luke 23:47)

Prayer to Begin the Lesson
Lord Jesus, You were a Righteous Man. You were always right in the way You acted. I do not want to act wrongly, and I also want to do what is right in a positive way. Teach me when and how to show positive emotions. Don't let me miss Your mind in these areas. Clothe me in Your righteousness. Amen.

Zeal
Hope
Glad

1. Begin today's lesson by reading the Bible verse and the name of Christ for today. Work on your memory verse. Then use the suggested prayer to begin your study.

2. As you read today's lesson, circle the emotions described. Below write the words for ready reference in the future.

_____

_____

_____

The New Testament names more positive emotions of Jesus than negative ones. At the casting out of the money-changers, Jesus' disciples primarily saw zeal (John 2:17), which controlled and overshadowed His anger. This was a messianic fulfillment of Psalm 69:9. Zeal is a deep emotion. Whatever Jesus felt, He felt deeply.

3. Read the following paragraph and underline the definition of *hope.*

Jesus expressed desire and anticipation prior to the Lord's Supper. He told the disciples, "I have earnestly desired to eat this Passover with you before I suffer" (Luke 22:15, NASB). Jesus actually had hoped for this time! Hope is a rare virtue. We sometimes think of hope only as a desperate resort: "I hope things finally turn out all right." In the New Testament, however, hope is the present enjoyment of a future blessing. Jesus knew how things would turn out. For Jesus, the Supper was a happy time. He had looked forward to it.

4. Name two positive emotions of Jesus: _____

Once Jesus said He was glad. Gladness is the celebration of continuing inner joy. Gladness occurs when joy expresses itself on a particular occasion. On His departure for Bethany to raise Lazarus from the dead, Jesus informed the disciples, "Lazarus is dead, and I am glad for your sakes that I was not there, so that you may believe" (John 11:14-15, NASB). Throughout His ministry, Jesus had been disappointed at the disciples' lack of faith. The resurrection undoubtedly would speak strongly to their struggling faith; Jesus was glad.

Joy

Joy characterized the conduct of Jesus' life. On the return of the 70 from their mission, Jesus "rejoiced greatly in the Holy Spirit" (Luke 10:21, NASB). Jesus even expressed joy on the evening of the Lord's Supper as He headed toward the cross. After Jesus told His followers that their obedience would cause them to remain in His love, He said: "These things have I spoken unto you, that my joy might remain in you, and that your joy might be full" (John 15:11). Of all the strange circumstances under which He could express joy, this evening of His betrayal, arrest, and trials seems the most unusual. Perhaps this is where many of us miss the mind of Christ more than any other area—we borrow tomorrow's hurt. The entire period of this Passover evening would normally have been a time of intense dread for any other human (had they been capable of understanding the events of the coming hours). Jesus deliberately did not enter that awesome dread until Gethsemane. During the last supper itself Jesus actually was cheerful. Jesus felt joy!

5. How can we miss the mind of Christ regarding the experience of joy?

_____

_____

_____

6. Can you remember a time when you "borrowed tomorrow's hurt"? Briefly describe it:

_____

_____

_____

_____

_____

Compassion

Five times the gospels record Jesus as having compassion. In three of these, His compassion is on a multitude (see Matt. 14:14; 9:36; Mark 8:2). Large crowds stirred His pity. Jesus saw the great need among the people. Once, as He began to heal a leper, Jesus was "moved with compassion" (Mark 1:41). When Jesus encountered the funeral procession of a young man in Nain, He halted it. The mother of the young fellow was a widow, and "He felt compassion for her" (Luke 7:13, NASB). His heart was tender toward need and hurt. On all of these occasions, Jesus met the need and healed the hurt.

7. Based on Jesus' example, what are some of the reasons you might demonstrate the mind of Christ by showing compassion?

_____

_____

Love

The highest emotion of Jesus is love. The love of Jesus is mentioned more than any other emotion. When the rich young ruler came to Jesus, "looking at him, Jesus felt a love for him" (Mark 10:21, NASB). When Lazarus became sick, Mary and Martha sent word to Jesus, "Lord, behold, he whom You love is sick" (John 11:3, NASB). Two verses later John tells us that "Jesus loved Martha, and her sister, and Lazarus." At the beginning of the Lord's Supper, "having loved his own which were in the world, he loved them unto the end" (John 13:1). Later in the meal, Jesus said to them, "As the Father has loved Me, I have also loved you" (John 15:9, NASB). To avoid mentioning his own name, John referred to himself as the disciple "whom Jesus loved" (John 13:23, again in John 19:26). Love is the central emotion in the mind of Christ.

Love is the central emotion in the mind of Christ.

8. **Turn to *Love* (page 233-34) and review the ways you can show love. Watch for opportunities this week to show the love of Christ.**

9. **Close this lesson's study time by asking God to develop in you the perfect expression of positive emotions. Ask God to reveal to you opportunities when He would like for you to express these emotions.**

DAY 4
CONTROLLING EMOTIONAL IMPULSES

1. **Begin today's lesson by reading the Bible verses and the name of Christ for today. Work on your memory verse. Then use the suggested prayer on the following page to begin your study.**

2. **As you read the following paragraph, circle some of the emotions that Jesus did NOT display.**

Note the absence in Jesus' mind of negative emotions such as doubt, pessimism, discouragement, cynicism, suspicion, and gloom. He had no phobias. Jesus never worried about the problems of His life, such as the frequent failures of His disciples, His troubled relations with authorities, His rejection in His own home town, or the dread of the cross.

According to Jesus' example, emotions are normal and typical of God's creation of humanity. Jesus' emotions, however, were resident and not subject to impulse. They find expression as occasion calls them out. We already have seen that God has holy anger, and that Jesus expressed anger. But God's anger does not come and go. God

Today's Bible Meditation
"It is God which worketh in you both to will and to do of his good pleasure. Do all things without murmurings and disputings: That ye may be blameless and harmless, the sons of God, without rebuke, in the midst of a crooked and perverse nation, among whom ye shine as lights in the world" (Phil. 2:13-15).

Name of Christ for Today
Wonderful Counselor
(Isa. 9:6, NASB)

never "gets mad." God's anger is a permanent, unchanging, holy part of His makeup. God reserves the expression of His emotions for those times when we need to know the significance of His holiness. We do not always perceive God's various emotions, but they always are present.

3. Which of the following best describes Jesus' emotions?

❏ Jesus' emotions were changeable and He expressed them impulsively.

❏ Jesus' emotions were resident and unchanging. He expressed emotions thoughtfully and deliberately.

Casting the money changers out of the temple was not an unthoughtful, impulsive action. Jesus made the whip Himself. Coolly and deliberately, Jesus expressed the righteous wrath of unchanging holiness. Until that absolute holiness consumes our entire being, we do well not to try to express righteous anger. Jesus' emotions were resident and unchanging.

**The greatest danger for those of us who
want the mind of Christ is acting from impulse.**

What emotions are subject to impulse? Those emotions which grip us with suddenness are nearly always negative—anger, lust, and revenge. These are also the hardest emotions to control. We act before we think. The Bible strongly emphasizes the will when it talks about the mind. The spiritual mind consciously places vengeance in the hands of the Lord (Heb. 10:30). The mind of Christ has both negative and positive resident emotions, but they are subject to the will. Their public display is subject to godly wisdom.

4. What is the best way for you to avoid impulsive expression of negative emotions? Check one.
   ❏ a. I wait until I feel an emotion coming on and hope I have the strength to do the right thing.
   ❏ b. I *set, renew,* and *gird up* my mind so I can use my will to choose the right action when a negative emotion arises.

We discovered our emotions falling into place after finding freedom (units 2-3) and after learning to interpret circumstances according to the blessings of the Sermon on the Mount (unit 6). More mature emotions grew out of these earlier lessons. Learn these lessons well, and you will be able to control emotional impulses by using godly wisdom and exercising your will to do right.

5. Take a few minutes to review the Bondage to Freedom Lists you have made. Does God want to set you free in other areas? Continue working on your lists until you sense Christ has set you free indeed.

6. Continue reviewing the Lifelong Helps (Virtues and Beatitudes) that God calls to your attention. Let God continue His work in those areas. Keep praying that God will mold you into the image of His Son Jesus Christ.

**Prayer to Begin
the Lesson**
Wonderful Counselor, I get myself into much trouble because of my emotional impulses. They seem uncontrollable at times. Will I ever be able to control those impulses? I turn to Your counsel today. Teach me from the example of Jesus how to express my emotions correctly. I want to honor You and shine as a light in a world of darkness. Thank You that You will help me want the right things and then enable me to do them. Amen.

DAY 5
JESUS AND WISDOM

1. Begin today's lesson by reading the Bible verses and the name of Christ for today. Work on your memory verse. Then use the suggested prayer on the left to begin your study.

Jesus never failed to use His intellect to the advantage of God's cause. Even at the age of 12, Jesus was about the affairs of His Father. In the temple, Jesus was receptive by listening to the teachers. The teachers questioned Jesus and were "amazed at His understanding and His answers" (Luke 2:47, NASB). Jesus had an unbelievable knowledge and use of the Old Testament.

2. As you read the following paragraph, circle the way Jesus responded to those who questioned Him. To what did He point them?

Jesus demonstrated a keen intellect and a quick response. He referred those who questioned Him to God's intent. When the chief priests, scribes, and elders demanded that He identify His authority, Jesus referred their question to John's baptism and God's divine purpose (see Luke 20:3-4). Jesus answered the question about giving tribute to Caesar by saying that both civil and divine authority should receive their due (Luke 20:22-25). Jesus baffled the Sadducees by pointing out their failure to comprehend Scripture (Luke 20:27-38). God's purposes were the source of His ready answers.

Most important to Jesus was the application of wisdom. Biblical wisdom is available to the uneducated person as well as to the scholar. Wisdom was important to the Jewish mind, and a section of their sacred writings is designated as "wisdom literature"—Job, Psalms, Proverbs, Ecclesiastes, Song of Solomon. As a child, Jesus "kept increasing in wisdom" (Luke 2:52, NASB). The difference and the depth of Jesus' teaching amazed His hearers (Matt. 7:28-29; Luke 4:32, 36). Speaking of His teaching, Christ claimed, "The words that I have spoken to you are spirit and are life" (John 6:63, NASB). Jesus often referred to the Scriptures as the reason for His actions. Jesus quoted the Scriptures as a means to resist Satan during His temptation in the wilderness. The Bible is a valuable source of wisdom for those willing to pay the price of time in God's Word to learn it.

3. How important were the Scriptures to Jesus? _____

4. If you are to have the mind of Christ, how important should the Scriptures be to you? _____

5. What are some practical ways you can allow the Scriptures to take their rightful place of importance in your mind? Check all that apply.

❏ a. Carry my study Bible with me at all times so I can look up what I need anytime I need it.
❏ b. Read and study the Scriptures.
❏ c. Listen to pastors and teachers as they explain the Scriptures.
❏ d. Meditate on the Scriptures.
❏ e. Memorize the Scriptures.
❏ f. Do not worry about knowing the Scriptures until the need arises, then hope God gives me a Word.
❏ g. Talk about the application of Scriptures with other believers.

Of these possibilities b., c., d., e., and g. are the most practical and reflect the pattern of Jesus' life. *A* is not all bad, but it may be impractical. Situations may arise that do not allow you that much time to make a right decision or response. *F* is presumptuous. God can give a word, but He has no obligation to make up for our laziness. The better choices are to "Study to shew thyself approved unto God, a workman that needeth not to be ashamed, rightly dividing the word of truth" (2 Tim. 2:15).

Paul said that in Christ "are hidden all the treasures of wisdom and knowledge" (Col. 2:3, NASB). So strongly identified with wisdom was Christ that Paul spoke of Him as "the wisdom of God" (1 Cor. 1:24). James 3:17 clearly describes the wisdom of God—that is Jesus! Demonstrating the mind of Christ is wise.

6. Reflect on your progress in becoming like Christ. Are you growing? Tell God what you are feeling and thinking right now. In prayer, make a fresh commitment to God to be a faithful student of His Word.

Demonstrating the mind of Christ is wise.

GROUP SESSION 8

JESUS AND EMOTIONS

SESSION GOALS

This session will help you understand ways to control emotional impulses and properly express both negative and positive emotions. You will demonstrate a desire to control all emotional expressions properly.

Hearing What the Spirit Is Saying (as you arrive)

1. (Individuals) Review what God has been saying to you during the study of unit 8.
   - Identify a Scripture and a name of Christ that have been meaningful this week.
   - Identify and mark the issue or subject in which God seems to be working most actively to develop the mind of Christ. (These will be shared later in the session.)
2. (Individuals) Write out any questions related to this unit you would like answered.

Magnifying the Lord and Exalting His Name (5 minutes)

1. (Volunteer) Open the session in prayer by asking God to teach us how to reflect Christ in the way we express emotions.
2. Pray as you feel led to worship God for Who He is and acknowledge Him for what He has done. Use the names of Christ to exalt His name together in prayer.
3. After prayer, share ways God revealed Himself to you this week through His names. Which name of Christ has been most meaningful to you and why?

Transforming by the Word (15 minutes)

1. (Pairs) Pair up and quote this week's memory verse, John 1:14. Then, as time permits, alternate quoting verses from previous units. Use your Scripture memory cards as a reference.
2. Share what God said to you through this week's memory verse or other Scripture that has been meaningful.
3. (Quads—or two groups) Distribute poster board or newsprint and markers to each of two groups. Make two lists related to characteristics of a Christlike mind. Focus on this unit's Scriptures only.
   - Group 1: Make a list of things, actions, or attitudes identified or implied in Scriptures during this unit that need to be cleansed from one's mind and life.
   - Group 2: Make a list of things, actions, or attitudes identified or implied in Scriptures during this unit that need to be incorporated into one's mind and life.
   - For example: We need to rid ourselves of *adultery* and *hatred* (group 1) (see Matt. 5:21-22,28); we need to add *wisdom* and *knowledge* (group 2) (see Col. 2:3).
4. Call on quads to read and comment on their lists. Place one on the Transformed From Wall and the other on the Transformed To Wall.
5. (Volunteer) Pray that God will cleanse members of your group and church.

Stimulating One Another to Love and Good Deeds (20 minutes)

1. Share testimonies of what God has done this week in your life that has been meaningful, challenging, or instructive.
2. Encourage members to ask questions or share concerns they have written for consideration. As time permits, guide the group in answering the questions.
3. As time permits, discuss one or more of the following questions:
   - In God's sight, is your inner or outer being more important? Why?
   - What are some of the ways Jesus expressed positive and negative emotions?
   - How can negative emotions be expressed in acceptable ways?

- In what ways are you able to express love like that described in 1 Corinthians 13? Give an example.
- Are emotional impulses wrong? Why or why not? How can a believer develop control for emotional impulses? What is your role? What is God's role?

5. Turn to page 153 and share your responses to activity 5.

Preparing the Bride for Her Bridegroom (5 minutes)

1. Read Matthew 24:36-51. Listen for ways the bride (church) needs to prepare for the return of Christ. List them in the margin.
2. As time permits, discuss these questions:
   - Since we do not know the day or the hour of Christ's return, how should we live our lives?
   - What cleansing, purifying, or preparation is needed in our church?
   - How can we apply this Scripture to our lives, families, and church?
3. Call on one member to pray aloud for your church to continue to prepare for the Lord's return.

Praying for One Another (10 minutes)

1. (Quads, preferably same gender) Share personal, family, church, or work-related prayer requests that primarily focus on developing the mind of Christ or purifying the bride.
2. (Quads) Pray specifically for one another for forgiveness, healing, encouragement, guidance, wisdom, knowledge, understanding, courage, strength, faithfulness, or for specific requests.

Closing the Session (5 minutes)

1. Share questions or concerns that came up during the session that we should remember in prayer.
2. Preview unit 9 on the following pages. Pay special attention this week to ways you relate to things and people.
3. Someone pray that God will guide and instruct us in a right way of relating to people and things, reserving our supreme love for God alone.

JESUS' RELATIONS WITH THINGS AND PEOPLE

Hymn Part 4
CHRIST'S HUMANITY
*"[Jesus] was made in the likeness of men:
and . . . found in fashion as a man"*
(Phil. 2:7-8).

DAY 1
Jesus and Materialism

DAY 2
Trusting God's Provision

DAY 3
Jesus' Sense of Timing

DAY 4
Jesus' Friendship

DAY 5
Jesus' Speech

Why You Will Find This Unit Helpful
Jesus had a perspective of material things that differs greatly from the common view in our world. Freedom from the bondage of possessions is vital to abundant living. You will find that you can trust God to provide for the needs of His children so you do not have to worry about the needs of tomorrow. By examining the example of Jesus you also will develop appropriate relationships to God's agenda, friendships, and speech.

Lifelong Goal
You will become like Christ in your relationship to material things, God's agenda for your life, friendships, and control of your speech.

Summary of God's Work in You

Christ's life in you springs from the mental quality of sincerity, which deals only with reality. God's goal for you is found in His original intention for a perfect humanity. Your spiritual growth can be measured only by Christ's relations with His Father and with other people. Christ enables your growth as God intended it in His role as Son of man.

Unit Learning Goals

- You will understand Jesus' teaching on materialism and the way Jesus related to friends.
- You will demonstrate your determination and commitment to lay up for yourself treasures in heaven.
- You will understand that God provides for the needs of His servants and children.
- You will demonstrate your confidence in God's provision for His children.
- You will understand that Jesus based His actions on the schedule of events planned by His Father.
- You will demonstrate your desire to know and follow God's agenda for your life.
- You will demonstrate your gratitude for Your friend Jesus.
- You will understand the way Jesus controlled His talk for divine purposes.
- You will demonstrate your commitment to developing temperance regarding your speech.

What You Will Do to Develop Appropriate Relationships to People and Things

- You will evaluate your relationship to things according to the teachings of Christ and you will seek freedom from possessions.
- You will study God's provision for His children and work at developing a deeper trust in His provision for your needs.
- You will evaluate the single-mindedness of your life and determine to follow God's agenda.
- You will review the Christlike virtue of temperance and seek God's help in the discipline of your tongue.

Scripture Memory Verses

"Lay up for yourselves treasures in heaven, where neither moth nor rust doth corrupt, and where thieves do not break through nor steal: For where your treasure is, there will your heart be also."

Lifelong Helps Related to This Unit

Bondage to Freedom Lists—Possessions (p. 226)
Christlike Virtues—Temperance (p. 239)

The Mind of Christ Card Related to This Unit

5A. Unit 9: Scripture Memory—Matthew 6:20-21

DAY 1
JESUS AND MATERIALISM

Today's Bible Meditations
"Take heed, and beware of covetousness: for a man's life consisteth not in the abundance of the things which he possesseth" (Luke 12:15).

"Lay not up for yourselves treasures upon earth, where moth and rust doth corrupt, and where thieves break through and steal: But lay up for yourselves treasures in heaven, where neither moth nor rust doth corrupt, and where thieves do not break through nor steal: For where your treasure is, there will your heart be also" (Matt. 6:19-21).

Name of Christ for Today
Heir of All Things
(Heb. 1:2)

Prayer to Begin the Lesson
Lord Jesus, You are the Heir of All Things; and I am a joint heir with You. I confess that I live like a poor person rather than like an heir of the kingdom. I have not learned to understand and appreciate the riches and treasures You make available to me. I confess that I have far too much attachment to the things of the world. Teach me to deny myself and give up my ownership to my things. I want to be completely free from attachment to things so I may follow You and Your example. Amen.

1. **Begin today's lesson by reading the Bible verses and the name of Christ for today. Work on your memory verse. Then use the suggested prayer on the left to begin your study.**

Jesus' Example

Both by example and by teaching, Jesus left no doubt that He placed little value on this world's goods. The divine choice for His birth was a stable. For most of His life, Jesus was a working man, a carpenter. During His ministry Jesus said, "Foxes have holes, and birds of the air have nests; but the Son of man hath not where to lay his head" (Luke 9:58). At His death, Jesus' only material possession was the garment for which the soldiers cast lots.

2. **Which of the following best describes Jesus' example regarding things? Check one.**

   ❏ Jesus was deeply attached to the things of the world and used His powers to accumulate many things for His personal comfort and pleasure.

   ❏ Jesus was detached and free from the love of the world's things. He chose a lowly life and saw no value in accumulating things.

Jesus' Teaching

In His teaching, Jesus contrasted *true riches* with *unrighteous mammon* (Luke 16:11). Jesus warned against storing up worldly wealth, and advised His followers to store up "treasures in heaven, where neither moth nor rust destroys, and where thieves do not break in or steal" (Matt. 6:20, NASB). In connection with this warning, He gave an important principle: "Where your treasure is, there will your heart be also" (Matt. 6:21).

3. **If you were completely honest with yourself, where would you say are most of your treasures? Check one.**

   ❏ In heaven   ❏ On earth   ❏ I don't think I have any treasures

Jesus' principle is evident in the parable of the rich fool (Luke 12:16-21). The foolish farmer kept storing his crops in bigger barns—accumulating his wealth. Then the farmer said to himself, "Take your ease, eat, drink and be merry" (Luke 12:19, NASB). That same night the Lord required his life, and his accumulated wealth was valueless. How foolish!

Jesus said, "No one of you can be My disciple who does not give up all his own possessions" (Luke 14:33, NASB). When he was called to be a disciple, Matthew "left everything behind, and rose and began to follow Him" (Luke 5:28, NASB). In the next verse, however, Matthew had a house in which to entertain Jesus and fellow tax collectors (see Luke 5:29). His "leaving everything" indicates that he left his profitable job rather than merely his possessions. The gospels, however, do not record that

Matthew ever returned to that house. He is always pictured following Jesus in the various trips around Galilee, Perea, and Judea.

Jesus required the rich young ruler to "Go and sell all you possess, and give to the poor, and you shall have treasure in heaven; and come, follow Me" (Mark 10:21, NASB). The young man was promised treasure in heaven immediately upon divesting himself of earthly treasure. Following Jesus came after the heavenly treasure. Jesus realized that this young man had made wealth his god. He loved it more than he loved God. Essentially, Jesus was telling him to put away his false god.

The story of the rich young ruler is the only case when the Bible explicitly says that Jesus loved a would-be follower (see Mark 10:21). The man's refusal must have been painful to the Lord. Jesus exclaimed, "How hard it will be for those who are wealthy to enter the kingdom of God!" (Mark 10:23, NASB). When questioned about this, Jesus said, "all things are possible with God" (Mark 10:27, NASB).

4. **Turn to the Lifelong Helps (p. 226) and review the Bondage to Freedom list related to possessions. Pray as you read through that list. Is there anything God is asking you to get rid of because it has become a false god to you? Respond in whatever way God may direct you. Below briefly describe your freedom (or lack of freedom) that you sense regarding possessions.**

_____

_____

_____

Jesus drew a hard and fast line in connection to materialism. He said, "No man can serve two masters: for either he will hate the one, and love the other; or else he will hold to the one, and despise the other. Ye cannot serve God and mammon [money]" (Matt. 6:24). One of the greatest rivals God has is worldly monetary success. We can have possessions and use them wisely like the women who supported Jesus and His disciples in ministry. But the grave danger is that the possessor of wealth will worship it. Jesus sternly warned, "That which is highly esteemed among men is detestable in the sight of God" (Luke 16:15, NASB).

One of the greatest rivals God has is worldly monetary success.

The mind of Christ places God above everything in the world.

A Remedy to Materialism

Greed will cause us to hold on to things for self-use. Greed is described in Ephesians 5:5 as idolatry—worshipping a false god. Jesus instructed the rich young ruler to give away his wealth because it had become a false god. The best remedy for materialism is cheerful giving.

Repeatedly, Jesus urged joyful giving. In the Sermon on the Mount, He commanded, "Give to him who asks of you, and do not turn away from him who wants to borrow from you" (Matt. 5:42). Jesus also warned that giving should be secret. We are not to announce it publicly (see Matt. 6:2-4). God is interested only in the motivation of our heart.

5. What is one way to avoid or get rid of a materialistic spirit?

_____

Money can become a powerful god that demands allegiance in a subtle but effective way. The mind of Christ allows involvement with money, but warns us that it can be dangerous. Money itself is neither good nor evil and can be used for worldly purposes or for God. We must be wise and heavenly-minded in its use. We must be ready to give as faithful stewards of God's resources.

6. Ask God if there is anything He wants you to give away as a way to keep materialism in check. If God reveals something, ask Him where or to whom you are to give it. You may need to set your mind and heart to give and then watch for the opportunity God brings your way. If God guides you to give in a special way, describe below what and to whom.

_____

_____

DAY 2
TRUSTING GOD'S PROVISION

Today's Bible Meditation
"If God so clothe the grass of the field, which to day is, and to morrow is cast into the oven, shall he not much more clothe you, O ye of little faith? Therefore take no thought, saying, What shall we eat? or, What shall we drink? or, Wherewithal shall we be clothed? (For after all these things do the Gentiles seek:) for your heavenly Father knoweth that ye have need of all these things. But seek ye first the kingdom of God, and his righteousness; and all these things shall be added unto you" (Matt. 6:30-33).

1. Begin today's lesson by reading the Bible verses and the name of Christ for today. Work on your memory verse. Then use the suggested prayer on the following page to begin your study.

Jesus taught that God provides for the needs of His children. In two similar passages (see Matt. 6:25-34 and Luke 12:22-32), Jesus said that God provides for the birds and the lilies. Since God provides for them, certainly He will provide for His children who are far more valuable. In the Luke passage, Jesus promised more than things like food and clothing: "Do not be afraid, little flock, for your Father has chosen gladly to give you the kingdom" (Luke 12:32, NASB).

2. Why should God's children not worry about food, drink, or clothing?

_____

3. Read again the Bible Meditation for today and look for the condition of God's provision. What should you seek first, after which God will provide?

_____

During the latter part of His adolescence and young manhood, Jesus worked as a carpenter. He showed that a working profession is valid and useful. After Jesus began His ministry, God supplied His material needs through the ministry of some women followers, who "were contributing to their support out of their private means" (Luke 8:3). Jesus did not require them to give away their wealth like He did the rich young ruler. Their wealth was not their god. Their love and devotion was given to Jesus. Through this provision, God freed Jesus and His disciples to devote their entire time to ministry. Jesus, therefore, was not worried about meeting His daily needs. God did that. Jesus says God will do that for us as well.

Learning to Trust

When I was first invited to teach *The Mind of Christ* publicly, I developed a booklet with charts to make the concepts memorable. I received a shock when I checked printing costs. The printer estimated the initial printing would be about $1,000. We checked our bank book and found that we had $37. Public ministry was new to me, and I could see no way to pursue what seemed to be a calling from God.

My studies of Jesus' life had convinced me that God will supply where there is genuine ministry need. This was the way Jesus functioned. My wife and I knew that the printing of the booklet would require a miracle. Somehow we had the faith and courage to ask God to print the booklet. We based our request on Jesus' example.

The treasurer of my church called with an unusual message. He told me, "T. W., we have a businessman in our church who just finished a major transaction. He came by this morning to tell us that he had an unexpected surplus. He says that God told him to give you the surplus." The check he had for me turned out to be $1,000!

With joy I took the booklet to the printer. Although I never have been excited about getting a bill, this time I could hardly wait for the bill to come. God was showing me that He supplies the needs of His children. Three weeks later, the bill was the top envelope in my mail! Joyfully I tore open the bill—but the bill was for $1,097. My heart sank. We had the thousand, but not the $97. With a heavy heart, I opened the rest of the mail. The third envelope was from a fellow who told me he had been praying for my ministry. He said that God had impressed on him that I had a need, and that he was to meet it. He enclosed a check for $100. That money arrived in the same mail as the bill! I knew that God had provided!

Over the years, God repeatedly has supplied the money that I have needed for ministry. The supply is usually exact, and it comes at the time of the need—seldom early. We are only able to please God when we walk with Him by faith (see Heb. 11:6). Jesus lived a life of faith, and He wants us to do the same.

4. **Can you remember a specific time when God provided for you in a way that you knew it was God? If so, briefly describe that time and prepare to share a summary with your group.**

_____

_____

_____

_____

Name of Christ for Today

Leader and Commander of the People (Isa. 55:4)

Prayer to Begin the Lesson

Lord Jesus, not only are You Head of our church; but You also are the Leader and Commander of Your People. Our church is an army intended to follow You into battle against the enemy. I pray that You will enable us to follow Your leadership so that even the gates of hell will not prevail against Your church. I pledge my allegiance to You as my Commander in Chief. Give me such confidence in Your provision that I will not worry about tomorrow. Give me the faith to trust You to provide. Amen.

HEBREWS 11:6

"BUT WITHOUT FAITH IT IS IMPOSSIBLE TO PLEASE HIM: FOR HE THAT COMETH TO GOD MUST BELIEVE THAT HE IS, AND THAT HE IS A REWARDER OF THEM THAT DILIGENTLY SEEK HIM."

Don't Worry About Things

Worry is pointless in view of God's care and provision for His children. Jesus expressly forbade worry about daily needs, and He even called anxiety pagan (Matt. 6:25-32). Jesus pictures the heathen world as eagerly seeking their needs (see Luke 12:30), but tells His followers to "make yourselves purses which do not wear out" (Luke 12:33, NASB). Treasure in heaven cannot be corrupted or lost.

Treasure in heaven cannot be corrupted or lost.

Worry accomplishes nothing, wastes mental effort, and does not characterize the mind of Christ.

5. **Which of the following best describes you? Check one or write your own.**

❑ I have learned the lesson about God's provision and I seldom worry about my need for things. I trust God to provide for my needs.

❑ I have such desperate needs I worry about things all the time. After all, my family has needs and I have a responsibility to provide for them.

❑ I am like a boat on the sea. When my needs are met, my confidence is high. But when things get tight, I shift my worry into high gear.

❑ Other: _____

6. **Confess to God exactly what you are thinking and feeling about His provision. Confess to Him that you are His child. Ask God to give you the faith and confidence to trust His provision even when things are difficult. Ask God to develop your trust in Him so that you will not worry like pagans do. Pray for God's honor and glory through your life.**

DAY 3
JESUS' SENSE OF TIMING

Today's Bible Meditations

"And he said . . . 'My time is at hand; I will keep the passover at thy house with my disciples' " (Matt. 26:18).

"Then cometh he to his disciples, and saith unto them, Sleep on now, and take your rest: behold, the hour is at hand, and the Son of man is betrayed into the hands of sinners" (Matt. 26:45).

1. **Begin today's lesson by reading the Bible verses and the name of Christ for today. Work on your memory verse. Then use the suggested prayer on the following page to begin your study.**

Jesus never appeared rushed. He never exhibited signs of worry or concern about schedule. Even on the way to heal Jairus's daughter, Jesus interrupted His trip to deal with the woman with the issue of blood (see Luke 8:43-48) in full knowledge that the little girl would die if He delayed. Neither imminent sickness nor death threatened Jesus' schedule. When He received notice that Lazarus was sick, "He stayed then two days longer in the place where He was" (John 11:6, NASB). Jesus knew what He would do, and He had more concern for the ultimate work of God than for the momentary illness of Lazarus. The resurrection of Lazarus was the decisive factor in the Sanhedrin's decision to kill Jesus (see John 11:53).

2. Check all of the words below that normally describe your feelings and thoughts about your schedule. Check those that apply most of the time.

❏ angry   ❏ calm   ❏ can't wait to get started
❏ confident   ❏ cool   ❏ excited
❏ frustrated   ❏ hurried   ❏ over loaded
❏ relaxed   ❏ rushed   ❏ stressed
❏ worried   ❏ want to quit   ❏ too much time

Name of Christ for Today
King Eternal, Immortal, Invisible (1 Tim. 1:17)

Prayer to Begin the Lesson
King Jesus, I exalt You. You are Eternal, Immortal, and Invisible; but You also are personal. I worship You and thank You that You care about me. I pray that You will help me to understand and discern the signs of the times and to follow You wisely. Help me to be watchful, active, and ready for Your soon return. Amen.

Do you feel and think like Jesus concerning your schedule? Because Jesus set His mind on the Kingdom, He focused attention on His purpose for ministry. Every miracle, teaching, and parable fit into a purposeful progression. Jesus was living His life according to His Father's agenda.

Jesus' referred to "His time" as one of great sacrifice. After Jesus' brothers tried to get Him to go to the Feast of Tabernacles and get the attention of the crowds, He told them, "My time is not yet come: but your time is alway ready" (John 7:6). Jesus timed every phase of His ministry in relation to that event. Later, during that same Feast of Tabernacles, Jesus met some challenges from the religious leaders. Jesus declared that to know Him was to know His Father. Though this enraged the leaders, "no man laid hands on him; for his hour was not yet come" (John 8:20). After claiming: "Before Abraham was, I am . . . Jesus hid Himself" (John 8:58-59). Still later, after saying that He was the Son of God, Jesus slipped out of their hand to avoid being captured (John 10:34-39). After He raised Lazarus from the dead, "Jesus therefore no longer continued to walk publicly among the Jews, but went away from there" (John 11:54, NASB).

Toward the end, "when the days were approaching for His ascension, . . . He resolutely set His face to go to Jerusalem" (Luke 9:51, NASB). Probably on Monday of Holy Week, Jesus said, "The hour is come, that the Son of man should be glorified" (John 12:23).

When Jesus sent the disciples to prepare the room for that final Passover, He instructed them to say to the host, "My time is at hand" (Matt. 26:18). Jesus began the greatest of all recorded prayers, "Father, the hour is come" (John 17:1). In Gethsemane, Jesus awakened the sleeping disciples by telling them, "The hour has come" (Mark 14:41, NASB). Jesus' entire life concentrated on the precise timing of His great sacrifice.

3. Would you describe Jesus as single-minded or double-minded? Circle one.

This knowledge and determination seem to be beyond our imitation. Yet God is present and able to guide you just as clearly. Spiritual concentration and time with Him are necessary.

4. Turn to unit 1 (p. 14) and read again the description of single-minded. Would you describe yourself as single-minded or double-minded? Circle one.

5. Conclude today's lesson by spending time with your heavenly Father. Tell God about your desire to work only on His agenda for your life. Agree to follow God one day at a time using His timetable and not your own.

DAY 4
JESUS' FRIENDSHIP

Today's Bible Meditation
¹³"Greater love hath no man than this, that a man lay down his life for his friends. ¹⁴Ye are my friends, if ye do whatsoever I command you. ¹⁵Henceforth I call you not servants; for the servant knoweth not what his lord doeth: but I have called you friends; for all things that I have heard of my Father I have made known unto you" (John 15:13-15).

Name of Christ for Today
Friend of Publicans and Sinners (Matt. 11:19).

Prayer to Begin the Lesson
Jesus, I'm so glad that You choose to be a friend of sinners. Otherwise, I'd miss out on Your friendship. I do want to be Your friend, so I pledge to do the things You command me. As I study Your Word, help me to identify the things You desire of me so I may obey. I yearn for fellowship with You. I open my life and invite You to come in and fellowship with me. Amen.

1. **Begin today's lesson by reading the Bible verses and the name of Christ for today. Work on your memory verse. Then use the suggested prayer on the left to begin your study.**

Jesus was a person who made many friends, and made them easily. He was invited to the wedding of family friends and blessed the wedding (see John 2:1-11). Jesus often accepted dinner invitations. He celebrated friendship. His friendships were profound. Jesus often visited the family of Mary, Martha, and Lazarus in Bethany. John tells us that Jesus loved them (John 11:5). Mary and Martha felt free to send for Jesus when Lazarus became ill (John 11:3). We already have discussed the virtue of being entreatable. Jesus displayed this virtue in relation to His friends. Jesus also was faithful to His friends. He stood by them in times of need, and He ministered to their needs. When Jesus visited the house of Simon Peter, He healed Peter's mother.

2. **Name at least two virtues Jesus displayed in relationship to His friends.**

   Jesus was _____ and _____.

Jesus loved His friends, and He was faithful and entreatable. Jesus' friends in turn were loyal to Him. Women remained at the cross through terrifying circumstances (Matt. 27:55) and later went to the tomb (Matt. 28:1; Luke 24:10). Joseph of Arimathea, facing the possible ridicule of his peers, bravely requested permission to bury Jesus (Matt. 27:57-58). Nicodemus also participated in the burial (John 19:39). Jesus inspired steadfastness in His friends.

Jesus' friends were His disciples. He appointed them "that they might be with Him" (Mark 3:14, NASB). Jesus indicated His supreme love in laying down His life for His friends (see John 15:13). Jesus told them, "No longer do I call you slaves, for the slave does not know what his master is doing; but I have called you friends, for all things that I have heard from My Father I have made known to you" (John 15:15, NASB).

3. **Read John 15:13-15 again and answer these questions.**
   Based on verse 13, what demonstrates the supreme love of a friend?

   _____

   _____

   What does Jesus expect of His friends? (v. 14) _____

   What is the difference between a servant and a friend? (v. 15)

   _____

   _____

Giving one's life for a friend is the ultimate expression of love. That is what Jesus did for His friends—and for us! Jesus expected obedience from His friends. When Jesus moved from a master-slave relationship with His disciples to a Friend-friend relationship, He revealed to them the will and heart of His Father.

4. Based on this passage, how would you rate your Friend-friend relationship with Christ? Check one or write in your own.

❏ I don't think I meet the criteria to be a friend of Christ.

❏ Sometimes I sense intimacy with Christ, and He reveals the Father's will to me. But at other times I seem distanced from the relationship.

❏ Right now I feel a deep closeness to Christ. I could almost say I would be willing to die for Him if need be.

❏ Other: _____

Within the intimate circle of the 12 disciples, Jesus developed an even closer bond with Simon Peter, James, and John. These men sometimes were allowed to witness private works (see Mark 5:37). Jesus took them to the Mount of Transfiguration (Mark 9:2), and allowed them to gain a glimpse of divine glory. Jesus also took them with Him into the inner recesses of His Gethsemane prayers (see Mark 14:33). In view of the extraordinary labor of His prayers there, Jesus expected them to watch, that is, to enter into His own work of prayer (see Mark 14:34).

John called himself the disciple whom Jesus loved. Jesus singled out Simon in His prayer in which He announced that Satan had asked permission to sift the disciples as wheat (see Luke 22:31-32). Later the angel had special instructions to inform Peter about the resurrection (see Mark 16:7), probably because Peter had denied the Lord.

Jesus made special provisions for His friends. Jesus' friendships lasted; His friends felt tremendous loyalty to Him; and Jesus' cared for the needs of His friends.

5. Conclude today's lesson by spending some time with your holy Friend—Christ Jesus. Follow the example of the disciples who were with Him. Consider taking a walk outside with your Friend. Express to Him your gratitude for His friendship. Walk and talk with Him. Share with your Friend your joys and concerns. Respond to His love. Ask Jesus to guide you in cultivating friendships with those around you.

DAY 5
JESUS' SPEECH

1. Begin today's lesson by reading the Bible verses and the name of Christ for today. Work on your memory verse. Then use the suggested prayer to begin your study.

2. Read again 1 Peter 2:22-24. Underline three things these verses tell you about Jesus' speech.

Peter tells us that there was no "guile [or deceit] found in His mouth" (v. 22). "When he was reviled" (reproached, verbally abused), Jesus did not retaliate with words. "When he suffered," He did not lash back with threatening words. Jesus demonstrated perfect temperance and self-control in His speech.

Much of Jesus' speech was in teaching and preaching. He was the Master Teacher, and He went about "all the cities and the villages, teaching in their synagogues" (Matt. 9:35). Some of His teaching was conceptual, as in the Sermon on the Mount. Frequently Jesus also taught by parables (see Mark 4:2). The precepts were concerned with the spiritual nature of the Kingdom of God, and were so radically different from the legalism of the day that often the crowds were amazed (see Mark 6:2).

3. What is one way Jesus used His speech? He _____

Jesus' commission to ministry was to preach (see Luke 4:18). He went about "preaching the gospel of the kingdom" (Matt. 9:35). Teaching instructs; preaching is intended to convince. John the Baptist had been a proclaimer. Jesus regarded John the Baptist's work as a specific preparation for His own work, and He continued that work of proclamation. Jesus placed high value on preaching. Later Jesus said that His gospel would be preached in the whole world (see Matt. 24:14).

4. What is a second way Jesus used His speech? He _____

Listed below are other ways Jesus used His speech.

- Jesus showed phenomenal skill in the use of questions as a teaching device.
- Sometimes Jesus warned people about coming difficulties or temptations.
- Jesus usually answered the questions that were asked Him. He did not, however, answer the demand of the Pharisees for a sign.
- Jesus answered the accusation with great logic that He cast out demons by Beelzebub (Matt. 12:24-29).
- At times Jesus severely reproached unresponsive people and cities.
- Jesus even reproached His disciples for their lack of faith.
- Jesus denounced the hypocrisy of the Pharisees.
- On a few rare occasions Jesus paid compliments to people for faith or faithfulness.
- The Lord frequently gave reassurances not to be afraid.

Jesus' use of words was economical but not timid. They were always appropriate and timed perfectly. If encouragement were necessary, Jesus spoke as the occasion demanded. Jesus' words were sharp and to the point. He said, "I say to you, that every careless word that men shall speak, they shall render account for it in the day of judgment" (Matt. 12:36, NASB).

5. How important is it for you to be careful about the way you speak? Check one.

❏ Not very important. I'm forgiven. What I do now doesn't really matter.

❏ Very important. God is keeping track of my every careless word, and I will have to give Him an explanation on the day of judgment.

Having the mind of Christ, we are to be careful and appropriate in our use of words.

6. Turn to page 239 and review the Lifelong Help on Temperance.

7. Close today's session by talking to the Lord. Confess any careless or inappropriate words you recently used that come to mind. Ask God to strengthen you with a Christ-controlled tongue that never dishonors Him.

Having the mind of Christ, we are to be careful and appropriate in our use of words.

GROUP SESSION 9

JESUS' RELATIONS

SESSION GOALS

This session will help you understand Jesus' teachings on materialism and the ways He related to people. You will demonstrate determination to lay up treasures in heaven and to live like Christ in your relationship to people.

Hearing What the Spirit Is Saying (as you arrive)

1. (Individuals) Review what God has been saying to you during the study of unit 9.
   - Identify a Scripture and a name of Christ that have been meaningful this week.
   - Identify and mark the issue or subject in which God seems to be working most actively to develop the mind of Christ. (These will be shared later in the session.)
2. (Individuals) Write out any questions related to this unit you would like answered.

Magnifying the Lord and Exalting His Name (5 minutes)

1. (Volunteer) Open the session in prayer by asking God to reveal every relationship to people or things that does not reflect a Christlike quality.
2. Pray as you feel led to worship God for Who He is and acknowledge Him for what He has done. Use the names of Christ to exalt His name together in prayer.
3. After prayer, share ways God revealed Himself to you this week through His names. Which name of Christ has been most meaningful to you and why?

Transforming by the Word (15 minutes)

1. (Pairs) Pair up and quote this week's memory verse, Matthew 6:20-21. Then, as time permits, alternate quoting verses from previous units. Use your Scripture memory cards as a reference.
2. Share what God said to you through this week's memory verse or other Scripture that has been meaningful.
3. (Quads—or two groups) Distribute poster board or newsprint and markers to each of two groups. Make two lists related to characteristics of a Christlike mind. Focus on this unit's Scriptures only.
   - Group 1: Make a list of things, actions, or attitudes identified or implied in Scriptures during this unit that need to be cleansed from one's mind and life.
   - Group 2: Make a list of things, actions, or attitudes identified or implied in Scriptures during this unit that need to be incorporated into one's mind and life.
   - For example: We do not need to *worry over food and clothes* (group 1); we do need to *seek the Kingdom above all else* (group 2) (see Matt. 6:30-33).
4. Call on quads to read and comment on their lists. Place one on the Transformed From Wall and the other on the Transformed To Wall.
5. (Volunteer) Pray that God will cleanse members of our group and church.

Stimulating One Another to Love and Good Deeds (20 minutes)

1. Share testimonies of what God has done this week in your life that has been meaningful, challenging, or instructive.
2. State questions or concerns you have written for consideration. As time permits, seek to answer the questions as a group.
3. Turn to page 133. Ask volunteers to share their response to the second activity. Was there anything in the activity on pages 133-134 that God has indicated you must get rid of? What? Have you obeyed Him?
4. Now turn to page 134 and share their responses, if any, to the last activity.

6. Turn to page 139 and share their responses to the activity which rated your Friend-friend relationship with Christ.

7. As time permits, discuss one or more of the following questions:
   - If greed is idolatry, how does God view the way many Christians love the world and the things of the world?
   - What are some ways God has been your Provider? (see pp. 160-62).
   - What can you do to be more single-minded rather than double-minded?
   - How does the way a person treats other people reflect or fail to reflect the mind of Christ?

Preparing the Bride for Her Bridegroom (5 minutes)

1. Read Revelation 2:1-18. Listen for ways the bride (church) may need to repent and return to Christ. List them in the margin.

2. As time permits, discuss these questions:
   - What in these messages of Christ to His churches applies to our church?
   - How can our church repent and return in these areas?
   - What cleansing, purifying, or preparation is needed in our church?
   - How can we apply this Scripture to our lives, families, and church?

3. Call on one member to pray aloud for your church to continue to prepare for the Lord's return.

Praying for One Another (10 minutes)

1. (Quads, preferably same gender) Read James 5:16 from your session segment poster and Share personal, family, church, or work-related prayer requests that primarily focus on developing the mind of Christ or purifying the bride.

2. (Quads) Pray specifically for one another for forgiveness, healing, encouragement, guidance, wisdom, knowledge, understanding, courage, strength, faithfulness, or for specific requests.

Closing the Session (5 minutes)

1. Share questions or concerns that came up during the session that we should remember in prayer.

2. Preview unit 10 on the following pages. Encourage each group member to pay special attention to his or her relationship to the Father and Holy Spirit.

3. Close by praying that God will teach and enable members to live in the fullness of the Spirit.

UNIT TEN

LIVING IN THE SPIRIT

Hymn Part 4
CHRIST'S HUMANITY
"[Jesus] was made in the likeness of men:
and ... found in fashion as a man"
(Phil. 2:7-8).

DAY 1
The Spiritual Controls the Material

DAY 2
Christ's Statements of Purpose

DAY 3
Christ and the Father

DAY 4
Christ and the Holy Spirit

DAY 5
Christ, the Scriptures, and Prayer

Why You Will Find This Unit Helpful
You will understand how Christ lived in the Spirit while He lived in the material world. As you study the example of Christ, you will learn ways to give greater control to the spiritual dimensions of life. You will be able to identify with Christ and follow His example in your relationship to the Father and Holy Spirit.

Lifelong Goal
In Christ you will seek to live a proper relationship to the Father and the Holy Spirit. You will continue to emphasize the spiritual over the material.

Summary of God's Work in You

Christ's spirituality in you begins in a mind-set that is first spiritual and second material. God's goal is that you have spiritual perception in order that He may guide you. Your growth in Christ can be measured only by Christ's dependence on the Holy Spirit. God directs your outer life through His inner Spirit.

Unit Learning Goals

- You will understand that the spiritual is more important than the material.
- You will demonstrate determination to emphasize the spiritual over the material.
- You will understand the source and nature of Jesus' purposes for His life and ministry.
- You will demonstrate your desire to know and do the will of your heavenly Father.
- You will understand the ways Jesus related to the Father and how you should relate to the heavenly Father.
- You will understand the ways Christ and the Holy Spirit are related and ways that you should relate to the Holy Spirit.
- You will understand the ways Jesus used the Scripture and the ways He practiced prayer.

What You Will Do to Begin Living in the Spirit

- You will study and seek to imitate the examples of Jesus.
- You will examine the Scriptures that speak clearly about your relationship to the Father and Holy Spirit.
- You will spend time meditating on the Scriptures and praying so God can conform your mind to reflect the image of His Son Jesus.

Scripture Memory Verse

"It is the spirit that quickeneth; the flesh profiteth nothing: the words that I speak unto you, they are spirit, and they are life" (John 6:63).

Lifelong Helps Related to This Unit

Your Relationship with Your Heavenly Father and the Holy Spirit (pp. 251-52)

The Mind of Christ Cards Related to This Unit

5A. Unit 10: Scripture Memory—John 6:63

DAY 1
THE SPIRITUAL CONTROLS THE MATERIAL

Today's Bible Meditation
" 'The first man, Adam, became a living soul.' The last Adam became a life-giving spirit. However, the spiritual is not first, but the natural; then the spiritual. The first man is from the earth, earthy; the second man is from heaven. As is the earthy, so also are those who are earthy; and as is the heavenly, so also are those who are heavenly. And just as we have borne the image of the earthy, we shall also bear the image of the heavenly"
(1 Cor. 15:45-49, NASB).

Name of Christ for Today
A Lamb without Blemish and without Spot
(1 Pet. 1:19)

Prayer to Begin the Lesson
Lord Jesus, I long to bear Your image more clearly. The worldly and the material have such a strong influence in my life. Teach me today to give priority to the spiritual like You do. Cleanse me from the contamination of the world and make me without blemish and spot. Amen.

1. Begin today's lesson by reading the Bible verses and the name of Christ for today. Work on your memory verse. Then use the suggested prayer on the left to begin your study.

The Spiritual Over the Material
The material world dominated my life at one time. I was told that I could be rich and successful in the career I had chosen. In 1956 I sought material success. That was my purpose. That period lasted three years. During that time, I was quite active in church and outwardly seemed to be serving the Lord. Inwardly my purposes were not God's purposes. The spiritual was subordinate.

2. Have you ever focused your attention on the material world to achieve success? ❏ Yes ❏ No
to become wealthy? ❏ Yes ❏ No
to experience pleasure? ❏ Yes ❏ No

3. If you answered yes, briefly describe your experience of focusing on the material world.

_____

_____

_____

_____

In 1959 one of my students gave me a German Bible. I happen to love languages and was delighted for the opportunity to practice my German. However, I wasn't excited about it being the Bible. Early one morning I began reading that Bible in the first chapter of John. I scarcely expected the exhilaration I encountered in the opening verses. Somehow, the old familiar concepts had an electrifying newness about them. The Word was in the beginning—and He was God!

I almost lost my breath on verse 4: "In Him was life." He has life in Himself; He is Self-existent! As I read with excitement, the most stimulating verse was John 1:14: "The Word was made flesh, and dwelt among us." The spiritual invaded the material! This miracle of God becoming a man overwhelmed me with great joy. God was using my love for languages to capture my attention! Day after day I pursued the story of Jesus with energizing intensity. The attraction of my material success began to fade as the majesty of the person of Christ increasingly overwhelmed me.

I decided to read the entire Bible in a modern translation. When I read about God's encounter with Moses at the burning bush (see Ex. 3), I had my own "burning bush" experience. Through His Word, God revealed Himself to me. A spiritual Being broke through the wall of materialism that I had built around my life. The spiritual is stronger than the material! I felt tremendous awe in the holiness

I experienced at my "burning bush" that morning. Spiritual glory is noble. In the early hours of that November day in 1959, I chose the spiritual glory of the Lord Jesus for my life. I forever rejected the glory of the material.

God showed me that I had made my career my god. Like the rich young ruler who treasured his possessions, I had to put away the false god of career. I had to leave that career. Since that time, I have chosen to make Christ's purposes my purposes. I never have regretted that decision!

4. **If God were to evaluate your life right now, how do you think He would rank your life on the following scales? Circle the number on the scale between the two extremes.**

| Focused on the Material World | 1 2 3 4 5 6 7 8 9 10 | Focused on the Spiritual World |

| Focused on My Purposes | 1 2 3 4 5 6 7 8 9 10 | Focused on Christ's Purposes |

Often many of us are focused on the material world in which we live. We have to be aware of it in order to make a living. The world places many demands on us to dress a certain way, make a certain impression, love certain things, and associate with certain people. Jesus said of the scribes and Pharisees: "Ye are of this world; I am not of this world" (John 8:23). The world system is one of controls with which Satan manipulates the people of the world for his desired ends. When you focus on your purposes rather than Christ's purposes, you are of this world.

We have seen that one of God's purposes in coming to earth was to show us how to live a truly human life—human as God intended it. That is the reason God became flesh. That is why you are seeking to imitate the perfect humanity seen in the life of Jesus. The most important of all aspects of humanity is the spiritual nature of humans as God intended. Jesus gave us the example of what that kind of life is like.

Jesus Emphasized the Spiritual Over the Material

Jesus had nothing to do with this world system. He told the Jews, "I am not of this world" (John 8:23). The disciples heard Jesus say, "The ruler of the world is coming, and he has nothing in Me" (John 14:30, NASB). He told Pilate, "My kingdom is not of this world" (John 18:36, NASB). Jesus trained His disciples so well that at the end of His time on earth He said of them, "They are not of the world, even as I am not of the world" (John 17:16, NASB). The world is against God's spiritual purposes.

5. **As Christ's disciple, which of the following should you be? Check one.**

❏ a. I am to live like the world with a focus on the material.

❏ b. I am to live like Christ with a focus on the spiritual.

Jesus lived His life perfectly in the spiritual realm. His work was done knowing that the spiritual has control over the material.

Jesus lived His life perfectly in the spiritual realm. His work was done knowing that the spiritual has control over the material. The material obeys the spiritual. Jesus' inner being radiated a power that affected everyone and everything He came close to. Jesus was able to call on and use spiritual forces. When He stilled the storm, the spiritual had control over the physical (see Mark 4:36-41). In the feeding of the five thousand, spiritual energies acted upon physical material. Disease and all kinds of physical infirmities yielded to the word of Jesus. Wherever Jesus went, the material world was touched and changed by the spiritual.

Jesus never said or implied that matter is evil. He enjoyed aspects of the material world. He blessed material human life. But Jesus subjected the material world to the spiritual world.

**The goodness of the material is at its best
when it serves spiritual purposes.**

6. Which is more important?   ❑ the spiritual   ❑ the material

7. Which controls the other? The _____ controls the

_____ .

Jesus emphasized the spiritual over the material and showed that the spiritual controls the material. Most important of all is the influence of the spirit over our relationships with God and with others. That influence touches all persons, for better or worse. We speak of a *spirit of anger* or a *spirit of love*. Jesus was sensitive to the spirits of people by responding more to their spirits than to their words or actions.

Expressing the Importance of the Spiritual

We who want the mind of Christ must be willing to express in tangible ways our conviction that the spiritual is greater than the material. The following illustrate ways a person can do that.

• Going without sleep or some other normal human activity can provide you extra time to accomplish spiritual aims. I have gone without sleep in order to accomplish spiritual aims. Usually this has been to pray all night. Jesus did that. Some of the most significant miracles I have seen have been in answer to a night of prayer.

• Fasting (denying food to your body for a period of time) says, "My body is subject to my spirit." Fasting forgoes eating in order to give you time for spiritual concerns like praying.

• Giving can demonstrate the value you place on the spiritual over the material. Providing financially or materially for spiritual concerns may be helpful in gaining victory over a materialistic spirit. If your love for things is great, giving things away for spiritual purposes will help. "Lay up for yourselves treasures in heaven" (Matt. 6:20).

Our works, however, should be done like Jesus' works were done—with intelligence and balance. We must never pervert the spiritual by causing damage to the material. Only godly wisdom can help us know how to do that.

8. Ask God to help you identify areas where the material may have too much importance or influence in your life. Are any of the following areas too important? Which ones? Check all that apply. If you know of others write them on the blank line.

❏ career/work   ❏ cars   ❏ clothes
❏ collections   ❏ eating   ❏ furniture
❏ hobbies   ❏ house   ❏ investments
❏ money   ❏ recreation   ❏ sports
❏ television   ❏ others: _____

9. Ask the Lord to guide you to victory over the areas you checked above. Do the following:

- Set your mind on things above—the spiritual.
- Allow God to renew your mind with a Christlike mind-set.
- Deny yourself and the importance of the material.
- Follow Christ in giving priority and emphasis to the spiritual.
- Ask God to help you emphasize the spiritual in practical ways.
- Write notes to yourself about the things you sense God is guiding you to do.

10. Conclude today's lesson with this prayer:

Father, I want to see life as You see it, as Jesus sees it. Give me spiritual perception. Then give me through Your Spirit the spiritual energy to follow and do all You want me to follow and do. Jesus showed me how, and gave me His name to offer You. So accept His gift to me—the name of Jesus—as Your authorization to answer this prayer. Amen.

DAY 2
CHRIST'S STATEMENTS OF PURPOSE

1. Begin today's lesson by reading the Bible verses and the name of Christ for today (in the margin on pp. 176-77). Work on your memory verse. Then use the suggested prayer on page 176 to begin your study.

During Jesus' ministry, He made several statements that indicated His purpose. None of these come from the world. Neither do they indicate a preoccupation with personal advancement, wealth, or earthly power.

Jesus' entire motivation was to advance those causes which cannot be measured physically or materially. These causes can be perceived only by people who are spiritually sensitive.

Today's Bible Meditations
"I came down from heaven, not to do mine own will, but the will of him that sent me" (John 6:38).

"As my Father hath sent me, even so send I you" (John 20:21).

Name of Christ for Today
The Power of God
(1 Cor. 1:24)

**Prayer to Begin
the Lesson**
Heavenly Father, You have placed Your Son in me. He is the Power of God. You have also given me the calling to follow in His steps by living my life with a purpose that reflects His purposes for life and ministry. Please grant me the wisdom to know Your purposes for my life and ministry and then work through me to accomplish them in Your power. Amen.

2. **Read the following purpose statements of Jesus and underline words or phrases that indicate what Jesus saw as His purposes for life and ministry.**

Purpose Statements of Jesus

- Isaiah 61:1-2—"The Spirit of the Lord is upon Me, because He anointed Me to preach the gospel to the poor. He has sent Me to proclaim release to the captives, and recovery of sight to the blind, to set free those who are downtrodden, to proclaim the favorable year of the Lord" (NASB).
- "My meat is to do the will of him that sent me, and to finish his work" (John 4:34).
- "I came down from heaven, not to do mine own will, but the will of him that sent me" (John 6:38).
- "I must preach the kingdom of God to other cities also: for therefore am I sent" (Luke 4:43).
- "The Son of man is come to seek and to save that which was lost" (Luke 19:10).
- "To this end was I born, and for this cause came I into the world, that I should bear witness unto the truth." (John 18:37).

3. **Jesus used statements like "The Spirit of the Lord . . . anointed Me," "him that sent me," and "I came down from heaven" to describe the source of His purposes. Check the source of Jesus' purposes.**

❏ **the world and worldly concerns**   ❏ **God and spiritual concerns**

Jesus described His purposes as coming from heaven and from the One who sent Him. Jesus' purposes did not come from the world system. They began with God Himself. These purpose statements help us understand the following:

1. The Spirit's anointing begins with the preaching of good news to the poor. For Jesus, the good news had to do with His advent and work. Jesus preached that in His coming, the kingdom had come.

2. The poor welcomed Jesus, while the high-ranking and the powerful did not. The authorities did not perceive that they needed good news, other than the loosing of the Roman yoke. The poor needed immediate good news, and Jesus brought it. The miserable of the earth were the ones who responded quickly to Jesus. Jesus' way is the opposite of the world's way. Our flesh prefers to cater to the rich and influential. Recognizing God's heart for the poor is profoundly spiritual. Jesus is concerned with the poor, the prisoners, the blind, and the oppressed.

3. Jesus' occupation with the will of His Father indicates Jesus' great concentration on the spiritual.

4. Jesus decided to leave the crowds in Capernaum. His first intention was to fulfill the Father's purpose in sending Him. Jesus also wanted to cover the main geographical sections of Israel with a spiritual message, leaving sparks to ignite the future church.

5. God sees people as they relate to Him. They are lost or saved. In reflecting the mind of God, Jesus is showing us the concerns of a spiritual mind. Jesus came to seek and save the lost.

6. Jesus said, "My kingdom is not of this world" (John 18:36). He indicated a profound preoccupation with the spiritual nature of things. In the intangible world of the spirit, truth alone reigns supreme.

4. John 20:21 says, "As the Father hath sent me, even so send I you." Since these are the purposes of Jesus and you have been sent as He was sent, what do you think God would want your purposes to be regarding the following?

poor, needy, and oppressed people _____

_____

the will of the Father _____

_____

carrying the good news to people in other geographic areas_____

_____

lost people_____

_____

the truth _____

_____

5. Conclude today's lesson by spending time talking to your Heavenly Father about the purposes He has for your life. Ask Him how those purposes might be fulfilled in your family, neighborhood, church, and workplace.

DAY 3
CHRIST AND THE FATHER

Today's Bible Meditation
"Behold, what manner of love the Father hath bestowed upon us, that we should be called the sons of God" (1 John 3:1).

Name of Christ for Today
Son of the Most High God (Mark 5:7)

Prayer to Begin the Lesson
Heavenly Father, You have indeed shown me great love by adopting me into Your family. I have never known love like this before. Thank You for sending Your Son Jesus as the sacrifice for my sins. Father, I want to move into a deeper and more personal love relationship with You. Teach me today how I can respond to You in a proper relationship. I ask this in Jesus' name. Amen.

1. Begin today's lesson by reading the Bible verse and the name of Christ for today. Work on your memory verse. Then use the suggested prayer on the left to begin your study.

Jesus not only established an identification with humans, He also identified with His Father. Just as Jesus identified with His Father, we identify with Jesus. Therefore we need to know Jesus' particular points of identification with His Father.

Jesus' work identified Himself with His Father. Jesus said, "Truly, truly, I say to you, the Son can do nothing of Himself, unless it is something He sees the Father doing; for whatever the Father does, these things the Son also does in like manner" (John 5:19, NASB). Jesus told the Jews, "I do nothing on My own initiative, but I speak these things as the Father taught Me . . . I always do the things that are pleasing to Him" (John 8:28-29, NASB). Jesus placed His work in opposition to that of the Jews: "I speak the things which I have seen with My Father; therefore you also do the things which you heard from your father" (John 8:38, NASB). The Father's work was Jesus' work.

2. What was one way Jesus identified with His Father? _____

3. Which of the following best describes one way you should relate to the Heavenly Father? Check one.

❑ I should watch to see what the Father is doing. When He chooses to show me what He is doing, I should become involved in His work. The Father's work should be my work.

❑ I should dream up what I want to do for my Father and then ask Him to assist me in doing it. He should adjust His work to what I want to do for Him.

The Father does not give us permission to set our own agendas. He does not adjust to us. God is the one working, and He invites us to become involved in His work.

Jesus' words also identified Himself with His Father. Jesus claimed, "I did not speak on My own initiative, but the Father Himself who sent Me has given Me commandment, what to say, and what to speak . . . therefore the things I speak, I speak just as the Father has told Me" (John 12:49-50, NASB). He also said, "The words that I say to you I do not speak on My own initiative, but the Father abiding in Me does His works" (John 14:10, NASB).

Jesus claimed that the Father's possessions were also His own. At the return of the seventy, Jesus told them, "All things have been handed over to Me by My Father" (Luke 10:22, NASB). Jesus prayed, "All things that are Mine are Thine, and Thine are Mine" (John 17:10, NASB). The Father could not have something that was not Christ's at the same time.

4. **What are two more ways Jesus identified with His Father? Jesus identified with His Father in His work,**

_____, and _____.

Christ is One with the Father in substance. Jesus claimed, "I and my Father are one" (John 10:30). Later He told Philip, "He that hath seen me hath seen the Father. . . . Believest thou not that I am in the Father, and the Father in me?" (John 14:9-10).

Jesus is One with the Father in unity. Jesus prayed for perfect unity among the disciples, just as He and the Father were One (see John 17:11, 22). We cannot identify with Christ in His divine substance, but in identifying with Jesus as human, we are one with one another and with Him. Jesus' identity with the Father, like His identity with man, is complete.

5. **Circle one of the items below in which you can identify with Christ and the Father.**

_____   Substance   Unity

The major point at which you cannot identify with Christ is in His divine substance. You can identify with Christ in the unity He expresses with the Father and His followers. Jesus' pattern of identification with His Father gives us a pattern for identifying with Him.

- We can identify with Him in His works—always reaching to the poor, the hurting, the needy.
- We can identify with His words—our words should be simple and direct (see Matt. 5:37), gracious (see Col. 4:6), purposeful (see Matt. 12:36), and exemplary (see 1 Tim. 4:12).
- We can identify with His possessions. Even Christ's possessions are ours, for we are joint-heirs with Him (see Rom. 8:17).
- We are in unity with Him (see John 17:21-23).

6. **Turn to pages 251-52 in the Lifelong Helps and complete the activity related to "Your Relationship with Your Heavenly Father." Close your study today with this activity and a time of prayer with the Heavenly Father.**

DAY 4
CHRIST AND THE HOLY SPIRIT

Today's Bible Meditation
"Be not drunk with wine, wherein is excess; but be filled with the Spirit" (Eph. 5:18).

Name of Christ for Today
Mediator of a New Testament (Heb. 9:15)

Prayer to Begin the Lesson
Jesus, my Lord, I am thankful that You did not leave us without another Comforter—the Holy Spirit. I realize, however, that I have probably never experienced the fullness of Your Spirit the way You have intended. I want to be filled with the Spirit and walk in the Spirit. Amen.

1. **Begin today's lesson by reading the Bible verse and the name of Christ for today. Work on your memory verse. Then use the suggested prayer to begin your study.**

Throughout His life and ministry, Jesus had a close relationship with the Holy Spirit. Before His birth, Jesus' mother was "found to be with child by the Holy Spirit" (Matt. 1:18, NASB). The work of the Spirit is indicated in Jesus' advanced insight and understanding at the temple at age 12. Mark describes the scene at His baptism: "Coming up out of the water, he saw the heavens opened, and the Spirit like a dove descending upon him" (Mark 1:10).

Jesus was "led up of the spirit" (Matt. 4:1) and "full of the Holy Spirit" (Luke 4:1, NASB) as He approached the temptation experience. His response to the temptations tells us that the Spirit was predominant in His mind. The Spirit had control over His mind as Jesus went through the experience. Then "Jesus returned in the power of the Spirit into Galilee" (Luke 4:14).

Jesus began His Galilean ministry by announcing: "The Spirit of the Lord is upon me" (Luke 4:18). This led to the mightiest spiritual work in the history of the world. Jesus' work was done through the Holy Spirit. Jesus expressly said, "I cast out devils by the Spirit of God" (Matt. 12:28). Jesus' life fulfilled the prophecy, "The Spirit of the Lord will rest on Him, the spirit of wisdom and understanding, the spirit of counsel and strength, the spirit of knowledge and the fear of the Lord" (Isa. 11:2, NASB).

Jesus had a special jealousy for the Spirit, and strongly forbade blaspheming the Holy Spirit (see Matt. 12:31-32). He had the highest regard for the Spirit, depended on the Spirit, and followed the Spirit closely throughout His life. This is the mind of Christ.

2. **In the list below are ways Jesus related to the Holy Spirit during His earthly life and ministry. Check all that apply.**

❑ Anointed by the Spirit   ❑ Ignored the Spirit
❑ Blasphemed the Spirit   ❑ Jealous for the Spirit
❑ Controlled by the Spirit   ❑ Led by the Spirit
❑ Depended on the Spirit   ❑ Quenched the Spirit
❑ Filled with the Spirit   ❑ Experienced the power of the Spirit
❑ Followed the Spirit   ❑ Resisted the leadership of the Spirit
❑ Grieved the Spirit

3. **Turn to pages 252 in the Lifelong Helps and complete the activity related to "Your Relationship with the Holy Spirit." Close your study today with this activity and a time of prayer seeking to rightly relate to the Holy Spirit. If time permits, review the Scriptures you read yesterday about your relationship to the Heavenly Father.**

DAY 5
CHRIST, THE SCRIPTURES, AND PRAYER

1. **Begin today's lesson by reading the Bible verse and the name of Christ for today. Work on your memory verse. Then use the suggested prayer to begin your study.**

Jesus' Use of Scripture

Jesus showed a remarkable familiarity with the Old Testament. During His ministry, Jesus quoted from 16 Old Testament books and referred to others. The Scriptures were clearly a vital part of His life and ministry. Jesus used the Scriptures in the following ways:

- Jesus frequently demonstrated a knowledge of Old Testament events, like His reference to David's eating consecrated bread (see Matt. 12:3-4, from 1 Sam. 21:3-6).
- Scripture sprang spontaneously from Jesus' lips. When He began His ministry by going to the desert, Satan tempted Him. He answered each of the temptations with commandments from Deuteronomy (see Matt. 4:4, from Deut. 8:3; Matt. 4:7, from Deut. 6:16; and Matt. 4:10, from Deut. 6:13).
- Jesus used Scripture to answer criticism. When the Pharisees asked Jesus' disciples why He ate with sinners, Jesus quoted Hosea 6:6, "I desire compassion, and not sacrifice" (Matt. 9:13, NASB).
- Scripture was the precise basis for Jesus' actions. To justify what He did, Jesus would quote Scripture. When Jesus cleansed the temple (see Mark 11:17) He used the term *house of prayer* from Isaiah 56:7, and accused the people of making it a den of robbers, as Jeremiah had stated (see Jer. 7:11).
- In His parables, Jesus drew freely from phrases used in the Old Testament. The parable of the vine-growers tending the vineyard derives from Isaiah 5:2.
- Christ used the Scriptures as a witness to Himself. When John the Baptist's disciples came inquiring about Jesus' role, He sent them back quoting Isaiah 35:5-6 (see Luke 7:22). In Caiaphas' court Jesus answered the question whether He was "the Christ, the Son of the Blessed One" with Scripture drawn from Psalm 110:1 and Daniel 7:13: "I am; and you shall see the Son of Man sitting at the right hand of Power, and coming with the clouds of heaven" (Mark 14:62, NASB).
- Jesus used Scripture to point to end times. In His explanation of the parable of the weeds (or tares), Jesus drew from Daniel 12:3 about the righteous who will shine in the kingdom of their Father (see Matt. 13:43).

2. **Without looking back, see if you can describe in your own words at least three ways Jesus used the Scriptures.**

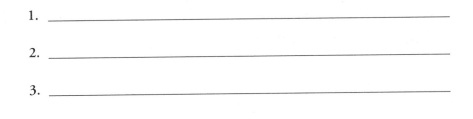

1. _____

2. _____

3. _____

Today's Bible Meditation
"They said one to another, Did not our heart burn within us, while he talked with us by the way, and while he opened to us the scriptures?" (Luke 24:32).

Name of Christ for Today
The Word of God
(Rev. 19:13)

Prayer to Begin the Lesson
Word of God, stir my heart by opening to me the Scriptures as You did to the disciples on the road. I long to know more about You and what You have to say to me through Your Word. Open my mind and give me understanding. Teach me how to relate to Your Word and pray in ways that will please You. Amen.

Jesus was especially concerned that His disciples understood Scripture. After the resurrection, Jesus reproved the two on the Emmaus road because they were "slow of heart to believe in all that the prophets have spoken" (Luke 24:25, NASB). Jesus then explained the Scriptures to them (v. 27).

The spiritual mind finds great light in the Scripture.

Jesus demonstrated that the spiritual mind finds great light in the Scripture. He said that "the Scripture cannot be broken" (John 10:35, NASB). His strongest affirmation is in the Sermon on the Mount: "Truly I say to you, until heaven and earth pass away, not the smallest letter or stroke shall pass away from the Law, until all is accomplished" (Matt. 5:18, NASB). Jesus revered the Scripture, based His actions on scriptural precedent, justified His actions with it, and even used it to point to the great consummation in His second coming.

Earlier I mentioned the fact that when I began these studies, the Lord led me to read nothing but the Bible for four years. During that time I discovered a technique that proved helpful in understanding the Bible. I memorized a passage and then spent months meditating on it. Most of what I learned comes from meditating on memorized Scriptures. If you want the mind of Christ, you must follow His example in His relation to Scripture.

3. **Pause for a few minutes and meditate on one or two of the Scripture verses you have been memorizing these past weeks. If you prefer, use The Mind of Christ Cards to meditate on Scriptures of your choosing. Ask the Lord to open your mind to understand these Scriptures.**

Jesus' Practice of Prayer

Prayer is a decisive factor in the life of a spiritual person.

Since the spiritual world dominates the material world, prayer is a decisive factor in the life of a spiritual person. Though we have more prayers by David and Paul, the Bible says more about the prayers of Jesus than any other biblical character. Jesus also taught more about prayer than any other person in the Bible. If we are to have the mind of Christ, we must imitate His prayer life.

- Jesus preferred to be alone and in a private place. He must have been tired after a busy day of healing. But "in the early morning, while it was still dark, He arose and went out and departed to a lonely place, and was praying there" (Mark 1:35, NASB). Hypocrisy cannot enter into private praying. When you choose to pray alone, God knows that it is real.
- Jesus prayed on all sorts of occasions and in groups of varying size.
- Jesus prayed before making important decisions. The entire night before He chose the 12 disciples was spent in prayer.
- Jesus prayed at important events like His baptism and His transfiguration.
- At least four of the miracles were accompanied by prayer.
- Jesus prayed all kinds of prayer except confession of sin. We find Him uttering praise (Matt. 11:25), thanksgiving (Matt. 14:19), petition or personal request (John 17:1-5), and intercession (John 7:6-26).

🖎 4. In your own words, describe the importance of prayer in the life and ministry of Jesus.

_____

_____

_____

_____

_____

The Gethsemane prayers stand in a class by themselves (Matt. 26:36-46). Christ was facing the greatest struggle any human has ever endured. Through the course of His great struggle, not once did Jesus depart from a firm resolution to do God's will (vv. 39, 42, 44). This agony made such an impression on the early Christians that the book of Hebrews also preserves it: "He offered up both prayers and supplications with loud crying and tears to One able to save Him from death, and He was heard because of His piety" (Heb. 5:7, NASB). Even with the mind of Christ, prayer may be a struggle.

🖎 5. Conclude today's study and this unit by practicing prayer. Find a place where you can be alone and talk to the Father. Use the following types of prayer.

- Confession. Seek God's cleansing before rushing into His presence.
- Praise. Offer praise to God for who He is. Praise His name.
- Thanksgiving. Thank God for His bounty. Be specific.
- Petition. Let God guide your asking so you can become like Him.
- Intercession. Join God in His work by praying for others according to His will.

GROUP SESSION 10

LIVING IN THE SPIRIT

SESSION GOALS

This session will help you understand ways you can practice living in the Spirit. You will demonstrate a desire to know and do the will of your Heavenly Father.

Hearing What the Spirit Is Saying (as you arrive)

1. (Individuals) Review what God has been saying to you during the study of unit 10.
   - Identify a Scripture and a name of Christ that have been meaningful this week.
   - Identify and mark the issue or subject in which God seems to be working most actively to develop the mind of Christ. (These will be shared later in the session.)
2. (Individuals) Write out any questions related to this unit you would like answered.

Magnifying the Lord and Exalting His Name (5 minutes)

1. (Volunteer) Open the session in prayer by asking God to fill members with His Holy Spirit and enable them to experience abundant life in Christ.
2. Pray as you feel led to worship God for Who He is and acknowledge Him for what He has done. Use the names of Christ to exalt His name together in prayer.
3. After prayer, share ways God revealed Himself to you this week through His names. Which name of Christ has been most meaningful to you and why?

Transforming by the Word (15 minutes)

1. (Pairs) Pair up and quote this week's memory verse, John 6:63. Then, as time permits, alternate quoting verses from previous units. Use your Scripture memory cards as a reference.
2. Share what God said to you through this week's memory verse or other Scripture that has been meaningful.
3. (Quads—or two groups) Distribute poster board or newsprint and markers to each of two groups. Make two lists related to characteristics of a Christlike mind. Focus on this unit's Scriptures only.
   - Group 1: Make a list of things, actions, or attitudes identified or implied in Scriptures during this unit that need to be cleansed from one's mind and life.
   - Group 2: Make a list of things, actions, or attitudes identified or implied in Scriptures during this unit that need to be incorporated into one's mind and life.
   - For example: We need to eliminate *being drunk with wine* (group 1) and add *being filled with the Spirit* (group 2) (see Eph. 5:18).
4. Call on quads to read and comment on their lists. Place one on the Transformed From Wall and the other on the Transformed To Wall.
5. (Volunteer) Pray that God will cleanse members of your group and church.

Stimulating One Another to Love and Good Deeds (20 minutes)

1. Read Hebrews 10:24 from your session segment poster.
2. Share testimonies of what God has done this week in your life that has been meaningful, challenging, or instructive.
3. State questions or concerns you have written for consideration. As time permits, seek to answer the questions as a group.
4. Turn to page 172. Ask volunteers to share their responses to activities 2 and 3.
5. As time permits, discuss one or more of the following questions:

- What are some of the differences in living in the ways of the world and living in the Spirit?
- What are some areas of your life where God has revealed that the material world has too much influence in your life and decision making?
- If you were to write a purpose statement for your life, what would it say? How well does it blend with or conflict with the purpose statements of Jesus? (See p. 147.)
- What have you learned about life from the ways Jesus related to His Father and the Holy Spirit? How should you relate to the Father and the Spirit?

Preparing the Bride for Her Bridegroom (5 minutes)

1. Read Revelation 2:19-29. Listen for ways the bride (church) may need to repent and return to the Lord. List them in the margin.
2. As time permits, discuss these questions:
   - What in these messages of Christ to His churches applies to our church?
   - What cleansing, purifying, or preparation is needed in our church?
   - How can we apply this Scripture to our lives, families, and church?
3. Call on one member to pray for your church to continue to prepare for the Lord's return.

Praying for One Another (10 minutes)

1. (Quads, preferably same gender) Read James 5:16 from your session segment poster and Share personal, family, church, or work-related prayer requests that primarily focus on developing the mind of Christ or purifying the bride.
2. (Quads) Pray specifically for one another for forgiveness, healing, encouragement, guidance, wisdom, knowledge, understanding, courage, strength, faithfulness, or for specific requests.

Closing the Session (5 minutes)

1. Share questions or concerns that came up during the session that we should remember in prayer.
2. Preview unit 11 on the following pages. If you are planning one or more sessions related to the crucifixion (unit 11) or the resurrection (unit 12) using *The Mind of Christ Worship Video Series*, discuss plans with the group. Identify resources that are available in the church media library that relate to these two events in the life of Christ that members may want to use in conjunction with the next two units.
3. Close by praying that God will clearly reveal the nature of His holiness and love that was demonstrated by Christ on the cross.

Hymn Part 5

CHRIST'S LOVE AND HOLINESS

Jesus "became obedient unto death,
even the death of the cross"
(Phil. 2:8).

᠕ ᠕

DAY 1

Reconciling Holiness and Love

DAY 2

The Character and Behavior of Holiness

DAY 3

Love Is a Verb, Part 1

DAY 4

Love Is a Verb, Part 2

DAY 5

Love As a Noun

Why You Will Find This Unit Helpful

You will understand that Christ exemplifies holiness and love. Christ desires that His disciples be like Him in these qualities. This unit will help you know how to cooperate with the Holy Spirit to be made holy and to practice love out of your inner being.

Lifelong Goal

In Christ you will be set apart from the world as holy. You will demonstrate Christlike love in your relationship to God, His people, and all humanity.

Summary of God's Work in You

Christ's holiness within you enables the spiritual quality of separation from the world. God's goal is your maturity. Your growth in holiness can be measured only by Christ's righteousness. Christ makes this possible in His office as Priest. Christ chose you.

Christ's love in you facilitates the spiritual quality of grace. God's goal is your oneness with Him and His people. Your growth in love can be measured only by Christ's sacrifice. Christ enables your love in His role as Bridegroom. Christ purchased you.

Holiness and love complement and strengthen one another. Christ's example is your goal in holiness and love. Christ brings together these qualities in you in His role as the Wisdom of God. Christ is perfecting you.

Unit Learning Goals

- You will understand the way holiness and love work together.
- You will understand the characteristics and behaviors of holiness.
- You will demonstrate your dedication to the Lord.
- You will know and begin to practice 15 behaviors of Christlike love.
- You will understand two ways you can aid the process of becoming like Christ and having love as a part of your inner being.

What You Will Do to Develop Holiness and Love

- You will examine your separation from the world and take necessary steps to display holiness in relation to the world.
- You will dedicate your body to the Lord to be used only for His purpose.
- You will begin seeking to perform at least 15 actions that demonstrate the Christlike love described in 1 Corinthians 13.
- You will review ways you can practice the principles of yearning and identification with Christ.

Scripture Memory Verses

"As he which hath called you is holy, so be ye holy in all manner of conversation. Because it is written, Be ye holy; for I am holy" (1 Pet. 1:15-16).

Lifelong Helps Related to This Unit

Christlike Virtues—*Love* (pp. 233-34)
Beatitudes—*Hungry* and *Persecuted* (pp. 246, 250)

The Mind of Christ Cards Related to This Unit

5B. Unit 11: Scripture Memory—1 Peter 1:15-16
13. Love Is — 1 Corinthians 13
23. A-4: Hungry
27. B-4: Persecuted

Optional DVD Messages by T. W. Hunt

- Session 5, Part 1: His Holiness and Love
- Session 5, Part 2: His Holiness and Love
- Session 7: The Crucifixion

DAY 1
RECONCILING HOLINESS AND LOVE

Today's Bible Meditation
"[He] became obedient unto death, even the death of the cross" (Phil. 2:8). "Having therefore these promises, dearly beloved, let us cleanse ourselves from all filthiness of the flesh and spirit, perfecting holiness in the fear of God" (2 Cor. 7:1).

Name of Christ for Today
He that Sanctifieth
(Heb. 2:11)

Prayer to Begin the Lesson
Holy Lord, I am not worthy to stand in Your presence. I once again need Your cleansing. Because You are love, I plead for Your mercy and forgiveness. Wash me that I may be clean and spotless before You. You are the One who makes me holy, who sanctifies me. Make me holy as You are holy. Teach me to love as You love. Amen.

1. **Begin today's lesson by reading the Bible verses and the name of Christ for today. Work on your memory verse. Then use the suggested prayer on the left margin to begin your study.**

Following a conference in Ohio, a man asked me a difficult question: "In the Old Testament, God is so terrifyingly holy that He seems distant, but in the New Testament, God is so warm and loving that He seems to be trying to get close to us. Those seem to be opposite pictures. Can those two opposites be reconciled?"

Yes they can. God is infinite and unchanging. Because our human minds cannot comprehend infinity, God reveals to us various aspects of His nature. Sometimes these aspects appear to be opposites. We cannot begin to understand the nature of God without accepting that He can have holiness and love at once.

God's holiness is a wonderful yet dreadful fact. In our sinful human condition, we find His holiness alarming. However, God is love, and "God so loved the world" (John 3:16). God took great pains to reach us with His love. God's love is a fact. Holiness causes us to fear God while His compassion and love draw us close. These attributes exist in the same magnificent Person.

The clearest example of God's holiness and love is what God did at Calvary. Nothing shows us God's holiness like Calvary. Because of sin, nothing less than Christ's shed blood on the cross could satisfy the requirements of God's awesome holiness. Nothing shows us how great God's love is like the sacrifice of Christ. The cross shows us how far God was willing to go to reach us in His infinite love.

2. **What event gives us the clearest picture of God's awesome holiness and His compelling love? Check one.**

   ❑ **Destruction of the world with the flood during Noah's time.**
   ❑ **The birth of Christ at Bethlehem.**
   ❑ **The crucifixion and death of Christ on the cross.**
   ❑ **The giving of the Holy Spirit at Pentecost.**

We risk irreverence and loss of perspective if we do not acknowledge the holiness of God. We miss God if we fail to see the immense love revealed through Jesus Christ. God's holiness and love were demonstrated best in the death of Christ on the cross.

3. **Because Christ's love and holiness are most clearly seen in His crucifixion, we want to give you an assignment to complete during the coming weeks. Your group leader may have announced plans to complete this activity as a large group. If not, consider viewing session 7, "The Crucifixion" from** *The Mind of Christ* **DVD Messages.**

Hymn Part 5: Christ's Holiness and Love

The fifth part of the hymn in Philippians 2 focuses on Christ's holiness and love as they are demonstrated in His sacrificial death on the cross. Jesus "became obedient unto death, even the death of the cross" (Phil. 2:8).

Not only is God holy and loving, but He expects holiness and love from us as well. The mind of Christ will manifest both characteristics.

According as he hath chosen us in him before the foundation of the world, that we should be holy and without blame before him in love (Eph. 1:4).

Put on therefore, as the elect of God, holy and beloved, bowels of mercies, kindness, humbleness of mind, meekness, longsuffering (Col. 3:12).

The Lord make you to increase and abound in love one toward another, and toward all men, even as we do toward you: To the end he may stablish your hearts unblameable in holiness before God, even our Father, at the coming of our Lord Jesus Christ with all his saints (1 Thess. 3:12-13).

Perfecting Holiness in Love

Only in the exemplary life of Jesus Christ do we see a perfect union of these two seemingly opposite attributes, holiness and love. Jesus' inner life was perfectly separated from the world: "I am not of this world" (John 8:23). No worldliness ever was seen in His actions or speech.

But Jesus came to the world to demonstrate perfect love. He became a friend of sinners. The outer members of Jesus' body served an inner purpose—His feet went, His tongue told, His hands healed. Jesus' inner life was separated from worldliness for the outer life to accomplish God's aims in love. The two poles, holiness and love, instead of being contradictory, are necessary to reveal the complete nature of God.

The holiness of God requires justice, yet His love consistently shows mercy and forgiveness. The perfect compounding of justice and mercy are seen in Christ. Holiness and love, which seem to be opposite, actually work together to reinforce each other.

The holiness of God requires justice, yet His love shows mercy and forgiveness.

Holiness will manifest itself in sanctification and righteousness. We derive our principles from holiness. Love cultivates holiness and renders it possible. Love manifests itself in grace and mercy. Holiness modifies love and prevents perversion. The mind of Christ cultivates both poles so that they are developed equally. If one or the other is neglected, perversion develops. Only wisdom can make holiness and love work together in perfect balance. In Christ we are holy. In Christ we are love. We are in a process of perfecting that holiness and love.

4. **Fill in the blanks below with holiness or love. Check your answers in the paragraph above.**

We derive our principles from _____.

_____ cultivates _____ and renders it possible.

_____ _____ modifies _____ and prevents perversion.

5. Which of the words below are related to holiness and which are related to love? Draw a line to match the word on the left with the related words on the right.

a. In the world
b. Separate from the world
HOLINESS
c. Mercy
d. Righteousness
LOVE
e. Sanctification
f. Grace
g. Justice

(Answers: Holiness—b., d., e., g.; Love—a., c., f.)

6. Conclude your study time in prayer for God to continue His work of making you holy as He is holy. Ask Him to enable you to love as He loves.

DAY 2
THE CHARACTER AND BEHAVIOR OF HOLINESS

Today's Bible Meditations
"Seeing then that all these things shall be dissolved, what manner of persons ought ye to be in all holy conversation and godliness, Looking for and hasting unto the coming of the day of God. . . . Be diligent that ye may be found of him in peace, without spot, and blameless"
(2 Pet. 3:11-12,14).

Name of Christ for Today
Holy One of God
(Luke 4:34)

1. Begin today's lesson by reading the Bible verses and the name of Christ for today. Work on your memory verse. Then use the suggested prayer on the following page to begin your study.

Men of the Bible saw God's holiness and reacted to it with terror. God told Moses to take off his shoes in the presence of holiness, and Moses hid his face (see Ex. 3:5-6). When Isaiah saw God's holiness, he cried, "Woe is me, for I am ruined! Because I am a man of unclean lips, and I live among a people of unclean lips" (Isa. 6:5, NASB). When Simon Peter realized the awesome power of Jesus, he pleaded, "Depart from me, for I am a sinful man, O Lord!" (Luke 5:8). When you come into the presence of holy God, your unworthy and sinful condition clearly will be evident.

Character of Holiness
Purity. One of the most striking attributes of holiness is purity: "Depart, depart, go out from there, touch nothing unclean; go out of the midst of her, purify yourselves, you who carry the vessels of the Lord" (Isa. 52:11, NASB). Even Jesus' enemies complimented one aspect of His purity when they said while trying to trap Him with trick questions, "Teacher, we know that . . . You are not partial to any" (Luke 20:21, NASB). How could Jesus be so pure that even His enemies had to acknowledge it? Because of His loving devotion to His Father's way! Purity is a quality of holiness, but Jesus' purity results from love for His Father!

2. What is one characteristic of holiness? _____

3. In your own words define purity.

Godliness. "What sort of people ought you to be in holy conduct and godliness, looking for and hastening the coming of the day of God?" (2 Pet. 3:11-12, NASB). Jesus' godliness can be seen in the reverence of His noble behavior during His trial. As the priests "began to accuse Him harshly" (Mark 15:3, NASB) of many charges, Pilate tried to get Jesus to answer His accusers. "But Jesus made no further answer; so that Pilate was amazed" (Mark 15:5, NASB). This is only one of four magnificent silences in Jesus' trial. The silences were a consequence of His dignity and reverence.

When Jesus did answer, however, His mind was quick; and His answers were appropriate (see Matt. 26:64; Luke 22:67; John 18:20,36; 19:11). Jesus held His tongue when occasion demanded. As other occasions required, Jesus gave immediate and fitting answers. How could He demonstrate such dignity and presence of mind that even a pagan governor was amazed? Throughout His life, including the period of the duress of the trials, Jesus had a loving reverence for His Father. We see dignity, reverence, and godliness in Jesus' trials. Behind them all was unfailing love!

4. What is a second characteristic of holiness? _____

5. In your own words define *godliness*.

_____

Glorious. Holiness is also glorious. Moses asked, "Who is like Thee among the gods, O Lord? Who is like Thee, majestic in holiness, awesome in praises, working wonders?" (Ex. 15:11, NASB). Jesus glorified His Father. At the end of His life, Jesus prayed, "I have glorified Thee on the earth, having accomplished the work which Thou hast given Me to do" (John 17:4, NASB). We already have seen several times that Jesus always sought the glory of His Father. In all that He did, Jesus practiced a loving exaltation of His Father. Once again, in holiness of character we see love behind the scenes, working to produce holiness.

6. What is a third characteristic of holiness? _____

7. Read Psalm 111:1-9 below and circle the words related to holiness and love.

Praise ye the Lord. I will praise the Lord with my whole heart, in the assembly of the upright, and in the congregation. The works of the Lord are great, sought out of all them that have pleasure therein. His work is honourable and glorious: and his righteousness endureth for ever. He hath made his wonderful works to be remembered: the Lord is gracious and full of compassion. He hath given meat unto them that fear him: he will ever be mindful of his covenant. He hath shewed his people the power of his works, that he may give them the heritage of the heathen. The works of his hands are verity and judgment; all his commandments are sure. They stand fast for ever and ever, and are done in truth and uprightness. He sent redemption unto his people: he hath commanded his covenant for ever: holy and reverend is his name.

Prayer to Begin the Lesson

Holy One of God, You will come again and judge the world. You already have told us that the evil world will be destroyed by fire. Since that is true, I want to live my life in holiness, godliness, and purity. I long for Your return, Lord Jesus. Enable me to live an exemplary life until You come. Amen.

Behavior of Holiness

Separate. Holiness not only has a certain character, it maintains a certain behavior. It separates itself from the world. The word holy means set apart. "If a man cleanses himself from these things [ignoble purposes], he will be a vessel for honor, sanctified, useful to the Master, prepared for every good work" (2 Tim. 2:21, NASB).

8. What is one behavior of holiness? _____

Dedicate. Closely related to holiness is dedication. The word *dedicate* means to set something aside for one use only. Solomon dedicated the temple: "Behold, I am about to build a house for the name of the Lord my God, dedicating it to Him" (2 Chron. 2:4). In this verse Solomon states that he is dedicating the temple for burning incense, for setting out the consecrated bread, and for offering sacrifices. Later Isaiah summarized the temple's purpose as a "house of prayer" (Isa. 56:7). The temple was dedicated for one purpose: to relate men to God through prayer. This was why Jesus had to drive the money changers from the temple. The temple had been dedicated to be a house of prayer; but, the priests had made it a den of robbers (see Mark 11:17).

9. What is a second behavior of holiness? _____

Sanctify. A word closely related to *dedication* is *sanctification*. To dedicate is to set apart; to sanctify is to render holy. At salvation we are sanctified; we are holy. The Bible sometimes speaks of sanctification as an event (2 Thess. 2:13; at salvation we become a saint, or *a holy one*), but sometimes as a process also (1 Thess. 4:3). Therefore, we are holy at salvation and we also grow in holiness (2 Cor. 7:1).

10. What is a third behavior of holiness? _____

Jesus prays for our sanctification. In the greatest of all intercessory prayers, Jesus prayed, "For their sakes I sanctify Myself, that they themselves also may be sanctified in truth" (John 17:19). Jesus continues to practice a loving cultivation of our holiness. Because Jesus loves us, He wants us to be holy. Once again, holiness and love cannot be separated.

Because Jesus loves us, He wants us to be holy. Once again, holiness and love cannot be separated.

Several years ago, when I began to realize the enormous action Jesus had taken in sanctifying Himself in order that I might be sanctified, I felt led to dedicate my body to Him. I went into my prayer closet, and dedicated my body parts to the Lord one by one. For example, I told God, "I dedicate my mouth to you. It will only speak that which is wholesome and of which You would approve. My tongue will serve Your purposes." In this way I dedicated to the Lord my mind, my hands, my feet, and even my stomach. I have had to guard what I put into my stomach since that day!

We urge you to do the same thing. Dedicate your body and its parts to the Lord Jesus. Just as Jesus was dedicated to the Father, so we must be dedicated to Him. Our body must never serve any purpose except those of its Creator. Dedicating our body is one way of ensuring that our entire being is given to God. For the rest of your life, then, you must always remember that you are holy, set apart.

11. If you are willing to dedicate your body part-by-part to the Lord Jesus, begin to do that now. Do not take this assignment lightly. You may want to prepare yourself and plan a special time for this dedication. If you are not willing, ask the Lord to make you willing. Ask the Lord to help you identify what is standing in the way of your willingness. Spend time in prayer regarding the dedication of your body to the Lord for His purposes. Once you have dedicated your body to the Lord, write and date an entry in the right margin.

(date)

On the above date I dedicated my body to the Lord for His purposes alone.

(signed)

DAY 3
LOVE IS A VERB, PART 1

1. Begin today's lesson by reading the Bible verses and the name of Christ for today. Work on your memory verse. Then use the suggested prayer to begin your study.

2. As you study Christlike love, several study aids have been prepared for you.
   • Review The Mind of Christ Cards 12 and 13 during the next few days.
   • Turn to and mark for future use the Lifelong Help on *Love* under the Christlike Virtues on page 233-34.

First Corinthians 13 often is referred to as the love chapter of the Bible. The New Testament uses several Greek words for *love*. The focus of 1 Corinthians 13 is *agape*. *Agape* is a God-like love that is holy. *Agape* love is seen as an act of the will and is not based on feelings or circumstances. First Corinthians 13:4-7 describe 15 characteristics of love. In Greek, all 15 characteristics are verbs. Shown in the chart below, each of these characteristics of love produce a measure of holiness.

CHARACTERISTICS OF CHRISTLIKE LOVE

Love	Holiness
Suffers long	Holy Relationships
Is kind	Holy Purposes
Does not envy	Holy Heart
Does not brag	Holy Speech
Is not arrogant	Holy Service
Does not act unbecomingly	Holy Behavior
Does not seek its own	Holy Desires
Is not provoked	Holy Temperament
Does not take into account a wrong	Holy Bookkeeping
Does not rejoice in unrighteousness	Holy Conscience
Rejoices in the truth	Holy Mind
Bears all things	Holy Stability
Believes all things	Holy Values
Hopes all things	Holy Expectations
Endures all things	Holy Sacrifice

Today's Bible Meditation
"Love is patient, love is kind, and is not jealous; love does not brag and is not arrogant, does not act unbecomingly; it does not seek its own, is not provoked, does not take into account a wrong suffered, does not rejoice in unrighteousness, but rejoices with the truth; bears all things, believes all things, hopes all things, endures all things" (1 Cor. 13:4-7, NASB).

Name of Christ for Today
Him that Loved Us and Washed Us from Our Sins in His Own Blood (Rev. 1:5-6)

Prayer to Begin the Lesson
Loving Lord Jesus, You have loved me with a perfect love. You have washed and forgiven me of my sins by Your own sacrifice on the cross. I love You for first loving me. Teach me to love like You loved. Amen.

3. **Turn to the Lifelong Help on Love (pp. 233-34) and read the section "Showing Love." The assignment to practice the behaviors of love will be long-term. Pray now and ask the Lord to enable you to love with this God-like love. Begin to watch for opportunities and keep a record of your actions. Ask the Lord to keep you from a spirit of pride or self-righteousness. Ask God to use this as a way to develop your capacity to love like He loves.**

On many occasions Jesus demonstrated through His actions and teachings the kind of *agape* love found in 1 Corinthians 13. The examples that follow illustrate each of the characteristics of Christlike love Paul listed.

4. **As you read the following seven behaviors of love, think of a way that you might display that behavior. Write it in the margin. For instance beside "Love Suffers Long" you might write: When I am tempted to lose my temper as a time you could show that kind of love.**

Love Suffers Long (Holy Relationships)

The verb used here means *to suffer long*. We would probably use the word *patient*. Jesus was remarkably longsuffering with the disciples; they were slow to comprehend His mind. Look how Jesus related to James and John:

> When his disciples James and John saw this, they said, Lord, wilt thou that we command fire to come down from heaven, and consume them, even as Elias did? But he turned, and rebuked them, and said, "Ye know not what manner of spirit ye are of. For the Son of man is not come to destroy men's lives, but to save them" (Luke 9:54-56).

I can show that love suffers long by:

_____

_____

Obviously, James and John were demonstrating a mind-set contrary to that of Christ. Jesus rebuked them. His relationship to the disciples constantly had to wait on their comprehension of His character and intentions. The real root in Jesus' longsuffering was the fact that He maintained holy relationships.

Love Is Kind (Holy Purposes)

After Jesus fed the five thousand (itself an act of kindness), He sent the disciples across the lake while He went up onto a mountain to pray. While on the mountain:

> He saw them toiling in rowing; for the wind was contrary unto them; and about the fourth watch of the night he cometh unto them, walking upon the sea, and would have passed by them. But when they saw him walking upon the sea, they supposed it had been a spirit, and cried out: For they all saw him, and were troubled. And immediately he talked with them, and saith unto them, "Be of good cheer: it is I; be not afraid" (Mark 6:48-50).

I can show the love is kind by:

_____

_____

Jesus' kindness is a demonstration of holiness of purpose. All of Christ's intentions were holy and loving.

Love Does Not Envy (Holy Heart)

Jesus owned nothing, and He did not seek after material things. "Jesus said unto him, 'Foxes have holes, and birds of the air have nests; but the Son of man hath not where to lay his head' " (Luke 9:58).

Not envying is an indication of a holy heart. Envy is unholy; self-denial for right purposes can be holy.

I can show that love does not envy by:

_____

_____

Love Does Not Brag (Holy Speech)

Love does not brag because it is more other-conscious than self-conscious. The central consciousness of love centers on others. Jesus said: "I can of mine own self do nothing: as I hear, I judge: and my judgment is just; because I seek not mine own will, but the will of the Father which hath sent me" (John 5:30).

Love cannot brag because its speech is holy. Here holiness cooperates with love.

I can show that love does not brag by:

_____

_____

Love Is Not Arrogant (Holy Service)

We see many times in the Bible that Jesus' life was lowly.

> Jesus called them to him, and saith unto them, "Ye know that they which are accounted to rule over the Gentiles exercise lordship over them; and their great ones exercise authority upon them. But so shall it not be among you: but whosoever will be great among you, shall be your minister: And whosoever of you will be the chiefest, shall be servant of all. For even the Son of man came not to be ministered unto, but to minister, and to give his life a ransom for many" (Mark 10:42-45).

Love actively seeks holy service. Arrogance is unholy.

I can show that love is not arrogant by:

_____

_____

Love Does Not Act Unbecomingly (Holy Behavior)

Jesus was to be the teacher of the day in Nazareth, at the beginning of His great Galilean ministry. Jesus read to them the prophecy of Isaiah 61:1-2 (a prophecy of the activity of the Messiah). After the reading of the scroll, Jesus began His teaching by announcing that He was fulfilling the prophecy. The townspeople were offended.

> All they in the synagogue, when they heard these things, were filled with wrath, and rose up, and thrust him out of the city, and led him unto the brow of the hill whereon their city was built, that they might cast him down headlong. But he passing through the midst of them went his way (Luke 4:28-30).

Jesus certainly had the power to do what we find among the mythical gods in other world religions—to kill His enemies, to disappear, or to fly away. But Luke tells us that Jesus simply passed through the crowd and went on His way. Do you see the elegance in this behavior? Jesus always exhibits a royal dignity that sets His nobility apart from that of any other man or so-called god. We see in all Jesus' actions uncommon grace and glory. Love always maintains a holy behavior.

I can show that love does not act unbecomingly by:

_____

_____

Love Does not Seek Its Own (Holy Desires)

After the Lord fed the five thousand, the crowd tried to make Him king. But: "When Jesus therefore perceived that they would come and take him by force, to make him a king, he departed again into a mountain himself alone" (John 6:15).

Many things were within His reach, but Jesus never reached for them. Love cannot seek its own position or pleasure. Love has only holy desires.

☙ Conclude this lesson by asking the Lord to fill you with His love and presence so that you will express that love in your relationships with others. Be specific in asking God to enable you to demonstrate these characteristics of love.

DAY 4
LOVE IS A VERB, PART 2

Today's Bible Meditation
"He that loveth not knoweth not God; for God is love. In this was manifested the love of God toward us, because that God sent his only begotten Son into the world, that we might live through him. Herein is love, not that we loved God, but that he loved us, and sent his Son to be the propitiation for our sins. Beloved, if God so loved us, we ought also to love one another" (1 John 4:8-11).

Name of Christ for Today
The Lamb of God
(John 1:29)

Prayer to Begin the Lesson
Lamb of God, You clearly showed Your love for me by paying the death penalty for my sins. Because I have been so greatly loved, I want to love others with Your kind of love. Live in me and love through me so others will experience Your redeeming love. Amen.

☙ 1. Begin today's lesson by reading the Bible verses and the name of Christ for today. Work on your memory verse. Then use the suggested prayer to begin your study.

Today we continue our look at love as Paul described it in 1 Corinthians 13. The following eight behaviors of love were true of Christ and His teachings.

☙ 2. As you read the following eight behaviors of love, think of a way that you might display that behavior. Write it in the margin. For instance beside "Love Is not Provoked" you might write: *When someone does something to me and I want to get even* is a time you could show that kind of love.

Love Is Not Provoked (Holy Temperament)
Jesus spoke an amazing warning to Judas one year prior to his betrayal: "Jesus answered them, Have not I chosen you twelve, and one of you is a devil?" (John 6:70).

Jesus continued to walk with Judas that year. Yet the Lord never demonstrated spite toward Judas. Even Jesus' last words to Judas were calm: "What you do, do quickly" (John 13:27, NASB). How could Jesus maintain such calmness in the face of monstrous treason? Love is not easily angered because it has a holy temperament.

Love Does Not Take into Account a Wrong (Holy Bookkeeping)
Jesus' family thought He was out of His mind: "When His own people heard of this, they went out to take custody of Him; for they were saying, 'He has lost His senses' " (Mark 3:21).

Jesus' brothers did not believe in Him, and their unbelief continued throughout His ministry (see John 7:2-5). Yet we are told in 1 Corinthians 15:7 that Jesus made a special, private resurrection appearance to His disbelieving brother James to bring him to faith. Apparently that appearance was enough to satisfy another brother, Jude (author of the epistle). Jesus did not take into account the wrongs of His half brothers. Our bookkeeping needs to be holy.

Love Does Not Rejoice in Unrighteousness (Holy Conscience)

Because of Annas's control of the Jewish priesthood, a corrupt procedure of selling animals for sacrifice was instituted in the temple courtyard. Pilgrims from other countries were not allowed to offer foreign currency in the temple. They could only give Jewish shekels. Annas instituted a system of exchanging money for these foreign Jews that probably made his family inordinately wealthy. Jesus drove the money changers from the temple because love cannot rejoice in unrighteousness. "When he had made a scourge of small cords, he drove them all out of the temple, and the sheep, and the oxen; and poured out the changers' money, and overthrew the tables" (John 2:15).

Love cannot rejoice when it finds evil in control. Holy love will cast out the money changers. The kind of divine love God wants us to have is holy. Jesus' conscience was holy.

I can show that love is not provoked by:

_____

_____

Love Rejoices in the Truth (Holy Mind)

After upbraiding the cities that rejected His works, Jesus spoke of His disciples: "I thank thee, O Father, Lord of heaven and earth, because thou hast hid these things from the wise and prudent, and hast revealed them unto babes" (Matt. 11:25).

Jesus was delighted with their recognition of truth regarding His person and works.

I can show that love does not take into account a wrong by:

_____

_____

I can show that love does not rejoice in unrighteousness by:

_____

_____

Love Bears All Things (Holy Stability)

One of the clearest examples of holy stability is Jesus' dealings with Simon Peter. No other disciple failed and succeeded so often. At times Peter demonstrated remarkable insight (see Luke 5:8, Matt. 16:16), but his failures were monumental (see Matt. 16:21-22; 26:69-74). Knowing that Peter would deny Him, Jesus said: "I have prayed for thee, that thy faith fail not: and when thou art converted, strengthen thy brethren" (Luke 22:32).

Jesus dealt with Peter's awkwardness often and rewarded him each time he demonstrated insight. Love does not come and go. Love has a holy stability.

I can show that love rejoices in the truth by:

_____

_____

I can show that love bears all things by:

_____

_____

Love Believes All Things (Holy Values)

Jesus had enormous faith in the people He chose. Perhaps the most questionable of all these strange choices was His selection of the despised tax collector, Zacchaeus: "When Jesus came to the place, he looked up, and saw him, and said unto him, Zacchaeus, make haste, and come down; for to day I must abide at thy house" (Luke 19:5).

Because Jesus believed in his holy potential, Zacchaeus acted out a total repentance. Most of us would not have selected the unpredictable persons Jesus chose. Often we choose high and mighty people. Jesus, however, did not choose as the world does. Jesus had holy values.

I can show that love believes all things by:

_____

_____

Love Hopes All Things (Holy Expectations)

Jesus' anticipation that the unstable Simon would become Peter, the rock, is an indication of the kind of hope He wants us to have: "I say also unto thee, That thou art Peter, and upon this rock I will build my church; and the gates of hell shall not prevail against it" (Matt. 16:18).

Love is not always required to think the best of a person's current condition. Love sees the full development of its own cultivation and knows that God's work in the individual will be completed. Love has holy expectations.

I can show that love hopes all things by:

_____

_____

Love Endures all Things (Holy Sacrifice)

The outstanding example of endurance in all the Bible is the fact that the mighty power of God did not interfere with Jesus finishing the work of the cross: "Thinkest thou that I cannot now pray to my Father, and he shall presently give me more than twelve legions of angels?" (Matt. 26:53). Jesus finished what He began. Jesus endured the most vigorous agony any human being has ever suffered. Love perseveres because only perfect love will make a holy sacrifice.

All these characteristics complement one another. A love which behaves royally will rejoice in the truth. A person who believes all things will also hope all things. The various operations of perfect love will enhance one another. The deeper we get into the mind of Christ, the more we see wholeness and unity.

I can show that love endures
all things by:

_____

_____

3. Conclude your study in prayer. Once again ask the Lord to fill you with His love and presence so that you will express that love in your relationships with others. Be specific in asking God to enable you to demonstrate these characteristics of love.

DAY 5
LOVE AS A NOUN

1. **Begin today's lesson by reading the Bible verses and the name of Christ for today. Work on your memory verse. Then use the suggested prayer to begin your study.**

The most significant statement in the Bible about love does not deal with the outwardly observable actions of love but in the essence of God Himself. First John 4:8, 16 tells us "God is love." Love is the essential characteristic of God's being. Ultimately, if we are to have the mind of Christ, God must be able to say of us, "They are love." Love will be the essential characteristic of our inner being.

When I tried to apply this test to myself by means of the Holy Spirit's examination, I discovered that I could more easily *carry out* the actions of love (1 Cor. 13) than I could *be* love. For example, I find it easy to behave according to 1 Corinthians 13 toward the unlovely. Most of us can *do* more easily than we can *be*.

Love Is a Fruit of the Spirit
Love as a verb is an act of the will. Love as a noun is a fruit of the Spirit.

2. **Which of the following statements relate to *love* as a verb and which relate to *love* as a noun? Write *verb* or *noun* in front of the related statements**

_____ Love is an act of the will.

_____ Love is a fruit of the Spirit.

_____ Love requires being.

_____ Love requires doing.

Love as a verb is an act of the will and requires doing. Love as a noun is a fruit of the indwelling Spirit and requires being. Any Christian is capable of exercising love-actions through the will. Fortunately, the Bible's commands usually are in the form of a verb (John 13:34; 15:12,17; 1 John 3:11; 4:7,21). Descriptions of love are usually in terms of action (1 Cor. 13:4-7; 1 John 2:9-11; 3:16-18; 4:7-12,16-21). Perhaps this is because, regardless of the development of the noun-fruit within us, we can obey the commands to carry out the various operations as an act of the will. Obedience does not depend on feelings. The will can overcome feelings. We can always obey. Jesus said, "If ye love me, keep my commandments" (John 14:15).

3. **Which of the following is the reason for us to carry out the actions of love? Check one.** ❏ **Feelings** ❏ **Obedience**

We are to act like Christ out of obedience. More than just acting like Christ, however, we are to become like Christ. We can aid this process of becoming if we understand more about the nature of *love*. Love is a fruit, a product of the indwelling Holy Spirit. We depend entirely on the Spirit to produce love in us. But this process of becoming love will not progress without prayer.

Today's Bible Meditation
"If we love one another, God dwelleth in us, and his love is perfected in us. Hereby know we that we dwell in him, and he in us, because he hath given us of his Spirit. And we have seen and do testify that the Father sent the Son to be the Saviour of the world. . . . And we have known and believed the love that God hath to us. God is love; and he that dwelleth in love dwelleth in God, and God in him" (1 John 4:12-14,16).

Name of Christ for Today
The Propitiation for Our Sins (1 John 2:2)

Prayer to Begin the Lesson
Jesus, You are the propitiation for my sins. You have done something for me that I could not do for myself. But it cost You great suffering and death on the cross. I cannot comprehend that depth of love. I am overwhelmed at how much You love me. I feel loved. I love You. Work through me to reveal Your love to others, no matter what it may cost me. What more could I give in return for Your love? Amen.

Can we cooperate with the Spirit? Can we put feet to our prayers to be love in any way? Two spiritual factors foster growth in the fruit and over which we have a certain amount of control. Many of us think that we are passive agents and only the Spirit is active—that we do nothing and the Spirit does everything. This would make us robots. God did not create robots.

Principle of Yearning

Yearning and Giving

The first ingredient of love into which we can introduce our will is *yearning*. We learn that from God. God greatly desired us. This yearning is the primary stimulus that causes love to take action. Love yearns for communion with and spiritual perfection for its object. Love yearns for the highest good of its object. Yearning is zealous and knows the secret of concentration. Love will take action; God took action. We yearn to commune with God and to become like Him—to "hunger and thirst after righteousness" (Matt. 5:6).

Matthew 5:6
"Blessed are they which do hunger and thirst after righteousness: for they shall be filled."

Giving is the most potent action that strong yearning can take. God is the great Giver, and we learn giving from Him. If we take action like God does, we, too, will be great givers. God provides us with countless opportunities to give: to His cause, to the needy, and to our brothers and sisters in Christ. We can give material goods, service, and ourselves. Love-givers understand this world and its inhabitants as destitute and impoverished, regardless of apparent material wealth. Love-givers are joyful in the opportunity to supply in the generous way God does.

4. What is one thing you can do to aid developing the fruit of love?

_____

_____

5. Turn to the Lifelong Help "A-4: Hungry" on page 246 and/or The Mind of Christ Card 23 and review the helps for developing this Beatitude.

Principle of Identification

Identification

The second factor in love over which we have control is identification. The most visible act of divine identification with us took place when Jesus became a man. God knows what it is like to be a human being! God knows what it is like to be hungry, thirsty, and tired. Jesus even experienced the pangs of death. God also knows the strength of human love. Jesus knows what genuine human friendship is like. He understands the eternal spiritual longings which stir our souls. God identified with us.

We practice identification when we identify ourselves with Christ—when we take His yoke and learn from Him (see Matt. 11:29-30). Paul expressed this idea of identification when he said, "That I may know him, and the power of his resurrection, and the fellowship of his sufferings, being made conformable unto his death" (Phil. 3:10). Paul wanted to identify with Christ in every way including sharing in Jesus' sufferings and, if necessary, His death.

Matthew 11:29-30
Take my yoke upon you, and learn of me; for I am meek and lowly in heart: and ye shall find rest unto your souls. 30 For my yoke is easy, and my burden is light.

6. What is a second thing you can do to aid in developing the fruit of love?

_____

Yearning is the culmination of God's work through us in circumstances that produce poverty of spirit, brokenness, and meekness—the first group of Beatitudes. Identification is the culmination of the work of the second group of Beatitudes—showing mercy, becoming pure, and making peace (see Matt. 5:10). God built into the way He works with us those factors which will facilitate our becoming love. If we cooperate with God, we are learning *to be* as well as *to do*.

> 7. **Turn to the Lifelong Help *B-4: Persecuted* on pages 250 and/or The Mind of Christ Card 27 and review the helps for developing this Beatitude.**

Our first yearning and identification must center on the person of God. We yearn for God first. That is the original work of the Spirit in our lives. We grow in that yearning through being poor in spirit, broken, and meek. We cannot identify with others until we identify with God. Then our identification with God through the Spirit enables us to show mercy, demonstrate purity, and make peace.

The Spirit's work causes us to love God first. By loving God, we learn to love others. We must especially love our brothers and sisters in Christ. The quality of our love for others is of the same quality as our love for God (1 John. 1:3,7). The greater our love for God, the greater will be our love for others. Love facilitates fellowship within the body of Christ. Yearning and identification are holy works. In loving as God loves, we are perfecting our own purity. Love is holy, and holy persons love in the same way that God loves.

Summary

Love and holiness can be reconciled. Each intensifies the meaning of the other. One is not possible without the other. Love that is not holy (pure, unadulterated) is meaningless. And if holiness did not love, it would be useless. As with all the vast attributes of the mind of Christ, each enhances and amplifies the effect of the other.

> 8. **Conclude by spending time in prayer. Pray this prayer:**

Heavenly Father, With this new understanding of the inter working of holiness and love, I feel that I almost understand how Your work makes sense on a grand scale. I understand that I cannot merely concentrate on holiness. If I do, I will pervert its purity and separation. Neither can I concentrate on love alone. If I do, impure elements will dilute it. The holiness I seek is like that of Jesus, perfectly coordinated with love. The only love I must have is that which is modified by holiness. I am looking to Jesus for my understanding of these qualities. Make me like Him. In Jesus' name. Amen.

MATTHEW 5:10
"BLESSED ARE THEY WHICH ARE PERSECUTED FOR RIGHTEOUSNESS' SAKE: FOR THEIRS IS THE KINGDOM OF HEAVEN."

1 JOHN 1:3,7
"THAT WHICH WE HAVE SEEN AND HEARD DECLARE WE UNTO YOU, THAT YE ALSO MAY HAVE FELLOWSHIP WITH US: AND TRULY OUR FELLOWSHIP IS WITH THE FATHER, AND WITH HIS SON JESUS CHRIST. . . . BUT IF WE WALK IN THE LIGHT, AS HE IS IN THE LIGHT, WE HAVE FELLOWSHIP ONE WITH ANOTHER, AND THE BLOOD OF JESUS CHRIST HIS SON CLEANSETH US FROM ALL SIN."

GROUP SESSION 11

HOLINESS AND LOVE

SESSION GOALS

This session will help you understand the nature of Christ's holiness and love. You will demonstrate a desire to exemplify Christ's love in your life.

Hearing What the Spirit Is Saying (as you arrive)

1. (Individuals) Review what God has been saying to you during the study of unit 11.
   - Identify a Scripture and a name of Christ that have been meaningful this week.
   - Identify and mark the issue or subject in which God seems to be working most actively to develop the mind of Christ. (These will be shared later in the session.)
2. (Individuals) Write out any questions related to this unit you would like answered.

Magnifying the Lord and Exalting His Name (5 minutes)

1. (Volunteer) Open the session in prayer asking God to convince every member of His holiness and unconditional love demonstrated on the cross.
2. Pray as you feel led to worship God for Who He is and acknowledge Him for what He has done. Use the names of Christ to exalt His name together in prayer.
3. After prayer, share ways God revealed Himself to you this week through His names. Which name of Christ has been most meaningful to you and why?

Transforming by the Word (15 minutes)

1. (Pairs) Pair up and quote this week's memory verses, 1 Peter 1:15-16. Then, as time permits, alternate quoting verses from previous units. Use your Scripture memory cards as a reference.
2. Share what God said to you through this week's memory verses or other Scripture that has been meaningful.
3. (Quads—or two groups) Distribute poster board or newsprint and markers to each of two groups. Make two lists related to characteristics of a Christlike mind. Focus on this unit's Scriptures only.
   - Group 1: Make a list of things, actions, or attitudes identified or implied in Scriptures during this unit that need to be cleansed from one's mind and life.
   - Group 2: Make a list of things, actions, or attitudes identified or implied in Scriptures during this unit that need to be incorporated into one's mind and life.
   - For example: We need to rid ourselves of the *filthiness of the flesh* (group 1) and strive to *perfect our holiness* (group 2) (see 2 Cor. 7:1).
4. Call on quads to read and comment on their lists. Place one on the Transformed From Wall and the other on the Transformed To Wall.
5. (Volunteer) Pray that God will cleanse members of your group and church.

Stimulating One Another to Love and Good Deeds (20 minutes)

1. Read Hebrews 10:24.
2. Share testimonies of what God has done this week in your life that has been meaningful, challenging, or instructive.
3. State questions or concerns you have written for consideration. As time permits, seek to answer the questions as a group.
4. Read John 13:1. Ask: If Christ loved us enough to die for us on the cross, how should we respond to Him? to each other?

5. As time permits, discuss one or more of the following questions:
   - How can God be both loving and holy? How are the two related?
   - How do you define holiness? What are some ways Jesus demonstrated holiness? How can we demonstrate holiness? Where does our holiness come from?
   - How do you define love? What are some ways Jesus demonstrated love? How can we demonstrate love?

Preparing the Bride for Her Bridegroom (5 minutes)

1. Read Revelation 3:1-22. Listen for ways the bride (church) may need to repent and return to the Lord. List them in the margin.
2. As time permits, discuss these questions:
   - What in these messages of Christ to His churches applies to our church? How do we need to respond?
   - What cleansing, purifying, or preparation is needed in our church?
   - How can we apply this Scripture to our lives, families, and church?
3. Call on one member to pray aloud for your church to continue to prepare for the Lord's return.

Praying for One Another (10 minutes)

1. (Quads, preferably same gender) Read James 5:16 from your session segment poster and Share personal, family, church, or work-related prayer requests that primarily focus on developing the mind of Christ or purifying the bride.
2. (Quads) Pray specifically for one another for forgiveness, healing, encouragement, guidance, wisdom, knowledge, understanding, courage, strength, faithfulness, or for specific requests.

Closing the Session (5 minutes)

1. Share questions or concerns that came up during the session that we should remember in prayer.
2. Preview unit 12 on the following pages.
3. If your group is going to view the additional DVD sessions related to the crucifixion or resurrection, discuss plans.
3. This week, prepare a brief written evaluation of the small-group study of *The Mind of Christ*. Share any suggestions you may have to improve the experience for group members in future studies. These will be received during the next session.
4. Someone pray that God will magnify and exalt His Son Jesus in our minds and hearts this week.

Hymn Part 6
CHRIST'S NAME

"Wherefore God also hath highly exalted him, and given him a name which is above every name: That at the name of Jesus every knee should bow, of things in heaven, and things in earth, and things under the earth; And that every tongue should confess that Jesus Christ is Lord, to the glory of God the Father"
(Phil. 2:9-11).

DAY 1
Prophet, Priest, and King

DAY 2
Names of Christ, Part 1

DAY 3
Names of Christ, Part 2

DAY 4
Victory in Christ

DAY 5
Pressing Toward the Mark

Why You Will Find This Unit Helpful
You will find that the names and offices of Christ will inspire you to worship and exalt Him. As your love for Christ increases, you will be drawn to surrender to His absolute lordship in your life. During this final unit, you will review what God has been doing in your life and you will set your mind on pressing toward the mark of the high calling of God in Christ Jesus.

Lifelong Goal
In Christ you will surrender to His lordship and worship Him in Spirit and truth.

Summary of God's Work in You

Christ's name before you at all times helps you think His thoughts and show His character. Knowing His position, authority, and work, you want to worship Him. Your worship can be measured only by His worth. Christ helps you worship in His role as Lord. God's goal is the lordship of Christ. Christ rules in your heart.

Unit Learning Goals

- You will understand three offices of Christ and principles by which His names can be grouped.
- You will demonstrate your surrender to His lordship over your life.
- You will demonstrate your worship, reverence, awe, and gratitude to Him in prayer.
- You will understand the nature and source of your victory in Christ.
- You will demonstrate your commitment to spend time daily with the Lord in prayer, Scripture study, and meditation for the rest of your life.

What You Will Do to Exalt Christ

- You will study the names and offices of Christ. You will worship, praise, and thank Him.
- You will spend time in prayer exalting Christ.
- You will respond to an invitation to bow and surrender to Christ's absolute lordship.
- You will understand the victory Christ already has provided for you, and you will learn about the weapons and armor He provides for spiritual warfare.
- You will review your study of *The Mind of Christ* and identify some of the areas God has been working in your life.
- You will begin praying for your church to be a pure and beautiful Bride of Christ.

Scripture Memory Verse

"He is the head of the body, the church: who is the beginning, the firstborn from the dead; that in all things he might have the preeminence" (Col. 1:18).

Lifelong Helps Related to This Unit

Names, Titles, and Descriptions of Jesus Christ (pp. 253-54)

The Mind of Christ Card Related to This Unit

5B. Unit 12: Scripture Memory—Colossians 1:18

Optional DVD Messages by T. W. Hunt

- Session 6, Part 1: His Name
- Session 6, Part 2: His Name
- Session8: The Resurrection

DAY 1
PROPHET, PRIEST, AND KING

Today's Bible Meditations
"God also hath highly exalted him, and given him a name which is above every name: That at the name of Jesus every knee should bow, of things in heaven, and things in earth, and things under the earth; And that every tongue should confess that Jesus Christ is Lord, to the glory of God the Father" (Phil. 2:9-11).

"The hour cometh, and now is, when the true worshippers shall worship the Father in spirit and in truth: for the Father seeketh such to worship him. God is a Spirit: and they that worship him must worship him in spirit and in truth" (John 4:23-24).

Name of Christ for Today
The Prophet (John 7:40)

Prayer to Begin the Lesson
Lord Jesus Christ, You are Prophet, Priest, and King. You do more for me than I can understand. Yet, I thank You for the privilege of being related to You, chosen by You. Draw me to Yourself in worship today. Teach me what You mean by worshiping in spirit and truth. Be exalted in my life for Your Father's glory. Amen.

1. Begin today's lesson by reading the Bible verses and the name of Christ for today in the left margin. Work on your memory verse. Then use the suggested prayer to begin your study.

Hymn Part 6: Christ's Name

The hymn in Philippians 2 concludes with verses 9-11 as God exalts His Son and gives Christ a name above every other name. God's goal is that every person (knee) shall bow and every person (tongue) shall confess that Jesus Christ is Lord for the glory of God the Father. During this final unit, we want to focus our attention on the names of Jesus and the Person those names represent. Our purpose is to worship Jesus Christ as Lord and thus bring glory to God the Father.

2. Why did God exalt His Son Jesus? _____

_____

_____

The sixth characteristic of a Christlike mind is *peaceful*. Christ's love took Him to Calvary. But in Christ's death He bought us peace with God. Peace is not the absence of conflict, but the harvest of love. The resurrection was Christ's victory over sin and death. His victory made peace a reality. Through Christ's death, resurrection, and exaltation, we can experience genuine peace.

3. What did Jesus purchase for you through His death on Calvary?

_____

4. Before you continue:

• Pray and thank God for providing peace for you through the sacrifice of His Son.

• Praise God for the victory Christ won over sin and death through His resurrection.

• Tell Christ how much you love Him for the supreme sacrifice He made for you.

Christ's Offices

The creed of the New Testament church was *Jesus Christ is Lord*. This is the confession of "every tongue" in Philippians 2:11. The confession of faith in Romans 10:9 is of Jesus as Lord. Paul wrote the Corinthian church, "No one can say, 'Jesus is Lord,' except by the Holy Spirit" (1 Cor. 12:3, NASB). The three titles, *Jesus, Christ,* and *Lord,* occur together many times in the New Testament. Each name refers to a special office Christ holds. God's intention is that *Jesus Christ is Lord* be the creed of today's New Testament church.

Jesus Is Prophet. *Jesus* was the name of God in the flesh. In this human nature, Jesus functioned as Prophet (see Acts 3:22), the first of His three great offices. God speaks through a prophet, and if a prophet speaks, we must listen.

ACTS 3:22,26
"A PROPHET SHALL THE LORD YOUR GOD RAISE UP UNTO YOU OF YOUR BRETHREN, LIKE UNTO ME [MOSES]; HIM SHALL YE HEAR IN ALL THINGS WHATSOEVER HE SHALL SAY UNTO YOU. . . . UNTO YOU FIRST GOD, HAVING RAISED UP HIS SON JESUS, SENT HIM TO BLESS YOU, IN TURNING AWAY EVERY ONE OF YOU FROM HIS INIQUITIES."

5. What is one of Jesus' offices? _____

6. Read Acts 3:22 and 26 in the right margin. What was the purpose of Jesus' coming as a prophet?

_____

_____

Christ Is Priest. As Prophet, Jesus came to bless us and to turn us away from our iniquities. The name *Christ* combines both His human and His divine natures. Christ is His name as Priest: "Christ being come an high priest of good things to come . . . by his own blood he entered in once into the holy place, having obtained eternal redemption for us" (Heb. 9:11-12).

Christ, our great High Priest, now functions in two ways. First, He is an Intercessor (see Heb. 7:25). We know that God will hear Christ as He prays for us. Second, Christ is our Mediator (1 Tim. 2:5). He mediated a new covenant relationship between us and God. Our Priest has given us an important observance, the Lord's Supper, as a reminder of what has been paid for our sin debt. This observance also helps us remember that Christ is coming again.

7. What are two ways Christ functions as our Priest?

I _____ and M_____

The Lord Is King. Jesus' third great office is that of King (see Rev. 19:16). His name as King is *Lord* (Phil. 2:11). This name brings in the divine nature. God rules through Christ as Lord, and we bow our knees to acknowledge His rule.

REVELATION 19:16
"AND HE HATH ON HIS VESTURE AND ON HIS THIGH A NAME WRITTEN, KING OF KINGS, AND LORD OF LORDS."

His three great offices, then, are contained in the formula: *Jesus Christ is Lord* (Phil. 2:11). As a human, Jesus was Prophet. This involves His past work. The name *Christ* brings in both His human and divine natures and shows Him as Priest. The priestly work is Jesus' present work for us. *Lord* shows Jesus to us as King. This speaks of a future day when every knee will bow. In this way, the creed contained every important idea in the work and nature of Christ: *Jesus* (Prophet) *Christ* (Priest) *is Lord* (King).

8. Beside the names below write the corresponding office.

Jesus _____

Christ _____

Lord _____

9. What is the creed of a New Testament church?

_____ J _____ C _____ is L _____

• Because Jesus is a Prophet, I listen to His Word.

• Because Jesus is a Priest, I believe Him.

• Because Jesus is King, I obey Him. I acknowledge Jesus' total lordship over every area of my life.

10. Jesus loved you so much that He gave His own life for your redemption. Out of love for Him, bow and confess to Him, "Jesus Christ, You are Lord." Take time as you conclude this lesson to worship Jesus in prayer as Prophet, Priest, and King.

DAY 2
NAMES OF CHRIST, PART 1

Today's Bible Meditation
"Because of the tender mercy of our God, with which the Sunrise from on high shall visit us, To shine upon those who sit in darkness and the shadow of death, To guide our feet into the way of peace" (Luke 1:78-79, NASB).

1. Begin today's lesson by reading the Bible verse in the margin and the name of Christ in the margin on the next page. Work on your memory verse. Then use the suggested prayer in the margin on the following page to begin your study.

Throughout this study, you have been given names of Christ from Scripture on which to focus your attention. We have found in the names of Christ ways to submit to Christ. We also have found ways to relate to Christ or abide in Him. Many of these ways help us love Him more fully and appropriately. The names of Christ help us worship Him.

2. Scan back through the previous lessons. Which name of Christ has been most meaningful to you and why?

_____

_____

Now we want to share with you a few principles that organize some of Christ's names. These principles are not mutually exclusive, because some names could be included under several of the principles.

Deity Names

Christ's deity or divine names refer to Him as God. Because of the deity names, we worship Christ as well as the Father and the Spirit. Any other worship is improper and idolatrous. God has revealed Himself through the incarnation, for Jesus is God. Listed below are some of His deity.

- Creator (Col. 1:16)

- Truth (John 14:6)

- Mighty God (Isa. 9:6)

- Son of God (John 1:49)

- Holy One of God (Luke 4:34)

- Lord from Heaven (1 Cor. 15:47)

- Image of the Invisible God (Col. 1:15)

- Emmanuel [God with us] (Matt. 1:23)

Perhaps the most important of the divine names is Jesus' own claim to be the "I Am" (John 8:58). In this way Jesus identified Himself with the eternal Self-Existent God who appeared to Moses (Ex. 3:14).

3. Take a few moments in prayer to worship Christ as God.

Functioning Names

These names indicate ways in which Jesus works for us, or functions on our behalf. Some of these names could be called Redemption Names. Jesus is:

- Deliverer (Rom. 11:26)

- He that Sanctifieth (Heb. 2:11)

- Shepherd and Bishop [Guardian, NASB] of your souls (1 Pet. 2:25)

- Saviour of the world (John 4:42)

- Wonderful Counsellor (Isa. 9:6, NASB)

4. In prayer acknowledge Christ for who He is, and thank Him for the things He does for you.

Name of Christ for Today
Emmanuel [God with us] (Matt. 1:23)

Prayer to Begin the Lesson
Emmanuel, how I praise You for coming to dwell among humanity in order to provide for my salvation on the cross. I cannot understand why You also have chosen to take up residence in my life—but I am glad You did. I enjoy Your presence and Your fellowship. Shine in me. Shine through me to reveal Your light to those who live in darkness. Guide my feet in the ways of peace. Amen.

Light Names

Jesus is the True Light. You have to look up in the sky to see all these manifestations of light. Listed below are celestial light names describing Jesus.

- Dayspring [Sunrise] (Luke 1:78)
- Day star (2 Pet. 1:19)
- Light of life (John 8:12)
- Light to lighten the Gentiles (Luke 2:32)
- Light of men (John 1:4)
- Light of the world (John 8:12)

In Jesus' last words in the New Testament He called Himself "The bright and morning star" (Rev. 22:16). This name signifies hope. In the New Jerusalem, "the city has no need of the sun or of the moon to shine upon it, for the glory of God has illumined it, and its lamp is the Lamb" (Rev. 21:23, NASB).

5. Close your time with the Lord today by praising Him for His glory.

DAY 3
NAMES OF CHRIST, PART 2

Today's Bible Meditation
"I am Alpha and Omega, the beginning and the end, the first and the last" (Rev. 22:13).

Names of Christ for Today
Alpha and Omega, the beginning and the end (Rev. 21:6)

1. Begin today's lesson by reading the Bible verse and the names of Christ for today. Work on your memory verse. Then use the suggested prayer in the margin on the next page to begin your study.

Complement Principle

One aspect of our submission to Christ (bowing the knee) is to fulfill a complementary role which His names suggest. Listed below are some of Christ's names and the role or relationship we have with Him.

CHRIST'S NAME	OUR ROLE
Shepherd (John 10:11)	Sheep
Father (Isa. 9:6)	Child
Brother (Heb. 2:11)	Brother or sister
Teacher (John 3:2)	Disciple
Master (2 Tim. 2:21)	Servant
Vine (John 15:1)	Branch
Bridegroom (Mark 2:19)	Bride of Christ (the church)

Identity Principle

When we apply the Identity Principle, we identify with Christ in certain of His names. We are to grow into His likeness. We are to become like Christ.

- God's Beloved (Matt. 12:18). We must be beloved by God (Rom. 1:7).

- Chosen One (Isa. 42:1, NASB). We are chosen (2 Tim. 2:10).

- Heir of All Things (Heb. 1:2). We are joint-heirs with Christ (Rom. 8:17).

- Last Adam (1 Cor. 15:45). We become fully human when we live like Christ lived.

- Lamb (John 1:29), Christ is pure. We are to be pure.

- Rock (1 Cor. 10:4). We are not to waver.

- Jesus Christ the Righteous (1 John 2:1). In Him we are righteous (Jer. 23:6).

2. Review the list and ask God if there is one particular area He would like to work on to bring you closer to Christ's likeness. Thank God that you are beloved, chosen, and a joint-heir with Christ.

The Life Principle

Some of the names for the Lord indicate that He is the Source of our Life. Whenever a name is repeated in various forms, God is emphasizing the concept illustrated in the use of that name. Christ is:

- The Bread of Life (John 6:35)
- Eternal Life (1 John 5:20)

- The Life (John 14:6)
- Our Life (Col. 3:4)

- Light of Life (John 8:12)
- Prince of Life (Acts 3:15)

- The Word of Life (1 John 1:1)
- The Resurrection and the Life (John 11:25)

3. Christ is your Life. Pause to agree that He is your life and ask Christ to do all that is necessary for His life to be clearly reflected in you.

Prayer to Begin the Lesson

Alpha and Omega, You began a good work in me, and You are able to finish it. You are far greater than my mind can comprehend. Holy Spirit, as I study more about Christ's names today, please continue to enlarge my knowledge and understanding of Him. Exalt Him in my life. Then enable me to lift Him up in the eyes of others as I declare His greatness to those around me. Amen.

The Sovereign Principle

Many names indicate the sovereignty and royalty of Christ.

- Governor (Matt. 2:6)

- King of Saints (Rev. 15:3)

- Thy King (Matt. 21:5)

- Good Master (Mark 10:17)

- Prince of Life (Acts 3:15)

- Prince of the Kings of the

  Earth (Rev. 1:5)

- King that Cometh in the
  Name of the Lord (Luke. 19:38)

- King of Kings (1 Tim. 6:15)

- King of the Jews (Matt. 27:11)

- Lord of Lords (1 Tim. 6:15)

- Messiah the Prince (Dan. 9:25)

- Prince of Peace (Isa. 9:6)

- King Eternal, Immortal,

  Invisible (1 Tim. 1:17)

- Leader and Commander to the
  People (Isa. 55:4)

The Preeminence Principle

Not only is Christ absolute Ruler, but He is to be preeminent (first or foremost) in all things.

- God of the Whole Earth (Isa. 54:5)

- Firstborn of Every Creature (Col. 1:15)

- Head of Every Man (1 Cor. 11:3)

- Firstborn among Many Brethren (Rom. 8:29)
- Head of the Body, the Church (Col. 1:18)

- Head of all Principality and Power (Col. 2:10)

- Lord over All (Rom. 10:12)

Paul expected Christ to be supreme in the New Testament church and in the lives of believers. If we will bow our knees today, we can place Christ above all earthly relations, institutions, past times, and business. Christ must be Lord over all.

4. **Christ is your ruler and the head of your church. Take a few moments in prayer to bow your knees and submit to His lordship in your life, your family, your work, and your church.**

🐚 5. Christ is great and greatly to be praised. Praise Him for His Preeminence.

The Alpha and Omega Principle

This designation is used for this series of names because it is biblical; it is a name Christ gave Himself. Alpha and Omega express well the idea contained in the principle. *Alpha* is the first letter of the Greek alphabet; *omega* is the last. We would say "the A and the Z." Some of the Alpha-names indicate Christ as Initiator—One who begins something. All initiative is with God. The Omega-names indicate Him as a Finisher—One who completes something. God always finishes what He starts. After Jesus said, "I am the Alpha and the Omega," He added "the first and the last, the beginning and the end" (Rev. 22:13, NASB).

🐚 6. In your own words define *Alpha* and *Omega* names.

Alpha names mean Christ is _____

Omega names mean Christ is _____

- Jesus is the Author (Initiator) and Finisher of our faith (Heb. 12:2).

  Author—Finisher

- Jesus is our Advocate with the Father (1 John 2:1)—our Defense Lawyer. This is an Alpha-name. We do not need to fear Satan's constant accusation (see Rev. 12:10), for Jesus initiated my salvation and stands ready to defend me. Jesus also has a corresponding Omega-name—Righteous Judge (2 Tim. 4:8). What an unbeatable combination—our Defense Lawyer is our Judge! Jesus begins and finishes the work on our behalf!

  Advocate—Judge

- As Alpha, Jesus is the Lamb of God who took away our sins (see John 1:29). He is meek, pure, and innocent. As Omega, Jesus is the Lion of the tribe of Judah (Rev. 5:5). As Lion, Jesus is bold, powerful, and strong.

  Lamb—Lion

- One of Jesus Alpha-names is Servant. As Servant, He submits to God and was even among the disciples as *One Who Serves* (see Luke 22:27). But Jesus as Omega is the Head of the Church (Eph. 5:23). As Head, Jesus directs the work of His servants.

  Servant—Head

- Another Alpha-name is Apostle—the Sent One who came to earth to begin a new work for all of us. But Jesus also has a corresponding Omega-name—the High Priest (Heb. 3:1) who now intercedes for us.

  Apostle—High Priest

- Jesus is the Son of Man (Matt. 11:19) and the Son of God (1 John 4:15).

  Son of Man—Son of God

🐚 7. Do you have a sense of awe at how great Jesus is? Take a moment in prayer to worship Him. Jesus is worthy of our worship.

Jesus is not only the A and the Z. He is the B-C-D-E-F-G-H-I-J-K-L-M-N-O-P-Q-R-S-T-U-V-W-X-Y! He who begins the work and finishes it also does the work through us throughout our lives (John 15:1-5). In the stages of life, Jesus is the Child (Isa. 9:6), the Man (1 Tim. 2:5), and the Eternal Father (Isa. 9:6). In regard to the building, He is the Foundation (1 Cor. 3:11), the Cornerstone (1 Pet. 2:6), and even the Builder (Heb. 3:3). If we see Jesus as Plant, He is the Seed from which we all spring (Gal. 3:16), the Root (Rom. 15:12), the Branch (Zech. 6:12), and the Vine (John 15:1). As to His churchly offices, Jesus is the Apostle (Heb. 3:1), the Prophet (Acts 3:22), the High Priest (Heb. 5:10), and the Overseer or Bishop (1 Pet. 2:25). Jesus is the Alpha and Omega, the summation of all God's work.

8. Review all the lists of the names of Christ. Conclude by expressing your worship, praise, and thanksgiving to Christ. God wants Christ to be exalted in your mind and in your life.

DAY 4
VICTORY IN CHRIST

Today's Bible Meditations
"For whatsoever is born of God overcometh the world: and this is the victory that overcometh the world, even our faith" (1 John 5:4-5).

"I beseech you therefore, brethren, by the mercies of God, that ye present your bodies a living sacrifice, holy, acceptable unto God, which is your reasonable service. And be not conformed to this world: but be ye transformed by the renewing of your mind, that ye may prove what is that good, and acceptable, and perfect, will of God" (Rom. 12:1-2).

Name of Christ for Today
Our Saviour Jesus Christ (2 Pet. 1:1)

1. Begin today's lesson by reading the Bible verses and the name of Christ for today on this and the following page. Work on your memory verse. Then use the suggested prayer on the following page to begin your study.

The Battles Continue

All of God's saints are engaged in battles that are part of a long war. The final outcome of the war is assured and is spelled out in the Book of Revelation. God and His saints will conquer Satan. Victory in the war is decided, but the battles continue. We are in their midst.

We are deceived if we do not take into account that "our struggle is not against flesh and blood, but against the rulers, against the powers, against the world forces of this darkness, against the spiritual forces of wickedness in the heavenly places" (Eph. 6:12, NASB). The battles we fight are in the mind—where Satan and his forces work with great determination. Jesus knew the thoughts of the Pharisees when He said, "A good man out of the good treasure of the heart bringeth forth good things: and an evil man out of the evil treasure bringeth forth evil things" (Matt. 12:35). Having the mind of Christ will involve struggle.

2. If you have the mind of Christ will you still face struggles and spiritual battles? _____

3. Where will those battles primarily be fought? _____

Spiritual Weapons and Armor

Paul shows in the verses below that the spiritual battles we fight are in the mind: "The weapons of our warfare are not of the flesh, but divinely powerful for the destruction of fortresses. We are destroying speculations and every lofty thing raised up against the knowledge of God, and we are taking every thought captive to the obedience of Christ" (2 Cor. 10:4-5, NASB).

God has given believers spiritual weapons that have divine power to demolish strongholds. Claim those weapons and use them to take captive every contrary thought and make it obedient to Christ. With spiritual armor (see Eph. 6:13-18), we are to "fight the good fight of faith" (1 Tim. 6:12).

4. Read Ephesians 6:10-18 below and circle items of spiritual armor you are to wear.

> Be strong in the Lord, and in the power of his might. Put on the whole armour of God, that ye may be able to stand against the wiles of the devil. For we wrestle not against flesh and blood, but against principalities, against powers, against the rulers of the darkness of this world, against spiritual wickedness in high places. Wherefore take unto you the whole armour of God, that ye may be able to withstand in the evil day, and having done all, to stand. Stand therefore, having your loins girt about with truth, and having on the breastplate of righteousness; And your feet shod with the preparation of the gospel of peace; Above all, taking the shield of faith, wherewith ye shall be able to quench all the fiery darts of the wicked. And take the helmet of salvation, and the sword of the Spirit, which is the word of God: Praying always with all prayer and supplication in the Spirit, and watching thereunto with all perseverance and supplication for all saints.

5. What is one thing you are always to do? _____

Paul used the spiritual weapons and armor to fight his spiritual battles. At the end of his life Paul claimed, "I have fought the good fight, I have finished the course, I have kept the faith" (2 Tim. 4:7, NASB). We pray that you, too, will be victorious.

The Battle and the Victory are the Lord's

Our present responsibility is to fight our battles in the Spirit of Jesus Christ. What Jahaziel told Jehoshaphat applies to all time: "The battle is not yours but God's" (2 Chron. 20:15, NASB). The New Testament consistently speaks of victory not as something we accomplish but as the appropriation of what Jesus already has accomplished!

Paul proclaimed, "But thanks be to God, who always leads us *in His triumph* in Christ, and manifests through us the sweet aroma of the knowledge of Him in every place" (2 Cor. 2:14, NASB, author's italics). Victory is not an outcome to be achieved, but steps to follow. When we walk in Christ, and He is shown and exalted

---

Prayer to Begin the Lesson

Jesus, You are my Savior. In You I have victory over the world. How can I say thanks? Nothing I can do would be adequate. However, I place my life on the altar as a living sacrifice to You in an act of worship. Continue to renew my mind that I may be pleasing to You. Please accept my humble thank you for the victory You give. Amen.

Victory is not an outcome to be achieved, but steps to follow.

Victory is when the Victor abides in us.

in our life, we walk in victory. For the spiritual Christian, victory is not an event. Victory is when the Victor abides in us.

"For whatever is born of God overcomes the world; and this is the victory that has overcome the world—our faith. And who is the one who overcomes the world, but he who believes that Jesus is the Son of God?" (1 John 5:4-5, NASB). The proof of faith is not in success or even in answered prayer, but in enduring. We do not have the privilege of giving up to Satan. Since the battle is not ours but God's, we are not the ones to make that choice. Paul urged Timothy, "Suffer hardship with me, as a good soldier of Christ Jesus" (2 Tim. 2:3, NASB). Moses persevered "as seeing Him who is unseen" (Heb. 11:27, NASB).

All spiritual forces are subject to Christ. The demons had to obey Christ because He had authority. Christ's final victory is the work of the cross. When the forces of evil succeeded in nailing the incarnate Second Person of the Trinity to the cross, they thought they had defeated God. But that cross proved to be their undoing. "When He [Jesus] had disarmed the rulers and authorities, He made a public display of them, having triumphed over them through Him" (Col. 2:15, NASB). Victory is not justice waiting to be accomplished, but a debt which has been fully paid.

6. **Which of the following best describes spiritual victory in Christ?**

❏ **Spiritual victory in Christ is a future hope. I hope He wins.**

❏ **Spiritual victory in Christ is a present reality. He has won already.**

Christ has won already. The final enemy to be vanquished will be death itself. The finality of death—the real meaning of death—will be realized for the unbeliever in what the Bible calls the "second death" (Rev. 20:14). But for the believer:

> When this perishable will have put on the imperishable, and this mortal will have put on immortality, then will come about the saying that is written, "Death is swallowed up in victory. O death, where is your victory? O death, where is your sting?" The sting of death is sin, and the power of sin is the law; but thanks be to God, who gives us the victory through our Lord Jesus Christ (1 Cor. 15:54-57, NASB).

For the Christian, real death (eternal, not momentary) happened two thousand years ago—and we do not dread the past!

For believers, death is momentary—a passage into the presence of Christ. Death is the path to full knowledge and the end of Satan's obstruction of our understanding. God manifests His final victory after indwelling our life of struggle. Beyond death is the reward we were seeking as we grappled with the forces of the world. Passing through this doorway, we at last experience safety and eternal sanctuary. For the Christian, real death (eternal, not momentary) happened two thousand years ago—and we do not dread the past!

Do not be surprised if Satan tries to thwart you in your effort to live by the principles of this course. Christ never promised that living His life would be easy. In one sense, the battles are won already. We have the mind of Christ. Our problem is knowing how to live by the mind of Christ in the context of this world. Remember that you gained the mind of Christ even at spiritual birth. Still, that baby mind in you must grow, and the growth process is beset by the habits of your old sin nature, the obstruction of Satan, and the appeal of the world. However, victory is yours. Your triumph was accomplished two thousand years ago when Christ fully satisfied the requirements of God on the cross, conquered death, and ascended to intercede for us until the final battle is over. Jesus has been interceding for you even as you have studied this material.

7. **Conclude in prayer. Claim your victory in Christ. Ask God to teach you to use your spiritual weapons to make every thought obedient to Christ.**

8. **As a follow-up to the previous assignment on page 188 to view the DVD on The Crucifixion, this is an appropriate time in your study to complete the following assignment either as a group or individually: session 8, "The Resurrection" from *The Mind of Christ* DVD Messages.**

DAY 5
PRESSING TOWARD THE MARK

1. **Begin today's lesson by reading the Bible verses and the names of Christ for today. Work on your memory verse. Then use the suggested prayer on the following page to begin your study.**

Conforming to Christ's Image

I believe the Lord had several purposes in leading me to write this course. He led me to write it, and I believe He led you to study it. The first group of purposes relate to you as an individual.

God's primary purpose in you as a believer is to conform you to the image of His Son.

Christ is your Creator (see Col. 1:16), your Redeemer, and your Sustainer (see Col. 1:14,17, NIV). He is the Head over every Rule and Authority (see Col. 2:10, NASB). Yet, great as Christ is, He is your Brother if you are redeemed (see Heb. 2:11). You are to look like your elder Brother. You are to resemble Christ and live a life that parallels His. Though you walk within a material world, you are really a spiritual, heavenly creature. God is molding you into that image: "Just as we have borne the image of the earthy, we shall also bear the image of the heavenly" (1 Cor. 15:49, NASB).

You can participate actively in that process of being conformed to Christ's image. Conforming to the pattern of Christ really is a matter of realizing in thought and deed all that which was born in you when you became a Christian. There are specifics in the mind of Christ to which you can conform:

Today's Bible Meditations
"Alleluia: for the Lord God omnipotent reigneth. Let us be glad and rejoice, and give honour to him: for the marriage of the Lamb is come, and his wife hath made herself ready. And to her was granted that she should be arrayed in fine linen, clean and white: for the fine linen is the righteousness of saints" (Rev. 19:6-8).

Names of Christ for Today
Author and Finisher of Our Faith (Heb. 12:2)

Prayer to Begin the Lesson

Jesus, Author and Finisher of my faith, I confess that You began a good work in my life when You redeemed me. You have been doing a good work in me these past few months. I now pray that You will continue to accomplish Your purposes in my life to mold and shape my life into Your image. I exalt You. I worship You. I adore You. I bow before You and proclaim that You are my Lord Jesus Christ! Amen.

• The virtues of godly wisdom in James 3:17.

• The fruit of the Spirit in Galatians 5:22-23.

• The characteristics of the servant mind.

• The qualities described in the Beatitudes of Matthew 5:3-10.

• The model of Christ in expressing emotions.

• The model of Christ in relationship to things and people.

• The model of Christ in relationship to the Father and the Holy Spirit.

• The model of Christ's use of the Scriptures and prayer.

• The character and behavior of holiness.

• The actions of Christlike love.

2. **Which area(s) found in this list did God emphasize in your life? Underline the area(s).**

3. **Do you sense that you are more or less like Christ than when you began this study?**

   ❏ More like Christ   ❏ Less like Christ

4. **Why?** _____

_____

_____

Conforming to the image of Christ is accomplished through a process (see Mark 4:26-29). You can and must cooperate in this process. This is why your will is so important. You must be "transformed by the renewing of your mind" (Rom. 12:2).

Knowledge of Christ

What we have given in this book is basic information about the mind and Person of Christ. If we are to be conformed, we must have specific information about what we are being conformed to. I have 21 personal notebooks (not to mention the many books in my library) full of information on the Person of Christ that I have gathered over the years. I included in this course only a part of the material which I have learned. Since Christ is inexhaustible, I have much yet to learn, and you do too. Jesus invites us, "Take My yoke upon you, and learn from Me" (Matt. 11:29, NASB).

5. **Of all the things you have learned about Christ during this study, what one thing seems to stand out as most interesting, meaningful, inspiring, or challenging?**

_____

This course is only a beginning. The knowledge you are to gain is contained in your primary textbook, the Bible. The Old Testament is full of God's actions, messianic prophecies, poetry about the various aspects of His work and being, and Christ's names. The New Testament tells of Jesus' earthly work (the Apostle work) and His heavenly work (the High Priestly work).

We pray that you will commit to spending time with God daily. Make Jesus and His purposes the basis of all you are and do. Embrace Jesus as you go through your daily routine, planning, budget, friendships, marriage, rearing of children, work, and all aspects of your life.

Getting to know Jesus Christ and becoming like Him requires:

• Time to talk with Jesus in prayer

• Time in prayer to listen to Jesus' instruction and guidance

• Time reading God's Word to know Jesus, His purposes, and His ways more certainly

• Time to meditate on the person and work of Christ as a model for your life

6. **We have one more long-term assignment for you. First, read the following verses:**

When thou vowest a vow unto God, defer not to pay it; for he hath no pleasure in fools: pay that which thou hast vowed. Better is it that thou shouldest not vow, than that thou shouldest vow and not pay (Eccl. 5:4-5).

7. **Consider the following request carefully and prayerfully. Will you commit yourself to spend time with the Lord in prayer, Scripture study, and meditation daily?**

_____ ❑ Yes   ❑ I'm not ready to do that yet.   ❑ No

8. **If you are willing, how much time are you willing to pledge to Jesus with the intention of keeping your vow to Him for the rest of your life? Check your response.**

❏ 15 minutes daily

❏ 30 minutes daily

❏ 45 minutes daily

❏ 60 minutes daily

❏ Other: _____ daily

Years ago, I committed to spend at least 30 minutes daily with the Lord. God has enabled me to keep that commitment to Him, and God has rewarded me with His presence and guidance. If you have just made a vow to the Lord, the Psalmist gives you a model prayer and God makes you a promise:

> "Thou, O God, hast heard my vows: thou hast given me the heritage of those that fear thy name. So will I sing praise unto thy name for ever, that I may daily perform my vows" (Ps. 61:5,8).

> "Offer unto God thanksgiving; and pay thy vows unto the most High: And call upon me in the day of trouble: I will deliver thee, and thou shalt glorify me" (Ps. 50:14-15).

The Bride of Christ

Another group of purposes which has pervaded my mind as I wrote has to do with His Bride, the church. One of the passions of my life is to see the church purified and cleansed. Will you join me and others as we pray for the Bride of Christ— the church?

• Pray that your church will be cleansed to be a suitable Bride for Christ's perfect purity. Some of our work in the church today is based on worldly techniques and methods. Our use of God's money is not always centered on His unique purposes. Sin persists in the lives of church members. Many members are not realizing the purpose God ordained for them to fulfill in the body. Ask God to purge from the church all sin, and to ready the church for her glorious Bridegroom.

• Pray that your church will come under the unconditional lordship of her Head— Christ. Lordship should begin with your life. If Christ is the Head, church members are the parts of His body. Each part must be obedient to the Head. Parts can function together as a unit only when all directives come from Christ. Pray that the various leaders of your church turn first to Christ for their direction.

• Finally, pray that the Bride will truly love her great Bridegroom. If the angels in heaven worship Christ (Heb. 1:6), how much more should we who are redeemed by His blood worship Him! Pray for your church's worship. Worldly music, insincere motives, an orientation to performance or pride in performance, mediocre or even indifferent execution of the components of worship—all these crowd out our adoration of a high and holy God. Ask the Lord to purify your worship so that only God will be glorified and Christ will be exalted.

9. **Take a moment now to pray these prayers for yourself and your church.**

We want to pray for you and your church.

> *Heavenly Father,*
> *I ask that my friends finishing this course today never forget the glory and accomplishments of Jesus. I pray that they will always glorify Christ in their lives above all else.*
> *I ask that You remind my friends of those things to be praying for in life and in the church. Purify the church through our prayers.*
> *I also plead with You that Jesus' church stop glorifying man and glorify only Jesus. Let Him be seen, not our talents or accomplishments. I pray that the day will come soon that only Jesus' glory will be perceptible in His church. I ask that no name be exalted except Christ's. Oh, great God, do exalt Jesus' name as it never has been exalted. Let it be high and holy in His body. Give us that much taste of heaven even now.*
> *Holy Father, fulfill the purpose You originally had in the writing of this course. In Jesus' name. Amen.*

Continuing the Process

You have concluded your study of this introduction to the lifelong process of letting the mind of Christ be developed in you. This is just a beginning. Continue to grow in grace and in a knowledge of your Lord and Savior Jesus Christ.

This is just a beginning. Continue to grow in grace and in a knowledge of your Lord and Savior Jesus Christ.

10. **Consider praying this prayer. Respond to God in whatever way you sense would be appropriate.**

> *Father God,*
> *I more clearly see now that Jesus was Your method of Self-revelation. In knowing Him, I know You and understand Your ways and nature. With all my heart, I thank You for revealing Yourself to us so clearly. I understand that all revelation is summarized in the Person of Christ.*
> *Because You want me to, I want to live His life today. Through Him, You are bringing many children to glory. I have begun a process. I ask You to carry that process through to the final glory You have for me, and pledge to work with You in accomplishing this Your purpose.*
> *I make Him absolute Lord of my life. I will not question Your directives through Him, for He is my Master.*
> *I love You very much, and I love Your Only Begotten Son. With all the adoration possible to me at this stage of my growth, I love You with my whole being. I commit myself to let You perfect fully all that You intend to finish in me. In Jesus' name, I am Yours. Amen.*

GROUP SESSION 12

EXALTING CHRIST

SESSION GOALS

This session will help you understand the names and offices of Christ. You will demonstrate a commitment to an ongoing process of developing the mind of Christ.

Hearing What the Spirit Is Saying (as you arrive)

1. (Individuals) Review what God has been saying to you during the study of unit 12.
   • Identify a Scripture and a name of Christ that have been meaningful this week.
   • Identify and mark the issue or subject in which God seems to be working most actively to develop the mind of Christ. (These will be shared later in the session.)
2. (Individuals) Write out any questions related to this unit you would like answered.
3. If you have prepared an evaluation of the study, give it to your group leader. If you have not prepared an evaluations, take a few moments to write down your comments or suggestions.

Magnifying the Lord and Exalting His Name (5 minutes)

1. (Volunteer) Open the session in prayer by asking God to exalt His Son Jesus in your hearts and minds. Ask God to exalt His Son through your church in your community.
2. Pray as you feel led to worship God for Who He is and acknowledge Him for what He has done. Use the names of Christ to exalt His name together in prayer.
3. After prayer, share ways God revealed Himself to you this week through His names. Which name of Christ has been most meaningful to you and why?

Transforming by the Word (15 minutes)

1. (Pairs) Pair up and quote this week's memory verse, Colossians 1:18. Then, as time permits, alternate quoting verses from previous units. Use your Scripture memory cards as a reference.
2. Share what God said to you through this week's memory verse or other Scripture that has been meaningful.
3. Ask group members to identify some of the attitudes, actions, or things that God has removed from their minds and lives during this study.
4. Describe attitudes, actions, virtues, and thoughts that God has added to their minds and lives during this study.
5. Take time as a group to thank God for what He has been doing to cleanse group members and your church. Ask God to continue to shape members into the image of His Son Jesus.

Stimulating One Another to Love and Good Deeds (20 minutes)

1. Lead the group in quoting Hebrews 10:24.
2. Share testimonies of what God has done this week in your life that has been meaningful, challenging, or instructive.
3. State questions or concerns you have written for consideration. As time permits, seek to answer the questions as a group.
4. Distribute the sheet or point to the poster with upcoming discipleship training opportunities. Encourage members to participate in one of these courses in order to continue their growth as disciples. Some may want to participate in the next study of *The Mind of Christ* as a means of review and continued growth.

5. As time permits, discuss one or more of the following questions:
   • What are some reasons we should worship Christ because of His offices of Prophet, Priest, and King? How can we worship Him?
   • Where will the greatest battles for having the mind of Christ be fought? What spiritual weapons and armor are available to you? What is your source of victory?
   • What is the most significant thing God has done in your life during the past 12 weeks?
   • How have other members of the body helped you become more of what God wants you to be?
   • What do you sense God is doing to prepare your church for His Son's return?
   • What do you sense God wants you to do next on your pilgrimage in developing the mind of Christ?

Preparing the Bride for Her Bridegroom (5 minutes)

1. Read Revelation 22:1-21. Listen for ways the bride (church) needs to prepare for the return of Christ. List them in the margin.
2. As time permits, discuss these questions:
   • What is the message of the bride in the last days? (v. 17)
   • What has God been saying to you or doing in your life related to the return of His Son?
   • What preparations have you seen our church making in purifying herself to prepare us for the marriage of the Lamb?
   • What cleansing, purifying, or preparation is still needed in our church?
   • How can we apply this Scripture to our lives, families, and church?
3. Call on one member to pray thanking God for the progress in purity these past weeks and asking God to continue His refining work.

Praying for One Another (10 minutes)

1. (Quads, preferably same gender) Identify one area of your life or minds that needs special attention. Ask each member to share (one person at a time) a way the quad can pray for him or her. Once a person has shared a request, let the quad pray for that request. Then repeat the process for each person, one at a time.

Closing the Session (5 minutes)

1. (Optional) Give members a copy of Philippians 2:5-11. Suggest they display it in their homes as a reminder of the work God is doing in your life to develop the mind of Christ.
2. Fill in the Christian Growth Study Plan form in the back of their books (p. 272). Provide guidance for those who have not previously participated in the Christian Growth Study Plan. Explain that members will receive a diploma as a symbol of the work invested in this study. Tell members about the video and audio approaches to The Mind of Christ and suggest they may want to participate in one of these.

Christ wants you to be free from every bondage to sin, self, and the mind-set of the world. Christ's freedom is the first step in developing the mind of Christ. I have found that making the following lists helps me to evaluate my thinking and my true mind-set. Under the supervision of the Holy Spirit, God has helped me identify things that are not like the mind of Christ. Then God has guided me toward thinking that is like the mind of Christ.

My personal experiences with making these lists and instructions for you to do so are located in units 2 and 3. This has been a long-term project in my life. It will be a lifelong process for you as God continually renews your mind.

I suggest that you keep a notebook for these lists. A loose-leaf notebook may work best so you can add and remove pages. Here are a few tips that may be helpful:

1. Title and date your lists and updates. Watch to see how God is working to remove and add items from your lists.
2. Be thoroughly honest with God as you make your lists.
3. Write down your list before using the suggested categories. Number the items on your list.
4. Use the following lists to help you identify other items.
5. Many of the standards for evaluating your lists come from Scripture or the life of Jesus as revealed in Scripture. You may need to study your Bible more closely to see what God has said about some of these items. When the Holy Spirit prompts you to question an area, study that topic to see what God has said to instruct you. For future use, write in your notebook what you discover.

    For example, you could do a study on possessions and stewardship or bitterness and forgiveness. A topical Bible, a concordance, and/or a word study book may be helpful. Daily Bible reading is another way to let God speak to you about His desires for your life.

6. Review and update these lists periodically to check your progress and to identify new areas of bondage that may have crept into your thinking.

LIST 1—Lusts/Wants/Desires

If you are having difficulty in making your list or want to be more thorough, consider wants or desires related to the following categories:\

- accomplishments
- control
- material things
- career
- attitudes/behaviors
- finances
- morality
- spiritual character

Evaluation of Your Desires—As you evaluate your desires, ask God to help you identify which ones are self-seeking and which ones are Kingdom-seeking. God's goal is to move your desires from selfish desires to Kingdom desires.

LIST 2—Habits

If you are having difficulty in making your list or want to be more thorough, consider habits related to the following categories:

- Bible study, prayer
- keeping promises
- reading
- speech/language
- exercise
- punctuality
- recreation
- use of free time

Evaluation of Your Habits—As you evaluate your habits, ask God to help you identify which ones are careless and which ones are Spirit-controlled. God's goal is to move your habits from being careless to Spirit-controlled.

LIST 3—Loyalties

If you are having difficulty in making your list or want to be more thorough, consider loyalties related to the following categories:

- boss/supervisor/manager
- friends
- co-workers
- denomination
- labor union
- church members
- relatives
- business, employer
- government
- para-church group

Evaluation of Your Loyalties—As you evaluate your loyalties, ask God to help you identify which ones are scattered and which ones are prayerful. God's goal is to move your loyalties from being scattered to being prayerful.

LIST 4—Relationships

If you are having difficulty in making your list or want to be more thorough, consider relationships related to the following categories:

- supervisor/boss
- church members
- friend
- relative
- pastor, church staff member
- business partner
- co-worker
- neighbor
- student
- teacher

Evaluation of Your Relationships—As you evaluate your relationships, ask God to help you identify which ones are serving self and which ones are serving God. God's goal is to move your relationships from serving self to serving God.

LIST 5—Prejudices

If you are having difficulty in making your list or want to be more thorough, consider prejudices related to the following categories:

- other ethnic backgrounds
- other para-church groups
- well-educated/poorly educated
- homosexuals/heterosexuals
- other denominations
- other gender
- homeless persons
- other religions
- rich or poor
- other professions

Evaluation of Your Prejudices—As you evaluate your prejudices, ask God to help you identify which ones are accidental and which ones are scriptural. If you don't know what the Bible has to say about a particular area, study the Bible to determine what your responses should be. God's goal is to move your prejudices from being accidental to being scriptural.

LIST 6—Ambitions

If you are having difficulty in making your list or want to be more thorough, consider ambitions (goals, purposes, objectives, hopes, dreams) related to the following categories:

- beauty/good looks
- control
- honor/praise
- popularity
- possession of things
- career ladder
- fame
- money
- position
- title

Evaluation of Your Ambitions—As you evaluate your ambitions, ask God to help you identify which ones are honoring self and which ones are honoring God. God's goal is to move your ambitions from honoring self to honoring God.

LIST 7—Duties

If you are having difficulty in making your list or want to be more thorough, try to think of the things that you do because you sense you have to. Consider duties related to the following categories:

- children
- citizenship (voting)
- God
- home maintenance
- school
- church
- civic organization
- job/work
- family members
- self

Evaluation of Your Duties—As you evaluate your duties, ask God to help you identify which ones are based on compulsion and which ones are based on eternity. God's goal is to move your duties from compulsion to eternity.

LIST 8—Debts

If you are having difficulty in making your list or want to be more thorough, consider debts (including favors owed) related to the following categories:

- bartered services
- church
- financial obligations
- phone calls
- taxes
- dinner invitations
- giving gifts
- showing hospitality

Evaluation of Your Debts—As you evaluate your debts, ask God to help you identify which ones are temporal and which ones are eternal. God's goal is to move your debts from temporal to eternal.

LIST 9—Possessions

If you are having difficulty in making your list or want to be more thorough, consider possessions related to the following categories:

- automobiles
- clothes
- insurance policies
- leisure time equipment
- money/bank accounts
- books
- furniture
- ewelry
- stocks/bonds
- real estate/land

Evaluation of Your Possessions—As you evaluate your possessions, ask God to help you identify which ones you relate to as owner and which ones you relate to as steward. God's goal is to move your relationship to possessions from ownership to stewardship.

This area may be one of the most difficult for Christians in the Western world. Because of our prosperity, we often do not sense a need for God. Have any of your possessions become sacred (an idol) to you? Like the rich young ruler who talked with Jesus, God may ask you to give away some of those things because you have fallen in love with them. Giving and sharing are ways God may help you to move from owner to steward. That is one reason God requires a portion (tithe) of your income—to help you remember that He is Provider of all you have.

Ask God if you have things He wants you to give to someone or to a cause. Are there things you have that God wants you to share with others? Can you sell a possession to give more generously? Be alert to opportunities God may give you to test you in these areas. You may come across the opportunity as you talk to a friend. Someone might seek your help. A report at church or on a newscast could alert you to a need. Be sensitive and responsive to those things God brings your way to renew your thinking regarding possessions.

LIST 10—Fears

If you are having difficulty in making your list or want to be more thorough, consider fears or worries related to the following categories:

- violence
- natural disaster
- health
- housing/home/shelter
- money, or lack of it
- death
- future
- people
- job security
- safety, security

Evaluation of Your Fears—As you evaluate your fears, ask God to help you move from a state of being self-protective to being secure in Christ. God's goal is to change you from being one who is self-protective to one who finds his security in Christ.

LIST 11—Weaknesses

If you are having difficulty in making your list or want to be more thorough, consider weaknesses related to the following categories:

- codependency
- uneducated, unskilled
- mental disability
- physical disability
- family background
- lack of knowledge
- minority status
- poor health

Evaluation of Your Weaknesses—As you evaluate your weaknesses, ask God to help you identify which ones are Satan's and which ones are God's. God's goal is to move your weaknesses from being tools of Satan to being tools of God.

LIST 12—Hurts

If you are having difficulty in making your list or want to be more thorough, consider hurts, grudges, or resentments related to the following categories:

- childhood experiences with family/relatives
- childhood experiences with friends/neighbors
- crime, fraud, injustice
- failure
- misunderstanding
- divorce
- job demotion, loss
- abuse

Evaluation of Your Hurts—As you evaluate your hurts, ask God to help you identify which ones you respond to with resentment and which ones you respond to with love. God's goal is to move your hurts from producing resentment to producing love.

PURE

For additional help on becoming pure see pages 66-67.

Possible Points of Temptation

The impurity Christians battle today touches primarily two areas: (1) Lust for the forbidden. This is expressed as a preoccupation with anything unlawful, immoral, or wrong. This might include things like engaging in improper sexual behavior, trusting the horoscope, watching x-rated movies, and other such activities. This is an "itch" for expression outside the realm of normal Christlike activity. (2) Lust for power. This is expressed either in lust for wealth or for position. The lust for power is recognizable in our motives. Temptation may come through attitudes expressed in television, movies, magazines, newspapers, radio, music, jokes, and gossip.

Becoming Pure

We can become pure by constantly practicing the presence of God.
- Recognize that God is present with you.
- Screen your thoughts, what you look at, and what you listen to.
- Mentally evaluate the purity of your thoughts, sights, and sounds by the standard of Christ's purity.
- When possible, avoid impure communication (turn off the TV or radio, close the book or magazine, leave the room).
- Identify regular problem areas (activities you do, places you go, things you watch or read that frequently cause you to have impure thoughts).
- Get rid of ever-present temptations.
- Find pure things to think about, watch, read, or do.

Scriptures for Meditation

As you read the following Scriptures, ask God to speak to you about the purity or impurity in your life. Watch for specific ways God may guide you to avoid impurities or to develop purity.

"Finally, brethren, whatsoever things are true, whatsoever things are honest, whatsoever things are just, whatsoever things are pure, whatsoever things are lovely, whatsoever things are of good report; if there be any virtue, and if there be any praise, think on these things" (Phil. 4:8).

Pure: blameless, clean, chaste, pristine, spotless, unblemished, innocent, unadulterated, stainless, not contaminated, beyond reproach

Opposites of *Pure:* lustful, carnal, fleshly, lewd, contaminated, tainted, corrupt, depraved, immoral, impure

Perversions of *Pure:* puritanical, pharisaical, rigid, severe, overly strict, prudish, austere, self-righteous

"Beloved, now are we the sons of God, and it doth not yet appear what we shall be: but we know that, when he shall appear, we shall be like him; for we shall see him as he is. And every man that hath this hope in him purifieth himself, even as he is pure" (1 John 3:2-3).

PEACEABLE

Peaceable: peaceful, friendly, harmonious, orderly, quiet, content, reconciling, calm, agreeable, compatible

Opposites of *Peaceable:* fussy, nit-picking, picky, contentious, combative, competitive, argumentative, cantankerous, ornery, controversial, litigious, contrary, cranky, disagreeable, mean, obstinate

Perversions of *Peaceable:* compromising, wishy-washy, goes with the flow, people-pleaser

For additional help on becoming peaceable see pages 68-70.

Possible Points of Temptation

Times when you are hungry, tired, or fatigued may cause you to test your peaceable spirit. Other times might be when your pride is strong and you seek to put others down or show them up, when you desire to impress others, or when you are around people who love to argue or debate meaningless issues.

Becoming Peaceable

You can become peaceable by bringing into harmony the perfections of Christ in you with those of others.

- Learn to recognize times when peace is needed.
- When you recognize times when peace is needed, pray to the Prince of Peace for godly wisdom in responding to the circumstances.
- Ask God to help you display a servant heart.
- Will a humble spirit or forgiveness dispel the tensions? If it is appropriate, do what you can to show such a spirit.
- Suggest a cooling-off time or call the people involved to prayer.
- Seek to maintain a spirit of unity in the bond of peace.
- See if people in the conflict have needs that can be met.
- Watch for ways to bring about consensus or agreement, but stop short of compromising on convictions or truth.

Scriptures for Meditation

As you read the following Scriptures, ask God to speak to you about your peaceable behavior. Watch for specific ways God may guide you to choose peace and harmony over strife.

"Follow peace with all men, and holiness, without which no man shall see the Lord" (Heb. 12:14).

"Be at peace among yourselves. Now we exhort you, brethren, warn them that are unruly, comfort the feebleminded, support the weak, be patient toward all men. See that none render evil for evil unto any man; but ever follow that which is good, both among yourselves, and to all men" (1 Thess. 5:13-15).

GENTLE

For additional help on becoming gentle see pages 70-71.

Becoming Gentle

You can become gentle by applying the perfect skill of Christ to the removal of the imperfections in the body of Christ.

- Examine yourself first (Matt. 7:3-5).
- Act only out of love, desiring the best for the body of Christ.
- Follow God's prescribed ways for church discipline. (See Matt. 18:15-20; 1 Cor. 5:6-13; 2 Cor. 7:8-11; Titus 3:10; 2 Tim. 4:2; 2 Thess. 3:14-15.)
- Pray carefully about when and how to respond.
- Treat others as brothers and sisters or as gently as children.

Scriptures for Meditation

As you read the following Scriptures, ask God to speak to you about gentleness or harshness in your life. Watch for specific ways God may guide you to respond to others with a gentle spirit.

"The servant of the Lord must not strive; but be gentle unto all men, apt to teach, patient" (2 Tim. 2:24).

"Put them in mind to be subject to principalities and powers, to obey magistrates, to be ready to every good work, To speak evil of no man, to be no brawlers, but gentle, shewing all meekness unto all men. For we ourselves also were sometimes foolish, disobedient, deceived, serving divers lusts and pleasures, living in malice and envy, hateful, and hating one another" (Titus 3:1-3).

ENTREATABLE

For additional help on becoming entreatable see pages 71-72.

Becoming Entreatable

You can become entreatable by making yourself available, knowing that God only allows circumstances in your life that build the body of Christ.

- See every circumstance as an event that God has permitted.
- Develop an intimacy with God so that you are always in a spirit of prayer—"pray without ceasing."
- When someone asks something of you, seek God's perspective on how to respond.

Gentle: fitting, equitable, fair, moderate, forbearing, considerate, humane, reasonable, pleasant, nurturing, tender, delicate, tactful, affable, amiable, genial, gracious, considerate, kindhearted

Opposites of *Gentle:* harsh, caustic, rough, abusive, hard, stiff, bitter, cruel, fierce, violent, blunt, brash, rude, short, snippy, grating

Perversions of *Gentle:* unkind restraint, negligent, lax, derelict, heedless, careless, delinquent, neglectful, inattentive, reckless, unchecked, unbridled, reticent

Entreatable: approachable, cordial, affable, helpful, accessible, available, open, reachable, cooperative, willing, inclined, amenable, accommodating, responsive

Opposites of *Entreatable:* unapproachable, distanced, cold, cool, reticent, uncooperative, inaccessible, closed, unresponsive, restrained, introverted

Perversions of *Entreatable:* yes-person, pushover, easy mark, dupe, chump, stooge, sucker

Scriptures for Meditation

Read the following Scriptures to prepare your mind to respond to requests in God's way.

"Whosoever shall compel thee to go a mile, go with him twain. Give to him that asketh thee, and from him that would borrow of thee turn not thou away" (Matt. 5:41-42). "If thine enemy be hungry, give him bread to eat; and if he be thirsty, give him water to drink" (Prov. 25:21).

MERCIFUL

Merciful: caring, forgiving, gracious, decent, chivalrous, noble, forbearing, sympathetic, tolerant, compassionate, charitable, benevolent

For additional help on becoming merciful see pages 72-73.

Possible Points of Temptation

The world encourages us to get even, to demand our rights, to look out for ourselves, to give others what they deserve. Kingdom ways are different. The basis for being merciful is to remember how much mercy God has shown us. Read Matthew 18:21-35 about an unmerciful servant.

Opposites of *Merciful:* merciless, unmerciful, unsympathetic, compassionless, hardened, uncaring, pitiless, spiteful

Becoming Merciful

You can become merciful by desiring to express the greatness of God.

Perversions of *Merciful:* indulgent, lenient, permissive

Scriptures for Meditation

As you read the following Scriptures, ask God to speak to you about being merciful. Watch for specific ways God may guide you to forgive someone or show mercy. "Be ye therefore merciful, as your Father also is merciful" (Luke 6:36).

"For if ye forgive men their trespasses, your heavenly Father will also forgive you: But if ye forgive not men their trespasses, neither will your Father forgive your trespasses" (Matt. 6:14-15).

FRUITFUL

Fruitful: productive, fertile, prolific, constructive, high yield

For additional help on becoming fruitful see pages 74-75.

Possible Points of Temptation

Opposites of *Fruitful:* fruitless, unproductive, non-productive, ineffective, ineffectual, unyielding, worthless, empty, hollow, profitless

Explaining away your fruitlessness by pointing to your circumstances indicates your lack of trust in God. Nothing is impossible to Him. Jesus said, "I will build my church; and the gates of hell shall not prevail against it" (Matt. 16:18). No opposition from the enemy will be able to thwart what God intends to do through His people.

Another danger in our world is to strive for success in the world's eyes and have still-born fruit. Rushing to decisions without making sure people are converted can make numbers look good, but is the fruit reproducing? The commission to make disciples includes teaching them to obey and practice all that Christ commanded. It is possible that God will grant you the success you desire without the blessing of His presence. God told Moses to go in and take the promised land. God said He would send an angel to drive out the inhabitants; God would not go with the people lest He destroy them for their rebellion. Moses could have success at the cost of God's presence. Moses was a wise spiritual leader, and he prayed:

> "If thy presence go not with me, carry us not up hence. For wherein shall it be known here that I and thy people have found grace in thy sight? is it not in that thou goest with us? so shall we be separated, I and thy people, from all the people that are upon the face of the earth" (Ex. 33:15-16).

Becoming Fruitful

You can become fruitful by cultivating processes and methods which produce godly results.

- Study the Scriptures with a ready heart to know God's ways. Watch for contrasts between God's ways and the world's ways.
- When God gives you an assignment, continue praying until He guides you in the way or method.
- Ask other believers to help you evaluate the fruit of your life.

Scriptures for Meditation

As you read the following Scriptures, ask God to speak to you about your fruitfulness. What is the quality and quantity of the fruit in your life? Watch for specific things in your life that God may want to prune away so that you will be more fruitful.

"Abide in me, and I in you. As the branch cannot bear fruit of itself, except it abide in the vine; no more can ye, except ye abide in me. I am the vine, ye are the branches: He that abideth in me, and I in him, the same bringeth forth much fruit: for without me ye can do nothing" (John 15:4-5).

"Ye have not chosen me, but I have chosen you, and ordained you, that ye should go and bring forth fruit, and that your fruit should remain: that whatsoever ye shall ask of the Father in my name, he may give it you" (John 15:16).

Perversions of *Fruitful:* fruit-obsessed, success-driven, obsessed with numbers, vain, showy

Steadfast: firm, unshakable, sure, never-failing, enduring, abiding, resolute, constant, adamant, devoted, staunch, steady, immovable, resolved, uncompromising

Opposites of *Steadfast:* wavering, unsure, unstable, vacillating, weak, wobbly, waffling, fickle, volatile, flimsy, shaky, faltering, halting, hesitant, indecisive, reluctant, wayward, capricious

STEADFAST

Perversions of *Steadfast:* inflexible, rigid, narrow-minded, obstinate, stubborn, unbendable, bullheaded, hardheaded, hard-line, inelastic, despotic, authoritarian, tyrannical, severe, iron-handed, intransigent

For additional help on becoming steadfast see page 75.

Possible Points of Temptation

Paul gave Timothy this advice: "Keep that which is committed to thy trust, avoiding profane and vain babblings, and oppositions of science falsely so called: Which some professing have erred concerning the faith" (1 Tim. 6:20-21). Avoid getting caught up in debates about truth which could lead you astray rather than keep you on track.

Becoming Steadfast

You can become steadfast by believing that God has a strong preference about your behavior for every circumstance He allows in your life.

• Agree with God that He has a right to dictate how you will live your life.

• Cultivate an intimate relationship with God in prayer.

• When you are faced with a situation that could cause you to waver, turn to Christ—your sure foundation.

Scriptures for Meditation

As you read the following Scriptures, ask God to speak to you about your steadfastness or wavering. Watch for specific ways God may guide you to avoid wavering or to develop steadfastness.

"Therefore, my beloved brethren, be ye steadfast, unmoveable, always abounding in the work of the Lord, forasmuch as ye know that your labour is not in vain in the Lord" (1 Cor. 15:58).

"Be sober, be vigilant; because your adversary the devil, as a roaring lion, walketh about, seeking whom he may devour: Whom resist steadfast in the faith, knowing that the same afflictions are accomplished in your brethren that are in the world. But the God of all grace, who hath called us unto his eternal glory by Christ Jesus, after that ye have suffered a while, make you perfect, stablish, strengthen, settle you" (1 Pet. 5:8-10).

HONEST

Honest: sincere, true, genuine, ethical, sound, trustworthy, upright, straightforward, factual, candid, forthright, real, plain dealing

For additional help on becoming honest see pages 75-77.

Possible Points of Temptation

Learn to say no at the slightest hint of dishonesty or falsehood. Temptation will lure you to get further and further from the truth until you find great difficulty in being honest. Don't let yourself stray even the slightest bit from the truth.

Becoming Honest

You can become honest by representing God appropriately to every person God allows in your life.

- Keep your life clean, pure, and holy so people who see you will be able to see the Christ who dwells in you.
- Allow God's love to flow through you in your relationships with others.
- Let every word out of your mouth be truthful so that people will not question your honesty or integrity.
- Let love guide your speech if God wants to speak words of correction through you.

Scriptures for Meditation

As you read the following Scriptures, ask God to speak to you about your honesty and sincerity. Watch for specific ways God may guide you to avoid hypocrisy and lying or to develop honesty.

"And this I pray, that your love may abound yet more and more in knowledge and in all judgment; That ye may approve things that are excellent; that ye may be sincere and without offence till the day of Christ" (Phil. 1:9-10).

"Having your conversation honest among the Gentiles: that, whereas they speak against you as evildoers, they may by your good works, which they shall behold, glorify God in the day of visitation" (1 Pet. 2:12).

LOVE

For additional help on showing love see pages 80-81.

Possible Points of Temptation

The great temptation is to base your love on feelings or circumstances. The challenge is to base your love on your will. Love is not just an emotion, it involves action. Love must be demonstrated.

Showing Love

You can show love by perfect giving of yourself to others. Try to apply the following 15 behaviors of love in your relationships and responses to others. Watch for opportunities God may bring across your life in order for you to learn to love more perfectly. Review this list (The Mind of Christ Card 13) periodically and ask God to help you evaluate your "love life" based on the perfect standard of Christ. Check the behaviors upon which you have opportunity to act. You may want to make space in your journal or notebook to describe the experiences where you demonstrate each behavior.

Opposites of *Honest:* lying, dishonest, hypocritical, counterfeit, fake, fraudulent, crooked, deceitful, scheming, shady, unscrupulous, corrupt

Perversions of *Honest:* brutal, cruel, callous, pitiless, unkind, ferocious, hard hearted, indifferent, ruthless, spiteful, unrelenting, vicious

Love: affection, charity, compassion, benevolence, adoration, fondness, commitment, caring deeply

Opposites of *Love:* hate, animosity, antipathy, aversion, dislike, enmity, hostility, ill-will, malice, vindictiveness, fear, dread, fright

Perversions of *Love:* possessive, overly protective, permissive, smothering love, manipulative

Love

- ❑ Suffers long (holy relationships).
- ❑ Is kind (holy purposes).
- ❑ Does not envy (holy heart).
- ❑ Does not brag (holy speech).
- ❑ Is not arrogant (holy service).
- ❑ Does not act unbecomingly (holy behavior).
- ❑ Does not seek its own (holy desires).
- ❑ Is not easily provoked (holy temperament).
- ❑ Does not take into account a wrong (holy bookkeeping).
- ❑ Does not rejoice in unrighteousness (holy conscience).
- ❑ Rejoices in the truth (holy mind).
- ❑ Bears all things (holy stability).
- ❑ Believes all things (holy values).
- ❑ Hopes all things (holy expectations).
- ❑ Endures all things (holy sacrifice).

Scriptures for Meditation

As you read the following Scriptures, ask God to speak to you about love. Watch for specific ways God may guide you to show your love to others.

"And thou shalt love the Lord thy God with all thy heart, and with all thy soul, and with all thy mind, and with all thy strength: this is the first commandment. And the second is like, namely this, Thou shalt love thy neighbour as thyself. There is none other commandment greater than these" (Mark 12:30-31).

"A new commandment I give unto you, That ye love one another; as I have loved you, that ye also love one another. By this shall all men know that ye are my disciples, if ye have love one to another" (John 13:34-35).

JOY

Joy: delight, gladness, calm, cheerfulness, bliss, enjoyment, contentment, radiance

Opposites of *Joy:* pain, hurt, wound, agony, anguish, distress, misery, torment, woe

Perversions of *Joy:* frenzy, crazed excitement, hysteria

For additional help on showing joy see pages 82-83.

Possible Points of Temptation

Joy is based on God's truth, not on your immediate circumstances. If you allow yourself to be tossed about by the storms of life, you may miss joy. Sin also destroys joy. David prayed in Psalm 51 for God to forgive him and restore the joy.

Showing Joy

You can show joy by choosing the glory of God in every circumstance.

- Quote Scriptures that remind you of God's truth.
- Ask God to give you understanding from His perspective about your circumstance.

Continue to trust God's sovereignty and love even if He does not give you an answer.

- Seek to gain God's perspective on suffering and trials.
- Think about your circumstances in light of eternity, not just for the present time.
- Remember that God's grace is sufficient for you even in times of weakness.
- Seek to bring glory to God in the way you respond to every circumstance.

Scriptures for Meditation

As you read the following Scriptures, ask God to speak to you about joy. Watch for specific ways God may guide you to show your joy in circumstances that are trying or difficult. Select Scriptures for memorization that may be helpful to you in trying times.

"Restore unto me the joy of thy salvation; and uphold me with thy free spirit. Then will I teach transgressors thy ways; and sinners shall be converted unto thee" (Ps. 51:12-13).

"Now the God of hope fill you with all joy and peace in believing, that ye may abound in hope, through the power of the Holy Ghost" (Rom. 15:13).

PEACE

For additional help on showing peace see pages 83-84.

Possible Points of Temptation

Peace comes from within. Peace does not come from outward circumstances. Sin destroys peace. War from within comes from lusts and desires that battle against each other.

Showing Peace

You can show peace by resting in the achievements and character of Christ. When peace is not present, ask God to help you identify the sin or the conflicting desires that are robbing you of the peace He wants to manifest in you.

Scriptures for Meditation

As you read the following Scriptures, ask God to speak to you about peace. Watch for specific opportunities God may allow you to experience where He can manifest His perfect peace in you—a peace that passes understanding.

"Thou wilt keep him in perfect peace, whose mind is stayed on thee: because he trusteth in thee. Trust ye in the Lord forever, for in the Lord Jehovah is everlasting strength" (Isa. 26:3-4).

"Therefore being justified by faith, we have peace with God through our Lord Jesus Christ" (Rom. 5:1).

Peace: rest, quietness, tranquility, harmony, concord, repose, serenity

Opposites of *Peace:* war, rage, havoc, discord, conflict, strife, rivalry, clash, feud, brawl, fracas, hassle, melee, rift

Perversions of *Peace:* neutrality, lukewarmness, indifference, detached, uncommitted, uninvolved

LONG-SUFFERING

Long-suffering: patience, endurance, constancy, steadfastness, perseverance, forbearance, slow in avenging wrongs

Opposites of *Long-suffering:* impatient, edgy, chafing, crabby, nagging, touchy, impetuous, restless, quick to avenge wrongs

Perversions of *Long-suffering:* lenient, indulgent, permissive

For additional help on showing long-suffering see pages 85-86.

Possible Points of Temptation

To suffer "long" you must not place limits on your willingness to endure. If you ever limit your willingness, the enemy knows and he will test those limits.

Showing Long-Suffering

You can show long-suffering by cooperating with God in the process of bringing others into the character of Christ.

Scriptures for Meditation

As you read the following Scriptures, ask God to speak to you about long-suffering or patience. Watch for specific ways God may guide you to show patience in your relationships with others. Look for Scriptures that tell you how God will be working to develop your patience. Submit to those circumstances; don't fight them. Cherish them. Thank God for them.

"Now we exhort you, brethren, warn them that are unruly, comfort the feebleminded, support the weak, be patient toward all men" (1 Thess. 5:14).

"My brethren, count it all joy when ye fall into divers temptations; Knowing this, that the trying of your faith worketh patience. But let patience have her perfect work, that ye may be perfect and entire, wanting nothing" (Jas. 1:2-4).

Gentleness: kindness, goodness of heart, integrity, goodness in deeds or actions, kindly disposition toward others

Opposites of *Gentleness:* severity, harsh, caustic, rough, abusive, hard, stiff, bitter, cruel, fierce, violent, blunt, brash, rude, short, snippy, grating

Perversions of *Gentleness:* soft, mushy, negligence, laxity, dereliction, heedless, careless, inattentive, unchecked, unbridled, reticent

GENTLENESS

For additional help on showing gentleness see pages 86-87.

Possible Points of Temptation

What is inside your mind and heart will show on the outside in your actions. If you have a hard heart or prejudices toward other people, you will not act with gentleness. If your actions are hard and reflect the opposites or perversions of gentleness, something is wrong on the inside. Ask God to examine your heart and mind and reveal the problem area.

Showing Gentleness

You can show gentleness by disposing your mind for the caress of God's touch on all His children.

Scriptures for Meditation

As you read the following Scriptures, ask God to speak to you about gentleness. Watch for specific ways God may guide you to show gentleness to others.

"For his merciful kindness is great toward us: and the truth of the Lord endureth for ever. Praise ye the Lord" (Ps. 117:2).

"And beside this, giving all diligence, add to your faith virtue; and to virtue knowledge; And to knowledge temperance; and to temperance patience; and to patience godliness; And to godliness brotherly kindness; and to brotherly kindness charity" (2 Pet. 1:5-7).

GOODNESS

For additional help on showing goodness see pages 88-89.

Possible Points of Temptation

The greatest temptation is to think that goodness comes from ourselves rather than from God. Because of sin, "there is none that doeth good, no, not one" (Rom. 3:12). Claiming a good life in your own self-righteousness is foolishness (see Prov. 20:6). Badness, unwholesomeness, or fruitlessness is an indication of a more serious problem. A good tree bears good fruit. A bad tree bears bad fruit. Your spiritual nature can be determined by the nature of the fruit you bear.

Showing Goodness

You can show goodness by working with God in His way.

Scriptures for Meditation

As you read the following Scriptures, ask God to speak to you about goodness. Watch for specific ways God may guide you to show goodness in your work with Him. Notice God's goodness as you read these Scriptures.

"Surely goodness and mercy shall follow me all the days of my life: and I will dwell in the house of the Lord for ever" (Ps. 23:6).

"I myself also am persuaded of you, my brethren, that ye also are full of goodness, filled with all knowledge, able also to admonish one another" (Rom. 15:14).

Goodness: uprightness of heart and life, moral goodness, wholesome, productive, functioning, in good working order

Opposites of *Goodness:* badness, unwholesome, non-productive, evil, corruption, depravity, immorality, wickedness

Perversions of *Goodness:* finicky nice, self-righteous

FAITH/FAITHFULNESS

Faith: faithfulness, trustworthiness, integrity, reliability, fidelity, ardor, loyalty, dependability, consistency

Opposites of *Faith:* faithlessness, fickleness, untrustworthiness, inconsistency, uncertainty, waywardness, capriciousness

Perversions of *Faith:* legalism, workaholism, over-committed, fanatical, overly zealous, extremism

For additional help on showing faith or faithfulness see pages 89-90.

Possible Points of Temptation

When you have been faithful for a long time and you are confronted with persecution, frustration, or weariness, you may be tempted to let up rather than persevere. The perversion of faithfulness also is common. People sometimes unconsciously think that the amount and difficulty of their "work for God" somehow earns His love or pleasure. But God's love is not for sale; it is unconditional. With the wrong motivation a person can move from faithfulness to being legalistic. Some Christians take every job that comes along, trying to do enough, and they turn into religious workaholics—very busy, but not very fruitful. God would prefer your faithfulness only to those assignments He gives. Avoid getting distracted by busywork devised by the initiative of men rather than the assignments God gives. Trust God to help you discern between the two.

Showing Faith/Faithfulness

You can show faithfulness by obeying God's commands and completing work He assigns to you.

- Begin by obeying the things you already know God has commanded.
- Be a faithful steward of the time and resources God gives you.
- When God gives you an assignment, keep doing it until the job is complete or God moves you to the next assignment.

Scriptures for Meditation

As you read the following Scriptures, ask God to speak to you about faithfulness. Watch for specific ways God may guide you to show or express faithfulness.

"A faithful man shall abound with blessings: but he that maketh haste to be rich shall not be innocent" (Prov. 28:20).

"His lord said unto him, Well done, thou good and faithful servant: thou hast been faithful over a few things, I will make thee ruler over many things: enter thou into the joy of thy lord" (Matt. 25:21).

MEEKNESS

Meekness: accepting God's dealings with us as good without resistance, a fruit of power, lowly before God and humble before man

For additional help on showing meekness see pages 90-91.

Possible Points of Temptation

The greatest temptation in this virtue is to let pride cause you to be self-assertive due to self-interest.

Showing Meekness

You can show meekness by disengaging the trappings of worldly power from your mind.

Scriptures for Meditation

As you read the following Scriptures, ask God to speak to you about meekness. Watch for specific ways God may guide you to show meekness.

"Take my yoke upon you, and learn of me; for I am meek and lowly in heart: and ye shall find rest unto your souls" (Matt. 11:29).

"Brethren, if a man be overtaken in a fault, ye which are spiritual, restore such an one in the spirit of meekness; considering thyself, lest thou also be tempted" (Gal. 6:1).

TEMPERANCE

For additional help on showing temperance see page 91.

Possible Points of Temptation

Human appetites may be your point of weakness. Watch out for those areas where intemperance or even addiction is common: eating, gossip, strong drink, drugs, gambling, pleasure seeking, television watching, overdoing any activity.

Showing Temperance

You can show temperance by accepting and applying the Holy Spirit's guidance as you master your desires and sensual appetites.

Scripture for Meditation

As you read the following Scripture, ask God to speak to you about temperance. Watch for specific ways God may guide you to develop or show temperance. Then confess, repent, and turn to the Lord for help.

"And every man that striveth for the mastery is temperate in all things. Now they do it to obtain a corruptible crown; but we an incorruptible. I therefore so run, not as uncertainly; so fight I, not as one that beateth the air: But I keep under my body, and bring it into subjection: lest that by any means, when I have preached to others, I myself should be a castaway" (1 Cor. 9:25-27).

"Let not sin therefore reign in your mortal body, that ye should obey it in the lusts thereof" (Rom. 6:12).

Opposites of Meekness: arrogance, haughtiness, pride, cockiness, egotism, self-assertiveness, self-interest, vanity, conceit

Perversions of Meekness: weakness, "wimpy," cowardly, spinelessness, timidity

Temperance: strength, controlling power of the will under the operation of the Spirit of God, self-control, mastery over desires or sensual appetites, endisciplined by God

Opposites of Temperance: undisciplined, self-indulgent, slothful, lazy, lackadaisical, sluggish, laid back

Perversions of Temperance: fleshly effort, self-effort

🔖 The following instrument is provided for you to measure your growth as a servant of Christ. Read each of the statements. Evaluate the attitudes of your servant mind. Use the following scale and place the appropriate number in each blank. The higher your total score, the closer you believe you are to attaining servanthood.

1–No, that's not me.
2–That's me sometimes.
3–That's me often.
4–Yes, that's definitely me.

Humble—Proper attitude toward the Master's work in others.
_____ I see my work as a part of God's plan.

Obedient—Understanding the authority of the Master over my time and life.
_____ I am obeying all known commands of Scripture.

Willing—Identity with the Master's attitudes.
_____ My great desire is to be about the Father's business.

Loyal—Unswerving devotion to the Master.
_____ I get my joy from the company of the Master, rather than what will enrich me.

Faithful—Confidence that anticipates the Master continuing His plan.
_____ God has enriched His kingdom through my work.

Watchful—Attentiveness to the Master's voice.
_____ I have learned recently something new about God.

Courageous—Conviction about the Master's priorities.
_____ My conviction is so strong that I cannot deny Christ any request He makes of me.

Not Quarrelsome—Peace that awaits the Master's work in others.
_____ I have no quarrel with any brother or sister in God's family.

Gentle—Respect that enhances the work of others for the Master.
_____ My desire is to enhance the work of my brothers and sisters, not that they make me look good.

Able to Teach—Understanding the Master's work.
_____ My concern is the authority of Christ. I desire His Word and will, not my opinion.

Patient—Forbearance that values the Master's purposes for others.
_____ I am willing to wait on the growth process in others.

Meek—Disciplined sensitivity to the Master.
_____ I am sensitive to the Master.

Good—Applied trust in the Master's excellence.
_____ All the fruit you can see in my life was produced by the Holy Spirit.

Wise—Dependence on the Master's method.
_____ I use God's method in doing my work rather than my method.

[ ] **Total Score (range: 14-56)**

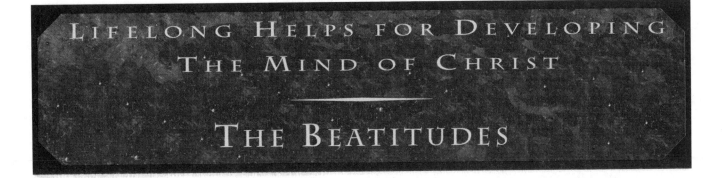

THE BEATITUDES

A—FIRST FOUR BEATITUDES

1. Blessed are the poor in spirit: for theirs is the kingdom of heaven.
2. Blessed are they that mourn: for they shall be comforted.
3. Blessed are the meek: for they shall inherit the earth.
4. Blessed are they which do hunger and thirst after righteousness: for they shall be filled.

```
A-1: Poor in Spirit . . . . Principle of Need
A-2: Mourn . . . . . . . . Principle of Brokenness
A-3: Meek . . . . . . . . . Principle of Submission
A-4: Hungry. . . . . . . . Principle of Yearning
```

- *Basis for Happiness*—Your need
- *Keys* to God's Heart
- *Focus*—Turn your mind toward God. You learn about God. You learn that God is God.
- *Command*—Love God–"Thou shalt love the Lord thy God with all thy heart, and with all thy soul, and with all thy mind, and with all they strength" (Mark 12:30).
- *Object*—God gives according to your need to mold and shape you into the image of Christ. He equips you with the character of Christ.
- *Door* to Greatness
- *Worship*—Lower Levels of Worship–Praise to God comes out of your need and His sufficiency to meet your need.

B—SECOND FOUR BEATITUDES

5. Blessed are the merciful: for they shall obtain mercy.
6. Blessed are the pure in heart: for they shall see God.
7. Blessed are the peacemakers: for they shall be called the children of God.
8. Blessed are they which are persecuted for righteousness' sake: for theirs is the kingdom of heaven. Blessed are ye, when men shall revile you, and persecute you, and shall say all manner of evil against you falsely, for my sake. Rejoice, and be exceeding glad: for great is your reward in heaven: for so persecuted they the prophets which were before you.

```
B-1: Merciful . . . . . . . Principle of Reciprocity
B-2: Pure in Heart. . . . . Principle of Perfect Heart
B-3: Peacemakers. . . . . . Principle of Reconciliation
B-4: Persecuted . . . . . . Principle of Identification
```

- *Basis for Happiness*—Your giving
- *Keys* to Christ's Character
- *Focus*—Turn your mind toward others. You serve in Christ's spirit. You reflect Christ to a watching world.
- *Command*—Love Others–"Thou shalt love thy neighbor as thyself" (Mark 12:31).
- *Object*—God works through you to reveal Himself to a watching world. You become identified with Christ as you reveal His character to others.
- *Practice* of Greatness
- *Worship*—Higher Levels of Worship–Praise to God comes from the exercise of your character as you reveal the character of Christ to others.

God's Training for Royalty and Nobility

Circumstances in life become opportunities for God to work in and through you. God uses circumstances in life to develop these qualities (Beatitudes) in your life. Every circumstance in life can become an adventure as you turn to God to see what He may want to do to develop your character or to work through you to reveal His character to others. God is working to train you for a noble future. You are a child of the King. God will take you through this cycle over and over again in order to train you for your royal and noble future reign with Christ.

> Pause and pray. Ask God to take you through circumstances in order to train you fully for your royal and noble future reign with Christ.

Using This Lifelong Helps

The following pages describe each of the eight Beatitudes in detail. Following the same format for each Beatitude, you can study each one to understand what it would look like in your life.

- You will see what the Beatitude is and what it is not.
- You will look at an example from the life of Jesus as He manifested this quality in His life.
- You will look at one or more examples from the Bible of other people who demonstrated this quality.
- God is going to be taking you through circumstances to mold this quality into your life. "What God Is Doing in Me" will help you see the goal God has in mind for you.
- "Circumstances Through Which God May Work" will give you an idea of the kinds of circumstances God may use to develop this trait in your life. If these circumstances come to you, consider them as God's invitation for spiritual growth. They may not all be pleasant. However, happy is the one who submits to God's process. Even when "bad" things happen, "God causes all things to work together for good to those who love God, to those who are called according to His purpose" (Rom. 8:28, NASB).
- "How I Express This Attitude" will give you some ideas of practical ways this attitude might show in your life. You may intentionally choose some of these as an "action plan" to work on developing the quality in your daily living.

- "Prayers" will give you an idea of ways you can express this attitude before God (First Four Beatitudes). Or how you may seek God's assistance as you express these attitudes toward others (Second Four Beatitudes).
- "Response in Worship" describes the way this attitude would be reflected in your worship. This section includes such things as a definition, biblical commands, promised blessings, biblical prayers, and biblical applications.

The Mind of Christ Cards

The Mind of Christ Cards summarize the following helps. Carry these cards with you for meditation, review, or application of the attitudes in your life. Cards related to the Beatitudes are:

6. Scripture Memory—Matthew 5:3-10
20. Poor in Spirit
21. Mourn
22. Meek
23. Hungry
24. Merciful
25. Pure in Heart
26. Peacemakers
27. Persecuted

For more information on the Beatitudes see unit 7—The Beatitudes (pp. 110-120).

A-1
POOR IN SPIRIT

"Blessed are the poor in spirit: for theirs is the kingdom of heaven" (MATT. 5:3).

Examples

Jesus: "Jesus said, Suffer little children, and forbid them not, to come unto me: for of such is the kingdom of heaven" (Matt. 19:14).

The Pharisee and the Publican: "Two men went up into the temple to pray; the one a Pharisee, and the other a publican. The Pharisee stood and prayed thus with himself, God, I thank thee, that I am not as other men are, extortioners, unjust, adulterers, or even as this publican. I fast twice in the week, I give tithes of all that I possess. And the publican, standing afar off, would not lift up so much as his eyes unto heaven, but smote upon his breast, saying, God be merciful to me a sinner. I tell you, this man went down to his house justified rather than the other: for every one that exalteth himself shall be abased; and he that humbleth himself shall be exalted" (Luke 18:10-14).

What God Is Doing in Me

God prepares me to be merciful to others (see B-1, pp. 208-209).

Prayers

• I am needy, Lord.
• I am nothing and can do nothing without You.
• I need You to …
• I need You because…
• What do I need You to do in me?
• What do You have that I need?

Response in Worship: Fear God

Definition: Respect God, reverence God, display piety toward God; not a fear of God's power or His righteous retribution, instead a sense of obedience to God because He is God.

"The fear of the Lord is to hate evil: pride, and arrogancy, and the evil way, and the froward mouth, do I hate" (Prov. 8:13).

Command: "Ye shall walk after the Lord your God, and fear him, and keep his commandments, and obey his voice, and ye shall serve him, and cleave unto him" (Deut. 13:4).

Blessings: "Let all the earth fear the Lord: let all the inhabitants of the world stand in awe of him.… Behold, the eye of the Lord is upon them that fear him, upon them that hope in his mercy" (Ps. 33:8,18).

"The fear of the Lord is the beginning of wisdom: a good understanding have all they that do his commandments" (Ps. 111:10).

"The fear of the Lord tendeth to life: and he that hath it shall abide satisfied; he shall not be visited with evil" (Prov. 19:23).

"The fear of the Lord is a fountain of life" (Prov. 14:27).
Prayer: "Teach me thy way, O Lord; I will walk in thy truth: unite my heart to fear thy name" (Ps. 86:11).

Applied: "Submitting yourselves one to another in the fear of God" (Eph. 5:21).

"Wherefore we receiving a kingdom which cannot be moved, let us have grace, whereby we may serve God acceptably with reverence and godly fear" (Heb. 12:28).

A-2

MOURN

"Blessed are they that mourn: for they shall be comforted" (MATT. 5:4).

Examples

Jesus: "He is despised and rejected of men; a man of sorrows, and acquainted with grief: and we hid as it were our faces from him; he was despised, and we esteemed him not" (Isa. 53:3).

Mary, Martha, and Jesus: "Then when Mary was come where Jesus was, and saw him, she fell down at his feet, saying unto him, Lord, if thou hadst been here, my brother had not died. When Jesus therefore saw her weeping, and the Jews also weeping which came with her, he groaned in the spirit, and was troubled, And said, Where have ye laid him? They said unto him, Lord, come and see. Jesus wept" (John 11:32-35).

What God Is Doing in Me

God uses difficult circumstances to purify me. Like a Refiner's Fire, God works in me to develop a pure heart (see B-2, pp. 209-210).

Prayers

- I need Your comfort, Lord. Would You just hold me for a little while?
- How can I bring glory to Your name through this painful experience?
- What impurities in me do You want to burn out through this experience?
- What do You want to do in me to cause this experience to work together for good?
- What needs to be broken in my life or broken away from me?

Response in Worship: Ascribe Credit to God

Definition: To give credit to God; to bestow, report, mention, or utter.

Commend: "Ascribe to the Lord, O mighty ones, ascribe to the Lord glory and strength. Ascribe to the Lord the glory due his name; worship the Lord in the splendor of his holiness" (Ps. 29:1-2, NIV).

"Ascribe ye strength unto God: his excellency is over Israel, and his strength is in the clouds" (Ps. 68:34).

Prayer: "The Lord is my rock, and my fortress, and my deliverer; my God, my strength, in whom I will trust; my buckler, and the horn of my salvation, and my high tower" (Ps. 18:2).

Applied: "Because I will publish the name of the Lord: ascribe ye greatness unto our God. He is the Rock, his work is perfect: for all his ways are judgment: a God of truth and without iniquity, just and right is he" (Deut. 32:3-4).

A-3
MEEK

"Blessed are the meek: for they shall inherit the earth" (MATT. 5:5).

Examples

Jesus: "Take my yoke upon you, and learn of me; for I am meek and lowly in heart: and ye shall find rest unto your souls" (Matt. 11:29).

Mary: "And Mary said, My soul doth magnify the Lord, And my spirit hath rejoiced in God my Saviour. For he hath regarded the low estate of his handmaiden: for, behold, from henceforth all generations shall call me blessed. For he that is mighty hath done to me great things; and holy is his name. And his mercy is on them that fear him from generation to generation. He hath shewed strength with his arm; he hath scattered the proud in the imagination of their hearts. He hath put down the mighty from their seats, and exalted them of low degree. He hath filled the hungry with good things; and the rich he hath sent empty away. He hath holpen his servant Israel, in remembrance of his mercy; As he spake to our fathers, to Abraham, and to his seed for ever" (Luke 1:46-55).

John the Baptist: "He must increase, but I must decrease" (John 3:30).

David: "From the end of the earth will I cry unto thee, when my heart is overwhelmed: lead me to the rock that is higher than I" (Ps. 61:2).

What God Is Doing in Me

Through opportunities of submission to God, I learn the value of submission to others. God develops in me the character of a peacemaker (see B-3, pp. 210-211).

Prayers

- Not my will, but Thine be done.
- In what ways can I decrease so You may increase?
- In what areas of my life do I need to learn greater submission to You?
- How can I magnify and exalt You more than I do?
- Show me times when I should stand up for You in the face of opposition.

Response in Worship: Magnify, exalt

Definition: Magnify: to make great, to enlarge, to cause to grow. We magnify God when we focus attention on His greatness. Exalt: To raise, lift, lift up, set on high.

Command: "I will bless the Lord at all times: his praise shall continually be in my mouth. My soul shall make her boast in the Lord: the humble shall hear thereof, and be glad. O magnify the Lord with me, and let us exalt his name together" (Ps. 34:1-3).

"Exalt ye the Lord our God, and worship at his footstool; for he is holy. Exalt the Lord our God, and worship at his holy hill; for the Lord our God is holy" (Ps. 99:5,9).

Prayers: "Thine, O Lord, is the greatness, and the power, and the glory, and the victory, and the majesty: for all that is in the heaven and in the earth is thine; thine is the kingdom, O Lord, and thou art exalted as head above all. Both riches and honour come of thee, and thou reignest over all; and in thine hand is power and might; and in thine hand it is to make great, and to give strength unto all. Now therefore, our God, we thank thee, and praise thy glorious name" (1 Chron. 29:11-13).

"Let all those that seek thee rejoice and be glad in thee: and let such as love thy salvation say continually, Let God be magnified" (Ps. 70:4).

"O Lord, thou art my God; I will exalt thee, I will praise thy name; for thou hast done wonderful things; thy counsels of old are faithfulness and truth" (Isa. 25:1).
"Be thou exalted, Lord, in thine own strength: so will we sing and praise thy power" (Ps. 21:13).
Applied: "I will praise the name of God with a song, and will magnify him with thanksgiving" (Ps. 69:30).

A-4

HUNGRY

"Blessed are they which do hunger and thirst after righteousness: for they shall be filled" (MATT. 5:6).

Examples

Jesus: "Jesus saith unto them, My meat is to do the will of him that sent me, and to finish his work" (John 4:34).

The Bereans: "The brethren immediately sent away Paul and Silas by night unto Berea: who coming thither went into the synagogue of the Jews. These were more noble than those in Thessalonica, in that they received the word with all readiness of mind, and searched the scriptures daily, whether those things were so. Therefore many of them believed; also of honourable women which were Greeks, and of men, not a few" (Acts 17:10-12).

What God Is Doing in Me

God is causing me to seek after Him so He can mold and shape me into the image of His Son Jesus.

Prayers

- "As the hart panteth after the water brooks, so panteth my soul after thee, O God. My soul thirsteth for God, for the living God: when shall I come and appear before God?" (Ps. 42:1-2).
- "God, thou art my God; early will I seek thee: my soul thirsteth for thee, my flesh longeth for thee in a dry and thirsty land, where no water is" (Ps. 63:1).
- "I remember the days of old; I meditate on all thy works; I muse on the work of thy hands. I stretch forth my hands unto thee: my soul thirsteth after thee, as a thirsty land. Hear me speedily, O Lord: my spirit faileth: hide not thy face from me, lest I be like unto them that go down into the pit. Cause me to hear thy lovingkindness in the morning; for in thee do I trust: cause me to know the way wherein I should walk; for I lift up my soul unto thee" (Ps. 143:5-8).

Response in Worship: Thanksgiving

Definition: To give thanks to God for what He has done, expressing gratitude for God's bounty.

Command: "O give thanks unto the Lord; for he is good: because his mercy endureth for ever" (Ps. 118:1). "O give thanks to the Lord of lords: for his mercy endureth for ever. To him who alone doeth great wonders: for his mercy endureth for ever" (Ps. 136:3-4).

Prayers: "O Lord, truly I am thy servant; I am thy servant, and the son of thine handmaid: thou hast loosed my bonds. I will offer to thee the sacrifice of thanksgiving, and will call upon the name of the Lord" (Ps. 116:16-17).

"Thou hast turned for me my mourning into dancing: thou hast put off my sackcloth, and girded me with gladness; To the end that my glory may sing praise to thee, and not be silent. O Lord my God, I will give thanks unto thee for ever" (Ps. 30:11-12).

Applied: "I will sacrifice unto thee with the voice of thanksgiving; I will pay that that I have vowed. Salvation is of the Lord" (Jonah 2:9).

B-1
MERCIFUL

"Blessed are the merciful: for they shall obtain mercy" (MATT. 5:7).

Examples

Jesus: "They brought to him a man sick of the palsy, lying on a bed: and Jesus seeing their faith said unto the sick of the palsy; Son, be of good cheer; thy sins be forgiven thee" (Matt. 9:2).

God's response to others: "With the merciful thou wilt shew thyself merciful, and with the upright man thou wilt shew thyself upright. With the pure thou wilt shew thyself pure; and with the froward thou wilt shew thyself unsavoury" (2 Sam. 22:26-27).

Pharaoh's hardened heart during the plagues in Egypt: "Pharaoh's heart was hardened, neither did he hearken unto them; as the Lord had said. And Pharaoh turned and went into his house, neither did he set his heart to this also" (Ex. 7:22-23).

"When Pharaoh saw that there was respite, he hardened his heart, and hearkened not unto them; as the Lord had said. And Pharaoh hardened his heart at this time also, neither would he let the people go" (Ex. 8:15,32). "The Lord hardened the heart of Pharaoh, and he hearkened not unto them; as the Lord had spoken unto Moses" (Ex. 9:12).

What God Is Doing Through Me

God reveals His mercy, grace, and forgiveness through the way I treat others. God in turn treats me with mercy, grace, and forgiveness in the same way I have treated others.

Prayers

- Who are the people around me to whom I need to show mercy, forgiveness, or grace?
- Lord, increase my faith to be forgiving "seventy times seven."
- You have forgiven me so much. I will forgive in a like manner.

Response in Worship: Reverence

Definition: A sense of honour, modesty, reverence, regard for others, respect.

Command: "Ye shall keep my sabbaths, and reverence my sanctuary: I am the Lord" (Lev. 19:30).

"Stand in awe, and sin not: commune with your own heart upon your bed, and be still" (Ps. 4:4).

"God is greatly to be feared in the assembly of the saints, and to be had in reverence of all them that are about him" (Ps. 89:7).

"Keep thy foot when thou goest to the house of God, and be more ready to hear, than to give the sacrifice of fools: for they consider not that they do evil" (Eccl. 5:1).

"Sanctify the Lord of hosts himself" (Isa. 8:13).

"The Lord is in his holy temple: let all the earth keep silence before him" (Hab. 2:20).

Applied: "He said, Draw not nigh hither: put off thy shoes from off thy feet, for the place whereon thou standest is holy ground" (Ex. 3:5).

"Wherefore we receiving a kingdom which cannot be moved, let us have grace, whereby we may serve God acceptably with reverence and godly fear" (Heb. 12:28).

B-2
PURE IN HEART

"Blessed are the pure in heart: for they shall see God" (MATT. 5:8).

Examples

Jesus: "He said unto them, Ye are from beneath; I am from above: ye are of this world; I am not of this world" (John 8:23).

David becoming king: "When he had removed him, he raised up unto them David to be their king; to whom also he gave testimony, and said, I have found David the son of Jesse, a man after mine own heart, which shall fulfil all my will" (Acts 13:22).

David's prayer after his sin with Bathsheba: "Purge me with hyssop, and I shall be clean: wash me, and I shall be whiter than snow. Make me to hear joy and gladness; that the bones which thou hast broken may rejoice. Hide thy face from my sins, and blot out all mine iniquities. Create in me a clean heart, O God; and renew a right spirit within me. Cast me not away from thy presence; and take not thy holy spirit from me. Restore unto me the joy of thy salvation; and uphold me with thy free spirit. Then will I teach transgressors thy ways; and sinners shall be converted unto thee. Deliver me from bloodguiltiness, O God, thou God of my salvation: and my tongue shall sing aloud of thy righteousness. O Lord, open thou my lips; and my mouth shall shew forth thy praise. For thou desirest not sacrifice; else would I give it: thou delightest not in burnt offering. The sacrifices of God are a broken spirit: a broken and a contrite heart, O God, thou wilt not despise. Do good in thy good pleasure unto Zion: build thou the walls of Jerusalem. Then shalt thou be pleased with the sacrifices of righteousness, with burnt offering and whole burnt offering: then shall they offer bullocks upon thine altar" (Ps. 51:7-19).

What God Is Doing Through Me

God reveals His holiness, righteousness, and purity through my behavior. God responds to me by allowing me to have a greater intimacy with Him. God reveals more of Himself to me.

Prayer

- Lord, cleanse my heart and purify my mind.
- I choose to do Your will, O Lord.
- I love You with all my heart, mind, soul, and strength.
- Lead me not into temptation and deliver me from evil.

Response in Worship: Glorify

Definition: To make honourable, honour, to give glory.
Command: "Ye that fear the Lord, praise him; all ye the seed of Jacob, glorify him; and fear him" (Ps. 22:23).

"Let your light so shine before men, that they may see your good works, and glorify your Father which is in heaven" (Matt. 5:16).

"Ye are bought with a price: therefore glorify God in your body, and in your spirit, which are God's" (1 Cor. 6:20).

Blessings: "Call upon me in the day of trouble: I will deliver thee, and thou shalt glorify me" (Ps. 50:15).

Prayer: "All nations whom thou hast made shall come and worship before thee, O Lord; and shall glorify thy name. For thou art great, and doest wondrous things: thou art God alone" (Ps. 86:9-10).

"Who shall not fear thee, O Lord, and glorify thy name? for thou only art holy: for all nations shall come and worship before thee; for thy judgments are made manifest" (Rev. 15:4).

Applied: "Now the God of patience and consolation grant you to be likeminded one toward another according to Christ Jesus: That ye may with one mind and one mouth glorify God, even the Father of our Lord Jesus Christ. Wherefore receive ye one another, as Christ also received us to the glory of God" (Rom. 15:5-7).

"Yet if any man suffer as a Christian, let him not be ashamed; but let him glorify God on this behalf" (1 Pet. 4:16).

B-3
PEACEMAKER

"Blessed are the peacemakers: for they shall be called the children of God" (MATT. 5:9).

Examples

Jesus: "Salt is good: but if the salt have lost his saltness, wherewith will ye season it? Have salt in yourselves, and have peace one with another" (Mark 9:50).

James: "When there had been much disputing, Peter rose up, and said unto them, Men and brethren, ye know how that a good while ago God made choice among us, that the Gentiles by my mouth should hear the word of the gospel, and believe. And God, which knoweth the hearts, bare them witness, giving them the Holy Ghost, even as he did unto us; And put no difference between us and them, purifying their hearts by faith. Now therefore why tempt ye God, to put a yoke upon the neck of the disciples, which neither our fathers nor we were able to bear? But we believe that through the grace of the Lord Jesus Christ we shall be saved, even as they.

Then all the multitude kept silence, and gave audience to Barnabas and Paul, declaring what miracles and wonders God had wrought among the Gentiles by them.

And after they had held their peace, James answered, saying, Men and brethren, hearken unto me: Simeon hath declared how God at the first did visit the Gentiles, to take out of them a people for his name. And to this agree the words of the prophets; as it is written, After this I will return, and will build again the tabernacle of David, which is fallen down; and I will build again the ruins thereof, and I will set it up: That the residue of men might seek after the Lord, and all the Gentiles, upon whom my name is called, saith the Lord, who doeth all these things. Known unto God are all his works from the beginning of the world. Wherefore my sentence is, that we trouble not them, which from among the Gentiles are turned to God: But that we write unto them, that they abstain from pollutions of idols, and from fornication, and from things strangled, and from blood. For Moses of old time hath in every city them that preach him, being read in the synagogues every sabbath day.

Then pleased it the apostles and elders, with the whole church, to send chosen men of their own company to Antioch with Paul and Barnabas; namely, Judas surnamed Barsabas, and Silas, chief men among the brethren: And they wrote letters by them after this manner; The apostles and elders and brethren send greeting unto the brethren which are of the Gentiles in Antioch and Syria and Cilicia" (Acts 15:7-23).

What God Is Doing Through Me

God reveals His wholeness to the world and restores wholeness among people. He shows the unity of the Godhead (Father, Son, and Spirit). Jesus is revealed as the Son of God: "That they all may be one; as thou, Father, art in me, and I in thee, that they also may be one in us: that the world may believe that thou hast sent me" (John 17:21).

Prayers

- Help me to know the peace that passes understanding.
- Lord, help me to live in peace with my fellow humans.
- Empower me to carry out the ministry of reconciliation You have assigned to me and the church.
- Bind us together, Lord.

Response in Worship: Extol

Definition: To rise, to lift up, to exalt.

Command: "Sing unto God, sing praises to his name: extol him that rideth upon the heavens by his name JAH, and rejoice before him" (Ps. 68:4).

Prayer: "I will extol thee, O Lord; for thou hast lifted me up, and hast not made my foes to rejoice over me. O Lord my God, I cried unto thee, and thou hast healed me" (Ps. 30:1-2).

Applied: "Now I Nebuchadnezzar praise and extol and honour the King of heaven, all whose works are truth, and his ways judgment: and those that walk in pride he is able to abase" (Dan. 4:37).

B-4
PERSECUTED

"Blessed are they which are persecuted for righteousness' sake: for theirs is the kingdom of heaven. Blessed are ye, when men shall revile you, and persecute you, and shall say all manner of evil against you falsely, for my sake. Rejoice, and be exceeding glad: for great is your reward in heaven: for so persecuted they the prophets which were before you" (MATT. 5:10-12).

Examples

Jesus: "Jesus said unto him, No man, having put his hand to the plough, and looking back, is fit for the kingdom of God" (Luke 9:62).

First Century Believers: "Beloved, think it not strange concerning the fiery trial which is to try you, as though some strange thing happened unto you: But rejoice, inasmuch as ye are partakers of Christ's sufferings; that, when his glory shall be revealed, ye may be glad also with exceeding joy. If ye be reproached for the name of Christ, happy are ye; for the spirit of glory and of God resteth upon you: on their part he is evil spoken of, but on your part he is glorified. But let none of you suffer as a murderer, or as a thief, or as an evildoer, or as a busybody in other men's matters. Yet if any man suffer as a Christian, let him not be ashamed; but let him glorify God on this behalf. For the time is come that judgment must begin at the house of God: and if it first begin at us, what shall the end be of them that obey not the gospel of God? And if the righteous scarcely be saved, where shall the ungodly and the sinner appear? Wherefore let them that suffer according to the will of God commit the keeping of their souls to him in well doing, as unto a faithful Creator" (1 Pet. 4:12-19).

Paul: "That I may know him, and the power of his resurrection, and the fellowship of his sufferings, being made conformable unto his death" (Phil. 3:10).

What God Is Doing Through Me

God allows me to be identified perfectly with Christ in His suffering as God's servant.

Prayers

- Thank You for allowing me to share in the sufferings of Christ.
- Defend me, O Lord. You are my Righteous Judge.
- If I live, I'll live for You. If I die, let me honor You.
- Into Your hands I entrust my life and reputation.

Response in Worship: Rejoice

Definition: To take pleasure in, to be glad, to exult, to express joy, to delight.

Command: "Rejoice in the Lord alway: and again I say, Rejoice" (Phil. 4:4).

"Let all those that put their trust in thee rejoice: let them ever shout for joy, because thou defendest them: let them also that love thy name be joyful in thee" (Ps. 5:11).

"Be glad in the Lord, and rejoice, ye righteous: and shout for joy, all ye that are upright in heart" (Ps. 32:11).

"Let the righteous be glad; let them rejoice before God: yea, let them exceedingly rejoice" (Ps. 68:3).

Blessings: "They that sow in tears shall reap in joy" (Ps. 126:5).

Prayer: "I have trusted in thy mercy; my heart shall rejoice in thy salvation" (Ps. 13:5).

"I will be glad and rejoice in thy mercy: for thou hast considered my trouble; thou hast known my soul in adversities" (Ps. 31:7).

"My lips shall greatly rejoice when I sing unto thee; and my soul, which thou hast redeemed" (Ps. 71:23).

Applied: "Who now rejoice in my sufferings for you, and fill up that which is behind of the afflictions of Christ in my flesh for his body's sake, which is the church" (Col. 1:24).

"Yea, and if I be offered upon the sacrifice and service of your faith, I joy, and rejoice with you all. For the same cause also do ye joy, and rejoice with me" (Phil. 2:17-18).

LIFELONG HELPS FOR DEVELOPING THE MIND OF CHRIST

YOUR RELATIONSHIP WITH YOUR HEAVENLY FATHER AND THE HOLY SPIRIT

HEAVENLY FATHER

Read the following verses that describe ways you should be related to your Heavenly Father and the Holy Spirit. Circle key words that describe the ways. Pray and ask God through the Holy Spirit to help you relate to Him completely. Review these Scriptures periodically to set your mind on your proper relationship.

"Now our Lord Jesus Christ himself, and God, even our Father, which hath loved us, and hath given us everlasting consolation and good hope through grace, Comfort your hearts, and stablish you in every good word and work" (2 Thess. 2:16-17).

"Behold, what manner of love the Father hath bestowed upon us, that we should be called the sons of God" (1 John 3:1).

"Ye have not received the spirit of bondage again to fear; but ye have received the Spirit of adoption, whereby we cry, Abba, Father. The Spirit itself beareth witness with our spirit, that we are the children of God: And if children, then heirs; heirs of God, and joint-heirs with Christ; if so be that we suffer with him, that we may be also glorified together" (Rom. 8:15-17).

"I am in my Father, and ye in me, and I in you. He that hath my commandments, and keepeth them, he it is that loveth me: and he that loveth me shall be loved of my Father, and I will love him, and will manifest myself to him" (John 14:20-21).

"The Father himself loveth you, because ye have loved me, and have believed that I came out from God" (John 16:27).

"The true worshippers shall worship the Father in spirit and in truth: for the Father seeketh such to worship him. God is a Spirit: and they that worship him must worship him in spirit and in truth" (John 4:23-24).

"All men should honour the Son, even as they honour the Father. He that honoureth not the Son honoureth not the Father which hath sent him" (John 5:23).

"I am the true vine, and my Father is the husbandman. Every branch in me that beareth not fruit he taketh away: and every branch that beareth fruit, he purgeth it, that it may bring forth more fruit" (John 15:1-2).

"If two of you shall agree on earth as touching any thing that they shall ask, it shall be done for them of my Father which is in heaven" (Matt. 18:19).

"When thou prayest, enter into thy closet, and when thou hast shut thy door, pray to thy Father which is in secret; and thy Father which seeth in secret shall reward thee openly" (Matt. 6:6).

"That they all may be one; as thou, Father, art in me, and I in thee, that they also may be one in us: that the world may believe that thou hast sent me" (John 17:21).

"Come out from among them, and be ye separate, saith the Lord, and touch not the unclean thing; and I will receive you, And will be a Father unto you, and ye shall be my sons and daughters, saith the Lord Almighty" (2 Cor. 6:17-18).

"Be ye therefore perfect, even as your Father which is in heaven is perfect" (Matt. 5:48).

"If ye forgive men their trespasses, your heavenly Father will also forgive you: But if ye forgive not men their trespasses, neither will your Father forgive your trespasses" (Matt. 6:14-15).

"Be ye therefore merciful, as your Father also is merciful" (Luke 6:36).

"If ye then, being evil, know how to give good gifts unto your children, how much more shall your Father which is in heaven give good things to them that ask him?" (Matt. 7:11).

"Every good gift and every perfect gift is from above, and cometh down from the Father of lights, with whom is no variableness, neither shadow of turning" (Jas. 1:17).

HOLY SPIRIT

"Repent, and be baptized every one of you in the name of Jesus Christ for the remission of sins, and ye shall receive the gift of the Holy Ghost" (Acts 2:38).

"Ye are not in the flesh, but in the Spirit, if so be that the Spirit of God dwell in you. Now if any man have not the Spirit of Christ, he is none of his" (Rom. 8:9).

"The Spirit itself beareth witness with our spirit, that we are the children of God" (Rom. 8:16).

"Know ye not that ye are the temple of God, and that the Spirit of God dwelleth in you?" (1 Cor. 3:16).

"Ye shall receive power, after that the Holy Ghost is come upon you: and ye shall be witnesses unto me" (Acts 1:8).

"The Comforter, which is the Holy Ghost, whom the Father will send in my name, he shall teach you all things, and bring all things to your remembrance, whatsoever I have said unto you" (John 14:26).

"When he, the Spirit of truth, is come, he will guide you into all truth: for he shall not speak of himself; but whatsoever he shall hear, that shall he speak: and he will shew you things to come" (John 16:13).

"All manner of sin and blasphemy shall be forgiven unto men: but the blasphemy against the Holy Ghost shall not be forgiven" (Matt. 12:31).

"And grieve not the holy Spirit of God, whereby ye are sealed unto the day of redemption" (Eph. 4:30).

"Quench not the Spirit." (1 Thess. 5:19).

"Walk in the Spirit, and ye shall not fulfil the lust of the flesh" (Gal. 5:16).

"Be not drunk with wine, wherein is excess; but be filled with the Spirit" (Eph. 5:18).

The following names, titles, and descriptions of Jesus Christ (the second Person of the Trinity) are from the King James Version of the Bible. This is not a complete list, but it may help you relate to Christ in different ways based upon His purposes and upon your needs. Use these names for meditation on the Person of Jesus Christ and in prayer through Him to the Heavenly Father.

From time to time, select one or a few names of Jesus on which to meditate. Read the Scripture listed or use a concordance to read other passages to see if the text gives you more detail about Christ's name and His function. Write the details on a card to carry with you throughout the day. Spend time with Jesus in prayer. Ask yourself questions like:

- What does this name tell me about Jesus Christ? about His nature? His work? (Christ is Faithful and True or He is a Judge.)
- Does this name call me to worship Christ for who He is or to thank Him for what He has done? (I can worship Jesus Christ as the King of Kings and Lord of Lords. I can thank Christ for His great sacrifice as the Lamb of God who took away my sins.)
- Does this name describe a relationship I have or can have with Christ? (Jesus is a Wonderful Counselor, and I can seek His counsel. He is Physician, and I can be His patient.)
- Is there a reason I need to experience Christ working in my life according to this name? (Jesus is the author of our faith and I need Him to give me faith to follow God in this situation.)
- Do I need to pray to Jesus in this name—to ask Him to function in this role? (Christ is the dayspring from on high, and I want Him to shine His light to my friend who lives in darkness and the shadow of death.)

JESUS CHRIST IS:
- an advocate with the Father (1 John 2:1)

- Alpha and Omega (Rev. 1:8)
- the Amen (Rev. 3:14)
- Ancient of days (Dan. 7:22)
- his anointed (Acts 4:27)
- Apostle and High Priest of our profession (Heb. 3:1)
- author and finisher of our faith (Heb. 12:2)
- the beginning and the end (Rev. 21:6)
- the beginning of the creation of God (Rev. 3:14)
- the only begotten of the Father (John 1:14)
- my beloved (Matt. 12:18)
- a righteous Branch (Jer. 23:5)
- bread of life (John 6:35)
- bridegroom (Matt. 9:15)
- the brightness of his [God's] glory (Heb. 1:3)
- chosen of God (Luke 23:35)
- Christ Jesus my Lord (Phil. 3:8)
- the Christ [Anointed One] (Matt. 16:16)
- chief cornerstone (Eph. 2:20)
- crown of glory (Isa. 62:3)
- the dayspring from on high (Luke 1:78)
- the Deliverer (Rom. 11:26)
- desire of all nations (Hag. 2:7)
- door of the sheep (John 10:7)
- Emmanuel [God with us] (Matt. 1:23)
- Faithful and True (Rev. 19:11)
- firstborn from the dead (Col. 1:18)
- firstborn of every creature (Col. 1:15)
- a sure foundation (Isa. 28:16)
- friend of publicans and sinners (Matt. 11:19)
- unspeakable gift (2 Cor. 9:15)
- God of the whole earth (Isa. 54:5)
- the only wise God our Saviour (Jude 1:25)
- a Governor (Matt. 2:6)
- head of the body, the church (Col. 1:18)
- head of the church (Eph. 5:23)
- head of all principality and power (Col. 2:10)
- the head (Eph. 4:15)

- heir of all things (Heb. 1:2)
- high priest (Heb. 4:15)
- a great high priest (Heb. 4:14)
- Holy One of God (Luke 4:34)
- our hope (1 Tim. 1:1)
- horn of salvation (Luke 1:69)
- image of God (2 Cor. 4:4)
- image of the invisible God (Col. 1:15)
- Jesus Christ (John 1:17)
- Jesus Christ of Nazareth (Acts 4:10)
- Jesus Christ our Saviour (Titus 3:6)
- Jesus of Nazareth (John 19:19)
- righteous judge (2 Tim. 4:8)
- King eternal, immortal, invisible (1 Tim. 1:17)
- King of kings (1 Tim. 6:15)
- King of saints (Rev. 15:3)
- King of the Jews (Matt. 27:11)
- thy King (Matt. 21:5)
- Lamb of God (John 1:29)
- the Lamb that was slain (Rev. 5:12)
- the last (Rev. 22:13)
- lawgiver (Jas. 4:12)
- leader and commander to the people (Isa. 55:4)
- eternal life (1 John 5:20)
- our life (Col. 3:4)
- light (1 John 1:5)
- light of life (John 8:12)
- light of men (John 1:4)
- the light of the world (John 8:12)
- true Light (John 1:9)
- lily of the valleys (Song of Sol. 2:1)
- Christ the Lord (Luke 2:11)
- Lord and Saviour Jesus Christ (2 Pet. 2:20)
- the Lord and Saviour (2 Pet. 3:2)
- the only Lord God (Jude 1:4)
- Lord God Almighty (Rev. 15:3)
- Lord Jesus Christ (Gal. 1:3)
- Lord both of the dead and living (Rom. 14:9)
- Lord of lords (1 Tim. 6:15)
- Lord of peace (2 Thes. 3:16)
- Lord of the harvest (Matt. 9:38)
- my Lord and my God (John 20:28)
- man of sorrows (Isa. 53:3)
- Good Master (Mark 10:17)
- your Master (Matt. 23:8)
- mediator (1 Tim. 2:5)
- the Messiah the Prince (Dan. 9:25)
- the most Holy (Dan. 9:24)

- a Nazarene (Matt. 2:23)
- an offering and a sacrifice to God (Eph. 5:2)
- our passover (1 Cor. 5:7)
- our peace (Eph. 2:14)
- Physician (Luke 4:23)
- a Prince and a Saviour (Acts 5:31)
- Prince of life (Acts 3:15)
- Prince of Peace (Isa. 9:6)
- the Prophet (John 7:40)
- the propitiation for our sins (1 John 2:2)
- Rabbi (John 3:2)
- Rabboni (John 20:16)
- as a refiner and purifier (Mal. 3:3)
- the resurrection, and the life (John 11:25)
- spiritual Rock (1 Cor. 10:4)
- Root of David (Rev. 5:5)
- root of Jesse (Rom. 15:12)
- thy salvation (Luke 2:30)
- our Saviour Jesus Christ (2 Pet. 1:1)
- Saviour of the world (John 4:42)
- my [God's] servant (Matt. 12:18)
- righteous servant (Isa. 53:11)
- Shepherd and Bishop of your souls (1 Pet. 2:25)
- great shepherd of the sheep (Heb. 13:20)
- chief Shepherd (1 Pet. 5:4)
- the good shepherd (John 10:11)
- son of Abraham (Matt. 1:1)
- son of David (Matt. 1:1)
- Son of God (John 1:49)
- son of Joseph (John 6:42)
- Son of man (Matt. 12:40)
- Son of the living God (Matt. 16:16)
- Son of God (John 10:36)
- the son of Mary (Mark 6:3)
- his only begotten Son (1 John 4:9)
- a Star (Num. 24:17)
- day star (2 Pet. 1:19)
- the bright and morning star (Rev. 22:16)
- the stone which the builders rejected (Matt. 21:42)
- the truth (John 14:6)
- the true vine, the vine (John 15:1,5)
- the way (John 14:6)
- a witness to the people (Isa. 55:4)
- faithful and true witness (Rev. 3:14)
- The Word of God (Rev. 19:13)
- the Word of life (1 John 1:1)
- the Word (John 1:1)

READINGS ON THE LIFE, TEACHING, AND PARABLES OF CHRIST

READINGS ON THE LIFE OF CHRIST

The following chart lists events from the life of Jesus. In many cases the references for an event are parallel passages (different accounts of the same event). In some cases a reference may be a related event that may or may not be describing the same event. As you read these passages, ask God to help you identify the mind of Christ at work in how Jesus thought or responded in various situations. The healings have been grouped together. Most of the other events are listed with priority given to the chronology of Matthew's Gospel.

	MATTHEW	MARK	LUKE	JOHN
1. Birth	❏ 1—2		❏ 2:1-40	❏ 1:1-18
2. Age 12 at the Temple			❏ 2:41-52	
3. Baptism	❏ 3:13-17	❏ 1:9-11	❏ 3:21-22	❏ 1:19-34
4. Temptation	❏ 4:1-11	❏ 1:12-13	❏ 4:1-13	
5. Begins Preaching Ministry	❏ 4:12-17	❏ 1:14-15	❏ 3:23	
6. Calling the First Disciples	❏ 4:18-22	❏ 1:16-20	❏ 5:1-11	❏ 1:35-42
7. Calling Philip, Nathaniel				❏ 1:43-51
8. Calling of Levi	❏ 9:9-13	❏ 2:13-17	❏ 5:27-32	
9. Naming the Twelve	❏ 10:2-4	❏ 3:13-19	❏ 6:12-16	
10. Turns Water to Wine				❏ 2:1-11
11. Jesus Heals Many	❏ 4:23-25	❏ 3:7-10	❏ 6:17-19	
	❏ 8:14-17	❏ 1:29-34	❏ 4:38-41	
	❏ 14:34-36	❏ 6:53-56		
12. Leprosy	❏ 8:1-4	❏ 1:40-45	❏ 5:12-15	
13. Evil Spirit		❏ 1:21-28	❏ 4:31-37	
14. Centurion's Servant	❏ 8:5-13		❏ 7:1-10	
15. Official's Son				❏ 4:43-54
16. Invalid at Bethesda Pool				❏ 5:1-15
17. Silences Evil Spirits		❏ 3:11-12		
18. Demon Possessed	❏ 8:28-34	❏ 5:1-20	❏ 8:26-39	
19. Paralytic	❏ 9:1-8	❏ 2:1-12	❏ 5:17-26	
20. Hemorrhaging Woman/ Dead Girl	❏ 9:18-26	❏ 5:21-43	❏ 8:40-56	
21. Two Blind Men	❏ 9:27-31			
22. Demon Possessed Mute	❏ 9:32-34			
23. Man with Withered Hand	❏ 12:9-14	❏ 3:1-6	❏ 6:6-11	
24. Demon Possessed, Blind, Mute	❏ 12:22-23			
25. Raises a Widow's Son			❏ 7:11-17	
26. Daughter of Canaanite Woman	❏ 15:21-28	❏ 7:24-30		

	MATTHEW	MARK	LUKE	JOHN
27. Deaf Mute	❑ 15:29-31	❑ 7:31-37	————	————
28. Blind Man at Bethsaida	————	❑ 8:22-26	————	————
29. Man Born Blind	————	————	————	❑ 9:1-41
30. Boy with Evil Spirit	❑ 17:14-21	❑ 9:14-29	❑ 9:37-43	————
31. Blind Men	❑ 20:29-34	❑ 10:46-52	❑ 18:35-43	————
32. Cripple Woman on Sabbath	————	————	❑ 13:10-17	————
33. Ten with Leprosy	————	————	❑ 17:11-19	————
34. Works Miracles	————	————	————	❑ 2:23-25
35. Must Preach	————	————	❑ 4:42-44	————
36. Prayer in Solitary Place	————	❑ 1:35-38	❑ 5:16	————
37. Calms the Storm	❑ 8:23-27	❑ 4:35-41	❑ 8:22-25	————
38. Questioned about Fasting	❑ 9:14-15	❑ 2:18-20	❑ 5:33-35	————
39. Workers Are Few/ Sends Out 72	❑ 9:35-38	————	❑ 10:1-12,17-20	————
40. Sends Out the Twelve	❑ 10:1—11:1	❑ 6:7-13	❑ 9:1-6	————
41. John's Testimony	————	————	————	❑ 3:22-36
42. Samaritan Woman at Well	————	————	————	❑ 4:1-42
43. John in Prison	❑ 11:1-6	————	❑ 7:18-23	————
44. God's Chosen Servant	❑ 12:15-21	————	————	————
45. Visits Mary and Martha	————	————	❑ 10:38-42	————
46. Accused of Working by Satan	❑ 12:24-37	❑ 3:20-30	❑ 11:14-22	————
47. Refuses to Give a Sign	❑ 12:38-45; 16:1-4	❑ 8:11-13	❑ 11:29-32	❑ 2:18-22
48. Teaches Nicodemus	————	————	————	❑ 3:1-21
49. Rejected at Home/Nazareth	❑ 13:53-58	❑ 6:1-6	❑ 4:14-30	————
50. Family Thinks He's Mad	❑ 12:46-50	❑ 3:20-21,31-34	❑ 8:19-21	————
51. Feeds 5,000	❑ 14:13-21	❑ 6:32-44	❑ 9:10-17	❑ 6:1-15
52. Feeds 4,000	❑ 15:29-39	❑ 8:1-10	————	————
53. Walks on Water	❑ 14:22-33	❑ 6:45-52	————	❑ 6:16-24
54. Many Desert Him	————	————	————	❑ 6:60-71
55. Jesus Anointed	❑ 26:6-13	❑ 14:3-9	❑ 7:36-50	❑ 12:1-8
56. Jesus the Christ	————	————	————	❑ 7:25-44
57. Unbelief of Leaders	————	————	————	❑ 7:45-52
58. Unbelief of Jews	————	————	————	❑ 10:22-42
59. Woman Caught in Adultery	————	————	————	❑ 8:1-11
60. Peter's Confession	❑ 16:13-20	❑ 8:27-30	❑ 9:18-21	————
61. Jesus Predicts His Death (1)	❑ 16:21-28	❑ 8:31—9:1	❑ 9:22-27	————
62. Transfiguration	❑ 17:1-13	❑ 9:2-13	❑ 9:28-36	————
63. Jesus Predicts His Death (2)	❑ 17:22-23	❑ 9:30-32	❑ 9:43-45	————
64. Paying the Temple Tax	❑ 17:24-27	————	————	————
65. Blessing Little Children	❑ 19:13-15	❑ 10:13-16	❑ 18:15-17	————
66. Rich Young Ruler	❑ 19:16-26	❑ 10:17-27	❑ 18:18-27	————
67. Samaritan Opposition	————	————	❑ 9:51-56	————
68. Zacchaeus	————	————	❑ 19:1-10	————
69. Lazarus Dies, Raised	————	————	————	❑ 11:1-44
70. Jesus Predicts His Death (3)	❑ 20:17-19	❑ 10:32-34	❑ 18:31-34	————
71. Triumphal Entry	❑ 21:1-11	❑ 11:1-10	❑ 19:28-40	❑ 12:12-19

	MATTHEW	MARK	LUKE	JOHN
72. Sorrow over Jerusalem	———	———	❑ 13:31-35	———
73. Weeps Over Jerusalem	———	———	❑ 19:41-44	———
74. Cleans the Temple	❑ 21:12-17	❑ 11:12,15-19	❑ 19:45-48	❑ 2:12-17
75. Fig Tree Withers	❑ 21:18-22	❑ 11:12-14,20-26	———	
76. Jesus' Authority Questioned	❑ 21:23-27	❑ 11:27-33	❑ 20:1-8	———
77. Widow's Offering	———	❑ 12:41-44	❑ 21:1-4	———
78. Predicts Crucifixion	❑ 26:1-2	———	———	❑ 12:20-36
79. Jews Still in Unbelief	———	———	———	❑ 12:37-50
80. Plot by Priests and Elders	❑ 26:3-5	———	———	❑ 11:45-57
81. Lord's Supper	❑ 26:17-30	❑ 14:12-26	❑ 22:7-23	❑ 13:1-30
82. Predicts Peter's Denial	❑ 26:31-35	❑ 14:27-31	❑ 22:31-38	❑ 13:31-38
83. Gethsemane and Arrest	❑ 26:36-56	❑ 14:32-52	❑ 22:39-53	❑ 18:1-11
84. Trial Before Sanhedrin	❑ 26:57-68	❑ 14:53-65	❑ 22:63-71	❑ 18:12-14,19-24
85. Peter's Denial	❑ 26:69-75	❑ 14:66-72	❑ 22:54-62	❑ 18:15-18,25-27
86. Trial Before Pilate	❑ 27:11-31	❑ 15:1-20	❑ 23:1-25	❑ 18:28-19:16
87. Crucifixion	❑ 27:32-56	❑ 15:21-41	❑ 23:26-49	❑ 19:17-37
88. Burial	❑ 27:57-66	❑ 15:42-47	❑ 23:50-56	❑ 19:38-42
89. Resurrection	❑ 28:1-15	❑ 16:1-14	❑ 24:1-12	❑ 20:1-9
90. Resurrection Appearances	———	———	❑ 24:13-49	❑ 20:10-21:14
91. Commissions Peter	———	———	———	❑ 21:15-25
92. Great Commission	❑ 28:16-20	❑ 16:15-16	———	———
93. Ascension	———	❑ 16:19-20	❑ 24:50-53	———

READINGS ON THE TEACHING OF CHRIST

The following passages relate to the teaching ministry of Jesus. Of course Jesus taught through what He did, and He taught through the parables which we have in a separate section that follows. Some of the references identify parallel passages while others are passages related to the same or similar topic.

	MATTHEW	MARK	LUKE	JOHN
1. The Beatitudes	❑ 5:3-12	———	❑ 6:20-26	
2. Salt and Light	❑ 5:13-16	❑ 9:50; 4:21-25	❑ 8:16-18; 11:33-36	———
			❑ 14:34-35	———
3. Fulfillment of the Law	❑ 5:17-20	———	———	———
4. Murder/Hatred	❑ 5:21-26	———	———	———
5. Adultery	❑ 5:27-30	———	———	———
6. Divorce	❑ 5:31-32; 19:1-9	❑ 10:1-12	❑ 16:18	———
7. Celibacy	❑ 19:10-12	———	———	———
8. Oaths	❑ 5:33-37	———	———	———
9. Eye for Eye	❑ 5:38-42	———	———	———
10. Love Enemies	❑ 5:43-48	———	❑ 6:27-36	———
11. Giving to Needy	❑ 6:1-4	———	———	———
12. Prayer	❑ 6:5-13;7:7-11	———	❑ 11:1-13	———
13. Forgiveness	❑ 6:14	———	❑ 17:3-4	———
14. Fasting	❑ 6:16-18	———	———	———
15. Treasures in Heaven	❑ 6:19-24	———	❑ 18:22	———
16. Don't Worry/Seek the Kingdom	❑ 6:25-34	———	❑ 12:22-34	———
17. Judging Others	❑ 7:1-6	———	❑ 6:37-42	———

	MATTHEW	MARK	LUKE	JOHN
18. Narrow Gate	❑ 7:13-14	————	❑ 13:22-30	————
19. Good and Bad Fruit	❑ 7:15-23	————	❑ 6:43-45	————
20. Cost of Following Jesus	❑ 8:18-22	————	❑ 9:57-62;14:25-33	————
21. Rewards for Following Jesus	❑ 19:27-30	❑ 10:28-31	❑ 18:28-30	————
22. Son Gives Life	————	————	————	❑ 5:16-30
23. Testimonies About Jesus	————	————	————	❑ 5:31-47
24. Jesus' Testimony	————	————	————	❑ 8:12-30,48-59
25. Children of Abraham/Devil	————	————	————	❑ 8:31-47
26. About John the Baptist	❑ 11:7-19	————	❑ 7:24-35	————
27. Woe to Unrepentant Cities	❑ 11:20-24	————	❑ 10:13-16	————
28. Jesus Reveals the Father	❑ 11:25-27	————	❑ 10:21-24	————
29. Rest for the Heavy Laden	❑ 11:28-30	————	————	————
30. Lord of the Sabbath	❑ 12:1-8	❑ 2:23-28	❑ 6:1-5	————
31. Obedience	————	————	❑ 11:27-28	————
32. Bread of Life	————	————	————	❑ 6:25-59
33. Clean and Unclean	❑ 15:1-21	❑ 7:1-23	————	————
34. Yeast of Pharisees/Sadducees	❑ 16:5-12	❑ 8:14-21	❑ 12:1-12	————
35. Greatness in the Kingdom	❑ 18:1-6	❑ 9:33-37	❑ 9:46-48	————
36. James and John	❑ 20:20-28	❑ 10:35-45	❑ 22:24-30	————
37. For or Against Us	————	❑ 9:38-41	❑ 9:49-50	————
38. Things that Cause Sin	❑ 18:7-9	❑ 9:42-48	❑ 17:1-2	————
39. Reconciliation	❑ 18:15-20	————	————	————
40. Faith	————	————	❑ 17:5-6	————
41. Servanthood	————	————	❑ 17:7-10	————
42. Humility	————	————	❑ 14:1-14	————
43. Good News of the Kingdom	————	————	❑ 16:16-17	————
44. Paying Taxes to Caesar	❑ 22:15-22	❑ 12:13-17	❑ 20:20-26	————
45. Marriage at the Resurrection	❑ 22:23-33	❑ 12:18-27	❑ 20:27-40	————
46. Greatest Commandment	❑ 22:34-40	❑ 12:28-34	❑ 10:25-28	————
47. Whose Son Is Christ	❑ 22:41-46	❑ 12:35-37	❑ 20:41-44	————
48. Authority of His Teaching	————	————	————	❑ 7:14-24
49. Good Shepherd	————	————	————	❑ 10:1-21
50. Woes to Teachers and Pharisees	❑ 23:1-39	❑ 12:38-40	❑ 20:45-47	————
51. Six Woes	————	————	❑ 11:37-54	————
52. Division not Peace	❑ 10:34-36	————	❑ 12:49-53	————
53. Interpreting the Times	————	————	❑ 12:54-59	————
54. Repent or Perish	————	————	❑ 13:1-5	————
55. Coming of the Kingdom	————	————	❑ 17:20-37	————
56. Signs of the End of the Age	❑ 24:1-35	❑ 13:1-31	❑ 21:5-38	————
57. Day and Hour Unknown	❑ 24:36-51	❑ 13:32-37	————	————
58. Teaches Disciples at the Supper	————	————	————	❑ 14—17
59. Preparing a place	————	————	————	❑ 14:1-4
60. Way to the Father	————	————	————	❑ 14:5-14
61. Promise of Holy Spirit	————	————	————	❑ 14:15-31
62. The Vine and Branches	————	————	————	❑ 15:1-17
63. World Will Hate You	————	————	————	❑ 15:18—16:4

	MATTHEW	MARK	LUKE	JOHN
64. Work of Holy Spirit	————	————	————	❏ 16:5-16
65. Grief Will Turn to Joy	————	————	————	❏ 16:17-33
66. Prayer for Himself	————	————	————	❏ 17:1-5
67. Prayer for Disciples	————	————	————	❏ 17:6-19
68. Prayer for All Believers	————	————	————	❏ 17:20-26

READINGS ON THE PARABLES OF CHRIST

The list below includes most of the parables of Jesus. However, some of His teaching includes comparisons or other stories that are considered parables by some. Most scholars believe each parable usually had only one primary theme. As you read and study a parable, ask God to give you understanding about the primary message.

	MATTHEW	MARK	LUKE
1. About teaching with parables	❏ 13:34-35	❏ 4:33-34	————
2. Good Samaritan	————		❏ 10:29-37
3. Growing Seed	————	❏ 4:26-29	————
4. Hidden Treasure	❏ 13:44		————
5. Lost Coin	————		❏ 15:8-10
6. Lost Sheep	❏ 18:10-14	————	❏ 15:1-7
7. Lost Son/Prodigal Son	————	————	❏ 15:11-32
8. Mustard Seed	❏ 13:31-32	❏ 4:30-32	❏ 13:18-19
9. Net	❏ 13:47-51	————	————
10. New and Old Treasures	❏ 13:52	————	————
11. New Wine/Old Wine Skins	❏ 9:17	❏ 2:22	❏ 5:37-39
12. Patched Garment	❏ 9:16	❏ 2:21	❏ 5:36
13. Pearl of Great Price	❏ 13:45-46	————	————
14. Persistent Widow	————	————	❏ 18:1-8
15. Pharisee and Publican	————	————	❏ 18:9-14
16. Rich Fool	————	————	❏ 12:13-21
17. Rich Man and Lazarus	————	————	❏ 16:19-31
18. Sheep and Goats	❏ 25:31-46	————	————
19. Shrewd Manager	————	————	❏ 16:1-15
20. Sower	❏ 13:1-23	❏ 4:1-20	❏ 8:4-15
21. Talents	❏ 25:14-30	————	❏ 19:12-27
22. Ten Virgins	❏ 25:1-13	————	————
23. Thief at Night/Be Watchful	————	————	❏ 12:35-48
24. Two Sons and Obedience	❏ 21:28-32	————	————
25. Unfruitfuquet	❏ 22:1-14	————	❏ 14:15-24
28. Weeds	❏ 13:24-30;36-43	————	————
29. Wicked Tenants	❏ 21:33-46	❏ 12:1-12	❏ 20:9-19
30. Wise Builder/Obedience	❏ 7:24-27	————	❏ 6:46-49
31. Workers in the Vineyard	❏ 20:1-16	————	————
32. Yeast	❏ 13:33	————	❏ 13:20-21

LEADER GUIDE
THE MIND OF CHRIST

This leader guide primarily is for use by the person who facilitates a small-group study of *The Mind of Christ*. If your church plans to offer other approaches to studying *The Mind of Christ*, the person coordinating these approaches also will find this guide helpful. If you fit one of those two descriptions, this guide is for you.

Overview

Paul said, "Let this mind be in you, which was also in Christ Jesus" (Phil. 2:5). *The Mind of Christ* resources help believers keep that command. In Luke 17:21 Jesus said, "the kingdom of God is within you." Jesus emphasized that the kingdom of God does not come with outward observance, but by an inner working that is not seen. That directs us to the mind, the area where God wants to work. The changes that God brings in a believer's life are secret and inward, but they will bear fruit that will be visible in life and lifestyle. When church leaders help members develop the mind of Christ, the body of Christ can function the way God intended to reveal His Son to a watching world. *The Mind of Christ* resources will help you lead members of your church to develop the mind of Christ under the leadership and empowering of the Holy Spirit.

The Hymn

The Mind of Christ resources examine the poem in Philippians 2:5-11. This poem was actually a hymn and probably was sung during times of worship in the early church. The hymn has been divided into six parts for this study:

Philippians 2:5-11

Part 1: Christ's Freedom
Part 2: Christ's Lifestyle
Part 3: Christ's Servanthood
Part 4: Christ's Humanity
Part 5: Christ's Holiness and Love
Part 6: Christ's Name

As members study each part of this hymn, they will understand how God wants to work to transform them into the image of His Son Jesus.

Resources for *The Mind of Christ*

The following resources support these three approaches.

- *The Mind of Christ* member's book (item 005173965)
- *The Mind of Christ Viewer Guide* (item 005174508) provides charts, diagrams, pages for participants to take notes on the DVDs, and a small-group discussion guide for 8 sessions.
- *The Mind of Christ Leader Kit* (item 005156923) provides a copy of the member book for use in a 13-session group study, as well the viewer guide and four DVDs featuring author T. W. Hunt for use in an 8-session DVD conference.
- *The Mind of Christ* hardback book (Broadman/Holman, item 001069699) Book version of T. W. Hunt's *The Mind of Christ*.

Ordering Resources

- WRITE LifeWay Church Resources Customer Service; One LifeWay Plaza; Nashville, TN 37234-0113;
- FAX order to (615) 251-5933;
- PHONE 1-800-458-2772;
- E-MAIL *orderentry@lifeway.com*;
- ONLINE at *www.lifeway.com*;
- VISIT the LifeWay Christian Store serving you.

Approaches to Studying *The Mind of Christ*

Because having the mind of Christ is essential for every believer, we recommend that you consider a variety of approaches that can help people at varied stages of maturity, levels of commitment, and with different learning styles. These approaches serve as an introduction to a lifelong process as God continually renews the minds and lives of Christians to reflect the image of His Son Jesus. Some members will benefit from participating in several or perhaps all of these approaches. With each approach, God works in different ways to orient more thoroughly a person to Himself.

Rather than choosing one approach, consider offering *The Mind of Christ* in as many ways as possible. You will be more likely to encourage everyone to participate in the study when they can choose their learning approach. Remember, interaction with other believers allows God to work through different members of the body of Christ to bring about change in the body. Encourage all church members to study *The Mind of Christ.*

☙ **1. Individual Study.** Individuals can study any of the resources at their own pace. They can either (1) read the Broadman & Holman book, (2) watch the DVD messages using the viewing guide or (3) study the member book. Making the resources available in the church media library and/or for sale to members will encourage individual study. Recommend that individuals consider participating in some group format to benefit from the encouragement and interaction with other believers.

☙ **2. DVD Conference.** For years T. W. Hunt has led weekend conferences on *The Mind of Christ* in churches across the country. Now you can have Dr. Hunt in your church leading the conference through DVD messages. You are not limited, however, by his schedule and availability. You can conduct the conference on a weekend, weekdays, week nights, spread it out over 8 weeks, or do all of the above! Let Dr. Hunt do the teaching and preaching on the DVD messages during the evening worship services. Many people have found that one time through is not enough, so you can repeat the conference as often as you choose at your convenience. Members who miss a session can make it up by checking out the DVDs for home viewing. The DVD conference will require at least eight 75-minute sessions if you include time for discussion of the messages. Group members can help each other in making application to their lives.

☙ **3. Individual and Small-Group Study Combination.** *The Mind of Christ* member book provides for an individual study with a small-group session once each week. This combination of more in-depth study and small-group interaction will enhance learning and contribute to greater application of the material. With this approach, you will need a small group for each eight to ten participants. If you have more than ten persons interested in the course, provide multiple groups in order to create the best possible learning environment. If you do not have sufficient leaders, start a waiting list for the next group. In the meantime, begin training new leaders within the group or groups you currently have.

Christian Growth Study Plan Diploma

Individuals may receive a Christian Growth Study Plan diploma (course CG-0174) for studying *The Mind of Christ* in one of two ways:

- Study *The Mind of Christ* member-leader book and participate in a small-group experience
- Attend the DVD Conference, utilize *The Mind of Christ Viewer Guide*, and participate in discussion of the messages.

The Christian Growth Study Plan form is found in the *Member Book* and the *Viewer Guide*. Keep attendance records and at the end of the conference or small-group study invite participants to complete the form at the back of their books. Follow the form instructions for submitting completed forms to LifeWay.

Getting Started

The more familiar you are with the message and the resources of *The Mind of Christ*, the better prepared you will be to guide the study. Complete the following activities to familiarize yourself with the course.

- ❑ Read the Preface and the Introduction (pp. 6-11).
- ❑ Read the table of contents (pp. 3-4) to get an overall view of the course.
- ❑ Read through the Lifelong Helps section (pp. 224-259) to get an idea of the learning aids available.
- ❑ Look at the cards in the back of the book to see the memory aids that can be used for review.
- ❑ Read the remainder of this leader guide and decide how you will conduct the study.

☙ **Decide when and where groups will meet.** We recommend one- to two-hour small-group sessions. One hour is a minimum. Groups should allow two hours if they intend to deal fully with Dr. Hunt's principles. Some groups may prefer to double the number of weeks and spend one hour each week on one half the recommended content for each unit.

Groups may meet at the church, in homes, community centers, a workplace, or other locations convenient to members. You may want to offer group studies at a variety of times and locations so more people will be able to participate. Consider these options:

• **Sunday Evenings**
–Begin one to two hours before evening worship.
–Meet in small groups before worship to process what members have learned during their study of the member book.

• **Weekdays**
–Meet at church at a convenient time to those involved. For instance, a senior adult group might meet before or after noon once a week and eat a sack lunch together in conjunction with their small-group study.
–Meet in homes at a convenient time to those involved. Homes often provide a quiet and more informal atmosphere for sharing and praying. Be sure to set guidelines about leaving times, so the group does not wear out its welcome.
–At the workplace. Some employees may want to meet before or after work once a week at their workplace provided their employer approves. Others may decide to bring lunch and spend two lunch breaks together each week.

☙ **Develop a time schedule.** A typical weekly session might look like this.

Small-group Study: One Hour/Two Hours

• Hearing What the Spirit Is Saying (as members arrive)
• Magnifying the Lord and Exalting His Name (5/10 minutes)
• Transforming by the Word (15/30 minutes)
• Stimulating to Love and Good Deeds (20/40 minutes)
• Preparing the Bride for Her Bridegroom (5/10 minutes)
• Praying for One Another (10/20 minutes)
• Closing the Session (5/10 minutes)

Consider kicking off the study during a weekend using *The Mind of Christ DVD Conference.* The member book study would begin shortly thereafter for interested participants using the small-group sessions in this book.

☙ **Decide on the number of groups needed.** Work with your pastor, discipleship director, minister of education, or other church leaders to determine how many individuals in your church want to study this course at this time. Adults who have surrendered their lives to Jesus Christ as Lord and Savior will benefit from this study. Survey your church members to determine the number of persons interested in a study to develop the mind of Christ. You may want to publicize the study using announcements in your church publications. Remember that you will need one group for every eight to ten participants.

☙ **Enlist leaders.** Each group will need a separate leader. Pastor, you may want to lead the first group and train eight to ten persons to provide leadership for future groups. If you need more leaders, you may want to take two or more groups through the course at different times during the week. Leading the first group will demonstrate your belief in what *The Mind of Christ* is about. It also will be enriching and helpful in your walk with the Lord. If you are unable to lead the first group, enlist another church staff member or lay leader.

Pray that God will help you identify those persons He wants to lead the groups. These leaders should be spiritually growing Christians and active church members. Leaders should have teachable spirits, the ability to relate well to people, a commitment to keep information private, and a willingness to spend the time necessary to prepare for the sessions. Also look for people who possess skills for leading small-group learning activities. Do *not* select someone who is having spiritual, marital, or physical difficulties that could hinder their effectiveness.

If you do not have enough leaders (maximum of 10 members per group) to accommodate all those who want to participate, enlist additional leaders from those who plan to participate. However, use the same criteria for all leaders. If you don't have qualified leaders, start a waiting list and encourage members to pray that God will call out additional leaders. Some leaders might be willing to lead a second group at a different time during the week since little additional preparation would be required.

☙ **Enlist participants.** Invite to the introductory session church leaders and other prospective participants. The introductory session provides enough information for persons to decide whether to participate in the study. At the end of the session, give those present an opportunity to sign up for the course. If persons are unwilling to make a commitment to individual and group study, encourage them not to participate at this time. Remind them of the other opportunities to study *The Mind of Christ* through the reading the hardback book and viewing the DVD messages.

≈ **Order resources.** Resources should be ordered for the course six to eight weeks prior to the introductory session. Although processing and shipping your order may take less time, leaders need time to prepare for the introductory session and time to enlist participants. Though you may not enlist participants until later, you can estimate the quantity needed by ordering eight to ten copies of the member book for each small group you anticipate. Husbands and wives will each need a personal copy of the member book. (See p. 260 for item numbers and ordering information.)

≈ **Set and collect fees.** We recommend that participants pay at least part of the cost of the materials so they make a commitment to the study with a financial investment. Announce the fee when you enlist participants so they will not be caught off guard or embarrassed at the introductory session. You may want to provide scholarships for those unable to participate due to lack of financial resources.

Guiding a Small-Group Study

Each of the group sessions includes three parts:
- **BEFORE THE SESSION**—Use the Standard Before the Session (p. 267) and the session-specific suggestions to prepare for each group session. These include actions for you to complete prior to the session. You may want to cut out this half page of your book and use it as a bookmark. The back side will have the Standard After the Session list.
- **DURING THE SESSION**—At the end of each unit, a two-page section provides a guide for the group session. (See pp. 30-31 for an example.) This section provides activities for you to use in conducting a one- to two-hour small-group session. Suggested times for each segment are for the one-hour experience. Double those times for a two-hour session. You probably will find that the activities suggested will require more than one hour to process effectively. Don't get frustrated if you are limited to one-hour sessions. Adapt the activities and use the ones that are most

helpful. The activities for the session follow a similar pattern each week. This simplifies your leadership role, but you should feel free to rearrange or adapt the sessions according to your group's needs. Since members have the session plans in their books you can assign activities to pairs or quads, and they will have the instructions or discussion questions available for use or review.
- **AFTER THE SESSION**—Use the Standard After the Session (p. 268) and the session-specific suggestions to evaluate the group session, your performance as a leader, and the needs of group members. These will help you improve your abilities to guide the group in their learning experience. The Standard After the Session list can be cut out and used as a bookmark for quick reference at the end of each session.

Ballot boxes (❑) are provided in the Specific Before the Session and Specific After the Session sections for you to check as you complete each action. Sessions require a minimum of leader preparation so you can give yourself to prayer and personal spiritual preparation. If you adapt the lesson plans or create activities of your own, remember to secure any resources that are required for these activities.

Each week you are encouraged to think about your group members and identify one or more who may need a personal contact from you. Do not neglect this aspect of your ministry. Your primary assignment in this study is to help people develop the mind of Christ, not just teach knowledge about Christ.

Seven Segments for Each Session

Each session is divided into seven segments. The following segment descriptions will give you an overview of the process suggested for each session. The purpose is to help believers practice "being" the body of Christ. Because the sessions are designed to provide help for one- and two-hour sessions, you may find that they include far more than can be accomplished if you only have one hour. Regardless of time, God can work in every session to help members grow in Christlikeness. Evaluate the learning activities and determine which ones will be most helpful for the members of your group. Every group may be different in its needs. Adapt these plans for your group's needs.

The segments below have a suggested time frame beside them. The first number indicates a recommended time in minutes for a one-hour session. The second number indicates the time recommended for a two-hour session.

1. Hearing What the Spirit Is Saying (as members arrive). "He that hath an ear, let him hear what the Spirit saith unto the churches" (Rev. 2:11). As members arrive before the session, guide them to review what God has been saying to them during the week. Ask members to identify a Scripture and a name of Christ that have been most meaningful this week. Ask them to identify and mark the issue or subject in which God seems to be working most actively to develop within them Christ's mind. Members will use these bits of information at various points in the session.

2. Magnifying the Lord and Exalting His Name (5/10 minutes). "O magnify the Lord with me, and let us exalt his name together" (Ps. 34:3). As you open each session in prayer, encourage members to worship God for Who He is and acknowledge Him for what He has done. Members may use the names of Christ to exalt His name together in prayer. Following the prayer time, give members a chance to share any ways God may have revealed Himself this week through His names. Be prepared to lead by example until members become familiar with the experience.

3. Transforming by the Word (15/30 minutes). "Christ also loved the church, and gave himself for it; that he might sanctify and cleanse it with the washing of water by the word, that he might present it to himself a glorious church, not having spot, or wrinkle, or any such thing; but that it should be holy and without blemish" (Eph. 5:25-27). Because the Scriptures reveal the nature, character, and standard for the mind and lifestyle of Christ, ask members to make two lists each week: (1) a list of things, actions, or attitudes identified in Scripture that need to be *cleansed from* one's mind and life, and (2) a list of things, actions, or attitudes that Scripture indicates need to be *incorporated into* one's mind and life. Ask members to review their memory verse for the week and share any Scripture that has been meaningful to them.

Because this activity may require more time than is allowed, you may want to try using it as an arrival activity. Let members begin the lists as they arrive. In this way you will be well along in the preparation of the lists by the starting time of the session. If you find, however, that members are consistently missing out on this activity, move it back to a time during the session.

4. Stimulating One Another to Love and Good Deeds (20/40 minutes). "Let us consider how to stimulate one another to love and good deeds" (Heb. 10:24, NASB). Because God did not intend for Christians to live their lives independently from the rest of the body, He made us dependent on one another. Use this period in each session to guide members in helping one another apply the truths of the Scriptures and the model of Christ to their own lives. This will be a time for discussion, testimony, encouragement, challenge, and accountability as members help one another respond to God's renewing process in their minds and lives.

Some people are far better at helping others than they are in receiving help themselves. For the body of Christ to function effectively, members need to learn to do both. If you see that some of your small group members tend to refuse help, you may want to take time to remind them about the importance of giving *and* receiving help. This is not to be a time for self-righteous people to "fix" everybody else. It is a time for humble servants to give and receive help.

5. Preparing the Bride for Her Bridegroom (5/10 minutes). "Let us be glad and rejoice, and give honour to him: for the marriage of the Lamb is come, and his wife hath made herself ready. And to her was granted that she should be arrayed in fine linen, clean and white: for the fine linen is the righteousness of saints. And he saith unto me, Write, Blessed are they which are called unto the marriage supper of the Lamb" (Rev. 19:7-9). As the marriage of Christ and His bride (the church) draws near, the bride must make herself ready. Christian churches must cleanse and purify themselves so they will be pleasing and acceptable to the Bridegroom. In each session, a Scripture will be examined that will help the bride prepare herself. Ask members to discuss and apply the Scripture to their lives, families, and church.

6. Praying for One Another (10/20 minutes). "Confess your faults one to another, and pray one for another, that ye may be healed. The effectual fervent prayer of a righteous man availeth much" (Jas. 5:16). Because God intends for a church to be a house of prayer (see Luke 19:46), members will take time each session sharing with one another in prayer. This will be an opportunity to share prayer requests for spiritual concerns; and confess faults, weaknesses, sins, struggles, and failures. But it will also be a time for praying fervently for one another for forgiveness, healing, encouragement, guidance, wisdom, knowledge, understanding, courage, strength, and faithfulness. Ideally you should use same-gender groups for these prayer times to maximize the sense of freedom to share openly with the group.

7. Closing the Session (5/10 minutes). At the conclusion of each session, summarize the questions that may still need answering and ask members to seek answers during the coming week. Take time to preview the coming unit and give any special instructions that may be helpful. Conclude the session in prayer.

The Role of the Small-group Leader

You may have some feelings of inadequacy in leading a study about the mind of Christ. You may not feel like a knowledgeable person in the field. That is OK. Your role in this small-group study is not that of a teacher. You are a facilitator of a group-learning process. You will be helping members help each other by applying "Let us consider how to stimulate one another to love and good deeds" (Heb. 10:24, NASB).

If God has led you to accept this assignment, you can trust Him to equip and enable you to accomplish the task. You are an instrument through which God wants to do His work. Without God you can do nothing of Kingdom value. With Him you can move spiritual mountains. Depend on God and "pray without ceasing." Keep in mind that the Holy Spirit of Christ is present in every session to work in and through you. You are not guiding this group alone!

Group members will be spending one to three hours each unit studying *The Mind of Christ* with T. W. Hunt as their personal guide or tutor. The Holy Spirit will serve as their Teacher, for no spiritual truth can be understood without His involvement. The content and learning activities will help members learn the basic truths and principles during the week. Members will be working on application of the truths even before coming to the group time. Your job is to help members review what they have learned, share with each other what God is doing in their lives, and help each other make practical application of the truths to life.

You should expect that members will ask some questions you cannot answer. What you do in response will help them learn to turn to the Lord, His Word, and other believers for assistance. When you do not have an answer (or perhaps even when you do), encourage the group to join you in praying and searching the Scriptures together for an answer. A question may become an extra homework assignment for members to study during the week. Together, ask God to guide you to His answer, to His perspective. Then trust God to do it. When God sends the answer through one or more people in the group, you and your members will come to trust Him more.

Grouping Members During the Session

In the session plans, each activity has a recommended grouping. The size of the sub-groups is based on the content to be shared and the amount of time available. You may decide to use different groupings. If you do make a change, evaluate what members will be sharing, how much time you have available, and what group size would provide for maximum member participation. The following descriptions explain the terms used in this guide.

- *Small Group*—Refers to a group of six to ten persons including the small-group leader. Unless a different group size is suggested, the activities during the session are for use with the entire small group.

- *Quads*—Refers to four people. Depending on the size of your group, each quad actually may have three, four, or five members. For instance, if you have eight members, you would have two quads of four each. For ten members we recommend two quads of three members and one quad with four. You could, however, have two groups of five. When you divide into quads, verbally give the assignment to all members. Ask one member in each quad to serve as the leader.

- *Pairs*—Refers to two people. If you have an odd number of people, one pair will need to have three members, or the extra person could work with you to form a pair.

Include yourself as you can in these small groupings for sharing and discussion. You will not only model a participating attitude, but you will also have the opportunity to share and grow with the group. They need to see you doing the same things you are asking them to do.

Preparing for a Group Study

As a small-group leader, you will need to prepare for the study, help enlist participants, guide group sessions, and provide follow-up at the end of the study. The following suggestions should help you accomplish these tasks.

🐚 **Prepare and secure resources.** Much of your course preparation can be completed at one time. First, complete the following actions:

❏ Prepare six session segment posters. Using poster board or newsprint prepare six posters—one for each of the first six segments of learning activities. Write a separate heading on each poster and copy the related Scripture passage. Display these posters on a focal wall for use during the Introductory Session. Then display them in your small-group room throughout the remainder of the study. The text for these posters is found in items 1-6 on page 264.

❏ Prepare headings for the "Transformed To" wall and the "Transformed From" wall. On poster board or using construction paper letters, place titles on the left and right walls for the "Transforming by the Word" activity. See the description and diagram of the room set up that follows.

❏ Provide two tables in the room at which members can work.

❏ Provide two pieces of poster board or newsprint, masking tape, and markers for every session for the Transformed To and Transformed From lists.

Read the SPECIFIC BEFORE THE SESSION suggestions on page 267 and prepare additional resources that are not listed here that you think you will need. If you add or adapt learning activities, you will need to prepare for those activities as well.

🐚 **Keep records.** Keep enrollment and attendance records so you can track completion of requirements for *The Mind of Christ* Diploma in the Christian Growth Study Plan. Your church may want attendance records for their own reporting purposes.

🐚 **Set up your room.** Each week, set up your room similar to the diagram below:

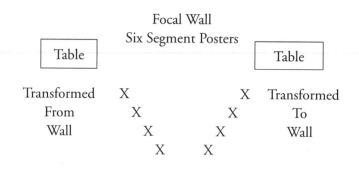

Place chairs (X) in a semi-circle or V shape with a focal wall at the open end. On the focal wall display the six posters that outline the segments of the small-group session. On the wall to the left place the title: *Transformed From.* On the wall to the right place the title: *Transformed To.* Add to these walls the lists that are prepared each week. Provide a table to the right and one to the left on which the quads can write their lists for Transforming by the Word. If possible, leave the lists in place throughout the study for the cumulative effect of reviewing what God is saying in His Word.

Help Members Memorize Scripture

One aspect of gaining the mind of Christ is implanting God's Word deeply in your mind. Some of your group may not be skilled at memorizing Scripture. Show them the cards in the back of the member book and challenge members to memorize the key passages in *The Mind of Christ.* Review the ideas on page 9 to help them further develop Scripture memorization.

Standard Before and After the Session

Cut on the dotted line and use these standard checklists on the following pages before and after each group session. You might want to laminate this cut-out section and use it as a bookmark.

SPECIFIC BEFORE THE SESSION PLANS

Session 1

❑ Provide copies of *The Mind of Christ* member book for any new members. Be prepared to give an orientation to the book and requirements for course participation.

Session 2

❑ Recommendation: After session 2 no new members should be accepted, since they will have too much work to do to catch up with the rest of the group. Be prepared to take names of interested persons for the next time the course is offered.

Session 6

❑ Prepare to discuss a possible get-together for your group or to share plans for such an event.

❑ Provide notebook paper and a pencil for each member to use in completing the Servanthood Instrument.

Session 7

❑ Consider making enlarged posters of the contrasts between the first four and the second four Beatitudes.

Session 10

❑ Finalize plans for showing *The Mind of Christ* DVD messages on the crucifixion and resurrection (Sessions 7 and 8). If you have not done so, read "After the Session" for session 9. Be prepared to share specifics about when and where the videos will be shown.

Session 11

❑ Prepare to share plans (if any) for viewing *The Mind of Christ* DVD messages on the crucifixion and the resurrection.

Session 12

❑ Prepare a sheet or poster listing information about upcoming discipleship training opportunities in your church. See unit 11 "After the Session."

STANDARD BEFORE THE SESSION

The following suggestions for preparation are standard for each of the 12 small-group sessions. They will be referenced but not repeated.

❑ Complete the learning activities in the member book and become familiar with any Lifelong Helps used during this unit.

❑ Pause and pray for God's guidance as you prepare for this week's group session. Pray specifically for each member of your group.

❑ Read the specific suggestions on page 267 (if any) for the upcoming session.

❑ You will have more suggestions in the session plans than you will have time to complete. Select the activities and the order that best suits the learning and spiritual needs of your group. Adapt or develop other activities that will best help your group gain the greatest benefit from the unit. Decide on the amount of time to allow for each activity. Write a time in the margin to indicate when each activity should begin. (For example, write 6:20 beside "Stimulating to Love and Good Deeds.") Always be prepared to change your plans if the Holy Spirit should lead you in another direction.

❑ Arrange the room according to the chart on page 266. Display the six session segment posters on the focal wall. Display as many lists from previous sessions as you can on the Transformed From and the Transformed To walls. These will serve as a reminder of the way God is working to conform members to the mind of Christ.

❑ Prepare a one-minute preview of the next unit.

STANDARD AFTER THE SESSION

Use the following suggestions to evaluate each of the 12 small-group sessions.

❑ Record ways you can pray for each group member. Do you sense a need to pray for any one person in particular? If so, record your prayer concerns.

❑ Ask yourself the following. Jot down your answers on a separate sheet of paper or in a journal.
  • Do the activities need to be rearranged? Do some of them need more or less time?
  • Did the groupings (quads, pairs, and small group) best meet the needs for participation, or would a different grouping have worked better?
  • What spiritual or mental preparation do I need to make for the next session?
  • Which of the members need to be encouraged to participate more in the sharing and discussion times? When and how will I encourage them?
  • When could I have responded more appropriately to the needs of members or to the leadership of the Holy Spirit? What should I have done or said?
  • How did I do at beginning and ending on time?
  • Would adjustments in our schedule, location, or room setup facilitate a better learning environment?
  • Do I need to call or write one of the group members to offer encouragement, prayer, instruction, correction, or counsel? When shall I call? or write?
  • Were there any absentees this week? Do I need to call with instructions or to check on needs?
  • Did spiritual needs surface concerning our church or its need for purification that I should share with church leadership for prayerful consideration?

❑ Read the STANDARD and SPECIFIC BEFORE THE SESSION suggestions for the next session to get an idea of advance preparation.

❑ Spend time alone with the Lord to seek His evaluation of your group leadership. Are you allowing God to guide you? Are you trusting God to work in members' lives? Do you need to make any adjustments to follow God's leadership better?

SPECIFIC AFTER THE SESSION PLANS

Session 1
❑ Does everyone in your group have a *Member's Book?* If not, secure needed books and, if possible, deliver them to the members early in the week.

Session 2
❑ If you have others who want to begin the study, give their names to the discipleship director for enlistment in the next class. Explain that the homework requirements would be too heavy to catch up at this time. You may want to recommend use of the DVD conference messages for personal study.

❑ Are members having difficulty memorizing Scripture? If so, schedule time in the next session to review instructions for Scripture memorization (p. 9). You may want to invite volunteers to share their successes for Scripture memory with one another.

Session 3
❑ Did any difficulty or serious need arise during the sharing this week related to one of the areas like fears, hurts, or weaknesses? Do you need to follow up with a call or a visit? How can you pray for the need?

Session 5
❑ Consider having a social get-together about half way through the study (session 6 or 7). Involve group members in planning for the time together.

Session 6
❑ Finalize plans for the get-together.

Session 9
❑ Is God leading you to take actions that you have not responded to because you think "But I am the teacher"? Do you need to obey Him in an area of giving that would be a model for the members of your group? (Don't respond because it would be a nice thing to do; respond because God is leading you.)

❑ Consider using *The Mind of Christ DVD Conference* messages on the crucifixion (related to unit 11) and resurrection (related to unit 12). Since these require one hour or more each, plan for additional sessions if necessary. You may want to offer them as an option for participants before or after your regular session or at a separate time.

Session 10

❏ Finalize plans (if any) for viewing *The Mind of Christ DVD Conference* messages on the crucifixion and resurrection.

Session 11

❏ Who is the person in your church responsible for discipleship training? Find out from him or her when another small-group study of *The Mind of Christ* will be offered. Ask what other approaches to the study of *The Mind of Christ* will be offered in the future. Also find out what future training opportunities have been scheduled so you can share this information with your group in the final session.

Session 12

❏ Complete the Christian Growth Study Plan forms, sign and mail them to Christian Growth Study Plan; One LifeWay Plaza; Nashville, TN 37234-0117. When your church receives the diplomas, you and the pastor need to sign them. Plan for an appropriate time to award the diplomas to the small-group participants.

❏ Are any members in your group qualified and spiritually gifted to lead a future study of *The Mind of Christ*? If so, give their names to the discipleship director for possible use in future groups.

❏ Gather the six session segment posters and the headings for the Transformed To and Transformed From walls. Keep them for use in a future study of *The Mind of Christ*.

❏ If you received written evaluations from group members, take time to review their comments and suggestions for future small-group studies of *The Mind of Christ*.

❏ Take some time to evaluate your group study of *The Mind of Christ*. Use the following questions to start your thinking. Make notes for yourself on separate paper or in your journal. Begin this time with a prayer for God's perspective.
  • How has God used this course and small-group study to influence or improve my relationship with Him?
  • What personal progress have I made in developing the mind of Christ?
  • Did I reflect the mind and behavior of Christ as I led this study? If not, what are some ways I can improve if I lead the study again?

  • What changes have I observed in the lives of group members? Have other people observed these changes also?
  • What was the most meaningful experience for the group in the study?
  • What would I do differently in a future study of the course? Consider enlistment of members, size of group, meeting time and place, schedule, learning activities, prayer times, and so forth.
  • What shall I do next in my service or growth in discipleship? Shall I lead another group through The Mind of Christ? Should I participate in one of the other discipleship training courses?

❏ Conclude your time in prayer. Thank God for all He has done in your life and the lives of group members. Thank Him for His Son Jesus and the love He has shown to you through Christ. Take time to pray specifically for the continued spiritual growth of each member of your group.

INTRODUCTORY SESSION

THE MIND OF CHRIST

SESSION GOALS

This session will help potential members (1) understand the approach of the study and how it will help them more fully develop the mind of Christ; (2) understand the commitments required for participating in the course; and (3) demonstrate a commitment to complete the course requirements.

BEFORE THE SESSION

❏ Prepare yourself spiritually for the upcoming study through a season of prayer. Ask God to draw people to the introductory session that He wants to involve in this study.

❏ Gather the following items:
  • A copy of *The Mind of Christ* member book for each potential small-group participant.

- The six session segment posters (p. 266).
- The Transform From and Transform To headings for the side walls (p.266).
- Mark pages in your member book for the Course Overview or prepare electronic presentation slides.
- Create a poster or presentation slide of the four images of how God might work to develop in believers the mind of Christ. (See 3 under Arrival Activity below).
❏ Set up your room according to the anticipated size of the group. This session includes all persons from your church interested in the study. Place the six session segment posters on a focal wall and the Transform From and Transform To headings on side walls.
❏ If you plan to use an overhead projector, secure a screen, projector, and extension cord.
❏ Prepare for the theme interpretation.
❏ Mark in your Bible the Scriptures you plan to read so you can turn to them quickly.
❏ Be prepared to register those who decide to participate in the course. Decide how you will collect book fees. Enlist a person to receive the fees after the session.

DURING THE SESSION

Arrival Activity (as members arrive plus 10 minutes)
1. Greet prospective members as they arrive. Give a copy of *The Mind of Christ* member book to every two people. Ask each pair to examine the contents pages and the various sections in the member book that will help them in a lifelong process of developing the mind of Christ.

2. Opening Prayer. Pray that God will use this session to give insight into how members can develop the mind of Christ. Ask God to guide each person to respond to Him in making a decision about whether or not to study *The Mind of Christ*.

3. Theme Interpretation. Describe in your own words how God might work in a person's life to develop the mind of Christ. If you choose, you could have some actors briefly act out these four images in visual vignettes like charades.

- *Potter and the Clay.* Read Isaiah 64:8 and Jeremiah 18:6. Explain that just as a potter molds clay into a vessel of his choosing, God desires to mold us into the image of His Son Jesus Christ.
- *Husbandman and the Vine.* Read John 15:1-2. Explain that God acts as a husbandman (vine dresser or gardener) and we are the branches of the grapevine. God will prune (cut) away things (perhaps even good things) so that we may become more fruitful.
- *Washing of Water by the Word.* Read Ephesians 5:25-27. Explain that the Holy Spirit of Christ uses God's Word to wash His people in order to cleanse them and sanctify them.
- *Sculptor and Marble.* Read 1 Corinthians 2:16. A famous sculptor was once asked how he could take a formless block of marble and sculpt a beautiful angel from it. The sculptor replied: "I see an angel inside the marble. I just chip away everything that isn't angel." God has placed His Son in us. We already have the mind of Christ. God works to remove from our lives everything that is not like Christ.

Course Overview (25 minutes)
1. Overview the Content. Referring to the member book or presentation slides you have prepared, briefly explain the following content elements:
- The outline of the hymn in Philippians 2:5-11 (p. 8). Explain that the hymn provides an outline for studying various aspects of the mind of Christ.
- Six Characteristics of the Christlike Mind (p. 14). Explain that these six words describe characteristics of the Christlike mind and that the course will help members develop these characteristics as they respond to God.
- Three Stages in Developing the Mind of Christ (p. 23). Explain that the course will guide members from the beginning stage toward the readiness stage as they develop maturity in Christ. Ask a member to read Colossians 3:2 as you describe "Beginning," another member to read Romans 12:2 as you describe "Growing," and a third member to read 1 Peter 1:13 as you describe "Qualified."
- Unit Overviews (unit pages 12, 32, 52, 70, 90, 108, 128, 142, 156, 170, 186, 204). Use "Why You Will Find this Unit Helpful" to provide a brief summary of the units in the member book.

2. Course Requirements. Use the information in the introduction under Studying *The Mind of Christ* (p. 9) to explain the requirements of self study and participation in the small-group sessions. Emphasize that participants will be expected to spend 30 to 60 minutes per day five days a week in completing assignments. Suggest that members who are not able to commit their time to the individual and small-group study should not participate at this time or should make the necessary adjustments so that they can complete the requirements. Offer to put names on a list for announcements of future studies when schedules may be more conducive to participation.

3. Time and Place. Announce when groups will be meeting to study *The Mind of Christ*. If you are offering the DVD conference format for the study, describe it and announce the time and place. Explain how the member book and small group approach offers a more personal, in-depth approach to developing the mind of Christ.

4. Questions. Call for and answer any questions people may have regarding the content of the course or the course requirements.

Getting Ready for Next Week (20 minutes)
1. Individual Study. Ask pairs to open the member books to page 12. Using the following outline, describe the process for self-study that members will need to use during the coming week prior to the first small-group session.
• *Unit Pages.* Describe the various elements of the unit pages. Guide members through the process of finding all the cards related to this first unit. Mention that the Scripture Memory cards for Philippians 2:5-11 are for use throughout the course. They do not have to memorize that passage all at once.
• *Scripture Memory Verse.* Point out the Scripture memory verse on the unit page and on card 3A in the back of the book. Using the Scripture memory poster, suggest ways members can memorize Scripture.
• *Daily Assignments.* Explain how content is divided into five daily assignments. Encourage members to study only one day at a time, so they will have time to think about and apply the teachings in their lives.

Explain that if they decide to participate in the study their first assignment will be to complete the daily work for unit 1 before the first small-group meeting.
• *Learning Activities.* Point out one of the learning activities with the symbol (🐟) and boldface type. Encourage members to complete all learning activities.

2. Spiritual Journal. Suggest that members may want to get a notebook or journal for recording responses to some of the assignments in the Lifelong Helps section.

3. Prayer Partners. Suggest that every group member should enlist a person to be a prayer partner with him or her during this study. This person could be a group member, spouse, or a close friend. Ask members to share regularly with this person specific ways they can pray for him or her as they work at developing the mind of Christ.

Decision Time/Closing (5 minutes)
1. Registration, Books, and Fees. Describe the process for members to register for the course. Mention that those needing books should pick one up after the session. Announce the book fee and tell members how to pay the fee.

2. Closing Prayer. Call for a time of silent prayer. Ask those present to pray about their participation in the study of *The Mind of Christ*. After a period of time, lead in a closing prayer requesting God's guidance during the coming weeks of study.

AFTER THE SESSION
❑ Read and complete the evaluations and activities described in the Standard After the Session instructions (p. 268).
❑ Save all posters for use in later sessions.
❑ Give the information from the registration sheets to the appropriate person in your church. If you have more than ten people per group, enlist additional leaders for every eight to ten people prior to the first small-group session.
❑ Secure additional member books as needed.

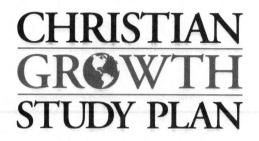

CHRISTIAN GROWTH STUDY PLAN

In the **Christian Growth Study Plan (formerly Church Study Course),** this book *The Mind of Christ* is a resource for course credit in the subject area Personal Life of the Christian Growth category of diploma plans. To receive credit, read the book, complete the learning activities, show your work to your pastor, a staff member or church leader, then complete the following information. This page may be duplicated. Send the completed page to:

Christian Growth Study Plan
One LifeWay Plaza
Nashville, TN 37234-0117
FAX: (615)251-5067; E-mail: *cgspnet@lifeway.com*
For information about the Christian Growth Study Plan, refer to the Christian Growth Study Plan Catalog. It is located online at *www.lifeway.com/cgsp*. If you do not have access to the Internet, contact the Christian Growth Study Plan office (1.800.968.5519) for the specific plan you need for your ministry.

The Mind of Christ
Course Number: CG-0174

PARTICIPANT INFORMATION

Social Security Number (USA ONLY-optional)	Personal CGSP Number*	Date of Birth (MONTH, DAY, YEAR)
— —	— —	— —

Name (First, Middle, Last)		Home Phone
		— —

Address (Street, Route, or P.O. Box)	City, State, or Province	Zip/Postal Code

Email Address for CGSP use

Please check appropriate box: ❏ Resource purchased by church ❏ Resource purchased by self ❏ Other

CHURCH INFORMATION

Church Name		

Address (Street, Route, or P.O. Box)	City, State, or Province	Zip/Postal Code

CHANGE REQUEST ONLY

☐ Former Name		

☐ Former Address	City, State, or Province	Zip/Postal Code

☐ Former Church	City, State, or Province	Zip/Postal Code

Signature of Pastor, Conference Leader, or Other Church Leader	Date

*New participants are requested but not required to give SS# and date of birth. Existing participants, please give CGSP# when using SS# for the first time. Thereafter, only one ID# is required. **Mail to:** Christian Growth Study Plan, One LifeWay Plaza, Nashville, TN 37234-0117. Fax: (615)251-5067.

Revised 4-05

Gentle

"The servant of the Lord must not strive; but be gentle unto all men, apt to teach, patient" (2 Tim. 2:24).

Gentle: equitable, fair, forbearing, considerate, reasonable, pleasant, nurturing, tender, delicate, tactful, considerate, kind

Opposites of *Gentle*: harsh, caustic, rough, abusive, bitter, cruel, fierce, violent, rude

Perversions of *Gentle*: unkind restraint, negligent, lax, derelict, careless, delinquent, neglectful, inattentive, unchecked, unbridled

9A

Scripture Memory—Matthew 5:3-6

3Blessed are the poor in spirit: for theirs is the kingdom of heaven.

4Blessed are they that mourn: for they shall be comforted.

5 Blessed are the meek: for they shall inherit the earth.

6Blessed are they which do hunger and thirst after righteousness—for they shall be filled.

6A

UNIT 1: Scripture Memory—Romans 12:2

"Be not conformed to this world: but be ye transformed by the renewing of your mind, that ye may prove what is that good, and acceptable, and perfect, will of God."

UNIT 2: Scripture Memory—Matthew 6:33

"Seek ye first the kingdom of God, and his righteousness; and all these things shall be added unto you."

3A

Pure

"Pure religion and undefiled before God and the Father is this, To visit the fatherless and widows in their affliction, and to keep himself unspotted from the world" (James 1:27).

Pure: blameless, clean, chaste, pristine, spotless, unblemished, innocent, unadulterated, stainless, not contaminated, beyond reproach

Opposites of *Pure*: lustful, carnal, fleshly, lewd, contaminated, tainted, depraved, immoral

Perversions of *Pure*: puritanical, pharisaical, rigid, overly strict, austere, self-righteous

8A

UNIT 9: Scripture Memory—Matthew 6:20-21

"Lay up for yourselves treasures in heaven, where neither moth nor rust doth corrupt, and where thieves do not break through nor steal: For where your treasure is, there will your heart be also."

UNIT 10: Scripture Memory—John 6:63

"It is the spirit that quickeneth; the flesh profiteth nothing; the words that I speak unto you, they are spirit, and they are life."

5A

Six Characteristics of a Christlike Mind

1. *Alive*—"The mind set on the Spirit is life and peace" (Rom. 8:6, NASB).

2. *Single-minded*—". . . the simplicity and purity of devotion to Christ" (2 Cor. 11:3, NASB).

3. *Lowly*—"In lowliness of mind let each esteem other better than themselves" (Phil. 2:3).

4. *Pure*—"Unto the pure all things are pure" (Titus 1:15).

5. *Responsive*—"He opened their minds to understand the Scriptures" (Luke 24:45, NASB).

6. *Peaceful*—"The mind set on the Spirit is life and peace" (Rom. 8:6, NASB).

2A

Eight Virtues of Godly Wisdom

"The wisdom that is from above is first pure, then peaceable, gentle, and easy to be intreated, full of mercy and good fruits, without partiality, and without hypocrisy" (Jas. 3:17).

- pure
- peaceable
- gentle
- entreatable
- merciful
- fruitful
- steadfast
- honest

7A

UNIT 5: Scripture Memory—Galatians 5:22-23

"The fruit of the Spirit is love, joy, peace, longsuffering, gentleness, goodness, faith, meekness, temperance: against such there is no law."

UNIT 6: Scripture Memory—Matthew 10:25

"It is enough for the disciple that he be as his master, and the servant as his lord."

4A

Scripture Memory—Philippians 2:5-8

5Let this mind be in you, which was also in Christ Jesus:

6Who, being in the form of God, thought it not robbery to be equal with God:

7But made himself of no reputation, and took upon him the form of a servant, and was made in the likeness of men:

8And being found in fashion as a man, he humbled himself, and became obedient unto death, even the death of the cross.

1A

Entreatable

"Whosoever shall compel thee to go a mile, go with him twain. Give to him that asketh thee, and from him that would borrow of thee turn not thou away" (Matt. 5:41-42).

Entreatable: approachable, helpful, accessible, cooperative, willing, inclined, amenable, accommodating, responsive

Opposites of *Entreatable:* unapproachable, distanced, cool, reticent, uncooperative, inaccessible, unresponsive, introverted

Perversions of *Entreatable:* Yes-person, pushover

Scripture Memory—Matthew 5:7-10

7Blessed are the merciful—for they shall obtain mercy.
8Blessed are the pure in heart—for they shall see God.
9Blessed are the peacemakers—for they shall be called the children of God.
10Blessed are they which are persecuted for righteousness' sake—for theirs is the kingdom of heaven.

UNIT 3: Scripture Memory—John 8:32,36

"Ye shall know the truth, and the truth shall make you free. . . . If the Son therefore shall make you free, ye shall be free indeed."

UNIT 4: Scripture Memory—James 3:17

"The wisdom that is from above is first pure, then peaceable, gentle, and easy to be intreated, full of mercy and good fruits, without partiality, and without hypocrisy."

Peaceable

"Be at peace among yourselves. Now we exhort you, brethren, warn them that are unruly, comfort the feebleminded, support the weak, be patient toward all men" (1 Thess. 5:13-14).

Peaceable: peaceful, friendly, harmonious, orderly, reconciling, agreeable, compatible

Opposites of *Peaceable:* fussy, nit-picking, picky, contentious, argumentative, ornery, cranky, disagreeable, mean, obstinate

Perversions of *Peaceable:* compromising, wishy washy, goes with the flow, man-pleaser

---

UNIT 11: Scripture Memory—1 Peter 1:15

"As he which hath called you is holy, so be ye holy in all manner of conversation. Because it is written, Be ye holy; for I am holy."

UNIT 12: Scripture Memory—Colossians 1:18

"He is the head of the body, the church: who is the beginning, the firstborn from the dead; that in all things he might have the preeminence."

Three Stages in Developing the Mind of Christ

1. Beginning—The Will Principle
   Set your mind on things above.
2. Growing—The River Principle
   Allow God to *renew* your mind.
3. Qualified—The Readiness Principle
   Gird up your mind for action.

Fruit of the Spirit

"The fruit of the Spirit is love, joy, peace, longsuffering, gentleness, goodness, faith, meekness, temperance: against such there is no law" (Gal. 5:22-23).

• Love
• Joy
• Peace
• Longsuffering
• Gentleness
• Goodness
• Faith
• Meekness
• Temperance

UNIT 7: Scripture Memory—Matthew 5:3

"Blessed are the poor in spirit: for theirs is the kingdom of heaven."

(For the other Beatitudes see card 6)

UNIT 8: Scripture Memory—John 1:14

"The Word was made flesh, and dwelt among us, (and we beheld his glory, the glory as of the only begotten of the Father,) full of grace and truth."

Scripture Memory—Philippians 2:9-11

9Wherefore God also hath highly exalted him, and given him a name which is above every name:
10That at the name of Jesus every knee should bow, of things in heaven, and things in earth, and things under the earth;
11And that every tongue should confess that Jesus Christ is Lord, to the glory of God the Father.

The Servant Mind 1

1. *Humble*—Proper attitude toward the Master's work in others. (Fleshly attitude: "Who do you think you are?")

2. *Obedient*—Understanding the authority of the Master over my time and life. (Fleshly attitude: "OK, in a minute." "I'll get around to it.")

3. *Willing*—Identity with the Master's attitudes. (Fleshly attitude: "You have to look out for yourself.")

4. *Loyal*—Unswerving devotion to the Master.

(Fleshly attitude: "You scratch my back, I'll scratch yours.")

18A

Meekness

"With all lowliness and meekness, with longsuffering, forbearing one another in love; Endeavouring to keep the unity of the Spirit in the bond of peace" (Eph. 4:2-3).

Meekness: accepting God's dealings with us as good without resistance, a fruit of power, lowly before God and humble before man

Opposites of *Meekness*: arrogance, haughtiness, pride, cockiness, egotism, vanity, conceit

Perversions of *Meekness*: weakness, "wimpy," cowardly, spinelessness, timidity

17A

Goodness

"For the fruit of the Spirit is in all goodness and righteousness and truth" (Eph. 5:9).

Goodness: uprightness of heart and life, moral goodness, wholesome, productive, functioning, in good working order

Opposites of *Goodness*: badness, unwholesome, evil, corruption, depravity, immorality, wickedness, non-productive

Perversions of *Goodness*: finicky nice, self-righteous

16A

Longsuffering

"The trying of your faith worketh patience. But let patience have her perfect work, that ye may be perfect and entire, wanting nothing" (Jas. 1:3-4).

Longsuffering: patience, endurance, constancy, steadfastness, perseverance, forbearance, slow in avenging wrongs

Opposites of *Longsuffering*: impatient, chafing, crabby, nagging, touchy, quick to avenge wrongs

Perversions of *Longsuffering*: lenient, indulgent, permissive

15A

Joy

"If ye keep my commandments, ye shall abide in my love. . . . These things have I spoken unto you, that my joy might remain in you, and that your joy might be full" (John 15:10-11).

Joy: delight, gladness, calm, bliss, cheerfulness, enjoyment, contentment, radiance

Opposites of *Joy*: pain, hurt, wound, agony, anguish, distress, misery, torment, woe

Perversions of *Joy*: frenzy, crazed excitement, hysteria

14A

Love Is — 1 Corinthians 13

1. Suffers long (holy relationships)
2. Is kind (holy purposes)
3. Does not envy (holy heart)
4. Does not brag (holy speech)
5. Is not arrogant (holy service)
6. Does not act unbecomingly (holy behavior)
7. Does not seek its own (holy desires)
8. Is not easily provoked (holy temperament)

13A

Love

"A new commandment I give unto you, That ye love one another; as I have loved you. . . . By this shall all men know that ye are my disciples, if ye have love one to another" (John 13:34-35).

Love: affection, charity (KJV), compassion, benevolence, adoration, fondness, commitment, caring deeply

Opposites of *Love*: hate, animosity, hostility, malice, vindictiveness, fear, dread, fright

Perversions of *Love*: possessive, overly protective, permissive, smothering, manipulative

12A

Steadfast

"Be ye steadfast, unmoveable, always abounding in the work of the Lord, forasmuch as ye know that your labour is not in vain in the Lord" (1 Cor. 15:58).

Steadfast: firm, unshakable, abiding, resolute, constant, devoted, staunch, steady, immovable, resolved, uncompromising

Opposites of *Steadfast*: wavering, unsure, unstable, vacillating, indecisive, reluctant

Perversions of *Steadfast*: inflexible, stubborn, bullheaded, despotic, authoritarian, tyrannical

11A

Merciful

"Be ye therefore merciful, as your Father also is merciful" (Luke 6:36).

Merciful: caring, forgiving, gracious, decent, chivalrous, noble, forbearing, sympathetic, tolerant, compassionate, charitable, benevolent

Opposites of *Merciful*: merciless, unmerciful, unsympathetic, compassionless, hardened, uncaring, pitiless, spiteful

Perversions of *Merciful*: indulgent, lenient, permissive

10A

The Servant Mind 2

5. *Faithful*—Confidence that anticipates the Master continuing His plan. (Fleshly attitude: "I'm tired of this.")

6. *Watchful*—Attentiveness to the Master's voice. (Fleshly attitude: "I wish I had not said that.")

7. *Courageous*—Conviction about the Master's priorities. (Fleshly attitude: "I'm not taking any chances.")

Gentleness

"To speak evil of no man, to be no brawlers, but gentle, shewing all meekness unto all men" (Titus 3:2).

Gentleness: kindness, goodness of heart, integrity, goodness in deeds or actions, kindly disposition toward others

Opposites of Gentleness: hard, severity, harsh, rough, abusive, cruel, rude, short, grating

Perversions of Gentleness: soft, mushy, negligent, careless, inattentive, unbridled

Love (continued)

"Ye have heard that it hath been said, Thou shalt love thy neighbour, and hate thine enemy. But I say unto you, Love your enemies, bless them that curse you, do good to them that hate you, and pray for them which despitefully use you, and persecute you" (Matt. 5:43-44).

"Owe no man any thing, but to love one another: for he that loveth another hath fulfilled the law. . . . Love worketh no ill to his neighbour: therefore love is the fulfilling of the law." (Rom. 13:8,10).

Temperance

"Add to your faith virtue; and to virtue knowledge; And to knowledge temperance; and to temperance patience; And to patience godliness; And to godliness brotherly kindness; and to brotherly kindness charity" (2 Pet. 1:5-7).

Temperance: strength, controlling power of the will under the operation of the Spirit, self-control, mastery over desires or sensual appetites

Opposites of Temperance: undisciplined, slothful, lazy, lackadaisical, sluggish, laid back

Perversions of Temperance: fleshly effort

Peace

"Thou wilt keep him in perfect peace, whose mind is stayed on thee: because he trusteth in thee. Trust ye in the Lord for ever: for in the Lord Jehovah is everlasting strength" (Isa. 26:3-4).

Peace: rest, quietness, tranquility, harmony, concord, repose, serenity

Opposites of Peace: war, rage, havoc, discord, conflict, strife, rivalry, clash, feud, brawl, fracas, hassle, melee, rift

Perversions of Peace: neutrality, lukewarmness, indifference, detached, uncommitted, uninvolved

Honest

"Having your conversation honest among the Gentiles: that, whereas they speak against you as evildoers, they may by your good works, which they shall behold, glorify God in the day of visitation" (1 Pet. 2:12).

Honest: sincere, true, genuine, ethical, sound, trustworthy, upright, straightforward

Opposites of Honest: lying, dishonest, fake, hypocritical, counterfeit, deceitful, scheming

Perversions of Honest: brutal, cruel, callous, pitiless, hard hearted, ruthless, vicious

---

Faith

"Moreover it is required in stewards, that a man be found faithful" (1 Cor. 4:2).

Faith: faithfulness, trustworthiness, integrity, reliability, fidelity, ardor, loyalty, dependability, consistency

Opposites of Faith: faithlessness, fickleness, untrustworthiness, inconsistency, uncertainty, waywardness, capriciousness

Perversions of Faith: legalism, workaholism, over-committed, fanatical, overly zealous, extremism

Love Is (continued)

9. Does not take into account a wrong (holy bookkeeping)

10. Does not rejoice in unrighteousness (holy conscience)

11. Rejoices in the truth (holy mind)

12. Bears all things (holy stability)

13. Believes all things (holy values)

14. Hopes all things (holy expectations)

15. Endures all things (holy sacrifice)

Fruitful

"I am the vine, ye are the branches: He that abideth in me, and I in him, the same bringeth forth much fruit: for without me ye can do nothing" (John 15:5).

Fruitful: productive, fertile, prolific, constructive, high yield

Opposites of Fruitful: fruitless, unproductive, non-productive, ineffective, ineffectual, unyielding, worthless, empty, hollow, profitless

Perversions of Fruitful: fruit-obsessed, success-driven, obsessed with numbers, vain, showy